Praise for
DESTINY DISRUPTED

"If you want to put today's headlines about jihadist suicide bombings into the much larger context of history, you'd be well advised to settle in with *Destiny Disrupted*. It's the story of a civilization that suddenly found itself upended by strangers and now wants to put itself right. And if author Ansary stops short of calling the result a clash of civilizations, he feels free to call it two one-sided views of world history. His book is a valuable tool for opening up a view of the other side."

—*St. Louis Post-Dispatch*

"Tamim Ansary has written a truly superb history of the Islamic world. His excellent analysis provides the reader with an insightful understanding of how that world and its people were shaped by events. This is a must-read for all those who want to understand the evolution of a significant global society and how it has interacted with the rest of the world."

—General Anthony C. Zinni, USMC (Ret)

"This is a marvelous book. Ansary has written an indispensable historical account of the last 1,500 years from a perspective that is all too often ignored in the West. *Destiny Disrupted* will be read for generations to come."

—Reza Aslan, author of *No god but God* and *How to Win a Cosmic War*

"A must-read for anyone who wants to learn more about the history of the Islamic world. But the book is more than just a litany of past events. It is also an indispensable guide to understanding the political debates and conflicts of today, from 9/11 to the wars in Iraq and Afghanistan, from the Somali pirates to the Palestinian/ Israeli conflict. As Ansary writes in his conclusion, 'The conflict wracking the modern world is not, I think, best understood as a clash of civilizations . . . It's better understood as the friction generated by two mismatched world histories intersecting.'"

—*San Francisco Chronicle*

"Ansary has written an informative and thoroughly engaging look at the past, present, and future of Islam. With his seamless and charming prose, he challenges conventional wisdom and appeals for a fuller understanding of how Islam and the world at large have shaped each other. And that makes this book, in this uneasy, contentious post 9/11 world, a must-read."

—KHALED HOSSEINI, author of *The Kite Runner* and *A Thousand Splendid Suns*

"A lively, thorough, and accessible survey of the history of Islam (both the religion and its political dimension) that explores many of the disconnects between Islam and the West."

—*Shelf Awareness*

"There's not a page where you won't learn something startling in *Destiny Disrupted*. Beautifully clear and endlessly engaging, it's a romp through science, poetry, politics, and religion, in the company of a wise and charming mind, the perfect antidote to the Islamophobia that clouds Europe and North America."

—RAJ PATEL, author of *Stuff* and *Starved* and visiting scholar, Center for African Studies, University of California at Berkeley

"Never apologist in tone, meticulously researched and balanced, often amusing but never glib, *Destiny Disrupted* is ultimately a gripping drama that pulls the reader into great, seminal events of world history, a book which offers a wealth of knowledge and insight to any reader who wants to understand the movements and events behind the modern-day hostilities wracking Western and Islamic societies." —*Portland Oregonian*

DESTINY DISRUPTED

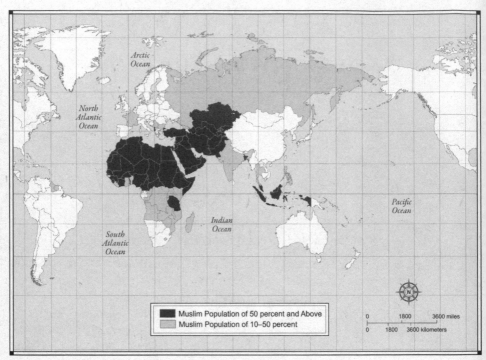

THE ISLAMIC WORLD TODAY

DESTINY
DISRUPTED

*A History of the World
Through Islamic Eyes*

TAMIM ANSARY

PUBLICAFFAIRS
New York

Hardcover edition first published in 2009 in the United States by PublicAffairs™,
a member of the Perseus Books Group.
Paperback edition first published in 2010 in the United States by PublicAffairs.

PublicAffairs books are available at special discounts for bulk purchases in the U.S.
by corporations, institutions, and other organizations. For more information, please
contact the Special Markets Department at the Perseus Books Group, 2300 Chestnut
Street, Suite 200, Philadelphia, PA 19103, call (800) 810-4145, ext. 5000, or e-mail
special.markets@perseusbooks.com.

Designed by Brent Wilcox
Text set in Adobe Garamond

A CIP catalog record for this book is available from the Library of Congress.
Hardcover ISBN: 978-1-58648-606-8
Paperback ISBN: 978-1-58648-813-0
LSC-C
Printing 23, 2022

For Amanuddin and Terttu

CONTENTS

LIST OF MAPS

NAMES AND DATES

Some writers are scrupulous about the system they use for transliterating Islamic names and words into English, insisting that one or another system is correct. I have to confess I am not among them. I have seen my own name spelled too many different ways in English to be picky. (People often ask me, which is correct, Ansari or Ansary—is it *y* or *i*? Well, neither, really: it's the letter *yaw.*) Given the arbitrary nature of transliteration, my guiding principle in this book has been to go for the simplest spellings and the most recognizable reductions.

Also many Arabic names include a series of patronymics preceded by Ibn, meaning "son of." Usually, I use the shortest form of the name by which a person is most commonly known. The profusion of unfamiliar names (and words) in this book will challenge many English-speaking readers; I wish to minimize such difficulties, so if a familiar form of a word or name exists in English, that's what I go with. Also, following a precedent set by Albert Hourani in *A History of the Arab Peoples,* I use the prefix *al*-the first time an Arabic name is used but drop it after that: al-Ghazali becomes Ghazali.

As for dates, two calendars apply to these events, the Islamic one and the so-called "common era" dating system, which actually derives from the Christian calendar. In the early decades after the birth of the Muslim community, I generally give the Islamic date (the number of years followed by AH which stands "After the Hijra"). I do so because I think that in this early period it's useful to convey a feel for how many years have passed since the crucial events of Islam. Later in time, I slide over to the "common

era" system, because that's the framework with which most readers are
familiar—and what's the point of giving a date if it doesn't place an event
in context and situate it relative to other events?

INTRODUCTION

Growing up as I did in Muslim Afghanistan, I was exposed early on to a narrative of world history quite different from the one that schoolchildren in Europe and the Americas routinely hear. At the time, however, it didn't shape my thinking, because I read history for fun, and in Farsi there wasn't much to read except boring textbooks. At my reading level, all the good stuff was in English.

My earliest favorite was the highly entertaining *Child's History of the World* by a man named V. V. Hillyer. It wasn't till I reread that book as an adult, many years later, that I realized how shockingly Eurocentric it was, how riddled with casual racism. I failed to notice these features as a child because Hillyer told a good story.

When I was nine or ten, the historian Arnold Toynbee passed through our tiny town of Lashkargah on a journey, and someone told him of a history-loving little bookworm of an Afghan kid living there. Toynbee was interested and invited me to tea, so I sat with the florid, old British gentleman, giving shy, monosyllabic answers to his kindly questions. The only thing I noticed about the great historian was his curious habit of keeping his handkerchief in his sleeve.

When we parted, however, Toynbee gave me a gift: Hendrick Willem Van Loon's *The Story of Mankind*. The title alone thrilled me—the idea that all of "mankind" had a single story. Why, I was part of "mankind" myself, so this might be my story, in a sense, or at least might situate me in the one big story shared by all! I gulped that book down and loved it, and the Western narrative of world history became my framework ever after.

All the history and historical fiction I read from then on just added flesh to those bones. I still studied the pedantic Farsi history texts assigned to us in school but read them only to pass tests and forgot them soon after.

Faint echoes of the other narrative must have lingered in me, however, because forty years later, in the fall of 2000, when I was working as a textbook editor in the United States, it welled back up. A school publisher in Texas had hired me to develop a new high school world-history textbook from scratch, and my first task was to draw up a table of contents, which entailed formulating an opinion about the overall shape of human history. The only given was the structure of the book. To fit the rhythm of the school year, the publisher ordained that it be divided into ten units, each consisting of three chapters.

But into what ten (or thirty) parts does all of time naturally divide? World history, after all, is not a chronological list of every damn thing that ever happened; it's a chain of only the most consequential events, selected and arranged to reveal the arc of the story—it's the arc that counts.

I tied into this intellectual puzzle with gusto, but my decisions had to pass through a phalanx of advisors: curriculum specialists, history teachers, sales executives, state education officials, professional scholars, and other such worthies. This is quite normal in elementary and high school textbook publishing, and quite proper I think, because the function of these books is to convey, not challenge, society's most up-to-date consensus of what's true. A chorus of advisors empanelled to second-guess a development editor's decisions helps to ensure that the finished product reflects the current curriculum, absent which the book will not even be saleable.

As we went through the process, however, I noticed an interesting tug and pull between my advisors and me. We agreed on almost everything *except*—I kept wanting to give more coverage to Islam in world history, and they kept wanting to pull it back, scale it down, parse it out as sidebars in units devoted mainly to other topics. None of us was speaking out of parochial loyalty to "our own civilization." No one was saying Islam was better or worse than "the West." All of us were simply expressing our best sense of which events had been most consequential in the story of humankind.

Mine was so much the minority opinion that it was indistinguishable from error, so we ended up with a table of contents in which Islam constituted the central topic of just one out of thirty chapters. The other two chapters in that unit were "Pre-Columbian Civilizations of the Americas" and "Ancient Empires of Africa."

Even this, incidentally, represented expanded coverage. The best-selling world history program of the previous textbook cycle, the 1997 edition of *Perspectives on the Past*, addressed Islam in just one chapter out of thirty-seven, and half of *that* chapter (part of a unit called "The Middle Ages") was given over to the Byzantine Empire.

In short, less than a year before September 11, 2001, the consensus of expert opinion was telling me that Islam was a relatively minor phenomenon whose impact had ended long before the Renaissance. If you went strictly by our table of contents, you would never guess Islam still existed.

At the time, I accepted that my judgment might be skewed. After all, I had a personal preoccupation with Islam that was part of sorting out my own identity. Not only had I grown up in a Muslim country, but I was born into a family whose one-time high social status in Afghanistan was based entirely on our reputed piety and religious learning. Our last name indicates our supposed descent from the Ansars, "the Helpers," those first Muslim converts of Medina who helped the Prophet Mohammed escape assassination in Mecca and thereby ensured the survival of his mission.

More recently, my grandfather's great-grandfather was a locally revered Muslim mystic whose tomb remains a shrine for hundreds of his devotees to this day, and his legacy percolated down to my father's time, instilling in our clan a generalized sense of obligation to know this stuff better than the average guy. Growing up, I heard the buzz of Muslim anecdotes, commentary, and speculation in my environment and some of it sank in, even though my own temperament somehow turned resolutely secular.

And it remained secular after I moved to the United States; yet I found myself more interested in Islam here than I ever had been while living in the Muslim world. My interest deepened after 1979, when my brother embraced "fundamentalist" Islam. I began delving into the philosophy of Islam through writers such as Fazlur Rahman and Syed Hussein Nasr as well as its history through academics such as Ernst Grunebaum and Albert Hourani, just trying to fathom what my brother and I were coming from, or in his case, moving toward.

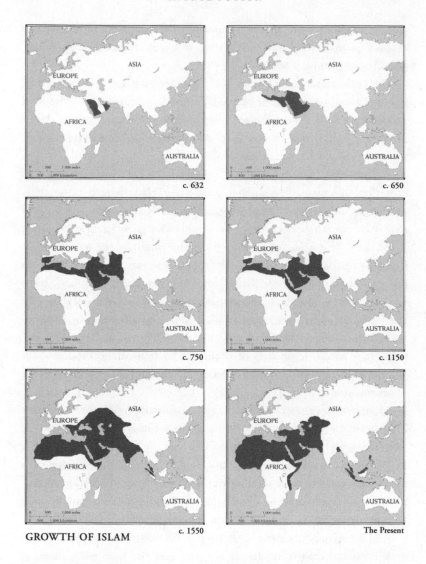

c. 632

c. 650

c. 750

c. 1150

GROWTH OF ISLAM   c. 1550   The Present

Given my personal stake, I could concede that I might be overestimating the importance of Islam. And yet . . . a niggling doubt remained. Was my assessment wholly without objective basis? Take a look at these six maps, snapshots of the Islamic world at six different dates:

When I say "Islamic world," I mean societies with Muslim majorities and/or Muslim rulers. There are, of course, Muslims in England, France, the United States, and nearly every other part of the globe, but it would be misleading, on that basis, to call London or Paris or New York a part of the Islamic world. Even by my limited definition, however, has the "Islamic world" not been a considerable geographical fact throughout its many centuries? Does it not remain one to this day, straddling the Asian-African landmass and forming an enormous buffer between Europe and East Asia? Physically, it spans more space than Europe and the United States combined. In the past, it has been a single political entity, and notions of its singleness and political unity resonate among some Muslims even now. Looking at these six maps, I still have to wonder how, on the eve of 9/11, anyone could have failed to consider Islam a major player at the table of world history!

After 9/11, perceptions changed. Non-Muslims in the West began to ask what Islam was all about, who these people were, and what was going on over there. The same questions began to bombinate with new urgency for me too. That year, visiting Pakistan and Afghanistan for the first time in thirty-eight years, I took along a book that I had found in a used bookstore in London, *Islam in Modern History* by the late Wilfred Cantwell Smith, a professor of religion at McGill and Harvard. Smith published his book in 1957, so the "modern history" of which he spoke had ended more than forty years earlier, and yet his analyses struck me as remarkably—in fact disturbingly—pertinent to the history unfolding in 2002.

Smith shone new light on the information I possessed from childhood and from later reading. For example, during my school days in Kabul, I was quite aware of a man named Sayyid Jamaluddin-i-Afghan. Like "everyone," I knew he was a towering figure in modern Islamic history; but frankly I never fathomed how he had earned his acclaim, beyond the fact that he espoused "pan-Islamism," which seemed like mere pallid Muslim chauvinism to me. Now, reading Smith, I realized that the basic tenets of "Islamism," the political ideology making such a clatter around us in 2001, had been hammered out a hundred-plus years earlier by this intellectual Karl Marx of "Islamism." How could his very name be unknown to most non-Muslims?

I plowed back into Islamic history, no longer in a quest for personal identity, but in an effort to make sense of the alarming developments among Muslims of my time—the horror stories in Afghanistan; the tumult in

Iran, the insurgencies in Algeria, the Philippines, and elsewhere; the hijackings and suicide bombings in the Middle East, the hardening extremism of political Islam; and now the emergence of the Taliban. Surely, a close look at history would reveal how on Earth it had come to *this*.

And gradually, I came to realize how it had come to this. I came to perceive that, unlike the history of France or Malta or South America, the history of the Islamic lands "over there" was not a subset of some single world history shared by all. It was more like a whole alternative *world* history unto itself, competing with and mirroring the one I had tried to create for that Texas publisher, or the one published by McDougall-Littell, for which I had written "the Islam chapters."

The two histories had begun in the same place, between the Tigris and Euphrates Rivers of ancient Iraq, and they had come to the same place, this global struggle in which the West and the Islamic world seemed to be the major players. In between, however, they had passed through different—and yet strangely parallel!—landscapes.

Yes, strangely parallel: looking back, for example, from within the Western world-historical framework, one sees a single big empire towering above all others back there in ancient times: it is Rome, where the dream of a universal political state was born.

Looking back from anywhere in the Islamic world, one also sees a single definitive empire looming back there, embodying the vision of a universal state, but it isn't Rome. It is the khalifate of early Islam.

In both histories, the great early empire fragments because it simply grows too big. The decaying empire is then attacked by nomadic barbarians from the north—but in the Islamic world, "the north" refers to the steppes of Central Asia and in that world the nomadic barbarians are not the Germans but the Turks. In both, the invaders dismember the big state into a patchwork of smaller kingdoms permeated throughout by a single, unifying religious orthodoxy: Catholicism in the West, Sunni Islam in the East.

World history is always the story of how "we" got to the here and now, so the shape of the narrative inherently depends on who we mean by "we" and what we mean by "here and now." Western world history traditionally presumes that here and now is democratic industrial (and postindustrial) civilization. In the United States the further presumption holds that world history leads to the birth of its founding ideals of liberty and equality and to its resultant rise as a superpower leading the planet into the future. This premise establishes a direction for history and places the endpoint somewhere down the road we're traveling now. It renders us vulnerable to the supposition that all people are moving in this same direction, though some are not quite so far along—either because they started late, or because they're moving more slowly—for which reason we call their nations "developing countries."

When the ideal future envisioned by postindustrialized, Western democratic society is taken as the endpoint of history, the shape of the narrative leading to here-and-now features something like the following stages:

1. Birth of civilization (Egypt and Mesopotamia)
2. Classical age (Greece and Rome)
3. The Dark Ages (rise of Christianity)
4. The Rebirth: Renaissance and Reformation
5. The Enlightenment (exploration and science)
6. The Revolutions (democratic, industrial, technological)
7. Rise of Nation-States: The Struggle for Empire
8. World Wars I and II.
9. The Cold War
10. The Triumph of Democratic Capitalism

But what if we look at world history through Islamic eyes? Are we apt to regard ourselves as stunted versions of the West, developing toward the same endpoint, but less effectually? I think not. For one thing, we would see a different threshold dividing all of time into "before" and "after": the year zero for us would be the year of Prophet Mohammed's migration from Mecca to Medina, his Hijra, which gave birth to the Muslim community. For us, this community would embody the meaning of "civilized," and perfecting this ideal would look like the impulse that had given history its shape and direction.

But in recent centuries, we would feel that something had gone awry with the flow. We would know the community had stopped expanding, had grown confused, had found itself permeated by a disruptive crosscurrent, a competing historical direction. As heirs to Muslim tradition, we would be forced to look for the meaning of history in defeat instead of triumph. We would feel conflicted between two impulses: changing our notion of "civilized" to align with the flow of history or fighting the flow of history to realign it with our notion of "civilized."

If the stunted present experienced by Islamic society is taken as the here-and-now to be explained by the narrative of world history, then the story might break down to something like the following stages:

1. Ancient Times: Mesopotamia and Persia
2. Birth of Islam
3. The Khalifate: Quest for Universal Unity
4. Fragmentation: Age of the Sultanates
5. Catastrophe: Crusaders and Mongols
6. Rebirth: The Three-Empires Era
7. Permeation of East by West
8. The Reform Movements
9. Triumph of the Secular Modernists
10. The Islamist Reaction

Literary critic Edward Said has argued that over the centuries, the West has constructed an "Orientalist" fantasy of the Islamic world, in which a sinister sense of "otherness" is mingled with envious images of decadent opulence. Well, yes, to the extent that Islam has entered the Western imagination, that has more or less been the depiction.

But more intriguing to me is the relative absence of any depictions at all. In Shakespeare's day, for example, preeminent world power was centered in three Islamic empires. Where are all the Muslims in his canon? Missing. If you didn't know Moors were Muslims, you wouldn't learn it from *Othello*.

Here are two enormous worlds side by side; what's remarkable is how little notice they have taken of each other. If the Western and Islamic worlds were two individual human beings, we might see symptoms of repression here. We might ask, "What happened between these two? Were they lovers once? Is there some history of abuse?"

But there is, I think, another less sensational explanation. Throughout much of history, the West and the core of what is now the Islamic world have been like two separate universes, each preoccupied with its own internal affairs, each assuming itself to be the center of human history, each living out a different narrative—until the late seventeenth century when the two narratives began to intersect. At that point, one or the other had to give way because the two narratives were crosscurrents to each other. The West being more powerful, its current prevailed and churned the other one under.

But the superseded history never really ended. It kept on flowing beneath the surface, like a riptide, and it is flowing down there still. When you chart the hot spots of the world—Kashmir, Iraq, Chechnya, the Balkans, Israel and Palestine, Iraq—you're staking out the borders of some entity that has vanished from the maps but still thrashes and flails in its effort not to die.

This is the story I tell in the pages that follow, and I emphasize "story." *Destiny Disrupted* is neither a textbook nor a scholarly thesis. It's more like what I'd tell you if we met in a coffeehouse and you said, "What's all this about a parallel world history?" The argument I make can be found in numerous books now on the shelves of university libraries. Read it there if you don't mind academic language and footnotes. Read it here if you want the story arc.[1] Although I am not a scholar, I have drawn on the work of scholars who sift the raw material of history to draw conclusions and of academics who sifted the work of scholarly researchers to draw meta-conclusions.

In a history spanning several thousand years, I devote what may seem like inordinate space to a brief half century long ago, but I linger here because this period spans the career of Prophet Mohammed and his first four successors, the founding narrative of Islam. I recount this story as an intimate human drama, because this is the way that Muslims know it. Academics approach this story more skeptically, crediting non-Muslim sources above supposedly less-objective Muslim accounts, because they are mainly concerned to dig up what "really happened." My aim is mainly to convey what Muslims *think* happened, because that's what has motivated Muslims over the ages and what makes their role in world history intelligible.

I will, however, assert one caveat here about the origins of Islam. Unlike older religions—such as Judaism, Buddhism, Hinduism, even Christianity—Muslims began to collect, memorize, recite, and preserve their history as soon as it happened, and they didn't just preserve it but embedded each anecdote in a nest of sources, naming witnesses to each event and listing all persons who transmitted the account down through time to the one who first wrote it down, references that function like the chain of custody validating a piece of evidence in a court case.

This implies only that the core Muslim stories cannot best be approached as parables. With a parable, we don't ask for proof that the events occurred; that's not the point. We don't care if the *story* is true; we want the *lesson* to be true. The Muslim stories don't encapsulate lessons of that sort: they're not stories about ideal people in an ideal realm. They come to us, rather, as accounts of real people wrestling with practical issues in the mud and murk of actual history, and we take from them what lessons we will.

Which is not to deny that the Muslim stories are allegorical, nor that some were invented, nor that many or even all were modified by tellers along the way to suit agendas of the person or moment. It is only to say that the Muslims have transmitted their foundational narrative in the same spirit as historical accounts, and we know about these people and events in much the same way that we know what happened between Sulla and Marius in ancient Rome. These tales lie somewhere between history and myth, and telling them stripped of human drama falsifies the meaning they have had for Muslims, rendering less intelligible the things Muslims have done over the centuries. This then is how I plan to tell the story, and if you're on board with me, buckle in and let's begin.

I

∞

The Middle World

LONG BEFORE ISLAM was born, two worlds took shape between the Atlantic Ocean and the Bay of Bengal. Each coalesced around a different network of trade and travel routes; one of them, mainly sea routes; the other, land routes.

If you look at ancient sea traffic, the Mediterranean emerges as the obvious center of world history, for it was here that the Mycenaeans, Cretans, Phoenicians, Lydians, Greeks, Romans, and so many other vigorous early cultures met and mingled. People who lived within striking distance of the Mediterranean could easily hear about and interact with anyone else who lived within striking distance of the Mediterranean, and so this great sea itself became an organizing force drawing diverse people into one another's narratives and weaving their destinies together to form the germ of a world history, and out of this came "Western civilization."

If you look at ancient overland traffic, however, the Grand Central Station of the world was the nexus of roads and routes connecting the Indian subcontinent, Central Asia, the Iranian highlands, Mesopotamia, and Egypt, roads that ran within a territory ringed by rivers and seas—the Persian Gulf, the Indus and Oxus rivers; the Aral, Caspian, and Black seas; the Mediterranean, the Nile, and the Red Sea. This eventually became the Islamic world.

Unfortunately, common usage assigns no single label to this second area. A portion of it is typically called the Middle East, but giving one part

1

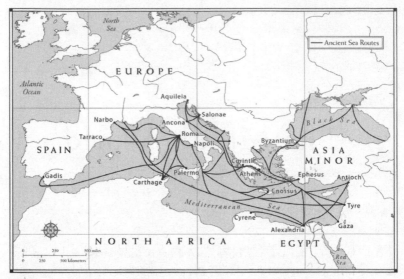

THE MEDITERRANEAN WORLD (Defined by Sea Routes)

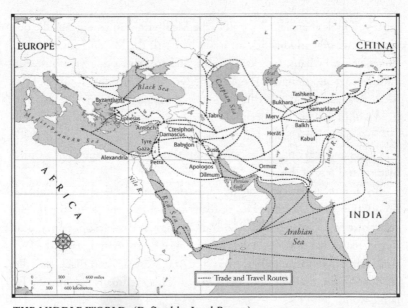

THE MIDDLE WORLD (Defined by Land Routes)

of it a name obscures the connectedness of the whole, and besides, the phrase *Middle East* assumes that one is standing in western Europe—if you're standing in the Persian highlands, for example, the so-called Middle East is actually the Middle West. Therefore, I prefer to call this whole area from the Indus to Istanbul the Middle World, because it lies between the Mediterranean world and the Chinese world.

The Chinese world was, of course, its own universe and had little to do with the other two; and that's to be expected on the basis of geography alone. China was cut off from the Mediterranean world by sheer distance and from the Middle World by the Himalayas, the Gobi Desert, and the jungles of southeast Asia, a nearly impenetrable barrier, which is why China and its satellites and rivals barely enter the "world history" centered in the Middle World, and why they come in for rare mention in this book. The same is true of sub-Saharan Africa, cut off from the rest of Eurasia by the world's biggest desert. For that matter, the Americas formed yet another distinct universe with a world history of its own, which is for geographic reasons even more to be expected.

Geography, however, did not separate the Mediterranean and Middle worlds as radically as it isolated China or the Americas. These two regions coalesced as different worlds because they were what historian Philip D. Curtin has called "intercommunicating zones": each had more interaction internally than it had with the other. From anywhere near the Mediterranean coast, it was easier to get to some other place near the Mediterranean coast than to Persepolis or the Indus River. Similarly, caravans on the overland routes crisscrossing the Middle World in ancient times could strike off in any direction at any intersection—there were many such intersections. As they traveled west, however, into Asia Minor (what we now call Turkey), the very shape of the land gradually funneled them down into the world's narrowest bottleneck, the bridge (if there happened to be one at the given time) across the Bosporus Strait. This tended to choke overland traffic down to a trickle and turn the caravans back toward the center or south along the Mediterranean coast.

Gossip, stories, jokes, rumors, historical impressions, religious mythologies, products, and other detritus of culture flow along with traders, travelers, and conquerors. Trade and travel routes thus function like capillaries, carrying civilizational blood. Societies permeated by a network of such capillaries are apt to become characters in one another's narratives, even if they disagree about who the good guys and the bad guys are.

Thus it was that the Mediterranean and Middle worlds developed somewhat distinct narratives of world history. People living around the Mediterranean had good reason to think of themselves at the center of human history, but people living in the Middle World had equally good reason to think they were situated at the heart of it all.

These two world histories overlapped, however, in the strip of territory where you now find Israel, where you now find Lebanon, where you now find Syria and Jordan—where you now, in short, find so much trouble. This was the eastern edge of the world defined by sea-lanes and the western edge of the world defined by land routes. From the Mediterranean perspective, this area has always been part of the world history that has the Mediterranean as its seed and core. From the other perspective, it has always been part of the Middle World that has Mesopotamia and Persia at its core. Is there not now and has there not often been some intractable argument about this patch of land: whose world is this a part of?

THE MIDDLE WORLD BEFORE ISLAM

The first civilizations emerged along the banks of various big slow-moving rivers subject to annual floods. The Huang Ho valley in China, the Indus River valley in India, the Nile Valley in Africa—these are places where, some six thousand years ago or more, nomadic hunters and herders settled down, built villages, and became farmers.

Perhaps the most dynamic petri dish of early human culture was that fertile wedge of land between the Tigris and Euphrates known as Mesopotamia—which means, in fact, "between the rivers." Incidentally, the narrow strip of land flanked by these two rivers almost exactly bisects the modern-day nation of Iraq. When we speak of "the fertile crescent" as "the cradle of civilization," we're talking about Iraq—this is where it all began.

One key geographical feature sets Mesopotamia apart from some of the other early hotbeds of culture. Its two defining rivers flow through flat, habitable plains and can be approached from any direction. Geography provides no natural defenses to the people living here—unlike the Nile, for example, which is flanked by marshes on its eastern side, by the uninhabitable Sahara on the west, and by rugged cliffs at its upper end. Geography gave Egypt continuity but also reduced its interactions with other cultures, giving it a certain stasis.

Not so, Mesopotamia. Here, early on, a pattern took hold that was repeated many times over the course of a thousand-plus years, a complex struggle between nomads and city dwellers, which kept spawning bigger empires. The pattern went like this:

Settled farmers would build irrigation systems supporting prosperous villages and towns. Eventually some tough guy, some well-organized priest, or some alliance of the two would bring a number of these urban centers under the rule of a single power, thereby forging a larger political unit—a confederation, a kingdom, an empire. Then a tribe of hardy nomads would come along, conquer the monarch of the moment, seize all his holdings, and in the process expand their empire. Eventually the hardy nomads would become soft, luxury-loving city dwellers, exactly the sort of people they had conquered, at which point another tribe of hardy nomads would come along, conquer them, and take over *their* empire.

Conquest, consolidation, expansion, degeneration, conquest—this was the pattern. It was codified in the fourteenth century by the great Muslim historian Ibn Khaldun, based on his observations of the world he lived in. Ibn Khaldun felt that in this pattern he had discovered the underlying pulse of history.

At any given time, this process was happening in more than one place, one empire developing here, another sprouting there, both empires expanding until they bumped up against each other, at which point one would conquer the other, forging a single new and bigger empire.

About fifty-five hundred years ago, a dozen or so cities along the Euphrates coalesced into a single network called Sumer. Here, writing was invented, the wheel, the cart, the potter's wheel, and an early number system. Then the Akkadians, rougher fellows from upriver, conquered Sumer. Their leader, Sargon, was the first notable conqueror known to history by name, a ferocious fellow by all accounts and the ultimate self-made man, for he started out poor and unknown but left records of his deeds in the form of clay documents stamped with cuneiform, which basically said, "This one rose up and I smote him; that one rose up and I smote him."

Sargon led his armies so far south they were able to wash their weapons in the sea. There he said, "Now, any king who wants to call himself my equal, wherever I went, let him go!" meaning, "Let's just see anyone else conquer as much as I have."[1] His empire was smaller than New Jersey.

In time, a fresh wave of nomadic ruffians from the highlands came down and conquered Akkad, and they were conquered by others, and they by others—Guttians, Kassites, Hurrians, Amorites—the pattern kept repeating. Look closely and you'll see new rulers presiding over basically the same territory, but always more of it.

The Amorites clocked a crucial moment in this cycle when they built the famous city of Babylon and from this capital ruled the (first) Babylonian Empire. The Babylonians gave way to the Assyrians, who ruled from the even bigger and grander city of Nineveh. Their empire stretched from Iraq to Egypt, and you can imagine how enormous such a realm must have seemed at a time when the fastest way to get from one place to another was by horse. The Assyrians acquired a nasty reputation in history as merciless tyrants. It's hard to say if they were really worse than others of their time, but they did practice a strategy Stalin made infamous in the twentieth century: they uprooted whole populations and moved them to other places, on the theory that people who had lost their homes and lived among strangers, cut off from familiar resources, would be too confused and unhappy to organize rebellion.

It worked for a while, but not forever. The Assyrians fell at last to one of their subject peoples, the Chaldeans, who rebuilt Babylon and won a lustrous place in history for their intellectual achievements in astronomy, medicine, and mathematics. They used a base-12 system (as opposed to our base-10 system) and were pioneers in the measurement and division of time, which is why the year has twelve months, the hour has sixty minutes (five times twelve), and the minute has sixty seconds. They were terrific urban planners and architects—it was a Chaldean king who built those Hanging Gardens of Babylon, which the ancients ranked among the seven wonders of the world.

But the Chaldeans followed the Assyrian strategy of uprooting whole populations in order to divide and rule. Their king Nebuchadnezzar was the one who first smashed Jerusalem and dragged the Hebrews into captivity. It was also a Chaldean king of Babylonia, Balshazzar, who, while feasting in his palace one night, saw a disembodied hand write on his wall in letters of fire, *"Mene mene tekel upharsin."*

His sycophants couldn't make heads or tails of these words, probably because they were blind drunk, but also because the words were written in some strange tongue (Aramaic, as it happens.) They sent for the Hebrew captive Daniel, who said the words meant "Your days are numbered; you've been weighed and found wanting; your kingdom will be divided." At least so goes the Old Testament story in the book of Daniel.

Balshazzar barely had time to ponder the prophecy before it came true. A sudden blistering bloodbath was unleashed upon Babylon by the newest gang of ruffians from the highlands, an alliance of Persians and Medes. These two Indo-European tribes put an end to second Babylonia and replaced it with the Persian Empire.

At this point, the recurrent pattern of ever-bigger empires in the heart of the Middle World came to an end or at least to a long pause. For one thing, by the time the Persians were done, there wasn't much left to conquer. Both "cradles of civilization," Egypt and Mesopotamia, ended up as part of their realm. Their suzerainty stretched west into Asia Minor, south to the Nile, and east through the Iranian highlands and Afghanistan to the Indus River. The perfumed and polished Persians probably saw no point in further conquest: south of the Indus lay steaming jungles, and north of Afghanistan stretched harsh steppes raked by bitter winds and roamed by Turkish nomads eking out a bare existence with their herds and flocks—who even wanted to rule that? The Persians therefore contented themselves with building a string of forts to keep the barbarians out, so that decent folks might pursue the arts of civilized living on the settled side of the fence.

By the time the Persians took charge, around 550 BCE, a lot of consolidation had already been done: in each region, earlier conquerors had drawn various local tribes and towns into single systems ruled by one monarch from a central capital, whether Elam, Ur, Nineveh, or Babylon. The Persians profited from the work (and bloodshed) of their predecessors.

Yet the Persian Empire stands out for several reasons. First, the Persians were the counter-Assyrians. They developed a completely opposite idea of how to rule a vast realm. Instead of uprooting whole nations, they resettled them. They set the Hebrews free from captivity and helped them get back to

Canaan. The Persian emperors pursued a multicultural, many-people-under-one-big-tent strategy. They controlled their enormous realm by letting all the different constituent people live their own lives according to their own folkways and mores, under the rule of their own leaders, provided they paid their taxes and submitted to a few of the emperor's mandates and demands. The Muslims later picked up on this idea, and it persisted through Ottoman times.

Second, the Persians saw communication as a key to unifying, and thus controlling, their realm. They promulgated a coherent set of tax laws and issued a single currency for their realm, currency being the medium of communication in business. They built a tremendous network of roads and studded it with hostels to make travel easy. They developed an efficient postal system, too, an early version of the Pony Express. That quote you sometimes see associated with the U.S. Postal Service, "Neither snow nor rain nor heat nor gloom of night stays these couriers from the swift completion of their appointed rounds," comes from ancient Persia.

The Persians also employed a lot of translators. You couldn't get away with saying, "But, officer, I didn't know it was against the law; I don't speak Persian." Translators enabled the emperors to broadcast written descriptions of their splendor and greatness in various languages so that all their subjects could admire them. Darius ("the Great"), who brought the Persian Empire to one of its several peaks, had his life story carved into a rock at a place called Behistun. He had it inscribed in three languages: Old Persian, Elamite, and Babylonian, fifteen thousand characters devoted to Darius's deeds and conquests, detailing the rebels who had tried and failed to topple him and the punishments he had meted out to them, essentially communicating that you did not want to mess with this emperor: he'd cut off your nose, and worse. Nonetheless, citizens of the empire found Persian rule basically benign. The well-oiled imperial machinery kept the peace, which let ordinary folks get on with the business of raising families, growing crops, and making useful goods.

The part of Darius's Behistun inscription written in Old Persian was decipherable from modern Persian, so after it was rediscovered in the nineteenth century, scholars were able to use it to unlock the other two languages and thus gain access to the cuneiform libraries of ancient

Mesopotamia, libraries so extensive that we know more about daily life in this area three thousand years ago than we know about daily life in western Europe twelve hundred years ago.

Religion permeated the Persian world. It wasn't the million-gods idea of Hinduism, nor was it anything like the Egyptian pantheon of magical creatures with half-human and half-animal shapes, nor was it like Greek paganism, which saw every little thing in nature as having its own god, a god who looked human and had human frailties. No, in the Persian universe, Zoroastrianism held pride of place. Zoroaster lived about a thousand years before Christ, perhaps earlier or perhaps later; no one really knows. He hailed from northern Iran, or maybe northern Afghanistan, or maybe somewhere east of that; no one really knows that, either. Zoroaster never claimed to be a prophet or channeler of divine energy, much less a divinity or deity. He considered himself a philosopher and seeker. But his followers considered him a holy man.

Zoroaster preached that the universe was divided between darkness and light, between good and evil, between truth and falsehood, between life and death. The universe split into these opposing camps at the moment of creation, they had been locked in struggle ever since, and the contest would endure to the end of time.

People, said Zoroaster, contain both principles within themselves. They choose freely whether to go this way or that. By choosing good, people promote the forces of light and life. By choosing evil, they give strength to the forces of darkness and death. There is no predestination in the Zoroastrian universe. The outcome of the great contest is always in doubt, and not only is every human being free to make moral choices, but every moral choice affects that cosmic outcome.

Zoroaster saw the drama of the universe vested in two divinities—not one, not thousands, but two. Ahura Mazda embodied the principle of good, Ahriman the principle of evil. Fire served as an iconic representation of Ahura Mazda, which has led some to characterize Zoroastrians as fire worshippers, but what they worship is not fire per se, it's Ahura Mazda. Zoroaster spoke of an afterlife but suggested that the good go there not as a reward for being good but as a consequence of having chosen that direction. You might say they lift themselves to heaven by the bootstraps of their choices. The Persian Zoroastrians rejected religious statues, imagery, and icons, laying the basis for the hostility toward representation in religious art that reemerged forcefully in Islam.

Sometimes Zoroaster, or at least his followers, called Ahura Mazda "the Wise Lord" and spoke as if he was actually the creator of the entire universe and as if it was he who had divided all of creation into two opposing aspects a short time after the moment of creation. Thus, Zoroaster's dualism inched toward monotheism, but it never quite arrived there. In the end, for the ancient Persian Zoroastrians, two deities with equal power inhabited the universe, and human beings were the rope in a tug of war between them.

A Zoroastrian priest was called a magus, the plural of which is *magi*: the three "wise men of the East" who, according to the Christian story, brought myrrh and frankincense to the infant Jesus in his stable were Zoroastrian priests. The word *magician* also derives from *magi*. These priests were thought by others (and sometimes themselves claimed) to possess miraculous powers.

In the late days of the empire, the Persians broke into the Mediterranean world and made a brief, big splash in Western world history. Persian emperor Darius sallied west to punish the Greeks. I say "punish," not "invade" or "conquer," because from the Persian point of view the so-called Persian Wars were not some seminal clash between two civilizations. The Persians saw the Greeks as the primitive inhabitants of some small cities on the far western edges of the civilized world, cities that implicitly belonged to the Persians, even though they were too far away to rule directly. Emperor Darius wanted the Greeks merely to confirm that they were his subjects by sending him a jar of water and a box of soil in symbolic tribute. The Greeks refused. Darius collected an army to go teach the Greeks a lesson they would never forget, but the very size of his army was as much a liability as an asset: How do you direct so many men at such a distance? How do you keep them supplied? Darius had ignored the first principle of military strategy: never fight a land war in Europe. In the end, it was the Greeks who taught the Persians an unforgettable lesson—a lesson that they quickly forgot, however, for less than one generation later, Darius's dimwitted son Xerxes decided to avenge his father by repeating and compounding his mistakes. Xerxes, too, came limping home, and that was the end of Persia's European adventure.

It didn't end there, however. About 150 years later, Alexander the Great took the battle the other way. We often hear of Alexander the Great conquering the world, but what he really conquered was Persia, which had already conquered "the world."

With Alexander, the Mediterranean narrative broke forcefully in upon the Middle World one. Alexander dreamed of blending the two into one: of uniting Europe and Asia. He was planning to locate his capital at Babylon. Alexander cut deep and made a mark. He appears in many Persian myths and stories, which give him an outsize heroic quality, though not an altogether positive one (but not entirely villainous, either). A number of cities in the Muslim world are named after him. Alexandria is the obvious example, but a less obvious one is Kandahar—famous now because the Taliban consider it their capital. Kandahar was originally called "Iskandar," which is how "Alexander" was pronounced in the east, but the "Is" dropped away, and "Kandar" softened into "Kandahar."

But the cut Alexander inflicted closed up, the skin grew over, and the impact of his eleven years in Asia faded. One night in Babylon he suddenly died, whether from the flu, malaria, too much drink, or poison, no one knows. He had stationed generals in various parts of the territory he had conquered, and the moment he died, the toughest ones claimed whatever terrain they happened to hold, fashioning Hellenic kingdoms that endured for a few hundred years. For example, in the kingdom of Bactria (now northern Afghanistan) artists made Greek-looking sculptures; later, when Buddhist influences seeped north from India, the two art styles mixed, resulting in what is now known as Greco-Buddhist art.

Eventually, however, those kingdoms weakened, Greek influence faded away, the Greek language fell out of use here, and the Persian substratum welled back to the surface. Another empire came to occupy much the same territory as that of the ancient Persians (though not as much of it). The new rulers called themselves Parthians, and they were formidable warriors. The Parthians battled Rome to a standstill, preventing their expansion east. Their armies were the first to include cataphracts—knights in full metal armor riding huge armored horses, much like the ones we associate with Europe's feudal ages. These Parthian knights were like mobile castles. But mobile castles are cumbersome, so the Parthians had another cavalry corps as well, lightly clad men riding naked horses. As a battle tactic, the light cavalry sometimes pretended to have been routed; in the hot middle of the fighting, they would suddenly turn tail and race away. The army they were fighting would break ranks and chase after them, losing all order as they clamored, "Get 'em, boys; they're on the run; let's finish 'em!" whereupon the Parthians would suddenly wheel around and fire into the disorganized rabble their opponents had become, annihilating them in minutes. This was later known as a Parthian shot, and when you hear the phrase "parting shot," you may actually be hearing a corruption of the phrase "Parthian shot."[2]

The Parthians were originally nomadic herders and hunters from the mountains northeast of Persia, but once they appropriated the frame of the old Persian Empire, they became, for all practical purposes, Persians. (Their name, Parthian, is probably a corruption or variation of "Persian.") This empire endured for centuries without leaving much of a trace, because they took little interest in art and culture, and mobile castles get recycled for scrap metal once the warriors inside them die.

While they lasted, however, the Parthians protected and promoted trade, and caravans moved freely within their borders. The Parthian capital was known to the Greeks as Hecatompylos, "the hundred gated," because so many roads converged there. In the bazaars of Parthian cities, you could probably hear gossip from all quarters of the empire and the societies it bordered: the Greco-Buddhist kingdoms in the east, the Hindus to the south of them, the Chinese of the further east, the waning Greek (Seleucid) kingdoms in the west, and the Armenians to their north. . . . The Parthians had little social intercourse with the Romans, unless fighting counts. The civilizational blood that made the Parthians Persian didn't get across that border, and so again the Mediterranean and Middle worlds diverged.

Around the time the Parthians began their rise, China was unified for the first time. In fact, the glory years of China's seminal Han dynasty coincide almost exactly with the period of Parthian dominance. In the West, the Romans began their great expansion near the beginning of the Parthian era. Just as Rome was beating Carthage for the first time, the Parthians were taking Babylonia. Just as Julius Caesar was tearing up Gaul, Parthian power was peaking in the Middle World. In 53 BCE the Parthians crushed the Romans in a battle, capturing thirty-four thousand legionnaires and killing Crassus who, along with Caesar and Pompey, had been coruler of Rome. Thirty years later, the Parthians dealt Mark Antony a stinging defeat and established the Euphrates River as the border between the two empires. The Parthians were still expanding east when Christ was born. The spread of Christianity went little noticed by the Parthians, who favored Zoroastrianism in a lukewarm sort of way. When Christian missionaries began trickling east, the Parthians let them in; they didn't care very much about religion, one way or another.

The Parthians always operated on a feudal system, with power distributed down through many layers of lords. Over time, imperial power leaked away into this ever more fragmented feudalism. In the third (Christian) century, a provincial rebel overthrew the last of the Parthians and founded the Sassanid dynasty, and this quickly expanded to occupy all the same territory as the Parthians and a little more besides. The Sassanids didn't alter the direction of cultural change; they only organized the empire more effectively, erased the last traces of Hellenic influence, and completed the restoration of the Persian fabric. They built monumental sculptures, enormous buildings, and imposing cities. Zoroastrianism enjoyed a huge resurgence—fire and ashes, sunlight and darkness, Ahura Mazda and Ahriman: it was the state religion. Missionary monks had been roaming west from Afghanistan, teaching Buddhism, but the seeds they dropped would not grow in the soil of Zoroastrian Persia, so they turned east, which is why Buddhism spread to China but not Europe. Countless Persian tales and legends of later times go back to this Sassanid period. The greatest of the Sassanid kings, Khusrow Anushervan, came to be remembered (by Persian speakers) as the archetype of the "just king," conflated perhaps with Kay Khosrow, the third king of Iran's mythical first dynasty, something like an Arthurian figure presiding over a Persian Camelot and served by noble warriors.[3]

The Roman Empire, meanwhile, was falling apart. In 293, the emperor Diocletian divided the empire in four parts for administrative purposes: it had grown just too huge and cumbersome to run from a single center. But Diocletian's reform ended up splitting the empire in two. The wealth was all in the east, it turned out, so the western part of the Roman Empire crumbled. As nomadic German tribes moved into the empire, government services shrank, law and order broke down, and trade decayed. Schools foundered, western Europeans stopped reading or writing much, and Europe sank into its so-called Dark Ages. Roman cities in places like Germany and France and Britain fell into ruin, and society simplified down to serfs, warriors, and priests. The only institution binding disparate locales together was Christianity, anchored by the bishop of Rome, soon known as the pope.

The eastern portion of the Roman Empire, headquartered in Constantinople, continued to hang on. The locals still called this entity Rome but to later historians it looked like something new, so retrospectively they gave it a new name: the Byzantine Empire.

Orthodox Christianity was centered here. Unlike Western Christianity, this church had no pope-like figure. Each city with a sizable Christian population had its own top bishop, a "metropolitan," and all the metropolitans were supposedly equal, although the top bishop of Constantinople was more equal than most. Above them all, however, stood the emperor. Western learning, technology, and intellectual activity contracted to Byzantium. Here, writers and artists continued to produce books, paintings, and other works, yet once eastern Rome became the Byzantine Empire it more or less passed out of Western history.

Many will dispute this statement—the Byzantine Empire was Christian, after all. Its subjects spoke Greek, and its philosophers . . . well, let us not speak too much about its philosophers. Almost any well-educated Westerner knows of Socrates, Plato, and Aristotle, not to mention Sophocles, Virgil, Tacitus, Pericles, Alexander of Macedon, Julius Caesar, Augustus, and many others; but apart from academics who specialize in Byzantine history, few can name three Byzantine philosophers, or two Byzantine poets, or one Byzantine emperor after Justinian. The Byzantine Empire lasted almost a thousand years, by few can name five events that took place in the empire during all that time.

Compared to ancient Rome, the Byzantine Empire didn't wield much clout, but in its own region it was a superpower, largely because it had no competition and because its walled capital of Constantinople was probably the most impregnable city the world had ever known. By the mid-sixth century, the Byzantines ruled most of Asia Minor and some of what we now call eastern Europe. They butted right up against Sassanid Persia, the region's other superpower. The Sassanids ruled a swath of land stretching

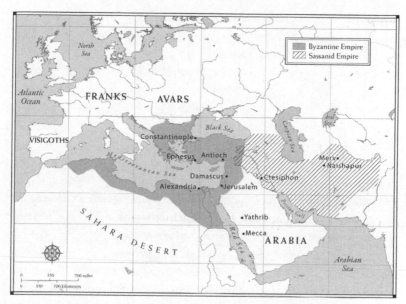

ON THE EVE OF ISLAM: THE BYZANTINE AND SASSANID EMPIRES

east to the foothills of the Himalayas. Between the two empires lay a strip of disputed territory, the lands along the Mediterranean shore, where the two world histories overlap and where disputes have been endemic. To the south, in the shadow of both big empires, lay the Arabian Peninsula, inhabited by numerous autonomous tribes. Such was the political configuration of the Middle World just before Islam was born.

2

The Hijra

Year Zero
622 CE

IN THE LATE sixth century of the Christian age, a number of cities flour-ished along the Arabian coast as hotbeds of commerce. The Arabians re-ceived goods at Red Sea ports and took camel caravans across the desert to Syria and Palestine, transporting spice and cloth and other trade goods. They went north, south, east, and west; so they knew all about the Chris-tian world and its ideas, but also about Zoroaster and his ideas. A number of Jewish tribes lived among the Arabs; they had come here after the Ro-mans had driven them out of Palestine. Both the Arabs and the Jews were Semitic and traced their descent to Abraham (and through him to Adam). The Arabs saw themselves as the line descended from Abraham's son Ish-mael and his second wife, Hagar. The stories commonly associated with the Old Testament—Adam and Eve, Cain and Abel, Noah and his ark, Joseph and Egypt, Moses and the pharaoh, and the rest of them—were part of Arab tradition too. Although most of the Arabs were pagan poly-theists at this point and the Jews had remained resolutely monotheistic, the two groups were otherwise more or less indistinguishable in terms of culture and lifestyle: the Jews of this area spoke Arabic, and their tribal structure resembled that of the Arabs. Some Arabs were nomadic Bedouins who lived in the desert, but others were town dwellers. Mohammed, the prophet of Islam, was born and raised in the highly cosmopolitan town of Mecca, near the Red Sea coast.

Meccans were wide-ranging merchants and traders, but their biggest, most prestigious business was religion. Mecca had temples to at least a hundred pagan deities with names like Hubal, Manat, Allat, al-Uzza, and Fals. Pilgrims streamed in to visit the sites, perform the rites, and do a little business on the side, so Mecca had a busy tourist industry with inns, taverns, shops, and services catering to pilgrims.

Mohammed was born around the year 570. The exact date is unknown because no one was paying much attention to him at the time. His father was a poor man who died when Mohammed was still in the womb, leaving Mohammed's mother virtually penniless. Then, when Mohammed was only six, his mother died too. Although Mohammed was a member of the Quraysh, the most powerful tribe in Mecca, he got no status out of it because he belonged to one of the tribe's poorer clans, the Banu ("clan" or "house of") Hashim. One gets the feeling that this boy grew up feeling quite keenly his uncertain status as an orphan. He was not abandoned, however; his close relatives took him in. He lived with his grandfather until the old man died and then with his uncle Abu Talib, who raised him like a son—yet the fact remained that he was a nobody in his culture, and outside his uncle's home he probably tasted the disdain and disrespect that was an orphan's lot. His childhood planted in him a lifelong concern for the plight of widows and orphans.

When Mohammed was twenty-five, a wealthy widowed businesswoman named Khadija hired him to manage her caravans and conduct business for her. Arab society was not kind to women as a rule, but Khadija had inherited her husband's wealth, and the fact that she held on to it suggests what a powerful and charismatic personality she must have had. Mutual respect and affection between Mohammed and Khadija led the two to marriage, a warm partnership that lasted until Khadija's death twenty-five years later. And even though Arabia was a polygynous society in which having only one wife must have been uncommon, Mohammed married no one else as long as Khadija lived.

As an adult, then, the orphan built quite a successful personal and business life. He acquired a reputation for his diplomatic skills, and quarreling parties often called upon him to act as an arbiter. Still, as Mohammed approached the age of forty, he began to suffer what we might now call a midlife crisis. He grew troubled about the meaning of life. Looking around, he saw a society bursting with wealth, and yet amid all the bustling prosperity, he saw widows eking out a bare living on charity and orphans scrambling for enough to eat. How could this be?

He developed a habit of retreating periodically to a cave in the mountains to meditate. There, one day, he had a momentous experience, the exact nature of which remains mysterious, since various accounts survive, possibly reflecting various descriptions by Mohammed himself. Tradition has settled on calling the experience a visitation from the angel Gabriel. In one account, Mohammed spoke of "a silken cloth on which was some writing" brought to him while he was asleep.[1] In the main, however, it was apparently an oral and personal interaction, which started when Mohammed, meditating in the utter darkness of the cave, sensed an overwhelming and terrifying presence: someone else was in the cave with him. Suddenly he felt himself gripped from behind so hard he could not breathe. Then came a voice, not so much heard as felt throughout his being, commanding him to "recite!"

Mohammed managed to gasp out that he could not recite.

The command came again: "Recite!"

Again Mohammed protested that he could not recite, did not know *what* to recite, but the angel—the voice—the impulse—blazed once more: "Recite!" Thereupon Mohammed felt words of terrible grandeur forming in his heart and the recitation began:

Recite in the name of your Lord Who created,
Created humans from a drop of blood.
Recite!
And your Lord is most Bountiful.
He who taught humans by the pen,
taught humans that which they knew not.

Mohammed came down from the mountain sick with fear, thinking he might have been possessed by a jinn, an evil spirit. Outside, he felt a presence filling the world to every horizon. According to some accounts, he saw a light with something like a human shape within it, which was only more thunderous and terrifying. At home, he told Khadija what had happened, and she assured him that he was perfectly sane, that his visitor had really been an angel, and that he was being called into service by God. "I believe in you," she said, thus becoming Mohammed's first follower, the first Muslim.

At first, Mohammed preached only to his intimate friends and close relatives. For a time, he experienced no further revelations, and it depressed him: he felt like a failure. But then the revelations began to come again. Gradually, he went public with the message, until he was telling people all around Mecca, "There is only one God. Submit to His will, or you will be condemned to hell"—and he specified what submitting to the will of God entailed: giving up debauchery, drunkenness, cruelty, and tyranny; attending to the plight of the weak and the meek; helping the poor; sacrificing for justice; and serving the greater good.

Among the many temples in Mecca was a cube-shaped structure with a much-revered cornerstone, a polished black stone that had fallen out of the sky a long time ago—a meteor, perhaps. This temple was called the Ka'ba, and tribal tales said that Abraham himself had built it, with the help of his son Ishmael. Mohammed considered himself a descendant of Abraham and knew all about Abraham's uncompromising monotheism. Indeed, Mohammed didn't think he was preaching something new; he believed he was renewing what Abraham (and countless other prophets) had said, so he zeroed in on the Ka'ba. This, he said, should be Mecca's only shrine: the temple of Allah.

Al means "the" in Arabic, and *lah,* an elision of *ilaah,* means "god." *Allah,* then, simply means "God." This is a core point in Islam: Mohammed wasn't talking about "this god" versus "that god." He wasn't saying, "Believe in a god called Lah because He is the biggest, strongest god," nor even that Lah was the "only true god" and all the other ones were fake. One could entertain a notion like that and still think of God as some particular being with supernatural powers, maybe a creature who looked like Zeus, enjoyed immortality, could lift a hundred camels with one hand, and was the only one of its kind. That would still constitute a belief in one god. Mohammed was proposing something different and bigger. He was preaching that there is one God too all-encompassing and universal to be associated with any particular image, any particular attributes, any finite notion, any limit. There is only God and all the rest is God's creation: this was the message he was delivering to anyone who would listen.

Mecca's business leaders came to feel threatened by Mohammed because they were making good money from religious tourism; if this only-one-god idea took hold, they feared, the devotees of all the other gods would stop coming to Mecca and they'd be ruined. (Today, ironically, over a million people come to Mecca each year to perform the rites of pilgrimage at the Ka'ba, making this the biggest annual gathering on earth!)

Besides, Mecca profited from drinking dens, gambling, prostitution, and other such attractions, and the tribal power brokers could not tolerate a man railing against the very entertainments that brought in their wealth, even if he had merely a smattering of followers, many of them powerless poor people and slaves. Well, for one thing, not *all* his followers were poor people and slaves: they included the wealthy and respected merchants Abu Bakr and Othman, and soon they even included the physically imposing giant Omar, who started out as one of Mohammed's most bitter enemies. The trend looked disturbing.

For nearly twelve years, Mohammed's uncle Abu Talib defended him against all criticism. According to most Muslims, Abu Talib never converted to Islam himself, but he stood up for his nephew out of personal loyalty and love, and his word had weight. Khadija also backed her husband unstintingly, which gave him precious comfort. Then, in the course of a single devastating year, both these major figures in Mohammed's life died, leaving God's Messenger exposed to his enemies. That year, seven elders of the Quraysh tribe decided to have Mohammed killed while he slept, thereby getting rid of the troublemaker before he could do real damage to the economy. One of Mohammed's several uncles spearheaded the plot. In fact, all seven plotters were related to Mohammed, but this didn't soften their resolve.

Fortunately, Mohammed caught wind of the plot and worked out how to foil it with help from two close companions. One was his cousin Ali, now a strapping young man, who would soon marry Mohammed's daughter Fatima and become the Messenger's son-in-law. Another was his best friend, Abu Bakr, Mohammed's first follower outside his immediate family circle and his closest adviser, soon to become Mohammed's father-in-law.

The Prophet had already been in contact with delegates from Yathrib, another town near the Red Sea coast, some 250 miles north of Mecca. It was an agricultural rather than a commercial town and it was torn by conflict because its inhabitants belonged to several quarreling tribes. The people of Yathrib wanted a fair-minded outsider to come in and oversee negotiations among the tribes; they hoped that if they ceded judicial authority to such a person, he would be able to bring about a peace. Mohammed had a reputation as a fair-minded and skillful arbitrator, a role he had played in several crucial disputes, and so the Yathribis thought he might be the man for the job. Several of them visited Mecca to meet Mohammed and found his charisma overwhelming. They converted to Islam and invited Mohammed to move to Yathrib as an arbiter and help put an end to all the quarrelling; the Prophet accepted.

Mohammed's murder was planned for a September night in the year 622 CE. That night, the Prophet and Abu Bakr slipped away into the desert. Ali crawled into Mohammed's bed to make it look like he was still there. When the would-be assassins burst in, they were furious to find Ali, but they spared the kid and sent a search party out to hunt down the Prophet. Mohammed and Abu Bakr had made it only to a cave near Mecca, but legend has it that a spider built its web across the mouth of the cave after they entered. When the posse came by and saw the web, they assumed no one could be inside, and so passed on. Mohammed and Abu Bakr made it safely to Yathrib, by which time some of Mohammed's other followers had moved there too, and the rest soon followed. Most of these Meccan emigrants had to leave their homes and property behind; most were making a break with family members and fellow tribesmen who had not converted. But at least they were coming to a place where they would be safe, and where their leader Mohammed had been invited to preside as the city's highest authority, the arbiter among the rival tribal chieftains.

True to his promise, Mohammed sat down with the city's fractious tribes to hammer out a covenant (later called the Pact of Medina.) This covenant made the city a confederacy, guaranteeing each tribe the right to follow its own religion and customs, imposing on all citizens rules designed to keep the overall peace, establishing a legal process by which the tribes settled purely internal matters themselves and ceded to Mohammed the authority to settle intertribal disputes. Most important, all the signatories, Muslim and non-Muslim, pledged to join all the others to defend

Medina against outside attack. Although this document has been called the first written constitution, it was really more of a multiparty treaty.

Mohammed also appointed one Yathribi Muslim to mentor and help each family of Meccan Muslims. The native was to host the newcomer and his family, get them settled, and help them start a new life. From this time on, the Yathribi Muslims were called the Ansar, "the helpers."

The name of the city changed too. Yathrib became Medina, which simply means "the city" (short for a phrase that meant "city of the prophet"). The emigration of the Muslims from Mecca to Medina, is known as the Hijra (often spelled *Hegira* in English.) A dozen years later, when Muslims created their own calendar, they dated it from this event because the Hijra, they felt, marked the pivot of history, the turning point in their fortunes, the moment that divided all of time into before the Hijra (BH) and after the Hijra (AH).

Some religions mark their founder's birthday as their point of origin; some, the day he died; and still others, the moment of their prophet's enlightenment or his key interaction with God. In Buddhism, for example, the religion begins with Siddhartha Gautama's achievement of enlightenment under the bodhi tree. Christianity attributes key religious significance to Christ's death and resurrection (as well as his birth.) Islam, however, pays little attention to Mohammed's birthday. Growing up as a Muslim, I didn't know when he was born, because nothing special happened that day in Afghanistan. Some countries, such as Egypt, commemorate the day more elaborately, but still, there's no analog to Christmas in Islam, no "Mohammedmas."

The revelation in the cave is commemorated as the most sacred night in Muslim devotions: it is the Night of Power, Lailut al-Qadr, which falls on or near the twenty-seventh day of Ramadan, the month of fasting. But in the Muslim calendar of history, that event occurred ten years before the really crucial turning point: the Hijra.

What makes moving from one town to another so momentous? The Hijra takes pride of place among events in Muslim history because it marks the birth of the Muslim community, the Umma, as it is known in Islam. Before the Hijra, Mohammed was a preacher with individual followers. After the Hijra, he was the leader of a community that looked to him for legislation, political direction, and social guidance. The word *hijra*

means "severing of ties." People who joined the community in Medina renounced tribal bonds and accepted this new group as their transcendent
affiliation, and since this community was all about building an alternative
to the Mecca of Mohammed's childhood, it was an epic, devotional social
project.

This social project, which became fully evident in Medina after the
Hijra, is a core element of Islam. Quite definitely, Islam is a religion, but
right from the start (if "the start" is taken as the Hijra) it was *also* a political entity. Yes, Islam prescribes a way to be good, and yes, every devoted Muslim hopes to get into heaven by following that way, but
instead of focusing on isolated individual salvation, Islam presents a plan
for building a righteous community. Individuals earn their place in
heaven by participating as members of that community and engaging in
the Islamic social project, which is to build a world in which orphans
won't feel abandoned and in which widows won't ever be homeless, hungry, or afraid.

Once Mohammed became the leader of Medina, people came to him
for guidance and judgments about every sort of life question, big or little:
how to discipline children . . . how to wash one's hands . . . what to consider fair in a contract . . . what should be done with a thief . . . the list
goes on. Questions that in many other communities would be decided by
a phalanx of separate specialists, such as judges, legislators, political leaders, doctors, teachers, generals, and others, were all in the Prophet's baili-
wick here.

Portions of the Qur'an recited in Mecca consist entirely of language
like this:

> *When earth is shaken with a mighty shaking*
> *and earth brings forth her burdens,*
> *and Man says, "what ails her?"*
> *upon that day she shall tell her tidings*
> *for that her Lord has inspired her.*
>
> *Upon that day men shall issue in scatterings to see their works*
> *and whoso has done an atom's weight of good shall see it*
> *and whoso has done an atom's weight of evil shall see it.*

When you look at the verses revealed in Medina, you still find much passionate, lyrical, and imprecatory language, but you also find passages like this one:

God charges you, concerning your children:
to the male the like of the portion
of two females, and if they be women
above two, then for them two-thirds
of what he leaves, but if she be one
then to her a half; and to his parents
to each one of the two the sixth
of what he leaves, if he has children
but if he has no children, and his
heirs are his parents, a third to his
mother, or, if he has brothers, to his
mother a sixth, after any bequest
he may bequeath, or any debt
Your fathers and your sons—you know not
which out of these is nearer in profit
to you. So God apportions; surely God is
All-knowing, All-wise.

This is legislation, and this is what the Muslim enterprise expanded to, once it took root in Medina.

After the Hijra, the native Arabs of Medina gradually converted to Islam, but the city's three Jewish tribes largely resisted conversion, and over time a friction developed between them and the Muslims. Among the Arabs, too, some of the men displaced by Mohammed's growing stature harbored a closely guarded resentment.

Meanwhile, the Quraysh tribe had not given up on assassinating Mohammed, even though he now lived 250 miles away. Not only did Quraysh leaders put a huge bounty of a hundred camels on Mohammed's head, they remained fixated on stamping out his whole community. To finance an assault on Medina, the wealthiest merchants of Mecca stepped up their trading expeditions. Mohammed countered by leading Muslims in raids on these Meccan caravans (which helped solve another problem the Meccan emigrants faced: how to support themselves now that they had lost their goods and businesses.)

After a year of these raids, the Meccans decided to raise the stakes. A thousand of them strapped on weapons and marched out to finish off the upstarts. The Muslims met them with a force of three hundred men at a place called Badr and defeated them soundly. The Qur'an mentions the battle of Badr as proof of Allah's ability to decide the outcome of any battle, no matter what the odds.

Before Badr, some of the bedouin tribesmen had worked for merchants in Mecca as contract bodyguards. After Badr, these tribes began to switch sides. The growing solidarity of the Muslim community in Medina began to alarm the Jewish tribes. One of the three renounced the Pact of Medina and tried to instigate an uprising against Mohammed and a return to the pre-Islamic status quo, but the uprising failed, and this tribe was expelled from Medina.

Now the Quraysh really did have cause to worry. Instead of eliminating Mohammed, it looked like they might have dug themselves the beginnings of a hole. In the year 3 AH, they decided to overwhelm the Muslims while they still had the numbers. They tripled the size of their army, heading for Medina with three thousand men. The Muslims could scratch up only 950 warriors. Again, they would be outnumbered three to one—but after Badr, how could this matter? They had the only asset that mattered: Allah was on their side.

The second of Islam's three iconic battles occurred at a place called Uhud. At first the Muslims seemed to be winning again, but when the Meccans fell back, some of the Muslims disobeyed one of Mohammed's explicit orders: they broke ranks and spilled across the field in a chaotic rush to scoop up their share of booty—at which point the Meccans struck from behind, led by Khaled bin al-Walid, a military genius who later converted to Islam and became one of the Umma's leading generals. The Prophet himself was wounded at Uhud, seventy Muslims were killed, and many of the rest fled. The Umma survived, but this battle marked a bad defeat.

These seminal battles of Islamic history were so small-scale, measured against most real wars, that they barely qualify as battles. Each one, however, was incorporated into Muslim theology and vested with meaning.

Thus, the battle of Badr showed that Allah's will, not material factors, determined victory in battle. But the battle of Uhud raised a thorny theological question. If Badr showed the power of Allah, what did Uhud show? That Allah could also lose battles? That He was not quite as all-powerful as Mohammed proclaimed?

Mohammed, however, found a different lesson in defeat. Allah, he explained, let the Muslims lose this time to teach them a lesson. The Muslims were supposed to be fighting for a righteous cause—a just community on earth. Instead, at Uhud they forgot this mission and went scrambling for loot in direct disobedience to the Prophet's orders, and so they forfeited Allah's favor. Divine support was not an entitlement; Muslims had to *earn* the favor of Allah by behaving as commanded and submitting to His will. This explanation for defeat provided a stencil that Muslims invoked repeatedly in later years, after the Mongol holocaust of the thirteenth century, for example, when nomadic invaders from Central Asia overwhelmed most of the Islamic world, and again in response to Western domination, which began in the eighteenth century and continues to this day.

The Quraysh spent two years planning their next assault. Recruiting allies from other tribes, they built an army of ten thousand men— inconceivably gigantic for that time and place. When Mohammed heard about this force marching on Medina, he had his Muslims dig a moat around their town. The Quraysh arrived on camels, which would not or could not cross the moat. The stymied Quraysh decided to starve Medina with a siege.

The siege strategy, however, scuttled a secret plan the Quraysh were counting on. After the disastrous battle of Uhud, another of Medina's Jewish tribes had been exposed as collaborating with the Meccans. Like the first Jewish tribe, they had been tried and sent into exile. The third tribe, the Banu Qurayza, then proclaimed its loyalty to the Pact of Medina. Now, however, in the run-up to the Battle of the Moat, its leaders had secretly conspired with the Quraysh to fall upon the Muslim forces from behind as soon as the Meccan forces attacked from the front.

When no frontal attack came, the conspirators within Medina lost their nerve. Meanwhile, the besieging force began to fragment, for it was a confederation of tribes, most of whom had come along only as a favor to their Qurayshi allies. With no battle to fight, they got restless. When a windstorm blew up—no small matter in this landscape—they drifted off, and soon the Quraysh gave up and went home too.

All this left the Banu Qurayza in a bad spot. Their plot had been discovered and now their allies were gone. Mohammed put the whole tribe on trial and appointed one of their former associates among the Medina tribes as judge. When the tribe was found guilty, the judge declared that the crime was treason, the punishment for which was death. Some onlookers protested against this sentence, but Mohammed confirmed the sentence, whereupon some eight hundred Jewish men were executed in the public square, and the women and children of the tribe were sent to live with the two tribes exiled earlier.

This whole drama sent a shock wave through Arabia. The trial and execution of the Banu Qurayza announced the grim resolution of the Muslims of Medina. In strictly military terms the Battle of the Moat was a stalemate, but the Quraysh had mustered a force of ten thousand with such fanfare that failing to win was as bad as losing, and this loss helped to stoke a growing myth of Muslim invincibility, communicating a broad impression that this community was not just another powerful tribe feeling its oats but something strange and new. The Muslims lived a distinctly different way of life, they practiced their own devotional rituals, and they had a leader who, when problems came up, went into a trance and channeled advice, he said, from a supernatural helper so powerful that Muslims had no fear of going into battle outnumbered three to one.

Who was this helper?

At first, many of the unconverted might have thought, *It's a really powerful god.* But gradually the Muslim message sank in: not *a* god but *the* God, the *only* one. And what if Mohammed was exactly what he claimed to be—the one human being on earth directly connected to the creator of the entire universe?

Recruiting people to kill the man grew ever more difficult. Recruiting warriors to go up against his forces grew difficult too. After the Battle of the Moat, the trickle of conversions to Islam became a flood. It's easy to suppose people were converting out of canny self-interest, a desire to join the winning side. Muslims, however, believe there was more to it. In Mohammed's presence, they believe, people were having a religious experience.

Mohammed never claimed supernatural powers. He never claimed the ability to raise the dead, walk on water, or make the blind to see. He only claimed to speak for God, and he didn't claim that every word out of his mouth was God talking. Sometimes it was just Mohammed talking. How could people tell when it was God and when it was Mohammed?

At the time, apparently, it was obvious. Today's Muslims have a special way of vocalizing the Qur'an called *qira'ut*. It's a sound quite unlike any other made by the human voice. It's musical, but it isn't singing. It's incantatory, but it isn't chanting. It invokes emotion even in someone who doesn't understand the words. Every person who performs qira'ut does so differently, but every recitation feels like an imitation or intimation or interpretation of some powerful original. When Mohammed delivered the Qur'an, he must have done so in *this* penetrating and emotional voice. When people heard the Qur'an from Mohammed, they were not just listening to words but experiencing an emotional force. Perhaps this is why Muslims insist that no translation of the Qur'an is *the* Qur'an. The true Qur'an is the whole package, indivisible: the words and their meanings, yes, but also the very sounds, even the look of the lettering when the Qur'an is in written form. To Muslims, it wasn't Mohammed the person but the Qur'an coming through Mohammed that was converting people.

One other factor attracted people to the community and inspired them to believe Mohammed's claims. In this part of the world, small-scale warfare was endemic, as it seems to be in any area populated by many small nomadic tribes among whom trading blends into raiding (such as North America's eastern woodlands before Columbus arrived, or the Great Plains shortly after). Add the Arabian tradition of blood feuds lasting for generations, add also the tapestry of fragile tribal alliances that marked the peninsula at this time, and you have a world seething with constant, ubiquitous violence.

Wherever Mohammed took over, he instructed people to live in peace with one another, and the converts did. By no means did he tell Muslims to eschew violence, for this community never hesitated to defend itself. Muslims still engaged in warfare, just not against one another; they expended their aggressive energy fighting the relentless outside threat to their survival. Those who joined the Umma immediately entered Dar al-Islam, which means "the realm of submission (to God)" but also, by implication, "the realm of peace." Everyone else was living out there in Dar al-Harb, the realm of war. Those who joined the Umma didn't have to watch their backs anymore, not with their fellow Muslims.

Converting also meant joining an inspiring social project: the construction of a just community of social equals. To keep that community alive, you had to fight, because the Umma and its project had implacable enemies. *Jihad* never meant "holy war" or "violence." Other words in Arabic mean "fighting" more unambiguously (and are used as such in the Qur'an). A better translation for *jihad* might be "struggle," with all the same connotations the word carries in the rhetoric of social justice movements familiar to the West: struggle is deemed noble when it's struggle for a just cause and if the cause demands "armed struggle," that's okay too; it's sanctified by the cause.

Over the next two years, tribes all across the Arabian peninsula began accepting Mohammed's leadership, converting to Islam, and joining the community. One night Mohammed dreamed that he had returned to Mecca and found everyone there worshipping Allah. In the morning, he told his followers to pack for a pilgrimage. He led fourteen hundred Muslims on the two-hundred-mile trek to Mecca. They came unarmed, despite the recent history of hostilities, but no battle broke out. The city closed its gates to the Muslims, but Quraysh elders came out and negotiated a treaty with Mohammed: the Muslims could not enter Mecca *this* year but could come back and perform their rites of pilgrimage *next* year. Clearly, the Quraysh knew the game was over.

In year 6 AH, the Muslims came back to Mecca and visited the Ka'ba without violence. Two years later, the elders of Mecca surrendered the city to Mohammed without a fight. As his first act, the Prophet destroyed all the idols in the Ka'ba and declared this cube with the black cornerstone the holiest spot in the world. A few of Mohammed's former enemies grumbled and muttered threats, but the tide had turned. Virtually all the tribes had united under Mohammed's banner, and all of Arabia was living in harmony for the first time in reported memory.

In year 10 AH (632 CE), Mohammed made one more pilgrimage to Mecca and there gave a final sermon. He told the assembled men to regard the life and property of every Muslim as sacred, to respect the rights of all people including slaves, to acknowledge that women had rights over men just as men had rights over women, and to recognize that among Muslims no one stood higher or lower than anyone else except in virtue. He also said he was the last of God's Messengers and that after him no further revelations would be coming to humanity.[2]

Shortly after returning to Medina, he fell ill. Burning with fever, he went from house to house, visiting his wives and friends, spending a moment or two with each one, and saying good-bye. He ended up with his wife Ayesha, the daughter of his old friend Abu Bakr, and there, with his head in her lap, he died.

Someone went out and gave the anxious crowd the news. At once, loyal Omar, one of Mohammed's fiercest and toughest but also one of his most hotheaded companions, jumped to his feet and warned that any man who spread such slander would lose limbs when his lie was exposed. Mohammed dead? Impossible!

Then the older and more prudent Abu Bakr went to investigate. A moment later he came back and said, "O Muslims! Those of you who worshipped Mohammed, know that Mohammed is dead. Those of you who worship Allah, know that Allah is alive and immortal."

The words swept away Omar's rage and denial. He felt, he told friends later, as if the ground had been cut out from under him. He broke down crying, then, this strong bull of a man, because he realized that the news was true: God's Messenger was dead.

3

∞

Birth of the Khalifate

11-24 AH

632-644 CE

D EVOTED MUSLIMS SEE the whole of Mohammed's life as a religious
metaphor illuminating the meaning of existence, but the religious
event does not end with the Prophet's death. It continues through the
terms of his first four successors, remembered as the Rashidun, "the rightly
guided ones": Abu Bakr, Omar, Othman, and Ali. The entire drama, from
the revelation in the cave through the Hijra to the death of the Prophet's
fourth successor almost forty years later, forms the core religious allegory
of Islam, analogous to the last supper, the crucifixion, and the resurrection
of Jesus Christ in Christianity.

Islam emerged well within literate times. People were writing journals,
diaries, letters, bureaucratic documents, and other works. For this period a
rich documentary record exists. It seems, then, as if the origins of Islam
should lie squarely within the realm of journalism rather than legend. And
yet, what we know about the life and times of these first four successors derives largely from a history written decades later by the writer Ibn Ishaq,
who died in 151 AH (768 CE).

Ibn Ishaq came from a long line of traditionists, the archivists of oral
culture: men and women whose job it was to gather, remember, and retell

significant events. He was the first of his line to write the whole story down, but most of his book has been lost. Before it disappeared, however, other writers quoted from it, referred to it, included excerpts from it in their own works, wrote synopses of it, or paraphrased its stories. (Recently, in fact, some academics have been trying to reconstruct Ibn Ishaq's work from the fragments of it found in other works.)

One historian who used Ibn Ishaq as his major source was Ibn Jarir al-Tabari, who died about three hundred years after the Hijra. He wrote the thirty-nine-volume *History of the Prophets and Kings* that begins with Adam and ends in the year 292 AH (915 CE). His work *has* survived into the present day, and most of the anecdotes and details we read about Mohammed and his successors come to us through him. It is he who tells us what color hair these men had, what their favorite food was, and how many camels they owned. He includes their key speeches and conversations as direct quotations. His history is not exactly a readable narrative, however, because each story is nested in a mind-numbing list of names, the *isnad*, or "chain of transmission": "X reports that Y told him that he heard from Z that . . . and finally the anecdote." After each anecdote comes a different version of the same anecdote, nested in a different isnad: "A reports that he heard from B that C said that D recounts that . . . [anecdote]." Tabari doesn't say which version is true; he just puts them out there for you the reader to decide. Over the centuries, writers have compiled their own versions of the most compelling anecdotes, some of which make their way into popular and oral accounts and eventually turn into the Islamic version of "Bible stories," told to kids like me at home by our elders and in grammar school by our religion teachers.

Overall, these stories chronicle a tumultuous human drama that unfolded in the first twenty-nine years after the Prophet's death, a story of larger-than-life characters wrestling with epic issues, a story filled with episodes that evoke wonder and heartbreak. It's quite possible to take sides in retelling these stories, for there are sides to take, and it's quite possible to speculate about motives and make judgments about people's decisions.

On the other hand, these anecdotes have acquired allegorical status: different judgments and interpretations support different doctrines and represent various theological positions. We cannot know the hard facts of this story in a journalistic way because no untouched eyewitness account has survived. We have only the story of the story of the story, a sifting process that has drawn the mythological significance of the raw events to the surface. Here, then, is *that* story of the succession.

THE FIRST KHALIFA (11–13 AH)

The moment Mohammed died, the community faced an overwhelming problem. It wasn't just "*Who* is our next leader?" but "*What* is our next leader?" When a saint dies, people can't simply name some other saint in his place, because such figures aren't created by election or appointment, they just emerge; and if they don't, oh well; people may be disappointed, but life goes on. When a king dies, by contrast, no one says, "Wouldn't it be nice if someday we had another king?" The gap must be plugged at once.

When Prophet Mohammed died, it was like a saint dying but it was also like a king dying. He was irreplaceable, yet someone *had* to take his place. Without a leader, the Umma could not hold together.

The new leader had to be more than a king, however, because this was not a community like any other. It was, its members believed, the embodiment of the revelations, existing to express Allah's will and thereby transform the world. The leader of *this* community could not get by on brains, bravery, strength, and such traits. He had to have some special religious grace or power. Yet Mohammed's successor would not be a God-guided messenger, because Mohammed himself had said there would be no more of those. So if the leader wouldn't be a king or a God-guided messenger, what *would* he be?

Curiously enough, the nascent Muslim community had given no consideration to this question before the Prophet died; and it gave no consideration to it in the hours immediately after his death either, for this was not a time for grand philosophical discussions. With the Prophet's body scarcely cold, Abu Bakr heard a disturbing report: the native Muslims of Medina were meeting to elect a leader of their own, as if they and the immigrants from Mecca were separate groups: here, quite possibly, was the beginning of the end of the Umma!

Abu Bakr gathered some of Mohammed's closest companions, crashed the meeting, and begged the Medinans to reconsider. Muslims should elect a single leader for the whole community. He pleaded, not a prophet, not a king, just someone to call meetings, moderate discussions, and hold the community together. "Choose one of these two," he suggested, pointing to the irascible Omar and to another of the Prophet's close companions.

Omar himself was appalled. Take precedence over Abu Bakr? Unthinkable! He grasped the older man's hand and told the assembly that only Abu Bakr could serve as leader, now that the Prophet himself was gone. Through tears, he swore allegiance to Mohammed's closest friend, a dramatic gesture that electrified the room. Suddenly Abu Bakr did seem like the obvious and only choice, this sensible, lovable man who had distinguished himself all his life by his wisdom, courage, and compassion. In a gush of enthusiasm, the meeting gave unanimous consent to letting Abu Bakr assume the modest title of khalifa (or, as most Western accounts would have it, "caliph"), which meant "deputy."

This title did not exist until Abu Bakr took it on. No tribe or nation at that time was headed by a khalifa. No one knew what the title meant or what powers it conferred. The first titleholder would have to fill in those details.

For now, Abu Bakr went to the mosque, where a crowd had gathered. His accession was announced. In a gracious inaugural speech he told that assembly, "I am not the best of you. If I do well, support me. If I make mistakes, do not hesitate to advise me. . . . If I neglect the laws of God and Prophet, I forfeit claim to your obedience." Everyone at the mosque gave him the same acclaim he had received from everyone at the meeting.

"Everyone," however, was not *at* the mosque or the meeting. One leading candidate for the role of successor did not even hear that the issue was being discussed. The Prophet's cousin Ali was washing the Prophet's body when the elders met. By the time he heard anything about the discussion, the decision had already been made.

You can see how this might have rankled. In the last months of Mohammed's life, Ali may well have felt like he *was* the Prophet's successor, no discussion needed, for he stood closest to the Prophet in every way. Mohammed had several cousins, but Ali was special because his father Abu Talib had adopted Mohammed and raised him as a son, which essentially made Ali and Mohammed brothers.

But Ali was almost thirty years Mohammed's junior, and in tribal Arab culture a much-older brother had a near paternal status with his sibling. In fact, as a little boy, Ali had moved in with Mohammed and Khadija and had grown up mostly in their household, so in addition to being practically like a brother to Mohammed, Ali was practically like a son to him too. What's more, Ali was the first person after Khadija to accept Islam: the first male Muslim.

When the assassins were coming to murder Mohammed in his bed, it was Ali who wrapped himself in the Prophet's blankets and risked taking the knife meant for Mohammed. In Medina, when the Muslims were in danger of annihilation, it was Ali who proved himself repeatedly as the virtual Achilles of Islam—for in those days, battles often began with individual challenges leading to single combat, and at each confrontation, when the Quraysh called on the Muslims to send out their best, Mohammed nominated Ali.

At the battle of Uhud, when all seemed lost and some Muslims fled for home, Ali was among those who rallied around the Prophet, and bore him home wounded but safe.

As the community flowered and the Prophet became a head of state, he kept Ali by his side as his right-hand man. Indeed, on the way home from his last sermon, Mohammed told the people, "Any of you who consider me your patron should consider Ali your patron." Now, didn't that amount to saying that after he was gone, the Umma should consider Ali their leader?

While all of Mohammed's close companions had charisma, Ali's glow seemed uniquely spiritual to a committed group of partisans, many of them younger Muslims, who felt something of the same authority radiating from Ali that everyone had felt radiating from Mohammed.

All the points mentioned marked Ali as special, but one further factor elevated him above all others, and it might have been the most important factor of all, or so it seemed in retrospect to later Muslims: Mohammed had no sons. Only one of his daughters produced sons who lived past childhood, and that one daughter was Fatima, who was married to Ali. Ali's sons were therefore Mohammed's grandsons, and Ali's descendents would be the prophet's descendents. Ali and Fatima were Mohammed's family.

Set all this aside, however, and picture Ali indoors with the womenfolk, drowning in grief as he bathed the Prophet's body. Then, picture him emerging finally into the terrible first day of the rest of his life, still reeling from the enormity of what had happened, only to find that while he was preparing Mohammed's body for burial, Mohammed's peer-group companions had been picking a successor for Mohammed, not only passing over Ali but failing even to consult him, failing even to inform him that the meeting was taking place. Surely, Ali felt he deserved some greater consideration than that!

On the other hand, every point in Ali's favor counted against him from another perspective. Ali was close to the Prophet? Part of his family? Good for him, but when did Allah ever say He was conferring special privileges upon a particular family? Dynastic succession was the old way, the sort of thing Islam proposed to overturn!

Besides, the Prophet had said there would be no more Messengers after him. If this was true, Ali's charisma had no religious significance, in which case, shouldn't Muslims separate the Prophet's bloodline from leadership roles in the community to prevent undue concentrations of power from distorting the egalitarian universalism of the Islamic message? Seen in that light, in fact, wasn't Ali's charisma precisely the quality that made him questionable? Might it not encourage his more fervid partisans to declare him a new prophet?

No, said Abu Bakr's proponents, what the community needed at this point was steady judgment, not youthful passion. Ali was just over thirty years of age at this time; Abu Bakr was almost sixty. In the Arabia of that time, choosing a thirty-year-old man as leader over a sixty-year-old probably struck most Arabs as unthinkable. Why, the word *sheikh,* the title for tribal leader, literally meant "old man."

Some say it took Ali six hard months to concede the election, during which some of Abu Bakr's more unruly followers threatened him and roughed up his family. In one such shove and scuffle, they say, a door was slammed against his wife Fatima's belly, who was pregnant at the time, and this manhandling may have caused her to miscarry what would have been Prophet Mohammed's third grandson.

Others claim that Ali swore allegiance to Abu Bakr just a few days after the latter took office; they minimize the abuse that Fatima suffered and attribute her miscarriage to an accident. A disagreement like this can never now be resolved by an appeal to evidence. It can only reflect the position one takes on the theological schism that developed out of the succession, for the disagreement between proponents of Abu Bakr and Ali eventually engendered two different sects of Islam, the Sunnis and the Shi'i, each of whom has a different version of these events. Ali's partisans developed into the Shi'i, a word that simply means "partisans" in Arabic, and they remain convinced to this day that Ali was the Prophet's only legitimate successor.

In either case, within six months the rift had closed, and just in time, for a new crisis was threatening the survival of Islam. All across Arabia, tribes were seceding from the alliance that Mohammed had forged. Most claimed they had never pledged allegiance to Abu Bakr or the Umma but only to Mohammed himself, and that pledge had been voided by Mohammed's death. Nominally, these tribespeople had all converted to Islam, and many of them insisted they were still Muslims. They still acknowledged the singleness of God and Mohammed's authority. They would still pray, still fast, still try to keep the drinking and debauchery under control—but zakat? The charity tax payable to the treasury at Medina? No, that they could no longer tolerate: no more payments to Medina!

A few tribal leaders went further. They claimed that they themselves were now Allah's living Messengers. They claimed they were receiving revelations and had permission to issue divinely authorized laws. These upstarts thought to use the model pioneered by Mohammed to forge sovereign "sacred" communities in competition with the Umma.

Had Abu Bakr allowed these departures, Islam would surely have gone in a very different direction. It might have evolved into a set of practices and beliefs that people embraced individually. But Abu Bakr responded to the crisis by declaring secession to be treason. The Prophet had said, "No compulsion in religion," and Abu Bakr did not deny that principle. People were free to accept or reject Islam as they pleased; but once they were in, he asserted, they were in for good. In response to a political crisis, Abu Bakr established a religious principle that haunts Islam to this day—the equation of apostasy with treason. Braided into this policy was the theological concept that the indissoluble singleness of God must be reflected in the indissoluble singleness of the Umma. With this decision Abu Bakr even more definitively confirmed Islam as a social project and not just a belief system. A Muslim community was not just a *kind* of community, of which there could be any number, but a *particular* community, of which there could be only one.

The new khalifa proved himself a formidable strategist. It took him a little over a year to end the rebellion known as the Apostate Wars and reunite

Arabia. At home, however, in his dealings with the Muslim community, he exhibited nothing but the modesty, affection, and benevolence people knew and loved him for. A stoop-shouldered man with deep-set eyes, Abu Bakr dressed simply, lived plainly, and accumulated no wealth. His one affectation was to dye his hair and beard red with henna. When disputes arose, he dispensed justice with an even hand, involving a council of elders in all his decisions, ruling as first among equals, and asserting no claim to religious elevation. His word had no greater weight than any other Muslim's, and his authority came only from his wisdom and his devotion to the revelation. No one was obliged to follow his rulings except when he was right, the caveat being, he was pretty much always right.

Back in Mecca, before the Hijra, Abu Bakr had been a prosperous merchant. By the time Muslims emigrated to Medina, however, he had spent much of his fortune on charitable causes, especially buying freedom for slaves who converted to Islam, and he forfeited the rest of his wealth in the course of the move. As khalifa, he took only a small salary for guiding the Umma and continued to ply his old trade to make a living, getting by as best he could on the fruits of his shrunken business. Sometimes, he even milked his neighbor's cow for extra cash.[1] As portrayed in the religious stories of Islamic tradition, children would run up to him shouting, "Papa! Papa!" when he walked through the streets of Medina, and he would pat their heads and give them candy—he was that kind of guy.

THE SECOND KHALIFA (13-24 AH)

One August day, two years into his khalifate, Abu Bakr stepped out of a hot bath into a blast of chill wind, and by nightfall he was running a high fever. Realizing that death was near, he called in a few of the community's top notables and told them he wanted to nominate Omar as his successor so there wouldn't be any arguments about it later.

The notables balked, because Omar could not have been more different from the gentle, understated Abu Bakr. He was a giant of a man, looming half a head above anybody else—in a crowd he was said to stand out like a man on horseback. His head was completely bald, his face ruddy, his whiskers huge. He was ambidextrous and strong as a bull, and he had an epic temper.[2]

Before his conversion, Omar had been known to do a certain amount of brawling and drinking. Back then, he had hated Islam and Mohammed. Then came his oft-recounted conversion: one day, tradition reports, he announced that he was going to kill the Messenger of God and be done with it. He grabbed a sword and went striding across town to commit the deed, but on the way he spotted his beloved sister sitting under a tree, studying a leaf with some sort of text on it. "What are you doing?"

"Reading," she said.

"Reading what?"

She looked up timorously. "The Qur'an. I've become a Muslim."

"What? Give me that!" He snatched away what she was reading. It was a verse called Ta Ha, and to Omar's astonishment the words seemed addressed directly to him. At that moment Omar went through a transformation. He dropped his sword, ran through the streets of Mecca, and banged on the Prophet's door, shouting, "I believe you! You *are* the Messenger of God! I believe!"

After that, he became one of Mohammed's closest companions, but he always remained a tough guy's tough guy, subject to outbursts of frightening rage, and though he had a good heart beneath it all, many wondered if the khalifate could be entrusted to a man whose very demeanor frightened children. At that critical moment, however, Ali stepped forward to endorse Omar, and his word tipped the scales: the Umma accepted their second post-Mohammed leader.

Upon taking office, Omar told the community that he knew he was more feared than loved, but he assured people, they had seen only one side of him so far. Both the Prophet and Abu Bakr had been tenderhearted men, he explained, yet leaders sometimes must take tough action, and when such a need had arisen, Omar had been their instrument. He had needed to be a sword all the time so that the Prophet, and later Abu Bakr, would have a sword available to them *any* time. Now that Omar was khalifa, however, he would not be a living sword all the time, because he knew that a leader must sometimes be gentle. From now on, therefore, the community would see both sides of him. Wrongdoers and tyrants who trampled on the weak would see the old Omar. The poor, the weak, the widows, the orphans, all who sought the good and needed protection, would see the tender Omar.

The Umma soon realized their second khalifa was a towering personality, even more imposing than Abu Bakr, perhaps. Omar directed the Umma for ten years, and during that time he set the course of Islamic theology, he shaped Islam as a political ideology, he gave Islamic civilization its characteristic stamp, and he built an empire that ended up bigger than Rome. Any one of these achievements could have earned him a place in a who's who of history's most influential figures; the sum of them make him something like a combination of Saint Paul, Karl Marx, Lorenzo di Medici, and Napoleon. Yet most people outside Islam know him only as a name and perhaps a one- or two-sentence descriptor: he's the second khalifa, a successor of Mohammed—that's about it.

Perhaps this is because Omar made lack of pretension his core principle. This is so much a part of his legend that Omar becomes in Islamic tradition the embodiment of a principle. His word was not law; his will did not rule; he ceded all authority to God—such was his storied claim. He envisioned Islam as an absolutely just and egalitarian community and he intended to make that vision a reality. In the Muslim community, he said, no one ever needed to fear the whims or will of any human power because this community had the Qur'an as its law, and the example of the Prophet's life as its guide, and nothing else was needed. Omar declared that his role was merely to keep the Umma united and moving forward along the track indicated by the revelations.

Omar had never been a rich man, but Ali and others urged him to take a suitable salary from the public treasury, arguing that since Islam now included all of Arabia, the Umma could no longer afford a part-time khalifa who milked a cow for extra cash. Omar agreed but appointed a commission to calculate how much he needed to live like the average Arab, no better and no worse, and supposedly set this amount as his salary. (Imagine the CEO of a modern multinational corporation doing that.)

In imitation of the Prophet, Omar habitually patched his own clothes, sometimes while conducting important state business. At night, after his official duties were done, the stories portray him shouldering a bag of grain and roaming through the city, personally delivering food to families in need. Once, somebody who saw him at this labor offered to carry the bag for him, but Omar said, "You can carry my burden for me here on Earth, but who will carry it for me on the Day of Judgment?"

It's easy to suppose such stories are purely apocryphal, or that, if true, they merely show Omar the politician demonstrating a common touch for show. Personally, I think he must have been strikingly pious, unpretentious, devoted, and empathic, just as the stories suggest: the anecdotes are too consistent to dismiss, and something must account for this man's overpowering impact on his contemporaries. Whatever the reality, however, the legend he planted in the Muslim imagination expresses an ideal of how rulers should behave.

Omar adopted a title that became an enduring addendum to khalifa: Amir al-Mu'mineen, or "commander of the faithful," a title that conflated his spiritual and military roles. As a big-picture military strategist, Omar ranked with Alexander and Julius Caesar, but how he acquired such savvy is hard to fathom. Until Islam came along, he was just another small-town merchant. He took part in those iconic early battles of Muslim history, but in military terms those were little more than skirmishes. Now, suddenly, he was studying "world" (i.e., Middle World) maps, calculating the flow of Byzantine or Sassanid resources, gauging what geography dictated for strategy, deciding where to force a battle and where to retreat—he was operating on a global scale.

Fortuitously, at this historical moment, the Umma produced an extraordinary array of brilliant field commanders such as Khaled bin al-Walid, hero of the Apostate Wars, Amr ibn al-A'as, conqueror of Egypt, and Sa'd ibn Abi Waqqas, who beat the Persians.

As soon as Omar took office, he finished a piece of military business that Abu Bakr had started. Toward the end of the Apostate Wars, seeing Arabia in turmoil, the Byzantines had moved troops to the border, intending to absorb this "troubled" territory. Abu Bakr had sent men to keep them at bay, but even before his death the Muslims had pushed the Byzantines back into their own territory. Shortly after Omar took the helm, they set siege to the city of Damascus. From that time on, Muslims had the Byzantines on the run, and in 636 CE, at a place called Yarmuk, they destroyed the main Byzantine army.

Meanwhile, the Persians were doing their best to unravel the upstart Muslim community with spies and provocateurs. Instead of swatting at individual Persian agents, Omar decided to throttle the threat at its source. He called on Muslims to topple the Sassanid empire, a proposal of breathtaking audacity: ants vowing to fell a mastiff.

Omar's decision to call a war of conquest a "jihad" has obvious ramifications for modern times and has been much debated. In Mohammed's day, the word *jihad* did not loom large. Etymologically, as I said, it didn't mean "fighting" but "striving," and though it could be applied to fighting an enemy, it could also be used to discuss striving against temptation, struggling for justice, or trying to develop one's compassion. The word *jihad* as "fighting" does come up in the Qur'an, bound explicitly to self-defense. Those verses were revealed at a time when the Quraysh were trying to erase Islam and Muslims from the face of the earth. In that context, it was no stretch to argue that fighting had a moral dimension: if the community of believers was what made justice possible on earth, then those who let hostile forces extinguish it were helping Satan, while those who put lives and property at risk to defend it were serving Allah.

But calling upon Muslims to leave home, travel to distant lands, and fight people with whom they had virtually no previous interaction—how could wars such as these be called defensive? And if they weren't defensive, how could they qualify as jihad?

They were connected through an idea that originated in Mohammed's time and that Muslim thinkers began fleshing out during Abu Bakr and Omar's khalifates: the idea that the world was divided into the mutually exclusive realms of Dar al-Islam and Dar al-Harb, "the realm of peace" and "the realm of war." This schema depicted Islam as an oasis of brotherhood and peace surrounded by a universe of chaos and hatred. Anything a person did to expand Dar al-Islam constituted action in the cause of peace, even fighting and bloodshed, because it shrank the realm of war.

Personally, I wonder how many people in the seventh century thought wars of conquest needed justification. In any case, calling a campaign of conquest a jihad met with no dispute among the Umma. Having survived the shock of Prophet Mohammed's death, they had regrouped, and Omar probably understood that setting them a heroic quest at this juncture would consolidate and deepen their unity.

In 15 AH (or thereabouts), near a town called Qadisiya, an Arab force traditionally numbered at thirty thousand warriors found itself facing a Sassanid army of sixty thousand crack troops. Only a river separated them. Several times, the Arab commander Waqqas sent envoys to negotiate with Rustum, the commander of the Sassanid force. As the story goes, General

Rustum asked one envoy if he headed up the Muslim army. The man replied, "No, we're Muslims. Among us, there is no highest and lowest."

Rustum said, "Look, I know you Arabs are hungry and poor, and I'm sure you've been causing trouble out of desperation. So I tell you what, I'll give each of you two suits of clothing and a bag of dates. Will that convince you to go back where you came from?"

The Muslim envoy said, "We're not here to take anything from you, General. We're here to give you Islam! You are headed to hell; we offer you an opportunity to go to heaven."

Rustum just laughed. "You remind me of the mouse that crept into the granary through a hole in the wall and ate till he could eat no more. Then he tried to go home, but he had grown too fat to fit back through the hole. His greed trapped him in the granary and the cat killed him. Now, you greedy Arabs have stolen into our granary and you're trapped. All of you will die here, like that mouse."

Eventually, in all this back and forth, the Muslims told Rustum, "If you don't want to convert, just pay the tax, and you won't be harmed."

"Harmed?" scoffed Rustum. "Tax?" He told his servants to give the Muslims a bag of dirt, by which he meant to symbolize the grave.

But the Muslims received it cheerfully. "You give us your soil? We accept!"

Both sides then prepared for battle. Despite his own greedy-mouse anecdote, Rustum made the mistake of crossing the river to attack the Muslims, so his were the forces backed up against the river with nowhere to flee. The battle of Qadisiya lasted four days, the Persians riding elephants, the Arabs camels. On the third day, the battle went on through the night and into the next day. When the Sassanids gave way at last, thousands of their routed warriors tried to swim the river in heavy armor and drowned.

Along with warriors, many poets (including some women) went to this battlefield and generated a rich trove of stories, elevating Qadisiya to a mythic status, like a (shorter) Trojan War.

For example, as soon as victory was certain, a courier jumped on a horse and headed for Arabia to deliver the good news. Approaching Medina, he passed a geezer by the side of the road, some simple fellow in a patched coat, who jumped to his feet and asked the courier if he had come from Qadisiya.

"Yes," said the courier.

"What's the news, then? What's the news?" the old man asked eagerly.

But the courier said he couldn't stop to chat and he rode on. The old man trotted after him, pestering him with questions. When they passed through the city gates, a crowd gathered. "Out of my way!" the courier yelled importantly. "I must see the khalifa at once. Where is Khalifa Omar?"

The crowd burst out laughing. "That's him right behind you."

No pomp—that was Omar's style, according to legend.

After Qadisiya, the Arabs took the Sassanid capital of Ctesiphon and then just kept marching, eating into the centuries-old Sassanid Empire, until the entire territory belonged to Muslims and the Sassanid Empire was no more: in three years they put an end to an empire that had gone toe-to-toe with Rome for centuries.

Meanwhile, other armies were routing the Byzantines along the Mediterranean coast, down through Egypt, and into North Africa. The crown jewel of these conquests was Jerusalem, which ranked just behind Mecca and Medina as a holy site for Muslims, in part because Mohammed had reported a vision of being briefly lifted to paradise from this city during his lifetime. One of the most famous Omar stories took place after this city fell. The khalifa made his way to Jerusalem to accept its surrender in person. He traveled with a servant, and since they had only one donkey between them, they took turns riding and walking. When they reached Jerusalem, the servant happened to be riding. The people of Jerusalem mistook him for the khalifa and hastened to pay him obeisance. They had to be told, "No, no, that's nobody; it's the other guy you should be saluting."

The Christians assumed that the khalifa of Islam would want to perform the Muslim prayer in their most hallowed church as a token of his triumph, but Omar refused to set foot in there. "If I do," he explained, "some future Muslim will use it as an excuse to seize the building and turn it into a mosque, and that's not what we've come here to do. That's not the sort of thing we Muslims do. Continue to live and worship as you please; just know that from now on we Muslims will be living among you, worshipping in our way, and setting a better example. If you like what you see, join us. If not, so be it. Allah has told us: no compulsion in religion."[3]

Omar's treatment of Jerusalem set the pattern for relations between Muslims and the people they conquered. Christians found that under Muslim rule they would be subject to a special poll tax called the *jizya*. That was the bad news. The good news: the jizya would generally be less than the taxes they had been paying to their Byzantine overlords—who *did* interfere with their religious practices (because the nuances of ritual and belief among various Christian sects mattered to them, whereas to the Muslims they were all just Christians.) The idea of lower taxes and greater religious freedom struck Christians as a pretty good deal, and so Muslims faced little or no local resistance in former Byzantine territory. In fact, Jews and Christians sometimes joined them in fighting the Byzantines.

By the time Omar died, Islamic rule covered more than 2 million square miles. How was this possible? Religious Muslims offer the simple explanation that Muslims had the irresistible supernatural aid of Allah. Academic historians explain that the Byzantine and Sassanid empires had just fought a ruinous war with each other, and despite their seeming might, they were both rotten to the core and ready to fall. Another often-cited explanation holds that Muslims fought more ferociously than others because they believed that they would go directly to heaven if they were killed and get seventy-two virgins. I can't comment on that, but I will suggest some other factors.

Those early Muslims had a sense that they were fighting for something apocalyptically great. They felt that fighting for their cause made their lives meaningful and would give their deaths meaning as well. People have proven time and again that they will attack extraordinary obstacles and endure tremendous hardships if they think the effort will impart *meaning* to their lives. The human hunger for meaning is a craving as fundamental as food and drink. Everyday life gives people little opportunity for this sort of nourishment, which is one reason why people get swept along by narratives that cast them as key players in apocalyptic dramas. Muslim warriors in the time of Khalifa Omar had that sense about their lives.

Developments back home kept their idealism alive, because Omar enforced what he practiced and practiced what he preached. Under his guidance, Medina did reflect the values that Muslims said they were bringing to the world: fellowship, fairness, harmony, decency, democratic participation in decision making, equality, and compassion. At the very least, the

Muslim community during the early khalifate exemplified these ideals so much more than ordinary empires, that later Muslims could easily polish the accounts of that time into a memory of lost perfection.

On the other side of the line, people heard story after story about Muslims scoring military victories against astounding odds. Resistance seemed useless against such a force; besides, common folk had little incentive to resist, since the conquest wouldn't affect their lives. Their potentates would lose their treasures, but the masses would keep what they had and go on as before. Had the Arabs been fighting civilian populations defending their homes, it would have been a tougher fight that probably would have eroded their idealism over time. But instead, even far from home they were mostly fighting mercenaries and draftees.

Let me not minimize a final factor intertwined with the hunger for meaning. War gave Muslims opportunities for plunder. Under Omar, however, soldiers had no permission to seize the fixed property of common citizens. They got battlefield loot and the treasuries of the monarchs they conquered—which, incidentally, was plenty. Four-fifths of whatever they won was divided equally among the soldiers, supposedly with no distinction among commanders and foot soldiers, generals and privates—that was the Muslim way.

One-fifth of the plunder went back to Medina. In the Prophet's day much of that money was distributed immediately to the needy, and this policy persisted though in ever more diluted form through Omar's day. Add all these factors together, and the sudden expansion of Islam was not so inexplicable after all.

Conquest led the surge but conquest was kept separate from conversion. There was no "conversion by the sword." Muslims insisted on holding political power but not on their subjects being Muslims. Instead, wherever Muslim armies flowed, cultural transmission followed. News of the Muslim social project proliferated quickly because the expansion covered pretty much exactly the world historical area sewn together by those ancient trade routes running between major seas and waterways. In its first fifty years, Islam expanded to the western edge of the Indian Ocean, to the eastern lip of the Mediterranean Sea, to the Nile, to the Caspian Sea, to the Persian Gulf. In this area, this intercommunicative zone so richly permeated with preexisting channels of interaction, Muslim stories and ideas went humming from person to person through gossip and tale-telling, street talk and scholarly debate, flowing easily because the ideas were not *that* new. The Zoroastrian world hovered on the brink of monotheism. The Byzantine world had come into it with Christianity. And of course, ages ago, Judaism had introduced radical monotheism to the Levant (the region between Mesopotamia and Egypt).

The whole time Omar the conqueror was directing the territorial expansion of Islam, Omar the spiritual leader was directing the consolidation of Muslim doctrine and defining the Islamic way of life. Abu Bakr had established that Islam was not just an abstract ideal of community, but one particular community with a world-changing destiny. Omar formalized this by declaring a new calendar that began, not with the birth of Mohammed, nor with the first revelations, but with the Hijra, the migration of Muslims to Medina. Omar's calendar enshrined the conviction that Islam was not just a plan for individual salvation, but a plan for how the world should run. Many religions say to their followers, "The world is corrupt, but you can escape it." Islam said to its followers, "The world is corrupt, but you can *change* it." Perhaps this was inherent from the earliest days of Mohammed's preaching, but Omar confirmed this course for Islam and set it on tracks of iron.

Abu Bakr had ruled with legendary humility, trying never to impose his own will but merely administering the directives set forth by the Qur'an and the Prophet. Omar made this attitude a cornerstone of Muslim doctrine, a seminal decision because in vowing to do only what the revelations directed, he committed Muslims to determining what the revelations directed in every possible case, great and small.

During Abu Bakr's khalifate, at Omar's suggestion, all the pieces of the Qur'an were compiled in one place. It was a miscellaneous collection at first, because when the revelations were coming in, people recorded them on anything that came to hand—a sheet of parchment, a piece of leather, a stone, a bone, whatever. As khalifa, Omar began a sorting process. In his presence, each written verse was checked against the memorized version kept by the professional reciters whom this society regarded as the most reliable keepers of information. Scribes then recorded the authorized copy of each verse before witnesses, and these verses were organized into one comprehensive collection.

Whenever a difficult decision came up, Omar looked here for the answer. If the Qur'an didn't provide an answer, he consulted with the community to find out what the Prophet had said or done in a similar situation. In this case, "the community" meant the several hundred men and women who had been Mohammed's "companions" during his lifetime. Every time the community made a ruling in this way, Omar had scribes record it and sent the ruling out to provincial governors to use as a basis for their decisions.

Omar funded a body of scholars to spend all their time steeping themselves in the revelations, the stories of Mohammed's life, and other pertinent data, so that when he needed expert advice he could get it from these "people of the bench," a seed that grew into one of Islam's major social institutions, the *ulama*, or "scholars."

Even as he was shaping Muslim law, Omar was busy applying the doctrine to social life in Medina, which brings us to his stern side. Omar had no tolerance for slackards. For example, he banned drinking outright, even though the Qur'an had been somewhat ambiguous on this question, seeming in some early verses to disapprove more of drunkenness than of drinking per se (although later verses ban it more definitely).

The Qur'an specified no particular punishment for drinking, but Omar deduced one by analogy. The analogy in this case went as follows: the Qur'an prescribed the lash for slander; drinking, said Omar, made a person spout slander. Therefore, the punishment for drinking must also be the lash. This mode of argument by analogy (*qiyas*) created a stencil used prolifically by later Muslim legal thinkers.

Dreading the destructive power of unlicensed sex, Omar enforced the sternest measures against adultery. In fact, he mandated stoning for adulterers, which is not mentioned in the Qur'an but does appear in the law of Moses, dating to pre-Qur'anic times (Deuteronomy 22:22). He also banned the Arab custom of temporary marriage, which allowed men to marry women for a few days: the khalifa recognized prostitution when he saw it. (Shi'ite jurists later relegitimized this practice in their codes.)

Omar's detractors charge him with misogyny, and his rulings do suggest that he held women responsible for the bad behavior of men. To defuse the disruptive power of sexuality, Omar took measures to regulate and separate the roles of men and women, mandating, for example, that women and men pray separately, presumably so they wouldn't be thinking about sex during that ritual.

This was, however, a far cry from the separation of the sexes and the disempowerment of women that developed in Islamic societies centuries later (and persists to this day). It's true, of course, that gender relationships in Medina did not conform to modern feminist ideals. Tribal Arabs (and most early cultures) saw separate and nonoverlapping roles for men and women, and Islam confirmed the separation. In Omar's day, however, education was compulsory for both boys and girls in the Muslim community. Women worked alongside men; they took part in public life; they attended lectures, delivered sermons, composed poetry for public orations, went to war as relief workers, and sometimes even took part in fighting. Important decisions facing the community were discussed in public meetings, Omar participated in those meetings as just another citizen of the community, and women as well as men engaged him fearlessly in debate. In fact, Omar appointed a woman as head of the market in Medina, which was a position of great civic responsibility, for it included duties such as regulating construction, issuing business permits, and policing the integrity of weights and measures. Even so, Omar did plant seeds that eventually developed into a severe constriction of women's participation in public life.

In the seventh century CE, every society in the world permitted slavery, and Arabia was no exception. Islam did not ban the practice, but it did limit a master's power over a slave, and Omar enforced these rulings strictly. No Muslim could *be* a slave. If a man impregnated a slave, he had to marry her, which meant that her child would be born a Muslim and therefore free. Slavery could not result in breaking up a family, which limited a master's options: he could only buy or sell whole families.

Masters could not abuse or mistreat slaves, who had the same human rights as free folks, a theme stressed in the Qur'an and specifically reaffirmed in Prophet Mohammed's final sermon. Omar ruled a master had to give his slaves the same food he was eating and in fact had to have his slaves eat with his family. If Omar's rulings had been carried to their logical conclusions, slavery might have ended in the Muslim world in the early days of the khalifate. (Instead, Muslim societies regressed in this matter.)

Ironically, Omar's own career ended when an emotionally unstable Persian slave drove a knife into his belly at the mosque. On his deathbed, some of the community's notables asked him to nominate his successor as Abu Bakr had done, in order to ensure a smooth transition. "How about your son?" they suggested.

Omar flew into his last rage: "Do you think I did this job to benefit myself and my family?" He died later that day, but before his death he established another consequential precedent. He named a six-man consultative committee (a *shura*) to select a new khalifa and seek the consensus of the Umma on their choice. Many later Muslim thinkers looked to the shura as the basis for democratic institutions in Islam. The shura discovered that two men, Ali and Othman, were everybody's first and second choices, some favoring Ali and some Othman. (Ali, remember, was Mohammed's son-in-law who had already been passed over twice.)

The chairman of the shura interviewed both men in front of an assembly of the people, posing one key question to each: "If you become khalifa, will you be guided by the Qur'an, the sunna, and the precedents set by Abu Bakr and Omar?"

Ali said yes to the Qur'an and yes to the sunna (the example set by Mohammed's life), but as for the decisions of his predecessors—no: Ali said he had a mind of his own and would consult his own conscience and best judgment for his decisions. Othman, by contrast, said yes to everything: "I am not an innovator." So the chairman declared him the right man to head the Umma, the people approved, and Ali, not wanting to rock the boat, took the oath of loyalty.

4

∞

Schism

24-40 AH
644-661 CE

Othman was Mohammed's fifth cousin once removed, and he took office as Islam's third khalifa at the age of sixty-eight. To understand his stormy twelve-year term, it's useful to look at who the man was and how he came to head up the community that ruled the Middle World.

Othman's father had been one of the richest men in Mecca, and Othman inherited his father's millions when he was twenty. With a deft touch for business, he managed to multiply that wealth many times over before he was even in his thirties, earning the nickname of Othman Ghani, "Othman the wealthy."

Chaste and modest even before his conversion, Othman never drank, smoked, or chased women. Around Mecca, he was famous for his good looks—people even went so far as to call him "beautiful"—yet an air of anxious melancholy always surrounded this austere, soft-spoken man.

He converted to Islam about a year after Mohammed began his preaching and nine years before the Hijra. His conversion story begins one evening when he was on his way home from a successful business trip.

Reputedly, Othman had stopped someplace for the night and was lying under the stars, looking up at the black dome of the sky, when the immensity of the universe suddenly overwhelmed him. Along with a crushing sense of his own insignificance came a conviction that *somebody* was in control, that this universe had a master, and what a master He must be! At that moment, even though he was alone, Othman heard a penetrating voice announce out loud that the Messenger of God was in the world. As soon as he got home, the story goes, Othman went to his friend Abu Bakr, who told him the curious tale of Mohammed and his message about a single, omnipotent God. Othman immediately announced himself a believer.

His conversion enraged his family. After all, his clan, the aristocratic Umayyads, was the most rabidly anti-Muslim faction of the Quraysh tribe. Othman's uncle Abu Sufyan would soon emerge as the leader of the anti-Muslim forces. Othman's stepfather had once attacked Mohammed in an alley and would have strangled him if Abu Bakr had not intervened. Othman's two wives reviled him for embracing Mohammed's faith. They would not convert, so Othman divorced them and married the Prophet's famously beautiful daughter Ruqayya. When she died, Othman married another daughter of Mohammed's, Um Kulthum.

The Muslims were no doubt glad to have a rich man in their ranks, and Othman was glad to help his fellow Muslims any way he could, but the main way he could think of was to provide money. Once, when abuse of Muslims was peaking in Mecca, Mohammed decided that a group of his followers should emigrate to Abyssinia, and Othman helped finance that. He himself emigrated with the group as well and in Abyssinia forged fruitful business connections that made him even richer than before. A few years later he returned to Mecca, where his Abyssinian connections— yes—served him so well he grew even richer.

For most Muslims, the Hijra meant losing everything they owned. They knew nothing about farming, the main occupation in Medina, so the move impoverished them. But not Othman. Although he emigrated with the others, he never quite severed his ties to business associates back home, and with those associates looking after his properties and business interests, Othman continued to prosper, even in Medina. There was never any suggestion that he came by his wealth dishonestly: quite the opposite. Some people simply have the golden touch, and Othman was such a man. Nor was he a miser.

He spent lavishly for the public good; for example, he expanded the mosque in Medina for Mohammed, and when the Muslims needed water, he bought a valuable well from one of the Jewish tribes and donated it to the public.

Staggering wealth, dazzling beauty, two of the Prophet's daughters for wives—what did this man lack? And yet Othman seemed haunted by the fear that he was not good enough. He spent much of his time fasting, praying, and reading the Qur'an. Perhaps his extravagant donations to the public good were attempts to deserve the extraordinary good fortune he already enjoyed.

Or perhaps he worried that his character was not quite at the level of the Prophet's other close companions. He missed the battle of Badr because his wife was sick. At the battle of Uhud, when a rumor spread that Mohammed had been killed, Othman was among the Muslims who abandoned hope and left the field. Othman redeemed himself at the Battle of the Moat, but shortly after that battle, his son died, and Othman seemed to feel that God was still punishing him. To earn forgiveness, he made a practice of buying slaves and liberating one each Friday.

After Mohammed died, Othman worried that the community might fall apart, but in addition he seemed particularly afraid for his own individual soul. "How will we now be safe from the snares of the devil?" he lamented. Fear of the hereafter consumed the poor man. "Every day is doomsday," he once said, by which he meant there is never an instant when it's safe to stop being good, so he for one stepped up his fasting and praying, and dispensed ever more extravagant contributions, trying desperately to deserve a place in paradise that the Prophet Mohammed had assured him was already his. This haunted giant of benevolence became the third khalifa of Islam.

When Omar began his khalifate, Islam had been a new kind of social organism still growing into its identity. Omar's khalifate was filled with a sense of spiritual adventure, invention, and discovery. By the time Othman took charge, the Islamic community was a government in control of a vast territory. It was no longer enough to preach, defend, attack, and spread holy excitement. Muslim leaders now had to collect taxes, run courts, keep bridges and highways in repair, set salaries, define duties for various positions—all that dull administrative stuff of daily life. Managing this transition fell to Othman.

One great project Othman saw to fruition during the first half of his khalifate was the preparation of a definitive edition of the Qur'an. He set scholars to work combing out redundancies among the copies that existed, resolving discrepancies, and evaluating passages whose authenticity was subject to doubt. The final product was compiled into a book in which the verses were arranged more or less in order of length (rather than thematically or chronologically). All other compilations, competing versions, and rejected verses were destroyed. From then on, every Qur'an would be the same, word for word, and that's the Qur'an all Muslims have today. You can see why this had to be done if the priority was to keep the community unified, but you can also see why this project might have disgruntled some Muslims, especially if they already had suspicions about Othman's intentions—as some did.

Next came the job of setting the community's finances in order. In the Prophet's time, there were basically no state expenditures. All money that flowed into Medina was distributed more or less immediately. Abu Bakr and Omar had operated in much the same way, although Abu Bakr did set up a treasury, and Omar did build up a surplus out of which he paid stipends to soldiers, the beginnings of a standing army for Islam. Under Othman, however, the treasury swelled into a regular organ of government, which financed an ever-proliferating array of state expenses.

This third khalifa dramatically increased the flow of tax revenues from his far-flung provinces. When Amr ibn al-A'as, the governor of Egypt, failed to send in enough money, Othman dismissed him and appointed his own foster brother Abdullah to the post. Abdullah succeeded in getting a great deal more money out of the province—in fact, doubling the revenue from Egypt—proving that Othman had made a wise business decision, but Amr ibn al-A'as grumbled that his successor was getting more milk out of the she-camel only by starving the camel's young. Islamic rule was acquiring hints of possible oppression and corruption.

Othman upheld Omar's prohibitions against confiscating land in conquered territories, but he lifted Omar's restrictions on Muslims *buying* land there, for Othman believed in economic freedom. In fact, he let eminent Muslims borrow money out of the public treasury to finance such purchases. Soon, Muslim elites, including most of the Prophet Mohammed's companions, were amassing fortunes and acquiring immense estates throughout the new Islamic empire. Othman's "economic reforms" tended to profit his own clan, the Umayyads, above all because they were best situated to take out loans from the treasury. This khalifa also appointed his relatives and "favorites" to many powerful political posts throughout the empire, simply because they were the people he knew best and trusted most. As a result, the Umayyads ended up acquiring disproportionate clout, both economically and politically.

The third khalifa continued to practice an austere lifestyle but demanded no such austerity from his officials. Being a rich man, he took no salary, but he did dole out grants to his favorites and spent lavishly on public works. His administration built over five thousand new mosques across the empire. Othman promoted a building boom that turned Medina into a city of broad streets and imposing buildings paved with fine tile, including a palatial mansion for Othman himself, a headquarters suitable to the dignity of his powerful office (within this palace Othman lived on bread, water, and prayer).

Throughout the empire, Othman demonstrated his business genius by ordering improvements beneficial to commerce. Canals were dug, highways built, irrigation systems improved. Ports got new facilities. Proliferating cities got new wells and water systems, and new bazaars regulated by government-appointed market officers. The Muslim enterprise didn't have quite the same flavor as it had in Omar's day, but who could argue with prosperity?

On questions of personal morality such as drinking and sex, Othman's asceticism put him beyond criticism. If piety consisted of penance and prayer, he had to rank among the top ten most pious men of his time, but Othman saw no ethical ambiguity in people making money, so long as their moneymaking promoted overall well being.

One of Othman's great favorites was his cousin Mu'awiya. Omar had appointed Mu'awiya governor of Damascus and its surroundings. Othman kept adding bits to his cousin's territory, until Mu'awiya governed everything from the headwaters of the Euphrates River down the Mediterranean coast to Egypt.

Mu'awiya was the son of Abu Sufyan, the Meccan tribal aristocrat who led the attack on Islam in two of those three iconic battles between Mecca and Medina. Mu'awiya's mother, Hind, followed her husband to those battles, and at Uhud, after the Muslims fled, she reputedly ate the liver of Mohammed's fallen uncle Hamzah in an act of triumphalist gloating. The Prophet, however, was never one to hold a grudge: as soon as someone embraced Islam, he or she became part of the family, and so it was with the Umayyads. The Prophet thought Mu'awiya especially competent and kept him close after his conversion.

No doubt Omar appointed Mu'awiya governor of Damascus because he got things done, but perhaps Omar should have paused to consider why Mohammed had kept the man so close: once ensconced in Damascus, Mu'awiya put his brilliance to work assembling a standing army loyal to himself. This would have grim consequences after Othman's untimely death.

Toward the end of Othman's twelve-year reign, grumbling began to sound throughout the empire. In Egypt, his foster brother was squeezing people so hard for money that riots broke out. Egyptian notables wrote to the khalifa, begging him to recall the governor. Hearing nothing back, they sent a delegation to petition him in person. As it happened, at this very time, groups of disgruntled citizens were converging on the city from the north as well. Apparently, Othman had displeased a lot of people.

All these petitioners made Othman nervous. He begged Ali to go out and talk to the malcontents on his behalf, placate them and persuade them to go home, but Ali refused, perhaps because he himself disapproved of the third khalifa's policies and practices. He advised Othman to secure himself by addressing the people's legitimate complaints. Finally, Othman gave in and met with the Egyptian delegation. He promised to replace his foster brother and told the Egyptians to go home and let the governor know a new man would soon be coming to replace him.

The Egyptians started back, feeling pretty good, but along the way they caught up with a slave of Othman's. Something about the man aroused their suspicions. They searched him and found a letter on his person, seemingly signed by the khalifa and addressed to the governor of Egypt, which told Governor Abdullah to arrest the delegation of malcontents as soon as they showed up at his court and to execute them as soon as it seemed politic!

The delegation returned to Medina in a fury. Othman came dithering out of the palace to meet them on the steps: Back so soon? What was wrong? They showed him the letter and Othman expressed shock. He swore he had never written such a thing, never heard of it until this moment. In fact, his troublemaking cousin Marwan, a relative and ally of the governor of Damascus, might have penned the letter and forged the khalifa's signature to it. Poor Othman, nearly eighty at this time, might well have been easy to manipulate.

In any case, the peaceful petitioners turned into an angry mob. First, they demanded that the khalifa deliver Mu'awiya's brother to them. The khalifa refused. Then they demanded that Othman step down and let some better man take over. Othman indignantly refused this too. His obligation was to God, he said, and quitting his office at the behest of a mob would be an affront to God! He then retired to his private chambers, where he lit a little lamp and settled in a corner to do what he always did in times of turmoil and doubt: humbly read his Qur'an.

Outside his palace, the rioters worked themselves into a frenzy, broke down palace doors, and burst in with a roar. They found the khalifa in his study, and there in the flickering twilight of the old man's lamp, in year 34 of the Muslim era, they beat their own leader to death. Suddenly, the succession conundrum had turned into a horrifying crisis that threatened the very soul of Islam.

For four days the mob rampaged through the city. The citizens of Medina cowered in their houses, waiting for the violence to die down. Even when the uproar faded, the leaders of the mob said they would not quit town until a new khalifa was appointed, someone they could trust. Now, at last, all thoughts turned to the one candidate who had been passed over time after time, the man some had always called the Prophet's only legitimate successor: Mohammed's son-in-law Ali.

At first, Ali refused the honor; but every other prominent member of the Muslim community turned down the khalifate as well, and the rebels threatened to launch a reign of terror unless Medina chose someone they could live with and chose him fast, so leading Muslims crowded into the mosque and begged Ali to take charge.

What a strange moment this must have been for Ali. For twenty-five agonizing years he must have felt like he was watching the ship drift off course. Three times, the Umma had rejected his leadership when he still would have had the power to make things right. Each time, he had been a good sport, because what else could he do? Trying to seize the helm would have split the community. He had to choose between causing trouble or watching the enterprise falter; killing it or letting it die. Only now, when things had gone so off kilter that Muslims had murdered their khalifa, *now* when his successor would face an impossible challenge, *now* the Umma was saying, "Take the reins, Ali."

THE FOURTH KHALIFA (36–40 AH, 656–661 CE)

Ali finally accepted the khalifate, but in his first oration to the people, he told them he had accepted this office under duress. He lamented the unraveling of the Umma in the single generation since the Prophet's death. It would take a stern hand to put things back in order, Ali said, and he gave the Umma fair warning: from him, what they could expect was stern.

One key segment of the community didn't hear him. The members of the Umayyad clan, Othman's close relatives, had fled to Damascus, where their kinsman Mu'awiya had quietly been assembling his military force. Mu'awiya began touring his province with a professional storyteller. At each stop, the storyteller aroused the crowd with a dramatic account of the murder in Medina. At the climactic moment, Mu'awiya himself would burst onstage, waving a bloody shirt, the very shirt in which (he claimed) the khalifa had been murdered. It was masterful political theater. Mu'awiya would then call upon the new khalifa to arrest and punish Othman's murderers or step down.

But how could Ali arrest the assassins? No one knew exactly who in that mob had dealt the actual blows. In any real sense, the whole mob was "the assassin." To meet Mu'awiya's demands, Ali would have had to arrest and punish the whole mob. This would never have been practical, but in the circumstances, it was utterly impossible: the mob still ruled the streets of Medina. Ali simply did not have the power to do as Mu'awiya demanded, and the governor knew it.

Besides, the rioters who murdered Othman had started out as victims of injustice and oppression. They had come to Medina with legitimate grievances, but in killing the khalifa, they had handed the higher moral ground to their oppressors. Now, Ali was forced to choose between aligning himself with the oppressors or the murderers—a heartbreaking choice!

He decided he would start by attacking the corruption rotting the empire. Win or lose, it was his only hope: by reversing Othman's policies and restoring rectitude, he might still pull the community back onto the Path, thereby acquiring the credibility and stature he needed to do all the other things that needed doing.

But a whole new class of nouveau riche had sprung out of the compost of the Muslim conquests, and this elite was not interested in Ali's idea of purity or his reforms. To them, Ali looked like a revolutionary threat, and Mu'awiya looked like the guardian of their wealth and safety, the new status quo.

Ali fired all the governors Othman had appointed and sent out new men to replace them, but none of the fired governors agreed to step down, except the one in Yemen, and he fled with all the money in the treasury, leaving a bankrupt province for Ali's appointee to take over.

Meanwhile, trouble cropped up in another quarter. The Prophet's youngest wife Ayesha happened to be in Mecca when Othman was assassinated. When Mu'awiya began his ruckus, Ayesha threw in with him, in part because there had always been bad blood between her and Ali. She announced her alignment with a fiery speech in Mecca. "O ye people! Rebels . . . have murdered the innocent Othman. . . . They violated the sanctity of the city of the Holy Prophet in the sacred month of hajj. They plundered and looted the citizens of Medina. By God, a single finger of Othman was more precious than the lives of all the assassins. The mischief has not been crushed, and the murderers of Othman have not been brought to book. . . . Seek satisfaction on these murderers. Only vengeance for the blood of Othman can vindicate the honor of Islam."

Capitalizing on the passion she aroused, she assembled an army, convened a war council, and mapped out a campaign. The ousted governor of Yemen pledged all his stolen treasure to her cause. Flush with funds, Ayesha led her troops north and stormed Basra, a key city in southern Iraq. She dispatched Ali's loyalists quickly and took over.

At this point, someone started a whispering campaign charging Ali himself with complicity in the assassination of Othman. Poor honest Ali admitted that he bore some responsibility for the crime because when Othman was pleading for protection, Ali had withheld his sword arm. The thought that he might have saved Othman tormented the fourth khalifa of Islam, and his honesty only fueled the rumors that undermined him.

Ali tried to raise an army to fight Ayesha, preaching that this was a jihad and that people should rally to defend Islam as they had in days of yore. But Muslims were confused, because Ayesha was calling for jihad too, against Ali. Both sides claimed to be fighting for truth, justice, and the Islamic way, yet each was calling on Muslims to fight other Muslims. This wasn't what they called jihad back in the good old days!

Curiously, Ayesha's cohorts included two men, Talha and Zubayd, companions of the Prophet, who may have been part of the mob that attacked Othman's palace that day. If not themselves assassins, they were certainly associated with the assassins—yet here they were, leading members of a force vowing to avenge the assassination of Othman by toppling Ali!

Ali marched out of Medina with the few troops he could muster, but various tribal warriors joined him on his way north, and his army grew to imposing size. When he reached Basra, he sent a trusted comrade into the city to negotiate with Ayesha. Remarkably, the spokesman's arguments got through to the fierce young woman. First, she admitted that she didn't really think Ali had anything to do with Othman's murder. What she blamed him for was failing to arrest the criminals responsible. Then, she agreed that the criminals were part of a mob, and that the mob, which was still in charge, drew its strength from chaos. Next, she admitted that by fighting Ali, she was promoting chaos and so, yes, in a sense she herself was helping the assassins escape justice. By the end of the day, she had agreed to lay down her weapons, disband her army, and join forces with Ali. She would meet with him in the morning to discuss terms.

The interaction reflected credit on both leaders: on Ali for seeking negotiation before battle, on Ayesha for the intellectual honesty that enabled her, even in the heat of anger, even while surrounded by the smell of war and the threat of death, to listen to Ali's case and admit the validity of points that eroded her position—just because they were true. In this, there was heroism.

The envoy returned to Ali's camp to give him the good news, and that night celebration rang out on both sides. There would be peace! There was just one problem that no one took into account: both armies contained members of the very mob that had killed Othman and would be brought to book if Ali and Ayesha made common cause. These men obviously could not afford to give peace a chance.

Early the next morning, a gang of them crept out of Ali's camp and launched a surprise attack on Ayesha's sleeping forces. By the time Ali woke up, Ayesha's men were striking back. Both Ali and Ayesha thought the other had double-crossed them, and thus began the Battle of the

Camel, so-called because Ayesha rode a camel right into the battlefield and directed her troops from its back; the battle ended only when her camel was cut down and she was captured. Ali won the day, but what a bitter victory! It's difficult to imagine how the two of them must have felt, meeting after the carnage ended, the Prophet's adored wife and the Prophet's beloved son-in-law, face to face on a blood-soaked field littered with ten thousand Muslim dead, many of them close companions of the Messenger of God.

As they pieced together how people and events had betrayed them both, these two survivors made some sort of peace with one another. Perhaps they found their way to a friendship, even. Perhaps, in some strange way, the tragedy that engulfed them both, and the horrors that neither could have wanted, drew them together. In any case, they never fought again. After the Battle of the Camel, Ayesha retired to Medina, and spent the rest of her life recording the sayings of the Prophet and writing commentaries on them. She ended her days as one of the most respected early scholars of Islam.

Ali never went back to Medina. He made the city of Kufa, in modern-day Iraq, his seat of government to reward the people of that city for supporting him, and he tried to piece together the remains of his khalifate, but the heartbreaking war with Ayesha only marked the beginning of his troubles. The master troublemaker still loomed in the wings, sharpening his scimitar and drilling his troops. Mu'awiya was getting ready for his final push.

By this time, Mu'awiya had formally refused allegiance to Ali and declared that the khalifate belonged to him. Both sides led armies into the field. In the year 36 AH, (657 CE), Ali confronted Mu'awiya at the battle of Siffin. It started when Mu'awiya's army tried to block Ali's access to water. A brief battle burst out, but Ali's men gained the river bank, and the fighting subsided into a stalemate that lasted for months, interrupted only by sporadic skirmishes. Both sides were holding back, looking for a way to win without brutality, because each side stood to lose religious authority by spilling Muslim blood.

The standoff ended with a four-day outburst of violence in which some sources reckon that sixty-five thousand people died. The slaughter led to calls that both armies pull back and let the two leaders settle the dispute with hand-to-hand combat. Ali, who was fifty-eight years old but still a fearsome physical specimen, eagerly accepted the challenge. Mu'awiya, who was about the same age as Ali, but dissipated and fat, said no.

Ali's troops renewed the attack, this time felling Mu'awiya's soldiers like weeds, but Mu'awiya devised a stratagem to give them pause: he had his soldiers attach pages of the Qur'an to their lance tips and march behind recitation experts who chanted Qur'anic verses and exhorted Ali to negotiate in the name of peace among Muslims. Ali's troops quailed at the prospect of defiling the Qur'an and Ali agreed to negotiations.

He probably didn't think of himself as giving into anything, since he had been calling for negotiation from the start; but no doubt he was thinking of talks that would end with Mu'awiya acknowledging his right to rule in exchange for some concession such as a guarantee to let him stay on as governor of Syria. Instead, when the representatives of the two leaders met, they agreed that the two men were equals, and that each should remain in charge of his own territories, Mu'awiya ruling Syria and Egypt, Ali ruling everything else.

This wasn't what Ali had been looking for, and it certainly infuriated his partisans, his *shi'i,* to use the Arabic word—a word that became the name of the sect that grew out of this rift. But Ali could not now reject the results without seeming to show bad faith. Mu'awiya had snookered him!

Besides, Ali was operating with a handicap. For twenty-six years Ali's shi'i had been declaring that he possessed God-given powers of leadership, powers that could save the Muslim community from its ills. Originally, this claim referred to his blood relationship with the Prophet, but over the decades, as the first three khalifas were shaping a new social order, Ali had been delivering mystical sermons that held forth rapturously on the nature of Allah's omnipotence, immensity, oneness, and beyondness. In short, while the other khalifas had made themselves the guardians of Mohammed's communitarian vision, Ali had established himself as the keeper of the inner flame. So his partisans' proposition came to be that unlike all other claimants to the khalifate, Ali had some mystical personal access to Allah's guidance. His whole case rested on this image.

Now he was . . . *negotiating?* With Mu'awiya, the utter embodiment of anti-Muslim materialism? What kind of God-gifted avatar of Allah-guided truth was he?

Compromising with the enemy disappointed a faction of Ali's most committed followers, and these younger, more radical of his partisans split away. They came to be known as Kharijites, "ones who departed." This splinter group reformulated the ideals of Ali's followers into a revolutionary new doctrine: blood and genealogy meant nothing, they said. Even a slave had the right to lead the community. The only qualification was character. No one was born to leadership, and mere election could not transform someone into the khalifa. Whoever exhibited the greatest authentic devotion to Muslim values simply *was* the khalifa, no election needed. He was, however, accountable to the people. If he ever fell a hair short of complete moral excellence, he forfeited his right to high office and someone else became khalifa. Through what actual machinery all this demotion and promotion was to occur, the Kharijites didn't say. Not their problem. They only knew that Ali had squandered his entitlement and needed to step down; and since he didn't step down, one young Kharijite took matters into his own hands. In the year 40 AH, this hothead assassinated Ali.

Ali's partisans immediately looked to his son Hassan as his successor, but Mu'awiya swept this challenge aside by offering Hassan a sum of money to renounce all claim to the khalifate. Mohammed's older grandson, heartbroken and war-weary at this point, stepped aside. He had no stomach for continuing the fight, and under the circumstances now prevailing, claiming the khalifate could only constitute a power grab, and what good was that? And so the Umayyad dynasty began.

Ali's death ended the first era of Islamic history. Muslim historians came to call the first four post-Mohammed leaders the Rightly Guided Khalifas. Life in their time was certainly not undiluted sweetness and wonder, but in calling them the Rightly Guided Ones, I don't think responsible Muslim historians mean to suggest such perfection. Rather, they're saying that the evolution of the community from the time of the Hijra to the assassination of Ali was a religious drama. Yes there was bloodshed and heartache, but the turmoil didn't stem from petty people vying for power, money, or ego gratification. The four khalifas and Mohammed's close companions who formed the core of the Umma in this period were honestly striving to make the revelations work. Each of them had a handle on some essential aspect of the project, but no one of them was big enough to grasp the whole of it, as Mohammed had done. The Prophet's immediate successors were like the six blind men trying to discern whether the elephant was more like a rope, a wall, a pillar, or what. All the struggles over the khalifate in the period of the Rightly Guided Ones had theological meaning because the issues they struggled with were essentially theological. After Ali's death, the khalifate was just an empire.

5

Empire of the Umayyads

40–120 AH
661–737 CE

O F COURSE, MU'AWIYA did not present himself as the man who ended the religious era. He titled himself khalifa and said he was continuing the same great mission as his predecessors. Toward the end of his life, however, he convened a council of Arab tribal leaders to discuss who *his* successor would be, a meeting that had the outward form of a *shura,* a consultative committee like the one Omar established. The chieftains thought their opinions were sincerely being solicited and began discussing the merits of this and that candidate. Suddenly one of the khalifa's henchmen jumped to his feet and glowered around the circle. "Right now," he scowled, "*this* is the commander of the faithful." He pointed to Mu'awiya. "After he dies, it's this one." He pointed to Yazid, the emperor's eldest son. "And if any of you object, it's *this* one!" He pulled out his sword."[1]

The chiefs got the point. They went on through all the proper Muslim-democratic forms and made all the appropriate noises and gestures, but in the end they dutifully chose Yazid to be their next khalifa, and when they went home that night, they all knew the principle of succession would never come up for discussion again.

When Yazid succeeded to the throne, however, he knew his father had not eliminated but merely suppressed rebellious elements. Yazid therefore kept close tabs on all who might challenge his power, especially Ali's relatives and descendents. Hassan had passed away by this time, but his brother Hussein was still alive, and just to be on the safe side, the emperor decided to have this man assassinated on his next pilgrimage to Mecca.

Hussein was now in his forties. He knew his father's partisans considered him to be the true khalifa; he knew that zealous Muslims looked to him to keep the spiritual revolution alive; but no one man could shoulder such a heavy mantle. Hussein had opted out of politics and lived a quiet life of prayer and contemplation all these years, meditating on his grandfather's mission.

But when he learned of the plot to have him killed, and that Yazid's assassins planned to murder him in the Ka'ba itself, Hussein could take no more. He had no troops and no military experience. Yazid had a network of spies, a treasury, and an army. Even so, in the year 60 AH (680 by the common calendar), Hussein announced that he was going to challenge Yazid and left Medina with a force of seventy-two people.

Actually, calling it a "force" goes too far: the seventy-two included Hussein's wife, his children, and some doddering elderly relatives. Only a handful of the company were fighting-age males. What was the man thinking? Did he really imagine he could topple the Umayyad monarch with this tiny band? Was he perhaps thinking that if he just started marching, he would ignite a firestorm of revolt and inspire the tribes to join him?

Probably not. In a final sermon before his departure, Hussein told his followers that he was sure to be slain but was not afraid, because death "surrounds Adam's offspring as a necklace surrounds a young girl's neck."[2] He noted a Qur'anic verse that told people to stand up to unjust rulers like Yazid. If the son of Ali and Fatima, the grandson of the Prophet himself, did not stand up to tyranny, who would? As portrayed in traditional accounts, therefore, Hussein was determined to make an example of his own life: right from the start, he saw himself as embarking on a pilgrimage with ritual significance. In a sense, he was committing noble suicide.

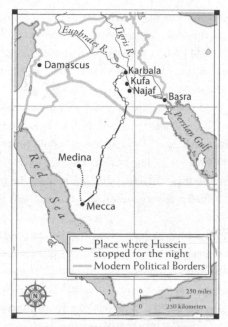

IMAM HUSSEIN'S ROUTE TO KARBALA

When Yazid heard that the Prophet's younger grandson was on the move, he sent an army to swat him down. Hussein posed no real threat to the empire, but Yazid wanted to crush him with overwhelming force as a warning to other radicals who might be tempted to play the God-chose-me card. The army he sent outnumbered Hussein's little group by enough to make it no contest. Legends put that number at anywhere from four hundred to forty thousand.

Whatever its size, this imperial army caught up with Hussein in the desert just south of Karbala, a city near the southern border of Iraq. If you glance at weather reports for that part of the world on any summer day, you'll see temperatures ranging upward of 115 degrees. On just such a sweltering day, the emperor's army trapped Hussein's little band within smelling distance of the Euphrates River but cut off from the water. Hussein, however, did what his father had failed to do. He refused to settle, compromise, or bargain. God had chosen him to lead the community of virtue, he said, and he would not disavow that truth.

One by one, the warriors in Hussein's band sallied forth to fight Yazid's army. One by one they fell. The women, children, and old folks, meanwhile, all died of thirst. When the last of the party was gone, the victorious general swooped in, cut off Hussein's head, and shipped it to the emperor with a gloating note.

The severed head arrived just as Yazid was entertaining a Byzantine envoy, and it spoiled the whole dinner party. The Byzantine envoy said, "Is this how you Muslims behave? We Christians would never treat a descendant of Jesus in this manner." The criticism angered Yazid, and he had the "Roman" thrown into prison. Later, however, he saw that keeping the severed head might be bad public relations, so he sent it back to Karbala to be buried with the body.

Yazid no doubt believed he had solved his problem: surely Ali's descendents would never make trouble again. He was quite wrong, however. By crushing Hussein at Karbala, this emperor lit a spark. The passionate embrace of Ali's cause now became a prairie fire called Shi'ism. What is Shi'ism? One often hears it summed up as if it were just another quarrel about dynastic succession, like the battles between Maud and Stephen in twelfth-century England. If that had really been the case, the movement would have faded out after Ali died. Who today calls himself a Maudist or a Stephenist? Who today even cares which of these two had the more legitimate claim to the English throne? Ali, however, kept gaining new adherents after his death. The ranks of his Shi'i kept on swelling. People who were not even born when Ali died grew up to embrace his cause and shape their identities around the conviction that he should have been the first khalifa. How could this be?

The answer, of course, is that the dispute about the khalifate was no mere dynastic struggle. Key religious issues were embedded in it, because the choice involved not just *who* but also *what* the leader would be. Ali's partisans saw in him something that they did not see in other claimants to the khalifate: a God-given spiritual quality that made him more than an ordinary mortal, a quality they had seen in Mohammed as well. No one said Ali was another Messenger of God. No one would have made that claim (at that point, anyway), and so they gave Ali a different title. They said he was the imam.

Originally, *imam* was simply the term for a person who led communal prayer. To most Muslims, that's still what the word means today. It's a title of respect, to be sure, but no more grandiose than, say, *reverend* or *honorable*. After all, every time a group of Muslims gathers to pray communally, one person among them has to lead the prayer; and he does nothing different than the others do; he just does it standing alone in front of the others to help keep the group moving in tandem through the ritual. Every mosque has an imam, and when he's not leading prayer, he might be sweeping the floor or patching the roof.

But when Shi'i say "imam," they mean something considerably more elevated. To Shi'i there is always one imam in the world, and there is never more than one. They proceed from the premise that Mohammed had some palpable mystical substance vested in him by Allah, some energy, some light, which they call the *baraka* of Mohammed. When the Prophet died, that light passed into Ali, at which moment Ali became the first imam. When Ali died, that same light passed into his son Hassan, who became the second Imam. Later, the spark passed into Hassan's younger brother Hussein, who became the third imam. When Hussein was martyred at Karbala, the whole "imam" idea flowered into a rich theological concept that addressed a religious craving left unnourished by the mainstream doctrines of that time.

The mainstream doctrine, as articulated by Abu Bakr and Omar, said that Mohammed was strictly a messenger delivering a set of instructions about how to live. The message was the great and only thing. Beyond delivering the Qur'an, Mohammed's religious significance was only his sunna, the example he set by his way of life, an example others could follow if they wanted to live in God's favor. People who accepted this doctrine eventually came to be known as Sunnis, and they comprise nine-tenths of the Muslim community today.

The Shi'i, by contrast, felt that they couldn't make themselves worthy of heaven simply by their own efforts. To them, instructions were not enough. They wanted to believe that direct guidance from God was still coming into the world, through some chosen person who could bathe other believers in a soul-saving grace, some living figure who would keep the world warm and pure. They adopted the term *imam* for this reassuring figure. His presence in the world ensured the continuing possibility of miracle.

When Hussein went to Karbala, he had no chance of winning. His only hope lay in the possibility of God producing a miracle—but then, the continuing possibility of miracle was the principle he embodied. He and his band chose death as symbolic refusal to disavow this possibility, and, in the final analysis, to Shi'i, a miracle did occur at Karbala, the miracle of Hussein's martyrdom.

To this day, Shi'i around the world commemorate the anniversary of Hussein's death with a day of cathartic mourning. They gather in "lamentation houses" to recount the story of the martyrdom, a religious narrative that casts Hussein in the role of a redemptive figure on an apocalyptic scale. By his martyrdom, Hussein has gained a place next to God and earned the privilege of interceding for sinners. Those who embrace him and believe in him will be saved and go to heaven, no matter what transgressions may foul their record. Hussein gave Shi'i this back door to the miracle they had hoped for all along. Believing in Hussein could not get you gold or high office or luck in love, but it could get you into heaven: that was the miracle.

And now for the political story that unfolded after Mu'awiya took power. The Umayyad ascension may have ended the birth of Islam as a religious event, but it launched the evolution of Islam as a civilization and a political empire. In the annals of conventional Western history, the Umayyads marked the beginning of Muslim greatness. They put Islam on the map by kicking off a golden age that lasted long after they themselves had fallen.

Whatever his shortcomings as a saint, Mu'awiya possessed tremendous political skill. The very qualities that helped him defeat the tormented Ali made him a successful monarch, and his reign institutionalized practices and procedures that would hold an Islamic empire together for centuries.

This is all very ironic because, let us not forget, when Mohammed's prophetic career began, the Umayyads were a leading clan among the rich elite of Mecca. When Mohammed as Messenger denounced the malefactors of great wealth who ignored the poor and exploited the widows and orphans, the Umayyads were some of the main people he was talking about. When Mohammed still lived in Mecca, the Umayyads outdid each other in harassing his followers. They helped plot the assassination of Mohammed before the Hijra and led some of the forces that tried to extinguish the Umma in its cradle after the Muslims moved to Medina.

But once Islam began to look like a juggernaut, the Umayyads converted, joined the Umma, and climbed to the top of the new society; and here they were again, back among the new elite. Before Islam, they were merely among the elite of a city. Now, they were the top elite of a global empire. I'm sure many among them were scratching their heads, trying to remember what they ever found to dislike in this new faith!

As rulers, the Umayyads possessed some powerful instruments of policy inherited from their predecessors, especially Omar and Othman. Omar had done them a great favor by sanctifying offensive warfare as jihad so long as it was conducted against infidels in the cause of Islam. This definition of jihad enabled the new Muslim rulers to maintain a perpetual state of war on their frontiers, a policy with pronounced benefits.

For one thing, perpetual war drained violence to the edges of the empire and helped keep the interior at peace, reinforcing the theory of a world divided between the realm of peace (Islam) and the realm of war (everything else), which developed in the days of the first khalifas.

Perpetual war on the frontiers helped to reify this concept of war and peace, first of all, by making the narrative *seem* true—the frontier was generally a violent place, while the interior was generally a place of peace and security—and second, by helping to make it actually *be* true. By unifying the Arab tribes against a surrounding Other, this concept of jihad reduced the incessant internecine warfare that marked Arab tribal life before Islam and thus really did help to make the Islamic world a realm of (relative) peace!

You can see this dynamic more clearly when you consider who fought the early wars of expansion. It wasn't so much a case of emperors dispatching armies of professional soldiers to do their bidding according to some master plan. The campaigns were fought by tribal armies who went off to battle more or less when they felt like it, as volunteers for the faith, responding more to the wishes than the orders of the khalifa. If they hadn't been fighting at the borders to expand the territory under Muslim rule, they might well have been fighting at home to wrest booty from their neighbors.

Perpetual war also worked to confirm Islam's claim to divine sanction, so long as it kept leading to victory. From the start, astonishing military and political success had functioned as Islam's core confirming miracle. Jesus may have healed the blind and raised the dead. Moses may have turned a staff into a snake and led an exodus for which the Red Sea parted. Visible miracles of this ilk proved the divinity or divine sponsorship of those prophets.

Mohammed, however, never really dealt in supernatural miracles such as those. He never solicited followers with displays of power that contradicted the laws of nature. His one supernatural feat, really, was ascending to heaven on a white horse from the city of Jerusalem, and this was not a miracle performed for the multitudes. It happened to him unseen by any public, and he reported it later to his companions. People could believe him or not, as they wished; it didn't impact his mission, because he wasn't offering his ascent to heaven as proof that his message was true.

No, Mohammed's miracle (aside from the Qur'an itself and the persuasive impact it had on so many who heard it) was that Muslims won battles even when outnumbered three to one. This miracle continued to unfold under the first khalifas as Muslim-ruled territory kept expanding at a breathtaking pace, and what could explain success like that except divine intervention?

The miracle continued under the Umayyads. The victories didn't come as fast, nor as dramatically, but then, the opportunity for truly dramatic victories diminished over time simply because Muslims rarely found themselves as outnumbered as they were at first. The bottom line was that the victories kept coming and the territory kept expanding—it never shrank. So long as this was true, perpetual war continued to confirm the truth of Islam, which fed the fervor that enabled the victories, which confirmed the truth that fed the fervor, which enabled the victories that confirmed the truth . . . and so on, round and round.

Perpetual war had some tangible benefits too. It brought in revenue. As Muslims told it, some Allah-defying potentate would tax his subjects until his coffers were overflowing; then the Muslims would appear, knock him off his throne, liberate his subjects from his greed, and take his treasures. This made the liberated people happy and the Muslims rich: everybody ended up ahead except the defeated princes.

One-fifth of the plunder was sent back to the capital, and at first all of it was distributed among the Umma, with the neediest taken care of first. But with each khalifa, an increasing percentage went into the public treasury; when the Umayyads took over, they started funneling virtually all revenue into the public treasury and using it to cover the costs of government, which included lavish building projects, ambitious public works, and extravagant charitable endowments. Revenue from the perpetual border wars thus enabled the Umayyad government to operate as a positive force in society, lavishing benefits on citizens without raising taxes.

Then there were precedents bequeathed to the Umayyads by Khalifa Othman, who allowed Muslims to spend their money any way they wanted, so long as they followed Islamic strictures. Based on Othman's rulings, the Umayyads allowed Muslims to purchase land in conquered territory with money borrowed from the treasury. Of course one had to be very well connected to get such loans, even more so than in Othman's time, and since Islam outlawed usury, these loans were interest-free, which is nice financing if you can get it.

Omar had ordered that Muslim Arab warriors moving into new territories stay in garrisons apart from local populations, in part to avoid trampling on the rights and sensibilities of the locals, in part to keep Muslims from being seduced by pagan pleasures, and in part to keep the minority Muslims from being absorbed into the majority locals. In Umayyad times, these garrisons evolved into fortified Arab cities housing a new landed aristocracy, who owned and profited from vast estates in the surrounding countryside.

Islamic society bore no resemblance to feudal Europe, however, where manors were largely self-sufficient economic units, producing for immediate consumption. The Umayyad Empire hummed with handicrafts, and it was sewn together by intricate trade networks. Wealth milked out of the vast estates didn't just sit there but proliferated into trade goods that flowed to distant lands and brought other trade goods flowing back. Garrison cities softened into busy commercial entrepôts. The Islamic world was dotted with vigorous cities. It was an urbane world.

Mu'awiya himself, reviled by the devout as a poor show next to such spiritual giants as the Rightly Guided Khalifas, proved himself no slouch as an economic manager and politician. Ruthless but charming, he gained the cooperation of fractious Arab chieftains, mostly with persuasion, using his military and police powers largely to put down revolts and impose law and order, which benefited him but also smoothed the way for civilized life.

Consider the mixture of stick and carrot in this warning to the people of Basra, issued by Mu'awiya's adopted brother Ziyad, whom he had appointed

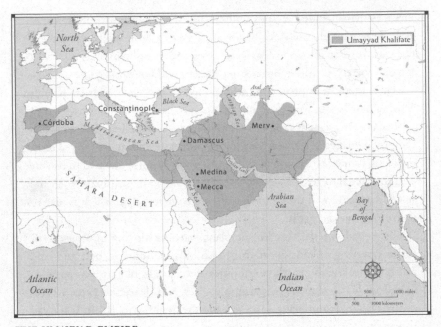

THE UMAYYAD EMPIRE

governor of Basra: "You allow kinship to prevail and put religion second; you excuse and hide your transgressors and tear down the orders which Islam has sanctified for your protection. Take care not to creep about in the night. I will kill every man found on the streets after dark. Take care not to appeal to your kin; I will cut off the tongue of every man who raises that call. . . . I rule with the omnipotence of God and maintain you with God's wealth. I demand obedience from you and you can demand uprightness from me . . . I will not fail in three things: I will at all times be there for every man to speak to me. I will always pay your pensions punctually and I will not send you into the field for too long a time or too far away. Do not be carried away by your hatred and anger against me; it would go ill with you. I see many heads rolling. Let each man see that his own head stays upon his shoulders!" [3]

Worldly tough guys though they were, the Umayyads nurtured the religious institutions of Islam. They supported scholars and religious thinkers, built mosques, and enforced laws that allowed the Islamic way of life to flourish.

Under the Umayyads, it wasn't just Arab-inspired commercial energy that permeated the Muslim world but also Islam-inspired social ideals. Nouveau riche lords made abundant donations to philanthropic religious foundations called *waqfs*. Social pressure drove them to it, but so did religious incentives: everyone wants the esteem of his or her society, and a rich man could garner such esteem by patronizing a waqf.

In theory, a waqf could not be shut down by its founder. Once born, it owned itself and had a sovereign status. Think of it as a Muslim version of a nonprofit corporation set up for charitable purposes. Under Muslim law, the waqfs could not be taxed. They collected money from donors and distributed it to the poor, built and ran mosques, operated schools, hospitals, and orphanages, and generally provided the burgeoning upper classes with a means for expressing their religious and charitable urges and to feel good about themselves even while lolling in wealth.

Of course, someone had to administer a waqf. Someone had to conduct its business, set its policies, and manage its finances, and it couldn't be just anyone. To possess religious credibility, a waqf had to be staffed by people known for piety and religious learning. The more famously religious its staff, the more prestigious the waqf and the more respect accrued to its founders and donors.

Since the waqfs ended up controlling real estate, buildings, and endowment funds, their management offered an avenue of social mobility in Muslim society (even though many waqfs became a device by which rich families protected their wealth from taxation). If you acquired a reputation for religious scholarship, you might hope to gain a position with a waqf, which gave you status if not riches, and you didn't have to hail from a famous family to become a famous religious scholar. You just had to have brains and a willingness to practice piety and study hard.

On the other hand, you did have to know Arabic, because it was the sacred language: to Muslims, the Qur'an itself, in Arabic, written or spoken, is the presence of God in the world: translations of the Qur'an are not the Qur'an. Besides, all the pertinent scholarly books were written in Arabic. And you did, of course, have to be Muslim. What's more, the Umayyads soon declared Arabic the official language of government, replacing Persian in the east and Greek in the west and various local languages everywhere else. So Umayyad times saw an Arabization and Islamification of the Muslim realm.

When I say Islamification, I mean that growing numbers of people in territories ruled by the khalifa abandoned their previous faiths—Zoroastrian, Christian, pagan, or whatever—and converted to Islam. Some no doubt converted to evade the poll tax on non-Muslims, but this probably wasn't the whole story, because after conversion people were liable for the charity tax incumbent on Muslims but not on non-Muslims.

Some may have converted in pursuit of career opportunities, but this, too, can be overstated, because conversion really only opened up the religion-related careers. The unconverted could still own land, operate workshops, sell goods, and pursue business opportunities. They could work for the government too, if they had skills to offer. The Muslim elite did not hesitate to take from each according to his abilities. If you knew medicine, you could be a doctor; if you knew building, you could be an architect. In the Islamic empire, you could become rich and famous even if you were a Christian or a Jew, the "Abrahamic" religions, or eventually Zoroastrian, even though this was more distant from Islam.

But most people, I think, in the world Muslims came to rule, converted to Islam because it looked like the Truth. Certainly, no other force or movement in the Middle World at this time had the muscular self-confidence and the aura of inexorable success of Islam. Who would *not* want to join the Umma if they could?

And they could. It was easy! All a person had to do was say *"La illaha il-Allah wa Muhammad ur-Rasulillah"*: "There is no god but God and Mohammed is his messenger." That's all it took to gain membership in this triumphant club.

But the core creed was much more loaded than it may have looked at first blush.

"No god but God"—that phrase alone has engendered countless thousands of volumes of commentary, and no one has yet come to the end of what it means.

And on top of that: "Mohammed is his messenger!" Sign on to that one, and you've accepted everything Mohammed prescribed as Messenger. You've committed yourself to five daily prayers; to avoidance of pork; to the Ramadan fast; to sobriety; and to much, much more.

6

∞

The Abbasid Age

120–350 AH
737–961 CE

THE DESCENDANTS OF Yazid ruled for a number of generations. They wove a skein of entrenched power over the Muslim world, extended their suzerainty to Spain in the west and India in the east. Under their administration, the doctrines of Islam were elaborated, written down, and sealed into codebooks. A body of religious scholars came to own those codebooks, the way lawyers in America own the constitution and the laws spun from it, and those religious scholars worked in tandem with the politicians and bureaucrats of the Umayyad court to forge a distinctly Islamic society.

Mainstream Western histories usually praise this process. The Umayyads introduced that wonderful quality called stability to the civilized world. Stability enabled farmers to plan next year's crop. It enabled businessmen to invest in long-term projects. It encouraged students to enter upon long courses of study with confidence that what they learned would still apply by the time they had graduated. Stability gave scholars the freedom to lose themselves in study and dig deep into the mysteries of nature without having to worry that their families were meanwhile getting killed by thugs.

All this came at a price however, the usual price of stability, which ensures that whatever is the case one day is even more the case the next day.
The rich got richer. The poor increased in numbers. Cities with magnificent architecture sprang up, but so did vast slums sunk in squalid poverty.
Justice became a commodity that only the rich could afford.

Other problems bubbled up too. The rapid expansion of Islamic rule
brought many different ethnicities under the Muslim umbrella, and there
was some question about how to make the Muslim promise of brotherhood and equality work for all of them.

Umayyad policies may have promoted Arabization and Islamification
but not both of them equally everywhere. In North Africa, Arabization
proceeded rapidly, perhaps because the patchwork of indigenous cultures
had long ago been fragmented by Phoenician colonization—the Romans
had deposited a Latin layer, the Vandals had come in with a Germanic
glaze, and finally Christianity had permeated the region. North Africa had
no single language or culture to bind it together; when the Arabs arrived
with their powerful conviction, no correspondingly unified and powerful
indigenous conviction was there to resist them. So the Arabs thoroughly
dissolved and absorbed whatever was there before.

Egypt and the Levant were somewhat easily digested too, because many
of these peoples shared a historical narrative with the Arabs, harking back
to common traditional ancestors such as Abraham, Noah, and Adam himself. Most of the inhabitants had already subscribed to the idea of
monotheism. Hebrew and Aramaic were Semitic languages, like Arabic.

Persia, however—ah, that was quite a different matter! The Persians
were an Indo-European people, not Semitic. They had an ancient civilization of their own, a proud history, and a language that would not be subdued. Many Persians accepted Islam, but they would not be Arabized.
Those who did convert to Islam presented the society with a challenging
religious contradiction. Islam claimed to make every Muslim equal to
every other. Join the Umma and you join an egalitarian brotherhood—
such was the promise of this new religion, this powerful movement. But
the Arab-dominated society forged by the Umayyads couldn't deliver on
the promise. Arabs were the rulers now; they were the aristocrats. Far from
making even a show of equal status for all, Umayyad society spawned formal institutions to discriminate among various gradations of folk in soci-

ety and to keep them layered: pure-blooded Arab Muslims at the top; below them, Muslims with one Arab and one non-Arab parent; then non-Arab Muslims; then non-Arab Muslims with non-Muslim parents; then non-Muslims who at least belonged to one of the monotheistic faiths; and so on down to the lowest of the low, rank polytheists born of polytheistic parents, who had virtually no legal rights.

Friction among all these designated social gradients, and especially the friction between the Arab nouveau aristocrats and the Persian former aristocrats, kept a sense of grievance smoldering beneath the surface in this portion of the Muslim realm.

Another shadow haunted the conscience of the Islamic world as well. Muslim sacred history was problematically rich with anecdotes about the simple, rugged lifestyle of the founders. Their simplicity and humbleness went to the very essence of their appeal as religious figures. Inevitably, therefore, a feeling started percolating in the lower reaches of this new society that something about all this splendor wasn't right. This prosperous, pleasure-plump society could not be what Allah had meant when he charged Mohammed with establishing a just community devoted to worship of the one God. Of course, the richer you were, the less likely that such considerations would trouble your dreams. For the poor, however, tales of luxury at court and the sight of perfumed Arab noblemen riding through the streets clad in silk had to evoke comparisons with Mohammed's simple blanket folded four times to provide both mattress and cover and Khalifa Omar at his cobbler's bench, mending his own shoes. Add to all this the odor left by the way in which the Umayyads came to power, a process that had generated two enduring opposition movements, the Shi'i and the Kharijites.

The Kharijites were the less numerous, but their movement was more radical. Their theology had come to focus on extravagant demands for purity. They said the leadership of the Muslim world belonged to the person who most assiduously practiced what the religion preached. No secular ruler could ever meet the standards of the Kharijites. In fact, quite probably, no ruler anywhere could ever meet their standards, period, so the Kharijites could preach revolution no matter what the circumstances. As long as anyone was in power, someone would feel oppressed, and as long as anyone felt oppressed, Kharijite agitators could use their doctrines to fuel insurgencies.

As time went on, however, Kharijites fizzled out because they were such extreme purists at a time when more and more people were acquiring a stake in the new prosperity. Society's losers might have been discontented, but they were even less ready to trade in the little they had for the joyless nothing the Kharijites offered. It was the Shi'i who remained the real threat to the established order, and after the death of Hussein and his followers at Karbala, this threat picked up force.

The Shi'ite imams no longer directly challenged the throne very much; they began to separate the meaning of *imam* from the meaning of *khalifa,* defining themselves ever more purely in religious terms. But Shi'ite rebels kept organizing trouble in the name of the imams, kept sparking rebellions aimed at bringing one or another of Ali's descendents to power, kept nurturing the notion that the khalifate did not belong to the Umayyads, kept undermining the legitimacy of Islam's secular rulers.

The Shi'ite threat metastasized because of an ominous synchronicity that developed in Umayyad times. It was this:

The Shi'i were the suppressed religious underdogs of Islam.

The Persians were the suppressed ethnic underdogs of Islam.

The Shi'i chaffed against the orthodox religious establishment.

The Persians chaffed against the Arab political establishment.

Inevitably, the one mapped onto the other. Persians began to embrace Shi'ism, and Shi'ite agitators began looking to the Persian east for recruits. When the two currents mingled, rebellion began to bubble. It bubbled ever harder the further east one traveled, for Umayyad police power ran ever thinner in that direction, while anti-Arab sentiment mounted ever higher.

One day, around 120 AH, a mysterious man blew into the city of Merv. This distant outpost of the empire lay almost fifteen hundred miles east of Damascus. Here in the wild, wild east, this stranger began to agitate against the Umayyads by promulgating a millennial religious narrative that spoke of an impending apocalyptic showdown between good and evil.

No one knew much about this fellow, not even his real name. He went by the handle Abu Muslim, but that was obviously a pseudonym, since it was short for Muslim abu Muslim bin Muslim, which means "Muslim man, son of a Muslim father, father of a Muslim son." As you can see, this man was at pains to assert that he had no-doubt-about-it Muslim credentials.

In truth, Abu Muslim was a professional revolutionary, dispatched to Merv by a secretive underground group based in Iraq, a group called the Hashimites. This group was a cross between a cult and a political party, whose core membership probably never exceeded thirty. Its name referred to the Prophet's clan, the Banu Hashim, and its purpose, supposedly, was to put a member of the Prophet's family at the head of the Muslim world. This was just one of many angry little hard-core bands of antigovernment conspirators active at this time, all preaching some version of the same message: the community had fallen off the track, history had gone off course, the Messenger's mission had been subverted, and toppling the Umayyads and empowering a member of the Prophet's family in their stead would set everything right again. Let me note that this narrative has been reinvented again and again in the Muslim world over the course of history, and some version of it is being recited even today, by revolutionaries who have substituted "the West" for "the Umayyads."

Sadly for the Hashimites, they didn't have an actual member of the Prophet's family to promote. They did, however, have Abu al-Abbas, a fellow who claimed descent from Abbas ibn Abd al-Muttalib, one of Prophet Mohammed's uncles, so he was at least related to the Prophet by blood and, more important, was willing to lend his name to the Hashimite enterprise.

The ancestral uncle in question, the original Abbas, was among the later converts to Islam, and in his day, inconveniently enough, no one had even considered him a candidate to succeed Mohammed, so he wasn't the *ideal* ancestor for a revolutionary purist. A direct descendant of Ali and Fatima would certainly have been better, but none of the Alids—that is, Ali's real and putative descendants—would make common cause with the Hashimites, so Abu al-Abbas would have to do. Sometimes you have to go into battle with the figurehead you have, not the figurehead you wish you had.

Abu Muslim didn't have much trouble tapping into the Shi'ite and Persian discontent seething in Khorasan, the province that stretched from Iran through Afghanistan. At key points in his speeches, Abu Muslim became a little vague about who exactly would become the khalifa once the revolution succeeded. Those who longed for a descendant of Ali could imagine that such a figure was waiting in the wings, anonymous for the moment only for security reasons.

Daring, ruthless, and charismatic, Abu Muslim quickly outgrew his role as anybody's agent and emerged as the leader of the Abbasid revolution (so named for its putative leader, Abu al-Abbas.) There in Khorasan, Abu Muslim recruited a revolutionary cadre, trained them to fight, and steeped them in Hashimite doctrines. His recruits could be recognized by the black clothes they wore and the black banners they carried. They even dyed their weapons black. The Umayyad army, incidentally, adopted white as its color. Lest you think this color coding strange for a cult that preached an apocalyptic showdown between good and evil, you should know that in Persia white was regarded as the color of mourning, the color of death. (The recent revolutionary Afghan Muslims called the Taliban favored black clothing as a uniform.)

In the year 125 AH (747 CE) Abu Muslim and his black-suited warriors began moving west. They encountered little resistance passing through Persian territory, where most people were eager to help topple the arrogant Umayyads. In fact, they gained recruits and momentum as they marched along.

In 750 CE, the armies of white and black clashed on the banks of the Great Zab River in Iraq. Although outnumbered, the men in black routed the emperor's forces, and the last Umayyad khalifa had to run for his life, south into Egypt; within the year, Abbasid agents hunted him down there and killed him.

The Hashimites proclaimed Abbas the new khalifa of Islam. Nobody really commented on the process that had just taken place: it wasn't an inevitable God-shaped outcome, nor an election, nor even a decision made by a council of wise men. No, the new khalifa was placed in power by one man with a tightly organized gang of enforcers. It didn't matter. Leadership was (phew!) back where it belonged at last, in the hands of a member of the Prophet's family. Now, finally, the Muslim social project could get back on course.

That was probably the happiest year of Abu Muslim's life, the year his life's work came to fruition at last! Perhaps he really thought that toppling the Umayyads would restore the quest for the lost community. Disillusionment soon set in, however. For one thing, the puppet did not, it

ABU MUSLIM AND THE ABBASID REVOLUTION

turned out, consider himself a puppet. Over the years, Abbas had built a real base within the movement that had chosen him as its figurehead, and now that Abu Muslim had done the donkey work, he said thank you very much and took the throne.

The new khalifa remembered that Mu'awiya had consolidated his power by slipping a velvet glove over his iron fist and winning over former foes with courtesy and charm. Accordingly, the new ruler invited leading members of the Umayyad clan to break bread with him, just to show that there were no hard feelings.

Well, I shouldn't say "break bread." That makes it sound like he was going to serve his guests a simple meal of barley bread and soup, such as the Prophet might have shared with Omar. That sort of thing was now out of fashion. No, the Umayyad survivors found themselves lolling on cushions while servants pranced in with lovely trays piled high with gourmet delicacies. The laughter rang out, the conversation turned spirited, and a sense of camaraderie swelled. Just as everyone was getting ready to tie into the meal, however, the waiters threw off their robes to reveal armor underneath. They weren't waiters, it turned out, but executioners. The Umayyads jumped to their feet, but too late: the doors had all been locked. The soldiers proceeded to club the Umayyads to death. From that time on, Abbas went by a new title, al-Saffah, which means "the slaughterer." Apparently, he took some pride in what he had done.

Little good it did him, however, for he soon died of smallpox and his brother al-Mansur took over. Mansur had to tussle with rivals a bit, but Abu Muslim stepped in and secured the throne for him, then returned to Khorasan. Abu Muslim made no bid for the khalifate on his own behalf, even though he had the military power to take what he wanted. He seemed to accept the legitimacy of Abbasid rule. Perhaps he really was a principled idealist.

And yet there was something Mansur just didn't like about this man, Abu Muslim. Well, perhaps it was one particular thing: Abu Muslim was popular. All right, two things: he was popular, and he had soldiers of his own. A ruler can never trust a popular man with soldiers of his own. One day, Mansur invited Abu Muslim to come visit him and share a hearty meal. What happened next illustrates the maxim that when an Abbasid ruler invites you to dinner, you should arrange to be busy that night. The men got together at a pleasant riverside campsite and Mansur spent the first day lavishly thanking Abu Muslim for all his selfless services; the next night he had his bodyguards cut Abu Muslim's throat and dump his body in the river.

Thus began the second dynasty of the Muslim khalifate.

Abbasid propagandists got busy creating a narrative about the meaning of this transition. They called it a revolutionary new direction for the Umma. Everything would be different now, they said. In fact, everything remained pretty much the same, only more so, both for better and for worse.

The Umayyads had steeped themselves in pomp and luxury, but the Abbasids made them seem by comparison like rugged yeomen living the simple life. Under the Umayyads, the Muslim realm had grown quite prosperous. Well, under the Abbasids, the economy virtually exploded with vigor. And like the Umayyads, the Abbasids were secular rulers who used spies, police power, and professional armies to maintain their grip.

Since the Abbasids had risen to power on a surge of Shi'ite discontent, you might suppose that in this regard at least they would have differed from the Umayyads, but in this supposition you would be dead wrong. The Abbasids quickly embraced the orthodox approach to Islam, probably because the orthodox religious establishment, all those scholars, had secured so much social power in Islam that embracing their doctrines was the politic thing to do. Indeed, it was only in Abbasid times (as we shall see in the next chapter) that the mainstream approach to Islam acquired the label Sunnism, since only now did it congeal into a distinct sect with a name of its own.

In the first days of the Abbasid takeover, many naïve Shi'i thought that Saffah and his family were going to put the recognized Shi'ite imam on the throne, thereby inaugurating the millennial peace predicted in Hashimite propaganda. Instead, the hunt for Alids intensified. In fact, when the third khalifa of this dynasty died, according to one of his maids, his successor found a secret room in his palace, which led to an underground vault where he had collected the corpses of all the Alids he had captured and killed. (They weren't necessarily Fatima's descendants, since Ali had other wives after Fatima died).

Yet the Abbasids also maximized everything that was good about Umayyad rule. The Umayyads had presided over a flowering of prosperity, art, thought, culture, and civilization. All this splendor and dynamism accelerated to a crescendo during the Abbasid dynasty, making the first two centuries or so of their rule the one that Western history (and many contemporary Muslims) remember as the Golden Age of Islam.

One of Mansur's first moves, for example, was to build himself a brand new capital, a city called Baghdad, completed in 143 AH (765 CE). The city he built has survived into the present day, though it has been destroyed and rebuilt several times over the centuries, and is in the process of being destroyed again.

Mansur toured his territories for several years before he found the perfect site for his city: a place between the Tigris and Euphrates where the rivers came so close together that a city could be stretched from the banks of one to the banks of the other. Smack dab in the middle of this space, Mansur planted a perfectly circular ring of wall, one mile in circumference, 98 feet high, and 145 feet thick at the base. The "city" within this huge doughnut was really just a single enormous palace complex, the new nerve center for the world's biggest empire.[1]

It took five years to build the Round City. Some one hundred thousand designers, craftspeople, and laborers worked on it. These workers lived all around the city they were building, so their homes formed another, less orderly ring of city around the splendid core. And of course shopkeepers and service workers flocked in to make a living selling goods and services to the people working on the Round City, which added yet another urban penumbra around the disorderly ring that surrounded that perfect circular core.

Within twenty years, Baghdad was the biggest city in the world and possibly the biggest city that had ever been: it was the first city whose population topped a million.[2] Baghdad spread beyond the rivers, so that the Tigris and Euphrates actually flowed through Baghdad, rather than beside it. The waters were diverted through a network of canals that let boats serve as the city's buses, making it a bit like Venice, except that bridges and lanes let people navigate the city on foot or on horseback too.

Baghdad might well have been the world's busiest city as well as its biggest. Two great rivers opening onto the Indian Ocean gave it tremendous port facilities, plus it was easily accessible to land traffic from every side, so ships and caravans flowed in and out every day, bringing goods and traders from every part of the known world—China, India, Africa, Spain. . . .

Commerce was regulated by the state. Every nationality had its own neighborhood, and so did every kind of business. On one street you might find cloth merchants, on another soap dealers, on another the flower market, on yet another the fruit shops. The Street of Stationers featured over a hundred shops selling paper, a new invention recently acquired from China (whom the Abbasids met and defeated in 751 CE, in the area that is now Kazakhstan). Goldsmiths, tinsmiths, and blacksmiths; armorers and stables; money changers, straw merchants, bridge builders, and cobblers, all could be found hawking their wares in their designated quarters of mighty Baghdad. There was even a neighborhood for open-air stalls and shops selling miscellaneous goods. Ya'qubi, an Arab geographer of the time, claimed that this city had six thousand streets and alleys, thirty thousand mosques, and ten thousand bathhouses.

This was the city of turrets and tiles glamorized in the *Arabian Nights,* a collection of folk stories transformed into literature during the later days of the Abbasid dynasty. Stories such as the one about Aladdin and his magic lamp hark back to the reign of the fourth and most famous Abbasid khalifa, Haroun al-Rashid, portrayed as the apogee of splendor and justice. Legends about Haroun al-Rashid characterize him as a benevolent monarch so interested in the welfare of his people that he often went among them disguised as an ordinary man, so that he might learn first-hand of their troubles and take measures to help them. In reality, I'm guessing, it was the khalifa's spies who went among the people disguised as ordinary beggars, not so much looking for troubles to right as malcontents to neutralize.

Even more than in Umayyad times, the khalifa became a near mythic figure, whom even the wealthiest and most important people had little chance of ever seeing, much less petitioning. The Abbasid khalifas ruled through intermediaries, and they insulated themselves from everyday reality with elaborate court rituals borrowed from Byzantine and Sassanid traditions. So, yes, Islam conquered all the territories ruled by the Sassanids and much that had once been ruled by the Byzantines, but in the end the ghosts of those supplanted empires infiltrated and altered Islam.

7

⊗

Scholars, Philosophers, and Sufis

10–505 AH
632–1111 CE

S O FAR I HAVE been recounting political events at the highest levels as
Muslim civilization evolved into the civilization of the middle world.
Big stories were unfolding, however, below that highest level, and none
was bigger than the development of Muslim doctrine, and the social class
it generated, along with the opposing and alternative ideas it engendered.

Looking back, it's easy to suppose that Mohammed left his followers
exact instructions for how to live and worship, complete in every detail.
How complete they were, however, is difficult to gauge. What's pretty certain is that, in his lifetime, Mohammed established the primacy of five
broad duties, now called the five pillars of Islam:

> *shahadah*, to attest that there is only one God and Mohammed is his
> messenger;
> *salaat* (or *namaz*), to perform a certain prayer ritual five times every
> day;

zakat, to give a certain percentage of one's wealth to the poor each year;
sawm (or *roza),* to fast from dawn to dusk during the month of Ramadan
   each year; and
hajj, to make a pilgrimage to Mecca at least once in a lifetime, if possible.

Notice both the simplicity and "externalness" of this program. Only one
of the five pillars is a belief, a creed, and even that is given in terms of an action: "to attest." The other four pillars are very specific things to do. Again,
Islam is not merely a creed or a set of beliefs: it is a program every bit as
concrete as a diet or an exercise regiment. Islam is something one *does.*

The five pillars were already part of life in the Muslim community by
the time of Mohammed's death, but so were other rituals and practices,
and any of them may have been parsed somewhat differently back then.
The fact is, when Mohammed was alive, there was no need to fix the details inflexibly because the living Messenger was right there to answer questions. Not only could people learn from him every day, but through him
they might receive fresh instructions at any time.

Indeed, Mohammed did receive revelations continually, not just about
general values and ideals but about practical measures to take in response
to particular, immediate problems. If an army was approaching the city,
God would let Mohammed know if the community should get ready to
fight, and if so, how. If Muslims captured prisoners and after the battle was
over wondered what to do with them: Kill them? Keep them as slaves?
Treat them as members of the family? Set them free? God would tell Mohammed, and he would tell everyone else.

It's well known that Muslims face Mecca when they pray, but this was
not always the case. At first, in fact, Muslims performed their prayers facing Jerusalem. At a certain point in the maturation of the community,
however, a revelation came down instructing them to shift direction, and
it has been Mecca ever since.

And it will always be Mecca from now on, because Mohammed is gone
and there will never be another Messenger, which means that no one will
ever again have the authority to change the direction of prayer. In short,
while Mohammed was alive, the Islamic project had an organic vitality. It
was constantly in the process of unfolding and evolving. Any element of it
might change at any time.

But the moment Mohammed died, Muslims had to ask themselves, "What exactly are we supposed to do? How are we supposed to do it? When we pray, should we hold our hands up here or down lower? In preparing for prayer, must we wash our feet all the way to the shins or would just to the ankles be enough?"

And, of course, there was a lot more to being a Muslim than the five pillars. Beyond individual duties such as fasting, alms, and the testament of faith, there was the social aspect of Islam, a person's obligations to the community, the good-citizenship behaviors that fed into making the community an instrument of God's will. For example, there was certainly a proscription against drinking. Certainly Muslims had some obligation to defend the community with their lives and fortunes when necessary in the obligation famously called jihad. In general, making sacrifices for the communal good devolved upon every Muslim because the community might not otherwise endure, and to many if not most Muslims, the community was the template of a new world, charged with an obligation to set a continuous example of how all people should live. Anyone, therefore, who contributed to the health of the community was doing God's work, and anyone who fell short was misbehaving. But what contributed to the health of the community? And how much contribution was enough?

Once Mohammed died, Muslims had to bring their obligations into focus and get the details down in writing to secure their faith from drift, divergence, and the whims of the powerful. That's why the first two khalifas collected every scrap of Qur'an in one place and why the third khalifa created that single authorized edition.

But the Qur'an did not explicitly address many questions that cropped up in real life. As a matter of fact, most of the Holy Book spoke in very general terms: Stop sinning; behave yourself; have a heart; you *will* be judged; hell is an awful place; heaven is wonderful; be grateful for all that God has given you; trust in God; obey God; yield to God—such is the gist of the message one gets from much of the Holy Book. Even where the Qur'an gets specific, it is often open to interpretation.

And "interpretation" portended trouble. If everyone were allowed to interpret the ambiguous passages for themselves, their conclusions might diverge wildly. People would move apart in as many different directions as there were people, the community would fragment, and the world might swallow up the pieces and who was to say the great revelation would not then vanish as if it had never been?

THE SCHOLARS

Clearly Muslims had to come to unified agreements about the ambiguous passages and do it fast, while the original excitement still burned in communal memory. No one in that early time wanted to offer a personal interpretation of the Truth backed only by his or her reason. If reason were enough, revelation would never have been needed. Certainly, none of the early khalifas laid claim to any such authority. They were devout people who refused to tamper with instructions from God. Their humble modesty was precisely what made them great. They wanted to get the instructions exactly right in letter and spirit—and by "right," they meant, "exactly as God intended."

From the start, therefore, Muslims tried to rely on their memories of the Prophet to fill in any gaps in the Qur'an's guidelines. It was Omar who really set the course here. Whenever a question came up for which no explicit answer could be found in the Qur'an, he asked, "Did Mohammed ever have to deal with a situation like this one? What did he decide?"

Omar's approach got people motivated to collect everything Mohammed had ever said and done, quotations and anecdotes known to Muslims as hadith. But many people had heard Mohammed say many things. Which ones were credible? Some quotations contradicted other quotations. Some people might have been making stuff up. Who could tell? And some, it turned out, hadn't actually heard a quotation themselves, but had it only on good authority—or so they claimed, which of course raised the question, who was the original source? Was that person reliable? What about the other people who had transmitted it? Were they all reliable? What, finally, constituted a "good authority?"

Omar, as I mentioned, established a body of full-time scholars to examine such questions, thereby establishing a consequential precedent: before Islam had a standing army of professional soldiers, it had a standing army of professional scholars (called "people of the bench" or sometimes "people of the pen").

Hadith, however, proliferated faster than any small group of scholars could control. New ones were constantly coming to light. By Umayyad times, thousands of remembered statements, quotations, and decisions of Mohammed's were floating around. Combing through this jungle and determining which ones were authentic provided employment for an ever-greater number of scholars. The court funded this sort of work, but so did rich men eager to earn merit in God's eyes. Independent scholars applied themselves to the great task on their own time, as well. If they gained enough fame, they attracted students and patrons. Informal groups of this type ripened into academies, sometimes as adjuncts to the *waqfs* mentioned earlier.

The word *hadith* is sometimes translated as "sayings," but that term can be misleading. The sayings of Mohammed are not like the sayings of Shakespeare or Einstein or the local wit. They're not remembered for their felicity of phrasing. No one would bother to record the sayings of the local wit, or even of Shakespeare, unless they were witty, pithy, or profound, but with hadith, what counts is the fact that Mohammed actually said them. It's true that some hadith have an epigrammatic quality. One can admire the economy of the admonition· "Food for one is enough for two, food for two is enough for three. . . . " But many hadith come off as ordinary, even casual, statements. They might have been remarks Mohammed tossed off in the course of daily life. One hadith reports the Prophet telling a fellow who had a sparse beard and had shaved those few scant hairs that he should not have shaved his beard. This comment from anyone else would have been forgettable and forgotten, but anything Mohammed said might offer one more clue about how to live a life pleasing to God.

Since the authenticity of a hadith was absolutely crucial, the authentication of hadith developed into an exacting discipline. At its core, it consisted of nailing down the chain of transmission and testing the veracity of every link. A hadith was only as good as the people who transmitted it. The chain of transmission had to extend to someone who knew the Prophet personally. Only then could a purported hadith be taken seriously. Ideally, it would trace to one of Mohammed's close companions, and the closer the companion the more sound the hadith. In addition, every person who transmitted it after that had to enjoy an impeccable reputation for piety, honesty, and learning.

I heard that once the great scholar Bukhari was investigating the chain of transmission for a particular hadith. He found the first link credible; the second man passed muster too; but when Bukhari went to interview the third man in the chain of transmission, he found the fellow beating his horse. That did it. The word of a man who beat his horse could not be trusted. That hadith had to be discarded.

In short, to gauge the credibility of the people who transmitted a hadith, a scholar had to know a great deal about them and about their times. A scholar also had to know the circumstances in which a hadith was spoken so that its intention might be judged from context. The "science of hadith" thus generated an elaborate discipline of critical historiography.

Some seven or eight decades after Mohammed's death, scholars across the Muslim world began compiling sifted collections of hadith grouped under specific topics, which functioned as organized statements of Islamic doctrine and as reference works on Islamic living. If you wondered, for example, what Prophet Mohammed had to say about diet, or clothing, or warfare, you could look it up in such a book. The enterprise began in late Umayyad times, but it matured in the Abassid era, and new collections kept emerging for centuries. (In fact, just last year, a distant Afghan acquaintance sent me a handwritten manuscript he was hoping I would translate into English. It constituted, he said, a new set of hadith he himself had collected—after fourteen centuries.)

Even though new hadith kept emerging, however, six collections achieved canonical status by the end of the third century AH. These complemented the Qur'an and came to constitute a second level of authority on the dos, don'ts, shoulds, and shouldn'ts of Muslim life.

Yet even the Qur'an and hadith together failed to give a definitive answer to *every* real-life question, as you can imagine. Sometimes, therefore, it was necessary for someone to make an original decision about a disputed situation. Given the legalistic spirit of Islam, Muslims conceded this right of original decision making only to scholars who had thoroughly absorbed Qur'an and hadith and had mastered the "science of hadith," the discipline of authentication. Only such folks could be sure their rulings did not contradict some point set forth in the revelations.

Even qualified scholars were to make decisions based strictly on *qiyas* or analogical reasoning, the method Khalifa Omar used to discover the punishment for drinking (and to make many other rulings). That is, for each unprecedented contemporary situation, scholars had to find an analogous one in classical sources and derive a judgment parallel to the one already made. And if ambiguities arose about the way to apply qiyas, the matter was settled by *ijma*, the consensus of the community—which really meant the consensus of all the recognized scholars of the time. Such a consensus could guarantee the veracity of an interpretation because Prophet Mohammed had once said, "My community will never agree on an error."

If a scholar had exhausted Qur'an, hadith, qiyas, and ijma, then and only then could he move on to the final stage of ethical and legislative thinking, *ijtihad*, which means "free independent thinking based on reason." Scholars and judges could apply this type of thinking only in areas not derived directly from revelation or covered by established precedents.

And over the centuries, even those cracks grew narrower, because once an eminently qualified scholar weighed in on some subject, his pronouncements also joined the canon. Scholars who came later had to master not just Qur'an, hadith, authentication, qiyas, and ijma, but also this ever-growing corpus of precedents. Only *then* were they qualified to exercise ijtihad!

In this way, an architectonic code took shape by the end of the third century AH, a set of proscriptions and prescriptions, obligations, recommendations, and warnings, guidelines, rules, punishments, and rewards covering every aspect of life from the grandest social and political questions to the minutest minutiae of daily life such as personal hygiene, diet, and sexual activity. This bill of particulars marks out the *shari'a*. The word comes from a cognate meaning "path" or "way," and shari'a refers to something bigger than "Islamic law." It is the whole Islamic way of life, which is not something to be developed but something to be discovered, as immutable as any principle of nature. All the specific legal points elaborated by scholars and jurists are markers that reveal this "path to Allah," the way stones, signs, and guideposts might show a traveler where the path is amid the brambles and brush of a wilderness.

On the Sunni side, four slightly different versions of this code took shape, and the Shi'i developed yet another one of their own, similar to the Sunni ones in spirit and equally vast in scope. These various codes differ in details, but I doubt that one Muslim in a thousand can name even five such details.

The four schools of Sunni law are named for the scholars who gave them final shape. Thus, the Hanafi school was founded by Abu Hanifa, from the Afghanistan area (though he taught in Kufa, Iraq); the Maliki school, by the Moroccan jurist Ibn Malik (though he worked and taught in Medina); and the Shafi'i school, by Imam al-Shafi'i of Mecca (though he settled finally in Egypt.) The last to crystallize was the Hanbali school, founded by the rigidly uncompromising Ahmed Ibn Hanbal, about whom I will say more later in this chapter.

The schools promote slightly different methods of deriving rulings, which has led to minor variations in the details of their laws, but ever since Abbasid times all four have been considered equally orthodox: a Muslim can subscribe to any of them without taint of heresy. Developing and applying this code in all its versions was itself a gigantic social enterprise that spawned and employed an entire social class of scholars known as the ulama—the title is simply the plural of *alim*, which means "learned one."

If you had a reputation for religious scholarship—if you were, that is, a member of the ulama—you might be invited to participate in the administration of a waqf. You might teach students, or even run a school. You might work as a judge, and not just one who heard particular cases, but a judge who issued rulings on broad social issues. In the khalifate, your scholarly status might well lead powerful officials to seek your advice, even though the government and the ulama tended to butt heads, being separate (sometimes even competing) loci of power. The ulama defined the law, controlled the courts, ran the educational system, and permeated Muslim social institutions. They had tremendous social power throughout the civilized world, the power to muster and direct the approval and disapproval of the community against particular people or behaviors. I emphasize *social* power, because in Muslim society, which is so community oriented, social pressure—the power of shaming—might be the most powerful of all forces, as opposed to political power, which operates through procedural rules, control of money, monopoly control of the instruments of force, and so on.

Let me emphasize that the ulama were not (and are not) appointed by anyone. Islam has no pope and no official clerical apparatus. How, then, did someone get to be a member of the ulama? By gaining the respect of people who were already established ulama. It was a gradual process. There was no license, no certificate, no "shingle" to hang up to prove that one was an alim. The ulama were (and are) a self-selecting, self-regulating class, bound entirely by the river of established doctrine. No single alim could modify this current or change its course. It was too old, too powerful, too established, and besides, no one could become a member of the ulama until he had absorbed the doctrine so thoroughly that it had become a part of him. By the time a person acquired the status to question the doctrine, he would have no inclination to do so. Incorrigible dissenters who simply would not stop questioning the doctrine probably wouldn't make it through the process. They would be weeded out early. The process by which the ulama self-generates makes it an inherently conservative class.

THE PHILOSOPHERS

The ulama, however, were not the only intellectuals of Islam. While they constructed the edifice of doctrine, another host of thoughtful Muslims were hard at work on another vast project: interpreting all previous philosophies and discoveries in light of the Muslim revelations and integrating them into a single coherent system that made sense of nature, the cosmos, and man's place in all of it. This project generated another group of thinkers known to the Islamic world as the philosophers.

The expansion of Islam had brought Arabs into contact with the ideas and achievements of many other peoples including the Hindus of India, the central Asian Buddhists, the Persians, and the Greeks. Rome was virtually dead by this time, and Constantinople (for all its wealth) had degenerated into a wasteland of intellectual mediocrity, so the most original thinkers still writing in Greek were clustered in Alexandria, which fell into Arab hands early on. Alexandria possessed a great library and numerous academies, making it an intellectual capital of the Greco-Roman world.

Here, the Muslims discovered the works of Plotinus, a philosopher who had said that everything in the universe was connected like the parts of a single organism, and all of it added up to a single mystical One, from which everything had emanated and to which everything would return.

In this concept of the One, Muslims found a thrilling echo of Prophet Mohammed's apocalyptic insistence on the oneness of Allah. Better yet, when they looked into Plotinus, they found that he had constructed his system with rigorous logic from a small number of axiomatic principles, which aroused the hope that the revelations of Islam might be provable with logic.

Further exploration revealed that Plotinus and his peers were merely the latest exponents of a line of thought going back a thousand years to a much greater Athenian philosopher named Plato. And from Plato, the Muslims went on to discover the whole treasury of Greek thought, from the pre-Socratics to Aristotle and beyond.

The Abbasid aristocracy took great interest in all of these ideas. Anyone who could translate a book from Greek, Sanskrit, Chinese, or Persian into Arabic could get high-paying work. Professional translators flocked to Baghdad. They filled whole libraries in the capital and in other major cities with classic texts translated from other languages. Muslims were the first intellectuals ever in a position to make direct comparisons between, say, Greek and Indian mathematics, or Greek and Indian medicine, or Persian and Chinese cosmologies, or the metaphysics of various cultures. They set to work exploring how these ancient ideas fit in with each other and with the Islamic revelations, how spirituality related to reason, and how heaven and earth could be drawn into a single schema that explained the entire universe. One such schema, for example, described the universe as emanating from pure Being in a series of waves that descended to the material facts of immediate daily life—like so:

Indivisible Being
↓
First Intelligence
↓
World Soul
↓
Primitive Matter
↓
Nature
↓
Spatial Matter
↓

Elements

↓

Minerals, Plants, and Animals

Plato had described the material world as an illusory shadow cast by a "real" world that consisted of unchangeable and eternal "forms": thus, every real chair is but an imperfect copy of some single "ideal" chair that exists only in the realm of universals. Following from Plato, the Muslim philosophers proposed that each human being was a mixture of the real and the illusory. Before birth, they explained, the soul dwelt in a realm of Platonic universals. In life, it got intertwined with body, which was made up of matter. At death, the two separated, the body returning to the world of all matter while the soul returned to Allah, its original home.

For all their devotion to Plato, the Muslim philosophers had tremendous admiration for Aristotle, as well: for his logic, his techniques of classification, and his powerful grasp of particularities. Following from Aristotle, the Muslim philosophers categorized and classified with obsessive logic. Just to give you a taste of this attitude: the philosopher al-Kindi described the material universe in terms of five governing principles: matter, form, motion, time, and space. He analyzed each of these into subcategories, dividing motion, for instance, into six types: generation, corruption, increase, decrease, change in quality, and change in position. He went on and on like this, intent on parsing all of reality into discrete, understandable parts.

The great Muslim philosophers associated spirituality with rationality: our essence, they said, was made up of abstractions and principles, which only reason could access. They taught that the purpose of knowledge was to purify the soul by conducting it from sensory data to abstract principles, from particular facts to universal truths. The philosopher al-Farabi was typical in recommending that students begin with the study of nature, move on to the study of logic, and proceed at last to the most abstract of all the disciplines, mathematics.

The Greeks invented geometry, Indian mathematicians came up with the brilliant idea of treating zero as a number, the Babylonians discovered the idea of place value, and the Muslims systematized all of these ideas, adding a few of their own, to invent algebra and indeed to lay the foundations of modern mathematics.

On the other hand, their interests directed the philosophers into practical concerns. By compiling, cataloging, and cross-referencing medical discoveries from many lands, thinkers like Ibn Sina (Avicenna to the Europeans) achieved a near-modern understanding of illness and medical treatments as well as of anatomy—the circulation of blood was known to them, as was the function of the heart and of most other major organs. The Muslim world soon boasted the best hospitals the world had ever seen or was to see for centuries to come: Baghdad alone had some hundred of these facilities.

These Abbasid-era Muslim philosophers also laid the foundations of chemistry as a discipline and wrote treatises on geology, optics, botany, and virtually all the fields of study now known as science. They didn't call it by a separate name. As in the West, where science was long called natural philosophy, they saw no need to sort some of their speculations into a separate category and call it by a new name, but early on they recognized quantification as an instrument for studying nature, which is one of the cornerstones of science as a stand-alone endeavor. They also relied on observation for data upon which to base theories, a second cornerstone of science. They never articulated the scientific method per se— the idea of incrementally building knowledge by formulating hypotheses and then setting up experiments to prove or disprove them. Had they bridged that gap, science as we know it might well have sprouted in the Muslim world in Abbasid times, seven centuries before its birth in western Europe.

It didn't happen, however, for two reasons, one of which involves the interaction between science and theology. In its early stages, science is inherently difficulty to disentangle from theology. Each seems to have implications for the other, at least to its practitioners. When Galileo promoted the theory that the earth goes around the sun, religious authorities put him on trial for heresy. Even today, even in the West, some Christian conservatives counterpose the biblical narrative of creation to the theory of evolution, as if these two are competing explanations of the same riddle. Science challenges religion because it insists on the reliability and sufficiency of its method for seeking truth: experimentation and reason without recourse to revelation. In the West, for most people, the two fields have reached a compromise by agreeing to distinguish their fields of inquiry: the principles of nature belong to science, the realm of moral and ethical value belongs to religion and philosophy.

In ninth and tenth century Iraq (as in classical Greece), science as such did not exist to be disentangled from religion. The philosophers were giving birth to it without quite realizing it. They thought of religion as their field of inquiry and theology as their intellectual specialty; they were on a quest to understand the ultimate nature of reality. That (they said) was what both religion and philosophy were about at the highest level. Anything they discovered about botany or optics or disease was a by-product of this core quest, not its central object. As such, philosophers who were making discoveries about botany, optics, or medicine did not hesitate to pronounce on questions we moderns would consider theological and quite outside the purview of, say, a chemist or a veterinarian—questions such as this one:

> If a man commits a grave sin, is he a non-Muslim, or is he (just) a bad Muslim?

The question might seem like a semantic game, except that in the Muslim world, as a point of law, the religious scholars divided the world between the community and the nonbelievers. One set of rules applied among believers, another set for interactions between believers and nonbelievers. It was important, therefore, to know if any particular person was *in* the community or outside it.

Some philosophers who took up this question said Muslims who were grave sinners might belong to a third zone, situated between belief and unbelief. The more rigid, mainstream scholars didn't like the idea of a third zone, because it suggested that the moral universe wasn't black-and-white but might have shades of gray.

Out of this third-zone concept developed a whole school of theologians called the Mu'tazilites, Arabic for "secessionist," so called because they had seceded from the mainstream of religious thought, at least according to the orthodox ulama. Over time, these theologians formulated a coherent set of religious precepts that appealed to the philosophers. They said the core of Islam was the belief in *tawhid*: the unity, singleness, and universality of Allah. From this, they argued that the Qur'an could not be eternal and uncreated (as the ulama proclaimed) because if it were, the Qur'an would constitute a second divine entity alongside Allah, and that would be blasphemy. They argued, therefore, that the Qur'an was among Allah's creations, just like human beings, stars, and oceans. It was a great book, but it was a book. And if it was just a book, the Qur'an could be interpreted and even (gasp) amended.

Tawhid, they went on to say, prohibited thinking of Allah as having hands, feet, eyes, etc., even though the Qur'an spoke in these terms: all such anthropomorphic references in the Qur'an had to be taken as metaphorical language.

God, they went on to say, did not have attributes, such as justice, mercy, or power: ascribing attributes to God made Him analyzable into parts, which violated tawhid—unity. God was a single indivisible whole too grand for the human mind to perceive or imagine. What human beings called the attributes of God only named the windows through which humans saw God. The attributes we ascribe to Allah, the Mu'tazilites said, were actually only descriptions of ourselves.

From their conception of Allah, the Mu'tazilites derived the idea that good and evil, right and wrong, were aspects of the unchanging reality of God, reflecting deep principles that humans could discover in the same way that human beings could discover the principles of nature. In short, this or that behavior wasn't good because scripture said so. Scripture mandated this or that behavior because it was good, and if it was already good before scripture said so, then it was good for some reason inherent to itself, some reason that reason could discover. Reason, therefore, was itself a valid instrument for discovering ethical, moral, and political truth *independently of revelation*, according to the Mu'tazilites.

This is where this quarrel among theologians has implications for the development of science, a mode of inquiry that depends on the application of reason without recourse to revelation. The Mu'tazilites were talking about reason as a way of discovering moral and ethical truths, but in this time and place, the principles of human conduct and the principles of nature all belonged to the same big field of inquiry: the quest for absolute truth.

The philosopher scientists generally affiliated themselves with the Mu'tazilite school, no doubt because it validated their mode of inquiry. Some of these philosophers even rated reason above revelation. The philosopher Abu Bakr al-Razi blatantly asserted that the miracles ascribed to prophets of the past were legends and that heaven and hell were mental categories, not physical realities.

You can see how beliefs such as these would put the philosophers and the ulama at odds. For one thing, the precepts of the philosophers implicitly rendered the ulama irrelevant. If any intelligent person could weigh in on whether a law was right or wrong, based on whether it made rational sense, why would anyone need to consult scholars who had memorized every quotation ever ascribed to Prophet Mohammed?

The ulama were in a good position to fight off such challenges. They controlled the laws, education of the young, social institutions such as marriage, and so on. Most importantly, they had the fealty of the masses. But the Mu'tazilites had advantages too—or rather, they had one advantage: the favor of the court, the imperial family, the aristocrats, and the top officials of the government. In fact, the seventh Abbasid khalifa made Mu'tazilite theology the official doctrine of the land. Judges had to pass philosophy tests and would-be administrators had to swear allegiance to reason, in order to qualify for office.

Then the Mu'tazilites and their supporters went further: they began using the power of government to persecute people who disagreed with them

Which brings me back to Ahmed Ibn Hanbal, founder of the Hanbali school of law, the last of the orthodox schools to develop, and the most rigidly conservative of them all. Ibn Hanbal was born in Baghdad in 164 AH, just thirty-six years after the Abbasid dynasty began. He came of age amid the disillusionment that must have permeated certain strata of society when people realized that Abbasids were going to be just as worldly as the Umayyads. He captured the imagination of the crowds by preaching that Islam had gone wrong and that the world was headed to hell unless the community corrected its course. The only hope of salvation, he said, lay in scraping away all innovations and going back to the ways of the first community, the Medina of Prophet Mohammed's time. Above all, he declared uncompromisingly that no one could know what was right or wrong on their own. They could guarantee their soul's safety only by following in the footsteps of Mohammed and trusting strictly to revelation. The other schools of Islamic law gave analogical reasoning (qiyas) a high place as a way to discover how the shari'a applied to new situations, but

Ibn Hanbal drastically demoted such methods: rely only on Qur'an and hadith, he said.

He was hauled into the imperial court and made to debate a leading theologian on the question of whether the Qur'an was created or uncreated, an issue that contained the whole question of the role of reason in moral inquiry. The philosopher hit Ibn Hanbal with logic, the scholar struck back with scripture. The philosopher tied him up in knots of argument, Ibn Hanbal burst free with invocations to Allah on high. Obviously, no one could really "win" a debate of this sort because the debaters did not agree on terms. When Ibn Hanbal refused to disavow his views, he was physically beaten, but it didn't change his mind. He was clapped into prison. Still he clung to his principles: never would he let reason trump revelation, never!

So the authorities ratcheted up the pressure. They beat Ibn Hanbal until his joints popped out of their sockets, bound him in heavy chains, and tossed him into prison for several years. Ibn Hanbal refused to renounce his views. As you might guess, the well-publicized abuse failed to discredit his ideas but instead gave them a certain prestige. Common folks, who already resented the Abbasids for their wealth and pomp, grew restive now; and when the masses grew restive, even the mighty Abbasids had to pay attention because almost every time a khalifa died, a scuffle broke out to determine his successor, a scuffle in which either side might use the passions of the crowd as artillery. When the aging, aching Ibn Hanbal was released from prison, reverent crowds greeted him and cheered him and carried him home. Seeing this, the imperial court developed some reservations about Islamic philosophy and the Greek ideas from which it derived. The next khalifa demoted the Mu'tazilites and heaped honors upon Ibn Hanbal, which signaled the waning prestige of the Mu'tazilites, and with them the philosophers. And it signaled the rising status of the scholars who maintained the edifice of orthodox doctrine, an edifice that eventually choked off the ability of Muslim intellectuals to pursue inquiries without any reference to revelation.

THE SUFIS

Almost from the start, however, as the scholars were codifying the law, some people were asking, "Is this all the revelation comes to in the end—

a set of rules? Because I'm not feeling it. Is there nothing more to Islam?" Instructions from God on high were all very well, but some people longed to experience God as a palpable living presence right now, right down here. What they wanted from the revelations was transformation and transcendence.

A few of these people began to experiment with spiritual exercises that went way beyond the requirements of duty. They read the Qur'an incessantly or spent hours reciting the names of Allah. In Baghdad, for example, there was a man named al-Junayd who habitually performed four hundred units of the Muslim prayer ritual after work every day. In reaction, perhaps, to the luxurious lifestyles of Muslim elite, some of these seekers embraced voluntary poverty, living on bread and water, dispensing with furniture, and wearing simple garments made of rough, uncarded wool, which is called *suf* in Arabic, for which reason people began to call these people Sufis.

They professed no new creed, these Sufis. They were not out to launch another sect. Sure, they opposed worldly ambition and corruption and greed, but so did every Muslim, in theory. The Sufis differed from the others only in saying, "How do you purify your heart? Whatever the exactly correct gestures and litanies may be, how do you actually get immersed in Allah to the exclusion of all else?"

They began to work out techniques for eliminating distractions and cravings not just from prayer but from life. Some spoke of engaging in spiritual warfare against their own meanest tendencies. Harking back to a hadith in which Mohammed distinguished between a "greater" and a "lesser" jihad, they declared that the internal struggle to expunge the ego was the real jihad, the greater jihad. (The lesser jihad they identified as the struggle against external enemies of the community.)

Gradually a buzz got started about these eccentrics—that some of them had broken through the barriers of the material world to a direct experience of Allah.

In Basra, for example, lived the poet Rabia al-Basri, whose life is now laced with legend. Born in the last years of Umayyad rule, she was a young woman when the Abbasids took over. As a little girl, she had been traveling somewhere with her family when bandits hit the caravan. They killed her parents and sold Rabia into slavery. That's how she ended up in Basra

as a slave in some rich man's household. Her master, the stories say, kept
noticing a luminous spirituality about her that made him wonder. . . . One
night, when she was lost in prayer, he observed a halo surrounding her
body. It struck him suddenly that he had a saint living in his house, and
awe took hold of him. He set Rabia free and pledged to arrange a good
marriage for her. He would get her connected to one of the best families in
the city, he vowed. She had only to name the man she wanted to marry,
and he would open up negotiations at once.

But Rabia said she could not marry any man, for she was already in
love.

"In love?" gasped her recent master. "With whom?"

"With Allah!" And she began to pour forth poetry of such rapturous
passion that her former owner became her first and lifelong disciple. Rabia
entered upon a life of ascetic contemplation, mystic musings that frequently erupted into a love poetry so intensely emotional it sounded almost carnal, except that the "lover" she addressed was Allah:

> O my own Lord, the stars glitter
> and the eyes of men are closed.
> Kings have locked their doors.
> Lovers are alone with their beloved ones . . .
> And here I am alone with You.[1]

How much poetry she poured forth, I don't know. The canon that survives
is slight, but in her day, her fame was great: many journeyed to Basra just
to see Rabia for themselves. Many came away convinced that she had
found the key to union with Allah. To her, the key was not fear but love,
utterly abandoned, reckless, and unlimited love.

Easy enough to say but how could one actually fall into such love?
Hungry seekers hung around with the charismatic mystic herself, hoping
to catch her passion like a fever. Some did catch it, they said, which of
course brought more seekers to her gates. I don't call them students, because no books were involved, no scholarship, no study. Rabia of Basra did
not teach. She simply radiated, and people in her vicinity changed. This
became the pattern in Sufism: direct transmission of techniques leading to
enlightenment from master to *mureed,* as would-be Sufis were called.

Until this time, most Muslim mystics were "sober" Sufis, rigorously de-voted to rituals and recitation. Their devotions focused on fear (of God). Rabia Basri put love at the center and helped spawn a long tradition of "God-intoxicated Sufis." Let's be clear, though: all of these people were Muslims first and Sufis next. I state this caveat simply because today lots of people call themselves Sufis when they're really just singing and dancing themselves into a state of euphoria. The Sufis were not after a mere emo-tion. They weren't trying to get high. Their spiritual practices began with the known devotions of Islam and then added more on top.

People flocked to Sufis with a definite goal in mind. They hoped to "get somewhere." Working with a Sufi master smacked of learning a method-ology. Indeed, what Sufis did came to be labeled the *tariqa*, the "method." Those who entered upon the method expected to move through distinct stages to annihilation of their egos and immersion in God.

The jurists and the orthodox scholars did not look kindly on the Sufis, especially the God-intoxicated variety. The language employed by these saints began to sound a bit heretical. Their claims grew ever more extrava-gant. Common folks began to ascribe magical powers to the most famous Sufis. The hostilities came to a head in the late tenth century CE with a Persian Sufi named al-Hallaj.

Hallaj means "cotton carder." This was his father's profession, and he too started out in the family trade; but the longing for union with God sank talons into his heart, and he abandoned his home to search for a master who would initiate him into Sufi secrets. At one point, he spent an entire year standing motionless in front of the Ka'ba, never uttering a sound. One year! Imagine the attention this might have drawn to him. Later, he went travel-ing to India and to Central Asia, and everywhere he went he spouted poetry and gave strange speeches, and he attracted countless followers.

But the sober Sufis began to back away from him, because Hallaj was saying things like, "My turban is wrapped around nothing but God." And again, "Inside my clothes you'll find nothing but God." And finally, in case someone didn't get his point, "I am God." Well, actually, he said, "I am Truth," but "Truth" was famously one of the ninety-nine names of God and given Hallaj's recent history, no one could miss what he was getting at.

This was too much. The orthodox scholars demanded action. The Ab-basid khalifa wanted to appease the scholars so they would get off his back about the philosophers. He therefore had Hallaj clapped in prison for eleven years, but Hallaj was so lost to the world by this time, he didn't care. Even in his cell he kept spouting his God-intoxicated utterances, sometimes associating himself with Jesus Christ, and often mentioning martyrdom. One thing was for sure: he recanted nothing. Finally, the orthodox establishment decided they had run out of options. They would have to pressure the state to apply the time-tested, never-fail method of discrediting a message: kill the messenger.

The authorities did not just execute Hallaj. They hung him, cut off his limbs, decapitated him, and finally burned his corpse. Oddly enough, it didn't work. Hallaj was gone, but Sufism continued to proliferate. Charismatic individuals kept emerging, hundreds of them, maybe thousands, all across the civilized world. Some were "sober" Sufis like Junayd and some were the God-intoxicated variety, like Rabia Basri and Hallaj.

In sum, by the mid-eleventh century, Muslims were hard at work on three great cultural projects, pursued respectively by scholar-theologians, philosopher-scientists, and Sufi mystics: to elaborate Islamic doctrine and law in full; to unravel the patterns and principles of the natural world; and to develop a technique for achieving personal union with God. Yes, the three groups overlapped somewhat, but overall they pulled in competing directions, and their intellectual disagreements had high and sometimes bloody political and financial stakes. At this juncture, one of the intellectual giants of world history was born of Persian-speaking parents in the province of Khorasan. His name was Abu Hamid Muhammad al-Ghazali.

By his early twenties, Ghazali had already earned acclaim as one of the foremost ulama of his age. No matter how many hadith you knew, he knew more. In his day, some ulama had elaborated a theology to compete with that of the Mu'tazilites. The Asharite school, as it was called, insisted that faith could never be based on reason, only on revelation. Reason's function was only to support revelation. Asharite theologians were constantly squaring off against prominent Mu'tazilites in public debates, but the Mu'tazilites knew fancy Greek tricks for winning arguments, such as logic and rhetoric, so they were constantly making the Asharites look confused.

Ghazali came to their rescue. The way to beat the philosophers, he decided, was to join them enough to use their tricks against them. He plunged into a study of the ancients, mastered logic, and inhaled the treatises of the Greek. Then he wrote a book about Greek philosophy called *The Aims of the Philosophers*. It was chiefly about Aristotle. In the preface, he said the Greeks were wrong and he would prove it, but first—in *this* book—he would explain what Greek philosophy was all about so that readers would know what he was refuting when they read his next book.

One has to admire Ghazali's fair-mindedness. He didn't set up a straw man for himself to knock down. His account of Aristotle was so lucid, so erudite, that even hard-core Aristotelians read the book and said, "Aha! Now at last I understand Aristotle!"

Ghazali's book made its way to Andalusia and from there into Christian Europe, where it dazzled those few who could read. Western Europeans had pretty much forgotten classical Greek thought since the fall of Rome. For most, this was their first exposure to Aristotle. Somewhere along the way, however, Ghazali's preface had dropped out, so Europeans didn't know Ghazali was *against* Aristotle. Some, indeed, thought he *was* Aristotle, writing under a pen name. In any case, *The Aims of the Philosophers* so impressed Europeans that Aristotle acquired for them an aura of imposing authority, and later Christian philosophers devoted much energy to reconciling church doctrines with Aristotelian thought.

Meanwhile, back in Persia, Ghazali had written his follow-up to *The Aims of the Philosophers*, a second seminal volume called *The Incoherence of the Philosophers*. Here, Ghazali identified twenty premises on which Greek and Greco-Islamic philosophy depended, then used syllogistic logic to dismantle each one. His most consequential argument, to my mind, was his attack on the notion of cause-and-effect relationships among material phenomena. No such connections exist, according to Ghazali: we think fire causes cotton to burn, because fire is always there when cotton burns. We mistake contiguity for causality. Actually, says Ghazali, it's God who causes cotton to burn, since He is the first and only cause of all things. The fire just happens to be there.

If I'm making Ghazali sound ridiculous here, it's only because I'm not as fair-minded as he was with Aristotle. I disagree with him. Not everyone does. Ghazali's case against causality was resurrected in the West, by the eighteenth-century Scottish philosopher David Hume; and in the 1970s, I read essentially the same argument made again by the American Zen Buddhist Alan Watts, who likened cause and effect to a cat walking back and forth past a narrow slit in a fence. If we're looking through the slit from the other side, Watts said, we keep seeing first the head of the cat and then the tail, which doesn't mean the head causes the tail. (Actually, I think it does, in a sense, but I won't get into that here.)

Take it however you will, the argument against causality undermines the whole scientific enterprise. If nothing actually causes anything else, why bother to observe the natural world in search of meaningful patterns? If God is the only cause, the only way to make sense of the world is to know God's will, which means that the only thing worth studying is the revelation, which means that the only people worth listening to are the ulama.

Ghazali allowed that mathematics, logic, and even the natural sciences could lead to true conclusions, but wherever they conflicted with the revelations, they were wrong. But if science is right only when it reaches the same conclusions as revelation, we don't need science. All the truth we need we can get from the revelations.

Some of the philosophers struck back. Ibn Rushd (known to Europeans as Averroes) wrote a riposte to Ghazali called *The Incoherence of the Incoherence*, but it did little good: when the smoke cleared, Ghazali had won the day. From his time forward, Greek-based Muslim philosophy lost steam and Muslim interest in natural science foundered.

Ghazali won tremendous accolades for his work. He was appointed head of the prestigious Nizamiya University in Baghdad, the Yale of the medieval Islamic world. The orthodox establishment acknowledged him as the leading religious authority of the age. Ghazali had a problem, however: he was an authentically religious man, and somehow, amid all the status and applause, he knew he didn't have the real treasure. He believed in the revelations, he revered the Prophet and the Book, he was devoted to the shari'a, but he wasn't feeling the palpable presence of God—the very same dissatisfaction that had given rise to Sufism. Ghazali had a sudden spiritual crisis, resigned all his posts, gave away all his possessions, abandoned all his friends, and went into seclusion.

When he came out of it many months later, he declared that the scholars had it right, but the Sufis had it righter: The Law was the Law and you had to follow it, but you couldn't reach Allah through book learning and good behavior alone. You needed to open your heart, and only the Sufis knew how to get the heart opened up.

Ghazali now wrote two more seminal books, *The Alchemy of Happiness* and *The Revival of the Religious Sciences*. In these, he forged a synthesis between orthodox theology and Sufism by explaining how the shari'a fit in with the tariqa, the Sufi method for becoming one with God. He created a place for mysticism within the framework of orthodox Islam and thus made Sufism respectable.

Before Ghazali came along, three intellectual movements were competing for adherents in the Islamic world. After Ghazali, two of those currents had come to an accommodation and the third had been eliminated.

I don't say the philosophers acknowledged that Ghazali had proved them wrong and as a result shriveled up and died. Nor do I even say that public opinion turned against the philosophers because Ghazali had proved them wrong. Public opinion rarely believes or disbelieves anything based on proof. Besides, hardly anything in philosophy is ever definitively proven right or wrong.

I say, rather, that some people *wanted* to turn away from philosophy and natural science in this era. Some *already* regarded reason as dangerous trickery leading only to chaos, and Ghazali gave such people the ammunition they needed to look respectable, and even smart while they were denouncing philosophy and reason.

In the years that followed, more and more people turned in this direction. The assumption that many shades of gray exist in ethical and moral matters allows people to adopt thousands of idiosyncratic positions, no two people having exactly the same set of beliefs, but in times of turmoil, people lose their taste for subtleties and their tolerance for ambiguity. Doctrines that assert unambiguous rules promote social solidarity because they enable people to cohere around shared beliefs, and when no one knows what tomorrow may bring, people prefer to clump together.

Sometime during this period, the status of women in Islamic society seems to have changed as well. Various clues suggest to me that in the early days of Islam, women had more independence and a greater role in public affairs than they had later on, or than many have in the Islamic world today. The Prophet's first wife Khadija, for example, was a powerful and successful businesswoman who started out as Mohammed's employer. The Prophet's youngest wife Ayesha led one major party during the schism that followed Othman's death. She even commanded armies in the field, and no one seemed surprised that a woman would take on this role. Women were present at the iconic early battles as nurses and support staff and even sometimes as fighters. In the battle of Yarmuk, the chronicles tell of the widow Umm Hakim fighting Byzantine soldiers with a tentpole for a sword.[2] Also, details about some of the battles come from women bards, who observed the fighting and composed poems about it, essentially acting as war correspondents.

Women must also have been present at crucial community meetings in those early days, since the fact of their public arguments with Khalifa Omar are recorded—and yet Omar appointed a woman to administer the market in Medina.[3] Besides all this, women figure prominently among the scholars of early Islam. In the first century after the Hijra, women such as Hafsa, Umm al-Darda, Amra bin Abdul Rahman, and others rose to eminence as authorities on hadith. Some were famous calligraphers. They and others taught classes, took in students of both sexes, and gave public lectures.

Clearly, these women were not shut out of public life, public recognition, and public consequence. The practice of relegating women to an unseen private realm derived, it seems, from Byzantine and Sassanid practices. Among the upper classes of those societies, women were sequestered as a mark of high status. Aristocratic Arab families adopted the same customs as a way of appropriating their predecessors' status. The average Muslim woman probably saw her access to public life markedly reduced in the fourth century AH (that is, after about 1000 CE) or at least that's what the tone of scholars' remarks on gender roles imply. The radical separation of gender roles into nonoverlapping spheres accompanied by the sequestration of women probably froze into place during the era of social breakdown that marked the latter days of the Abbasid khalifate. The same forces that squeezed protoscience out of Islamic intellectual life, the same forces that devalued reason as an instrument of ethical and social inquiry, acted to constrict the position of women.

Ghazali devotes one-fourth of his oeuvre, *The Revival of the Religious Sciences*, to a discourse on marriage, family life, and the proper etiquette for the sexes. Here, he says that a woman "should remain in the inner sanctum of her house and tend to her spinning; she should not enter and exit excessively; she should speak infrequently with her neighbors and visit them only when the situation requires it; she should safeguard her husband in his absence and in his presence; she should seek his pleasure in all affairs. . . . She should not leave his home without his permission: if she goes out with his permission, she should conceal herself in worn-out clothes . . . being careful that no stranger hear her voice or recognize her personally. . . . She should . . . be ready at all times for (her husband) to enjoy her whenever he wishes."[4] Ghazali also discusses men's obligations to their wives, but add up all his remarks and you can see that he's envisioning a social world divided strictly into public and private realms, with women restricted to the private one and the public realm reserved exclusively for men.

Anxiety about change and a longing for stability tend to deepen traditional and familiar patterns of society. In the Muslim world, these included patriarchal patterns inherent not just in Arabic tribal life but also in pre-Islamic Byzantine and Sassanid societies. Ghazali's ideas proved persuasive in his time and in the centuries following his death because this was a period of rising disorder, a time of anxiety that cast a pall over civilized life, a time of instability that came finally to a horrifying crescendo.

8

Enter the Turks

120–487 AH
737–1095 CE

WHAT GAVE RISE to all the anxiety? The answer lies in the political story unfolding alongside the intellectual movements I have described. From the Prophet's day through the first two centuries or so of Abbasid rule, people in the Muslim world had good reason to think they were living at the very center of world civilization. European culture barely existed. India had fragmented into many small kingdoms. Buddhism had receded into China, and although it's true that there in "Cathay" the Tang and Sung dynasties presided over a glorious renaissance almost exactly co-extensive with the Muslim one flowering in the middle world, China was too far away to have much resonance in places like Mesopotamia or Egypt.

If the Muslim realm was the heart of the world, then the underlying driving force of world history was the quest to perfect and universalize the Muslim community. All the major issues of the time—the struggle between Shi'ism and orthodoxy, philosophy and theology, Persians and Arabs—could be understood within this framework. For a long while, optimistic observers could look at world events and believe that things were generally moving forward. The implications of the holy miracle that blossomed in Mecca and Medina were still flowering. Islam had permeated deeply and rippled far. Even the Hindus of the Indian heartland were weakening. Even sub-Saharan Africa had Muslim converts now. Only Cathay and darkest Europe remained fully outside the realm. It seemed only a matter of time before Islam fulfilled its destiny and bathed even those regions with light.

But the dream of the universal community of piety and justice remained elusively out of reach and then began to slip away. At the very height of its power and glory, the khalifate began to crack. Indeed, looking back, historians could plausibly say the cracking began before the heights were achieved. It began when the Abbasids took power.

In that cataclysmic transition, the new rulers lured all the Umayyads into a room and clubbed them to death. Well, not quite all. One Umayyad nobleman skipped the party. This man, the last of the Umayyads, a young fellow by the name of Abdul Rahman, fled Damascus in disguise and headed across North Africa, and he didn't stop running until he got to the furthest tip of the Muslim world: Andalusian Spain. Any further and he would have been in the primitive wilderness of Christian Europe.

Abdul Rahman impressed the locals in Spain. A few hard-core Kharijite insurgent types skulking about there at the ends of the Earth pledged their swords to the youngster. There in Spain, so far from the Muslim heartland, no one knew much about the new regime in Baghdad and certainly felt no loyalty to them. Andalusians were accustomed to thinking of the Umayyads as rulers, and here was a real-life Umayyad asking to be their ruler. In a less tumultuous time, Abdul Rahman might simply have been posted here as governor and the people would have accepted him. Therefore, they accepted him as their leader now, and Andalusian Spain became an independent state, separate from the rest of the khalifate. So the Muslim story was now unfolding from two centers.

At first, this was only a political fissure, but as the Abbasids weakened, the Andalusian Umayyads announced that they were not merely independent of Baghdad but were, in fact, still the khalifas. Everyone within a few hundred miles said, "Oh, yes, sir, you're definitely the khalifa of Islam; we could tell from the very look of you." So the khalifate itself, this quasi-mystical idea of a single worldwide community of faith, was broken in two.

The Umayyad claim had some resonance because their Andalusian capital of Córdoba was far and away the greatest city in Europe. At its height it had some half a million inhabitants and boasted hundreds of bathhouses, hospitals, schools, mosques, and other public buildings. The largest of many libraries in Córdoba reputedly contained some five hundred thousand volumes. Spain had other urban centers as well, cities of fifty thousand or more at a time when the biggest towns in Christian Europe did not exceed twenty-five thousand inhabitants. Once-mighty Rome was merely a village now, with a population smaller than Dayton, Ohio, a thin smattering of peasants and ruffians eking out a living among the ruins.

At first, therefore, the political split in Islam did not seem to imply any loss of civilizational momentum. Andalusia traded heavily with the rest of the civilized world. It sent timber, grains, metals, and other raw materials into North Africa and across the Mediterranean to the Middle World, importing from those regions handcrafted luxury goods, ceramics, furniture, rich textiles, spices and the like.

Trade with the Christian countries to the north and east, by contrast, amounted to a mere trickle—not so much because of any hostility between the regions, but because Christian Europeans had virtually nothing to sell and no money with which to buy.

Muslims formed the majority in Andalusia, but many Christians and Jews lived there as well. Umayyad Spain may have been at odds with the Baghdad khalifate, but its rulers followed much the same social policies as in all the Muslim conquests so far. Both Christian and Jewish communities had their own religious leaders and judicial systems and were free to practice their own rituals and customs. If one of them got into a dispute with a Muslim, the case was tried in a Muslim court by Islamic rules but disputes among themselves were adjudicated by their own judges according to their own rules.

Non-Muslims had to pay the poll tax but were exempt from the charity tax. They were excluded from military service and the highest political positions, but all other occupations and offices were open to them. Christians, Muslims, and Jews lived in fairly amicable harmony in this empire with the caveat that Muslims wielded ultimate political power and probably radiated an attitude of superiority, stemming from certainty that their culture and society represented the highest stage of civilization, much as Americans and western Europeans now tend to do vis-à-vis people of third world countries.

The story of King Sancho illustrates how the various communities got along. In the late tenth century CE, Sancho inherited the throne of Leon, a Christian kingdom north of Spain. Sancho's subjects soon began referring to him as Sancho the Fat, the sort of nickname a king never likes to hear his subjects using with impunity. Poor Sancho might more accurately have been called Sancho the Medically Obese, but his nobles could not take the large view. They regarded Sancho's size as proof of an internal weakness that made him unfit to rule, so they deposed him.

Sancho then heard about a Jewish physician named Hisdai ibn Shaprut who reputedly knew how to cure obesity. Hisdai was employed by the Muslim ruler in Córdoba, so Sancho headed south with his mother and retinue to seek treatments. The Muslim ruler Abdul Rahman the Third welcomed Sancho as an honored guest and had him stay at the royal palace until Hisdai had shrunk him down, whereupon Sancho returned to Leon, reclaimed his throne, and signed a treaty of friendship with Abdul Rahman.[1]

A Christian king received treatments from a Jewish physician at the court of a Muslim ruler: there you have the story of Muslim Spain in a nutshell. When Europeans talk about the Golden Age of Islam, they are often thinking of the Spanish khalifate, because this was the part of the Muslim world that Europeans knew the most about.

But Córdoba was not the only city to rival Baghdad. In the tenth century, another city emerged to challenge the supremacy of the Abbasid khalifate.

When the Abbasids decided to rule as Sunnis, they revived the Shi'ite impulse to rebellion. In 347 AH (969 CE) Shi'i warriors from Tunisia managed to seize control of Egypt and declared themselves the true khalifas of Islam because (they said) they were descended from the Prophet's daughter Fatima, for which reason they called themselves the Fatimids. These rulers built themselves a brand new capital they called Qahira, the Arabic word for "victory." In the West, it is spelled Cairo.

The Egyptian khalifate had the resources of North Africa and the granaries of the Nile valley to draw upon. It was well situated to compete in the Mediterranean Sea trade, and it dominated the routes along the Red Sea to Yemen, which gave it access to markets bordering the Indian Ocean. By the year 1000 CE, it probably outshone both Baghdad and Córdoba.

In Cairo, the Fatimids built the world's first university, Al Azhar, which is still going strong. Everything I've said about the other two khalifates—big

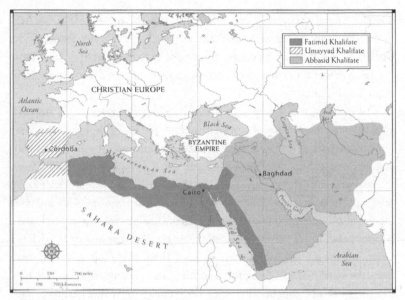

THE THREE KHALIFATES

cities, busy bazaars, liberal policies, lots of cultural and intellectual activity—
was true of this khalifate as well. Rich as it was, however, Egypt represented
yet another fragmentation of what was, in theory, a single universal community. In short, as the millennium approached, the Islamic world was divided
into three parts.

Each khalifate asserted itself to be the one and only true khalifate—
"one and only" being built into the very meaning of the word *khalifate.*
But since the khalifas were really merely secular emperors by this time, the
three khalifates more or less coexisted, just like three vast secular states.

The Abbasids had the most territory (at first), and theirs was the richest capital, but the very size of their holdings made them, in some ways,
the weakest of the three khalifates. Just as Rome grew too big to administer from any single place by any single ruler, so, too, did the Abbasid khalifate. A vast bureaucracy that developed to carry out the khalifa's orders
encrusted into permanence. The khalifa disappeared into the stratosphere
above this machinery of state until he became invisible to his subjects.

Just like the Roman emperors, the Abbasid khalifas surrounded themselves with a corps of bodyguards, which became the tail that wagged the

dog. In Rome, this group was called the Praetorian Guard, and it was (ironically) well staffed with Germans recruited from the territories of the barbarians north of the frontiers, those same barbarians with whom Rome had been at war for centuries and whose excursions posed a constant threat to civilized order.

The same pattern emerged in the Abbasid khalifate. Here, the imperial guards were called mamluks, which means "slaves," although these were not ordinary slaves but elite slave soldiers. Like Rome, the Abbasid khalifate was plagued by nomadic barbarians north of its borders. In the west, the barbarians of the north were Germans; here they were Turks. (There were no Turks in what is now called Turkey; they migrated to this area much later. The ancestral home of the Turkish tribes was the central Asian steppes north of Iran and Afghanistan.) As the Romans had done with the Germans, the Abbasids imported some of these Turks—purchasing them from the slave markets along the frontier—and used them as bodyguards. The khalifas did this because they didn't trust the Arabs and Persians whom they ruled and among whom they lived, folks with too many local roots, too many relatives, and interests of their own to push. The khalifas wanted guards with no links to anyone but the khalifas themselves, no home but their court, no loyalties except to their owners. Therefore, the slaves they brought in were children. They had these kids raised as Muslims in special schools where they were taught martial skills. When they grew up they entered an elite corps that formed something like an extension of the khalifa's own identity. In fact, since the public never saw the khalifa anymore, these Turkish bodyguards became, for most folks, the face of the khalifate.

Of course they were arrogant, violent, and rapacious—they were raised to be. Even while keeping the khalifa safe, they alienated him from his people, their depredations making him ever more unpopular and therefore unsafe and therefore ever more in need of bodyguards. Eventually, the khalifa had to build the separate soldier's city of Samarra just to house his troublesome mamluks, and he himself moved there to live among them.

Meanwhile, a Persian family, the Buyids, insinuated themselves into the court as the khalifa's advisers, clerks, helpers. Soon, they took control of the bureaucracy and thus of the empire's day-to-day affairs. Boldly, they passed the office of vizier (chief administrator) down from father to son as a hereditary title. (A similar thing happened in the Germanic kingdoms of Europe where a similar officer, the "mayor of the palace" developed into the real ruler of the land.) The Buyids, like the khalifas, began importing the children of Turkish barbarians to Baghdad as slaves and raising them in dormitories over which they had absolute control, to serve as *their* personal bodyguards. Once the Buyids had their system in place, no one could oppose them, for their Turkish bodyguards had come to town at such a young age they had no memory of their families, their fathers, their mothers, their siblings: they knew only the camaraderie of the military schools and camps in which they grew up, and they felt soldierly allegiance only to one another and to the men who had controlled their lives in the camps. The Buyids, then, became a new kind of dynasty in Islam. They kept the khalifa in place but issued orders in his name and enjoyed a high life behind the throne. Thus, Persians came to rule the capital of the Arab khalifate.

These Persian viziers couldn't rule the rest of the empire, however, nor did they even care to. They were perfectly content to leave distant locales to the domination of whatever lord happened to have the most strength there. Major governors thus turned into minor kings, and Persian mini dynasties proliferated across the former Sassanid realm.

You might think that training slaves to be killers, giving them weapons, and then stationing them outside your bedroom door would be such a bad idea that no one would ever do it, but in fact almost everyone did it in these parts: every little breakaway Persian kingdom had its own corps of Turkish mamluks guarding and eventually controlling its little Persian king.

As if that were not enough, the empire as a whole was constantly fighting to keep whole tribes of Turkish nomads from crossing the frontier and wreaking havoc in the civilized world, just as the Romans had struggled to keep the Germans at bay. At last the Turks grew too strong to suppress, both inside and outside the khalifate. In some of those little outlying kingdoms, mamluks killed their masters and founded their own dynasties.

Meanwhile, with the empire decaying and the social fabric fraying, barbarians began to penetrate the northern borders, much as the Germans had done in Europe when they crossed the Rhine River into Roman territory. Rude Turks came trickling south in ever growing numbers: tough warriors, newly converted to Islam and brutal in their simplistic fanaticism. Accustomed to plunder as a way of life, they ruined cities and laid waste to crops. The highways grew unsafe, small-time banditry became rife, trade declined, poverty spread. Turkish mamluks fought bitterly with Turkish nomads—it was Turks in power everywhere. This is part of why anxiety permeated the empire in Ghazali's day.

A light did shine at the edges, however, under a Persian dynasty called the Samanids. Their kingdom radiated from cities on either side of the Oxus River, which now forms the northern border of Afghanistan. Here, in the great urban centers of Balkh and Bokhara, the literary culture of ancient Persia revived, and Persian began to compete with Arabic as the language of learning.

But the Samanids, too, had mamluks, and one of their mamluk generals decided he would rather give orders than take them. Goodbye, Samanids; hello, Ghaznavids. The new rulers were called Ghaznavids because they moved their capital to the city of Ghazni, southeast of Kabul. The Ghaznavid dynasty peaked with a long-lived conqueror named Mahmud, a Charlemagne of the Islamic East. By the time this man was done, his empire sprawled from the Caspian to the Indus. Just as Charlemagne saw himself as a "most Christian emperor," Mahmud considered himself a most Muslim monarch. He appointed himself coruler of the Muslim world, giving himself the brand new title of sultan, which means something like "sword arm." As he saw it, the Arab khalifa was still the spiritual father of the Islamic community, but he, Mahmud, was the equally important military leader, the Enforcer. From his day until the twentieth century, there was always at least one sultan in the Muslim world.

Sultan Mahmud was bright enough to staff his imperial service with educated Persians who could read and write. He announced handsome rewards for men of learning, offers that attracted some nine hundred poets, historians, theologians, philosophers, and other literati to his court, which added to his prestige.

One of these literati was the poet Firdausi, who was writing *Shahnama* (*The Book of Kings*), an epic history of the Persian nation from the beginning of time to the birth of Islam, all in rhyming couplets. In the Middle World he has a stature comparable to Dante. Mahmud extravagantly promised this man one piece of gold for each couplet of his finished epic. He was shocked when Firdausi finally presented him with the longest poem ever penned by a single man: *The Book of Kings* has over sixty thousand couplets. "Did I say gold?" the sultan frowned. "I meant to say silver. One piece of *silver* for each couplet."

The offended Firdausi went off in a huff and offered his poem to another king. According to legend, Sultan Mahmud later regretted his penny-pinching and sent servants with trunk loads of gold to coax the poet back, but they were knocking on the front door of the poet's house while his corpse was being carried out the back for burial.[2]

The Book of Kings represents all of history as a struggle between the descendants of two legendary brothers, Iran and Turan, who (it is often thought) represent the Persians and the Turks, respectively: Iran is the good guy, and Turan the bad guy. Not surprisingly, *The Book of Kings* is now the national epic of Iran, and I wonder if it was actually the cost of the book that gave the sultan pause: maybe he didn't like seeing Turks presented as the bad guys of history.

Firdausi also heaped scorn on the Arabs and devoted a long passage at the end to detailing their primitive savagery as compared to the civilized grace of the Persians at the time Islam was born. His book was just one more sign of the decline of Arab power and the rising prestige of Persian culture within Islam. In fact, his attitude about Arabs was not unique. As another poet of the era wrote,

Arabs were eating crickets in the wasteland, living on the brink,
While in Mashad, even dogs had ice water to drink.[3]

Sultan Mahmud was not only first in patronage of the arts; he also prided himself on the number of Hindu temples he sacked and how thoroughly he sacked them and what quantities of loot he snatched away from infidel fingers. He hauled his plunder home to ornament his capital and pay the nine-hundred-plus literati living at his court. His invasions of India and his slaughter of Hindus made him, he felt, a hero of Islam.

Mahmud's son Masud built himself a winter capital on the banks of the Helmand River, about a mile downriver from my own boyhood town of Lashkargah. The ruins of the city are still there. Growing up, I often wondered if Masud might have hunted deer on the same wooded island in the middle of the river where my buddies and I used to roam, woods that in my day teemed with jungle cats, jackals, and wild boar.

Masud himself was a formidable specimen of a man. Too heavy for most horses, he customarily rode an elephant, of which he had a whole battalion penned up in the marshy canebrakes along the Helmand River. Make no mistake, however, his great girth was all muscle. He went into battle with a sword only he could swing and a battleaxe so huge, no one else could even lift it. Even the great Sultan Mahmud reputedly feared his boy.

When the father died, Masud happened to be in Baghdad. The courtiers proclaimed his brother the new king. Masud came rushing back, gathering up an army along the way, dethroned his brother lickety-split, and put out both his eyes to make sure he would never try anything like *that* again. Then he took over the Ghaznavid Empire and, like his father, welded art and war into a potent cultural combination of grandeur and gold and savagery. At that point, it must have seemed like Ghaznavid dominion would last forever.

Yet four times during Masud's reign, rugged Oghuz Turks from the north stormed across the Oxus River to attack Ghaznavid realms. Led by a family called the Seljuks, they made their way into Khorasan (eastern Iran, western Afghanistan). Four times Sultan Masud sallied forth to meet them on the field of battle. Three times he beat them back, but in the fourth battle, his forces got hammered. In 1040 he lost Lashkargah and his western strongholds to those Seljuks. I've described the dread demeanor of the frightening Masud; now imagine what kind of men it must have taken to beat him. Masud retreated to the city his father had built and lived out his reign, but the glory days of the Ghaznavids were done. The Seljuk era had begun.

The Seljuks moved west, nibbling away at the empire based in Baghdad. These chieftains couldn't read or write and saw no point in learning. A strong swordsman could command enough gold to hire a hundred tallow-faced clerks to read and write for him. They sacked cities and exacted tribute, but preferred to live in tents, which they furnished as gloriously as was possible for a people constantly on the move. (In time, they also funded the construction of wonderful architecture in their major cities.) Once they crossed the border, they dropped their ancient shamanistic religion and converted to Islam, but it was a rough-and-ready Islam that didn't concern itself with doctrines or ethical ideas very much: it was more a rah-rah locker-room ideology that marked off Us Guys from Them Guys.

In 1053 CE, a young Seljuk prince was sent to govern the province of Khorasan. His name was Alp Arslan, which means "heroic lion"—a nickname his troops gave him. Alp Arslan took along his Persian secretary, soon to be known as Nizam al-Mulk, which means "order of the realm." Alp Arslan stood out in any crowd, not only because he stood well over six feet tall, but because he had grown his moustache so long he could sling the two strands of it over his shoulders to hang down behind his back, and when he rode his white horse at top speed, the braids streamed behind him like whip-shaped banners.

His Persian adviser managed to set Khorasan in order and get the economy humming, which gave his sponsor such prestige that when the old Seljuk chieftain died and the usual fighting broke out among brothers, sons, and nephews, Alp Arslan quickly emerged triumphant, thanks in part to the crafty Nizam al-Mulk's advice. After crowning himself sultan, Alp Arslan began poring over maps to see what else he might conquer.

He extended Seljuk power into the Caucasus region and then kept moving west, finally leading his armies into Asia Minor, most of which was ruled by Constantinople, the fortress capital of an empire the Muslims were still calling Rome.

In 1071, on the outskirts of a town called Manzikert, Alp Arslan met the Byzantine emperor Romanus Diogenes in battle and smashed his hundred-thousand-man army. He took the emperor himself prisoner, sending a shock rippling through the Western world. Then he did the unthinkable; he released the emperor and sent him home to Constantinople with gifts and admonishments never to make trouble again, a courtesy that only underscored Seljuk might and added to the Christian emperor's humiliation. The battle of Manzikert was one of history's truly seminal battles. At the time, it seemed like the greatest victory these Seljuks could ever achieve. In fact, it may have been their biggest mistake, but no one would realize this for another twenty-six years.

Alp Arslan died the following year in Khorasan, but his son Malik Shah stepped right into his shoes, and under the expert tutelage of Nizam al-Mulk proved himself nearly the equal of his father. It was he who conquered Syria and the Holy Lands for the Turks.

The partnership between the Persian vizier and the two Seljuk sultans served both sides well. The sultans devoted themselves to conquests,

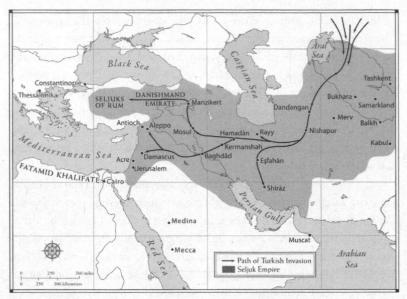

SELJUK EMPIRE: THE TURKS INVADE THE ISLAMIC WORLD

Nizam al-Mulk to organizing their conquests. There was much to organize because the sultans put diverse relatives in charge of various lands as they moved on, and the relatives regarded the territories given to them as their personal possessions. Fresh off the steppes, these Turks did not fully grasp the distinction between taxing and looting.

Nizam al-Mulk got the tax system straightened out and created a cadre of roving inspectors to make sure the tax collectors didn't cheat. He used the Sultan's war revenues to build roads and organized a police force to protect travelers, so that merchants might feel safe transporting goods. He also set up state-funded hostels spaced about a day's journey apart for their convenience. This great vizier also built a network of schools and colleges called madrassas to teach future officials of his Islamic society a uniform doctrine. He ensured the uniformity of it by putting the curriculum in the hands of orthodox Sunni ulama.

These measures were all part of his struggle against the centripetal forces of his times. Nizam al-Mulk hoped to weave a stable Islamic community out of three ethnic strands. The Turks would keep order with their military strength, the Arabs would provide unity by contributing religious doctrine, and the Persians would contribute all the remaining arts of civilization—administration, philosophy, poetry, painting, architecture, science—to elevate and beautify the world. The new ruling class would thus consist of a Turkish sultan and his army, an Arab khalifa and the ulama, and a Persian bureaucracy staffed by artists and thinkers.

The stability this engendered would, he hoped, let farmers and merchants generate the wealth needed to . . . provide the taxes needed to . . . fund the armies needed to . . . keep the order needed to . . . let farmers and merchants keep generating wealth.

But Nizam al-Mulk had a sinister opponent working to unravel his fabric, a ruthless genius named Hassan Sabbah, founder of the Cult of the Assassins. I call them a cult because "sect" seems too mainstream. They were a branch that split away from a branch that split away from Shi'ism, itself a branch of Islam.

Shi'is believe in a central guiding religious figure called an imam, of whom there is always one in the world. As soon as the imam dies, his special grace passes into one of his sons, making *him* the imam. The trouble is that every time an imam passes away, disagreements can arise about which of his sons is the next imam. Each such disagreement can lead to a split that gives birth to a new branch of the sect.

Just such a disagreement had broken out about who was the fifth imam, spawning the Zaidi sect, also known as the Fivers. A more serious disagreement arose after the death of the sixth imam, giving rise to a sect called the Isma'ilis, who became the dominant branch of Shi'ism for a while, since the Fatimids who captured Egypt and set up a rival khalifate were Isma'ilis.

In the late eleventh century the Isma'ilis themselves branched into two. The minority was a revolutionary offshoot angered by the wealth and pomp of the now-mighty Fatimid khalifate and dedicated to leveling rich and poor, empowering the meek, and generally getting the Islamic project back on course. The leaders of this movement sent an operative named Hassan Sabbah to Persia to recruit adherents.

In Persia, Sabbah developed his own power base. He took control of a fortress called Alamut ("the eagle's nest"), situated high in the Elburz mountains of northern Iran. No one could touch him there because the only approach to the fortress was a footpath too narrow to accommodate an army. How Sabbah conquered it, no one knows. Some legends say trickery was involved, some that he used supernatural means, some that he converted the staff of the fortress and then simply bought the place from its master for a small sum. Whatever the case, there at Alamut, Sabbah got busy organizing the Assassins.

Did his cult adopt this name because they were devoted to political murder? Quite the opposite: political murder is now called assassination because it was a tactic practiced by this cult. Centuries later, Marco Polo would claim that Sabbah's agents smoked hashish in order to hop themselves up for murder and were thus called hashishin, from which derived the word *assassin*. I doubt this etymology, and I'll tell you why.

Sabbah was the archetypal prototerrorist, using murder largely for its propaganda value. Since he lacked the resources and troops to fight battles or conquer cities, he sent individuals, or at most small groups, to assassinate carefully targeted figures chosen for the shock their death would spark. The Assassins plotted their killings for months or even years, sometimes contriving to make friends with the victim or enter his service and work their way up to a position of trust.

Where in this long process was the hashish smoking supposed to take place? It doesn't add up. The Lebanese writer Amin Malouf suggests that actually the word *assassin* probably derives from the Persian word *assas*, which means "foundation." Like most religious schismatics, Sabbah taught that the revelations had been corrupted and that he was taking his followers back to the foundation, the original. Of course, every schismatic has a different idea about what the founding revelation was. Sabbah's doctrine strayed pretty far from anything most scholars recognize as Islam. For one thing, he taught that while Mohammed was indeed the messenger of Allah, Ali was an actual incarnation of Allah—as were the succeeding imams.

Sabbah further taught that the Qur'an had a surface or exterior meaning but many levels of esoteric or interior meanings. The surface meaning prescribed the rituals of religion, the outward show, the rules of conduct, the ethical and moral mandates; all of this was for the brutal masses who couldn't aspire to deeper knowledge. The esoteric Qur'an—and every verse, every line, every letter had an esoteric meaning—provided a secret code that allowed cognoscenti to unlock the cryptogram of the created universe.

The Assassins were organized as the ultimate secret society. Out in the world, they gave no indication of their identity or their real beliefs. No one knew, therefore, how many Assassins there were or which of the people in the bazaar, or the mosque, or anywhere else was actually an Assassin. Recruits went through intensive indoctrination and training, but once accepted into the sect, each member had a rank reflecting his level of knowledge. Initiates moved from stage to stage as they presumably plumbed ever deeper levels of meaning in the Qur'an, until they reached the foundation upon which all was built, whereupon they were admitted to Sabbah's innermost circle.

Although they crafted their plots in utmost secrecy, the Assassins killed with utmost publicity: their object was not really to remove this or that person from power but to make people throughout the civilized world believe that the Assassins could kill *any* person, anytime, anywhere. Sabbah wanted people to worry that anyone they knew—their best friend, their most trusted servant, even their spouse—might actually be an Assassin. In this way, he hoped to control the policies of men who, unlike himself, did hold territory, did possess resources, and did command troops.

The agents who did the murders for him were called Fedayeen, which means "sacrificers." When they plotted a public assassination, they knew they would be caught and killed within moments of completing their deed, but they made no effort to evade this outcome. Indeed, dying was a key element of the ritual they were enacting: they were suicide knifers. By embracing death, they let the authorities know that not even the threat of execution could intimidate them.

The Assassins added to the anxiety of a world already in turmoil. Sunnis were struggling with Shi'i. The Abbasid khalifate in Baghdad was wrestling with the Fatimid khalifate in Cairo. Nearly a century of Turkish invasions had brutalized society. And now this cult of killers extending its secret tendrils throughout the Middle East injected society with a persistent underlying nightmare.

The Assassins announced themselves with a series of ever more spectacular assassinations. They killed Seljuk officials and well-known Sunni clerics. They killed two of the khalifas. As often as possible, they carried out their assassination in the biggest mosques during Friday prayer, when they could be sure of an audience.

Then in 1092 they murdered the recently retired Nizam al-Mulk himself. Scarcely a month later, they dispatched his master, Sultan Malik Shah, son of Alp Arslan. In the space of weeks, they had eliminated the two men most crucial to the shaky unity the empire enjoyed. These murders set off a debilitating power struggle among Seljuk sons, brothers, cousins, and relatives, as well as miscellaneous adventurers, a struggle that left the western portion of the empire in pieces. From Asia Minor to the Sinai, practically every city ended up in the hands of a different prince—Jerusalem, Damascus, Aleppo, Antioch, Tripoli, Edessa—each was a de facto sovereign state owing only nominal fealty to the sultan in Baghdad. Each petty prince huddled over his possession like a dog over a bone and eyed all the other princes with suspicion.

By 1095 CE, the dream of a universal community had failed at the political level. The ulama were barely holding society together with Qur'an, hadith, and shari'a. The philosophers were a scattered breed, still adding to the conversation, but with voices that were growing ever dimmer. This was the world in which Ghazali lived and worked, a world in which trusting to reason could easily seem unreasonable.

And then the catastrophes began.

9

⁂

Havoc

474-783 AH
1081-1381 CE

ASSAULT FROM THE WEST

Really, there were two catastrophes, one little, one big. The little one came from the west. At this time, the Muslim world knew as little of western Europe as Europeans later knew about the African interior. To Muslims, everything between Byzantium and Andalusia was a more or less primeval forest inhabited by men so primitive they still ate pig flesh. When Muslims said "Christians," they meant the Byzantine church or the various smaller churches operating in Muslim controlled territory. They knew that an advanced civilization had once flourished further west: a person could still make out traces of it in Italy and parts of the Mediterranean coast, which Muslims regularly raided; but it had crumbled during the Time of Ignorance, before Islam entered the world, and was now little more than a memory.

This Muslim view was not far wrong. Europe had been in terrible shape for a long time. Under attack for centuries from Germanic tribes, from Huns, from Avars, from Magyars, from Muslims, from Norsemen and others, it had sunk to a level of bare subsistence. Almost everybody in Europe was a peasant. Almost every peasant did backbreaking labor from dawn to dark just to scratch up enough food to keep from starving and support a thin upper class of military aristocrats and clerics (and since clerics couldn't marry, their ranks were replenished largely out of the military aristocracy.) Except for those few who went into the church, upper-class boys studied hardly anything except how to fight.

Sometime in the eleventh century, however, the consequences of various tiny technological innovations accumulated to a tipping point. These innovations were so subtle that they probably went all but unnoticed at the time. One was a modified, steel-tipped "heavy" plow that could cut through roots and, compared to the older models, dig a deeper furrow in the dense, wet soil of northern Europe. The heavy plow enabled peasants to clear forests and extend their fields into areas previously considered unsuitable for farming. In effect, it gave peasants more land.

A second invention was the horse collar, which was just a slight improvement of the yoke used to harness a beast of burden to a plow. The earlier version could be used only with oxen, due to its shape. If a horse were strapped to that yoke, the strap would press against the horse's neck and choke off its air supply. At some point, some unknown innovator modified that yoke just enough to have it press against a horse's shoulders and a lower spot on its neck. With this yoke, peasants could use horses instead of oxen to plow their fields, and since horses plow about fifty percent faster than oxen, they could till more land in the same amount of time.

A third innovation was three-field crop rotation. Farming the same plot of land year after year exhausts the soil, so farmers have to let their fields "rest" from time to time. But the stomach never rests, so European peasants customarily divided their land into two fields. Each year they planted crops in one field and let the other field lie fallow. The next year, they planted crops in the second field and let the first lie fallow.

Over the centuries, however, Europeans came to realize that a field didn't have to rest every second year. It stayed just as fertile if it lay fallow one year out of three. Gradually, peasants started dividing their land into three plots, and planting *two* of them each year while letting *one* lie fallow. In effect, this gave peasants one-sixth more arable land each year.

What did these little changes add up to? Not much. They merely allowed peasants to produce a slight surplus from time to time. When they had a surplus, they took it to certain crossroads on designated days and traded with peasants who had a surplus of something else. As the goods they had access to grew more various and more abundant, they were able to borrow some time from the backbreaking business of sheer subsistence to make handcrafted items to trade, whatever they were good at. Certain crossroads turned into more or less permanent market sites, which then developed into towns. Towns began to attract people who could work full time making things to sell for cash. Cash allowed some people to spend all their time going from market to market, just buying and selling. Money came back into use in Europe, and as money proliferated, the wealthiest Europeans acquired the means to travel.

And where did they travel? Well, this being a world steeped in religion and religious superstition, they went to shrines in search of miracles. If they had limited means, they visited local shrines, but if they could afford better, they went to the great shrines in the Holy Lands. This was a long and dangerous journey for western Europeans, and without a universal currency the only way to pay for it was with gold or silver, which made such travelers prime targets for bandits; so pilgrims often formed groups, hired bodyguards, and organized communal expeditions to Palestine. There, they visited the places where Christ and his disciples had walked and worked and lived and died. They begged forgiveness of the Lord, got a leg up in the quest for heaven, bought charms to treat their physical ills, purchased some of the marvelous items to be had in the bazaars of the east, acquired relics and souvenirs for their relatives, and headed home to contemplate their life's greatest adventure.

Then the Seljuk Turks wrested control of Palestine away from the tolerant Fatimids and the indolent Abbasids. As new converts, these Turks tended toward zealotry. They weren't zealous about sobriety, modesty, charity, and the like, but they ceded second place to none when it came to expressing chauvinistic disdain toward followers of other religions, especially those from faraway and more-primitive lands.

Christian pilgrims began to find themselves treated rather shabbily in the Holy Lands. It wasn't that they were beaten, tortured, or killed—nothing like that. It was more that they were subjected to constant little humiliations and harassments designed to make them feel second-class. They found themselves at the end of every line. They needed special permission to get into their own shrines. Every little thing cost money; shopkeepers ignored them; officials treated them rudely; and petty indignities of every sort were piled upon them.

When they got back to Europe, they had much to swear and gripe about, but they also had tales to tell about the opulence of the East: the gorgeous houses they had seen, the silk and satin even commoners wore, the fine foods, the spices, the perfumes, the gold, the gold . . . stories that stirred up both anger and envy.

The battle of Manzikert in 1071 CE, the one in which the Seljuk Turks crushed the Byzantines and took their emperor prisoner, came as stunning news. It also triggered a stream of messages from the Byzantines. The Byzantine emperors harangued the knights of the West to come to their aid in the name of Christian unity. The patriarch of Constantinople sent urgent messages to his diehard western rival, the pope, warning that if Constantinople fell, the heathen "Mohammedans" would stream right to Rome.

Meanwhile, with the European economy on the mend, the population was rising, but European customs had not kept pace in two crucial ways. First, productive labor was still considered unsuitable to the dignity of the noble born: their job was to own land and make war. Second, ancient custom still decreed that when a landowner died, his eldest son inherited the whole estate, leaving the younger sons to make their way as best they could. Ironically, this custom of "primogeniture" was only reinforced by an opposite process at the highest levels, the tendency of kings and princes to *divide* their realms among their sons, which fragmented kingdoms into ever-smaller units. France, for example, had dissolved into semisovereign units called counties and even smaller units ruled by really minor noblemen called castellans, whose nobility consisted of possessing one castle and whatever surrounding area it could dominate. A castle could not be divided among several sons, and so at this level, the level where knights were generated, the custom of "eldest son inherits all" became pervasive.[1]

Every generation therefore saw a larger pool of landless noblemen for whom there was no suitable occupation except war, and with the invasions sloping off, there wasn't even enough war to go around. The Vikings, the last major wave of invaders, no longer posed a threat because, by the eleventh century they had crammed into Europe and settled down. "They" had become "us." Even so, the system kept producing knights and more knights.

Enter the pilgrims, stage left, complaining of the indignities visited upon them by heathens in the Holy Lands. Finally, in 1095, Pope Urban II delivered a fiery open-air speech outside a French monastery called Claremont. There, he told an assembly of French, German, and Italian nobles that Christendom was in danger. He detailed the humiliations that Christian pilgrims had suffered in the Holy Lands and called upon men of faith to help their brethren expel the Turks from Jerusalem. Urban suggested that those who headed east should wear a cross-shaped red patch as a badge of their quest. The expedition was to be called a *croisade,* from *croix,* French for "cross," and from this came the name historians give to this whole undertaking: the Crusades.

By focusing on Jerusalem, Urban linked the invasion of the east to pilgrimage, thus framing it as a religious act. Therefore, by the authority vested in him as pope, he decreed that anyone who went to Jerusalem to kill Muslims would receive partial remission of his sins.

One can only imagine how this must have struck those thousands of restless, rowdy, psychologically desperate European knights: "Go east, young man," the pope was saying. "Unleash your true self as the awesome killing machine your society trained you to be, stuff your pockets with gold guilt-free, get the land you were born to own, and as a consequence of it all—get into heaven after you're dead!"

When the first crusaders came trickling into the Muslim world, the locals had no idea who they were dealing with. Early on, they assumed the interlopers to be Balkan mercenaries working for the emperor in Constantinople. The first Muslim ruler to encounter them was a Seljuk prince, Kilij Arslan, who ruled eastern Anatolia from the city of Nicaea, about three days' journey from Constantinople. One day in the summer of 1096, Prince Arslan received information that a crowd of odd-looking warriors had entered his territory, odd because they were so poorly outfitted: a few did look like warriors, but the rest seemed like camp followers of some kind. Almost all wore a cross-shaped patch of red cloth sewn to their garments. Arslan had them followed and watched. He learned that these people called themselves the Franks; local Turks and Arabs called them al-Ifranj ("the Franj"). The interlopers openly proclaimed that they had come from a distant western land to kill Muslims and conquer Jerusalem, but first they intended to take possession of Nicaea. Arslan plotted out the route they seemed to be taking, laid an ambush, and smashed them like so many ants, killing many, capturing many more, and chasing the rest back into Byzantine lands. It was so easy that he gave them no more thought.

He didn't know that this "army" was merely the ragtag vanguard of a movement that would plague Muslims of the Mediterranean coast for another two centuries. While Urban had been speaking to the aristocracy up at the monastery, a vagabond named Peter the Hermit had been preaching the same message out on the streets. Urban had addressed nobles and knights, but presumably any Christian who went crusading could get the remission of sins the pope was offering, so Peter the Hermit was able to recruit from all classes—peasants, artisans, tradespeople, even women and children. His "army" left before the formal army could get organized, in part because *his* "army" didn't feel much need to get organized. They were off to do God's work; surely God would take care of the arrangements. It was these tens of thousands of cobblers, butchers, peasants and the like that Kilij Arslan succeeded in crushing.

The next year, when Kilij Arslan heard that more Franj were coming, he dismissed the threat with a shrug. But the Crusaders in this next wave were real knights and archers led by combat-hardened military commanders from a land where the combat never stopped. Arslan's engagement with them came down to a battle of lightly clad mobile horseman firing arrows at the armored tanks that were the medieval knights of western Europe. The Turks picked off the Franj foot soldiers, but the knights formed defensive blocks that arrows could not penetrate and kept moving slowly, ponderously, and inexorably forward. They took Arslan's city and sent him running to one of his relatives for refuge. The knights then split up, some heading inland toward Edessa, the rest heading down the Mediterranean coast toward Antioch.

The king of Antioch sent a desperate appeal to the king of Damascus, a man named Daquq. The king of Damascus wanted to help, but he was nervous about his brother Ridwan, the king of Aleppo, who would swoop in and grab Damascus if Daquq were to leave it. The ruler of Mosul agreed to help, but he got distracted fighting someone else along the way, and when he did arrive—late—he got into a fight with Daquq who had also finally arrived—late—and these two Muslim forces ended up going home without helping Antioch at all. From the Muslim side, this was the story of the early Crusades: a tragicomedy of internecine rivalry played out in city after city. When Antioch fell, the knights took vengeance for the city's resistance with some indiscriminate killing, and then kept heading south, towards a city called Ma'ara.

Knowing what had happened at Nicaea and Antioch, the Ma'arans were terrified. They too sent urgent messages to nearby cousins, begging for help, but their cousins were only too glad to see the wolves from the west batter Ma'ara, each one hoping to absorb the city for himself once the Franj had blown by. So Ma'ara had to face the Franj alone.

The Christian knights set siege to the city and reduced it to desperation—but in the process reduced themselves to desperation as well, because they ate every scrap of food in the vicinity and then commenced to starve. Obviously, no one was going to feed these invaders, and that was the problem with setting a long siege in a strange land.

At last Franj leaders sent a message into the city assuring the people of Ma'ra that none of them would be harmed if they simply opened their gates and surrendered. The city notables decided to comply. But once the Crusaders made it into Ma'ara, they did more than slaughter. They went on a frightening rampage that included boiling adult Muslims up for soup and skewering Muslim children on spits, grilling them over open fires, and eating them.

I know this sounds like horrible propaganda that the defeated Muslims might have concocted to slander the Crusaders, but reports of Crusader cannibalism in this instance come from Frankish as well as Arab sources. Frankish eyewitness Radulph of Caen, for example, reported on the boiling and grilling. Albert of Aix, also present at the conquest of Ma'ara, wrote, "Not only did our troops not shrink from eating dead Turks and Saracens; they also ate dogs!"[2] What strikes me about this statement is the implication that eating dogs was worse than eating Turks, which makes me think that this Franj, at least, considered Turks a different species from himself.

Amazingly enough, even after this debacle, the Muslims could not unite. Examples abound. The ruler of Homs sent the Franj a gift of horses and offered them advice about what they might sack next (not Homs). The Sunni rulers of Tripoli invited the Franj to make common cause with them against the Shi'i. (Instead, the Franj conquered Tripoli.)

When the Crusaders first arrived, the Egyptian vizier al-Afdal sent a letter to the Byzantine emperor, congratulating him on the "reinforcements" and wishing the Crusaders every success! Egypt had long been locked in a struggle with both the Seljuks and the Abbasids, and al-Afdal really thought the newcomers would merely help his cause. It didn't seem to dawn on him until too late that he himself might be in the line of pillage. After the Franj conquered Antioch, the Fatimid vizier wrote to them to ask if there was anything he could do to help. When the Franj moved against Tripoli, Afdal took advantage of the distraction to assert control of Jerusalem in the name of the Fatimid khalifa. He posted his own governor there and assured the Franj they were now welcome to visit Jerusalem anytime as honored pilgrims: they would have his protection. But the Franj wrote back to say they were not interested in protection but in Jerusalem, and they were coming "with lances raised."[3]

The Franj marched through largely empty country, for their reputation had preceded them. Rural folks had fled at their approach, and small towns had emptied into larger cities with higher walls for protection. Jerusalem had some of the highest walls around, but after a forty-day siege, the Crusaders tried the same gambit they had run successfully at Ma'ara—open the gates, no one will be harmed, they told the citizens—and it worked here too.

Upon securing this city, the Franj indulged in an orgy of bloodletting so drastic it made all the previous carnage seem mild. One crusader, writing about the triumph, described piling up heads, hands, and feet in the streets. (He called it a "wonderful sight.") He spoke of crusaders riding through heathen blood up to their knees and bridle reins.[4] Edward Gibbon, the British historian who chronicled the fall of the Roman Empire, said the Crusaders killed seventy thousand people here over the course of two days. Of the city's Muslims, virtually none survived.

The city's Jewish denizens took refuge in their gigantic central synagogue, but while they were in there praying for deliverance, the Crusaders blockaded all the doors and windows and set fire to the building, burning up pretty much the entire Jewish community of Jerusalem in one fell swoop.

The city's native Christians did not fare so well either. None of them belonged to the Church of Rome but to various Eastern churches such as the Greek, Armenian, Coptic, or Nestorian. The crusading Franj looked upon them as schismatics bordering on heresy, and since heretics were almost worse than heathens, they confiscated the property of these eastern Christians and sent them into exile.

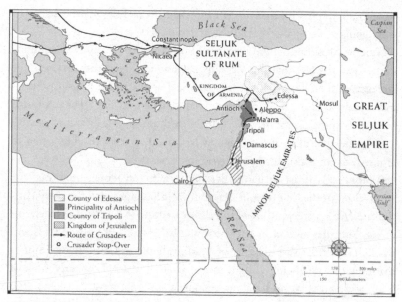

THE THEATER OF THE CRUSADES

The taking of Jerusalem marked the high-water mark of the Franj invasion. The victorious crusaders proclaimed Jerusalem a kingdom. It ranked the highest of the four small crusader states that took root in this area, the others being the principality of Antioch and the counties of Edessa and Tripoli.

Once these four crusader states had been established, a sort of deadlock developed, which ground on dismally for decades. The two sides continued to clash sporadically during these decades, and the Franj won some battles, but they also lost some battles. They pounded the Muslims, but also got pounded, and they quarreled with one another, just as the Muslims were doing among themselves. Sometimes they forged temporary alliances with some Muslim prince to gain an advantage against a rival Franj.

Strange alignments formed and died. In one battle Christian king Tancred of Antioch fought Muslim amir Jawali of Mosul. One third of Tancred's force that day consisted of Turkish warriors on loan from the Muslim ruler of Aleppo, who was allied with the Assassins, who had links with the Crusaders. On the other side, about one third of Jawali's troops were Franj knights on loan from King Baldwin of Edessa, who had a rivalry going with Tancred.[5] And this was typical.

On the Muslim side, the absence of unity was breathtaking. It stemmed partly from the fact that the Muslims saw no ideological dimension to the violence, at first. They felt themselves under attack not as Muslims but as individuals, as cities, as mini states. They experienced the Franj as a horrible but meaningless catastrophe, like an earthquake or a swarm of snakes.

It's true that after the carnage at Jerusalem, a few preachers tried to arouse Muslim resistance by defining the invasion as a religious war. Several prominent jurists began delivering sermons in which they used the word *jihad* for the first time in ages, but their harangues fell flat with Muslim audiences. The word *jihad* merely seemed quaint, for it had fallen out of use centuries earlier, in part because of the rapid expansion of Islam, which had left the vast majority of Muslims living so far from any frontier that they had no enemy to fight in the name of jihad. That early sense of Islam against the world had long ago given way to a sense of Islam *as* the world. Most wars that anyone could remember hearing of had been fought for petty prizes such as territory, resources, or power. The few that could be cast as noble struggles about ideals were never about Islam versus something else, but only about whose Islam was the real Islam.

Given the turmoil of the Muslim world, perhaps some disunity was inevitable: when the Franj dropped into this snake pit, fractious Muslims simply incorporated them into their ongoing dramas. Not all the disunity was spontaneous, however. The Assassins were busy behind the scenes, sowing turmoil, and quite successfully.

Just before the Crusades began, Hassan Sabbah had established a second base of operations in Syria, run by a subsidiary master whom the Crusaders came to know as the Old Man of the Mountains. By the time the Crusades began, virtually everyone who wasn't an Assassin hated the Assassins. Every power in the land was trying to hunt them down. The Assassins' enemies included the Shi'i, the Sunnis, the Seljuk Turks, the Fatimid Egyptians, and the Abbasid khalifate. As it happened, the Crusaders were making war against the same gallery—the Shi'i, the Sunnis, the Seljuk Turks, the Fatimid Egyptians, and the Abbasid khalifate. The Assassins and Crusaders had the same set of enemies so, inevitably, they became de facto allies.

During the first century of the Franj invasions, every time the Muslims began moving toward unity, the Assassins murdered some key figure and triggered turmoil anew.

In 1113 CE the governor of Mosul called a conference of Muslim leaders to organize a unified campaign against the Franj. Just before the meetings began, however, a mendicant approached the governor on his way to the mosque, pretended to beg for alms, then suddenly plunged a knife in his chest. So much for the unity campaign.

In 1124, Assassin agents murdered the second most influential cleric preaching the new jihad. The next year, a group of supposed Sufis attacked and killed another such preacher, the most influential proponent of jihad, the first of this era to revive the call.

In 1126, the Assassins killed al-Borsoki, the powerful king of Aleppo and Mosul who, by uniting these two major cities, had forged the potential core of a united Muslim state in Syria. Borsoki had even taken the precaution of wearing armor under his clothes—he knew that Assassins were lurking about. But as fake Sufis attacked him, one of them cried, "Aim for his head!" They knew about his armor. Borsoki died of neck wounds. His son immediately took command and might have saved the nascent state, but Assassins killed him too, and four rival claimants to the throne plunged this part of Syria back into war.

Murders of this sort happened an astounding number of times during the early Crusades. Some of the murders were not proven to have been the work of the Assassins, but once the terrorist narrative had been reified, the terrorists didn't need to commit all the terrorist acts. They could claim any murder that bore their stamp and use it to forward their cause. Apparently, they kept detailed records of their work, but because they were so very secretive, no outsiders had access to these records at the time, and when the cult was finally destroyed by the Mongols in 1256, it was destroyed so thoroughly its records were almost all erased from history. Therefore no one now knows how many of the murders attributed to Assassins were actually committed by them. Rumors and whispers tell us they cast a grim shadow over their times but we will never know the scope of their impact on the Crusades: the records are gone.

What finally turned the tide against the Franj was a series of Muslim leaders, each of whom was greater than the one before. The first of them was the Turkish general Zangi, who governed Mosul, then took Aleppo, and then absorbed many other cities into his domains until he could reasonably call himself the king of a united Syria. This was the first time in fifty years that a Muslim country larger than a single city and its environs had existed in the Levant (the region between Mesopotamia and Egypt).

Zangi's troops revered him because he was the archetypal soldier's soldier. He lived as ruggedly as his men, ate what they ate, and put on no airs. He soon decided that Muslims had a single common enemy and began to organize a unified campaign against this enemy. First, he squeezed the weakness out of his machine: he eliminated flatterers from his court and courtesans from his armies. More important, he built a network of informers and propagandists throughout Syria that kept his governors in line.

In 1144, Zangi conquered Edessa, which made him a hero to the Muslim world. Edessa wasn't the biggest city in the east, but it was the first sizable city the Muslims had taken *back* from the Franj, and with recapture of Edessa, one of the four "Crusader Kingdoms" ceased to exist. A wave of hope ran through the Levant. A wave of dismay and war fever swept western Europe, inspiring a group of monarchs to organize what turned out to be a dismally ineffectual Second Crusade.

Zangi supported preachers who promoted jihad because he saw jihad as an instrument for unifying the Muslims. Unfortunately Zangi could not very well put himself at the head of a new jihad because he was a hard-drinking, foulmouthed brawler; the very qualities that endeared him to his men offended many of the ulama. He did, however, create an anti-Franj movement that another more pious ruler could build into a real jihad.

His son and successor, Nuruddin, possessed the qualities his father had lacked. Though he shared his father's martial energy, Nuruddin was polished, diplomatic, and devout. He called on Muslims to unite around one set of religious beliefs (Sunni Islam) and make jihad their central objective in life. He revived the image of the just and pious man who fought not for ego, not for wealth, nor for power, but for the community. In restoring to Muslims this sense of themselves as a single Umma, he gave them back their sense of destiny, nurturing a fervor for jihad that another, greater ruler could use to craft a real political victory.

This greater ruler turned out to be Salah al-Din Yusuf ibn Ayub, commonly known as Saladin, the nephew of one of Nuruddin's top generals.

In 1163, Nuruddin sent Saladin's uncle off to conquer Egypt, just to keep it out of Franj hands, and the general took along his nephew. The general succeeded in taking Egypt, and then promptly died, leaving Saladin in charge. Officially, Egypt still belonged to the Fatimid khalifa, but real power belonged to his vizier, and the Egyptian court gladly accepted Saladin as the new vizier, mostly because he was only twenty-nine years old, and the courtiers thought his youth and inexperience would make him their tool.

Saladin had indeed shown little hint of greatness while living in his uncle's shadow. Retiring by nature and modest to a fault, he showed no inclination for war. As soon as he took charge of Egypt, Nuruddin told him to abolish the Fatimid dynasty, and the order distressed him. The Fatimid khalifa was a sickly twenty-year-old at this time, who didn't really rule anything anyway. He was just a figurehead, and Saladin was loathe to hurt his feelings. He obeyed his orders, but he abolished the khalifate so quietly, the khalifa never even knew about it. One Friday, Saladin simply arranged for a citizen to get up in the mosque and recite a sermon in the name of the Abassid khalifa in Baghdad. No one protested and so the deed was done. The frail young khalifa soon expired of natural causes without learning that he was a private citizen and that his dynasty had ended. His death left Saladin as the sole ruler of Egypt.

Now came a series of nonencounters with his supposed boss. Nuruddin kept arranging meetings; Saladin kept making excuses not to be there: his father was sick, he himself was feeling under the weather—it was always something. In truth, he knew that if he met his master face-to-face, he would have to break with him, because he was already the bigger man, king of a more powerful country, and incipient leader of the Muslim cause, and he didn't want to quarrel about it. So he maintained the fiction that he was Nuruddin's subordinate until the older man passed away. Then, Saladin proclaimed himself king of Syria as well as Egypt. Some of Nuruddin's followers cursed him then and called him a disloyal upstart and an arrogant young fool, but they were swimming against history. The Muslim savior had arrived.

He was a man of slight build, this Saladin. He had a pensive air and melancholy eyes, but when he smiled, he could light up a room. Charitable to the point of penury, he was humble with the humble, but majestic with men of might. No one could intimidate him, yet he never stooped to intimidating anyone over whom he had power. As a military leader, he was okay, but nothing special. His power ultimately lay in the fact that people simply adored him.

Saladin sometimes wept at sad news and often went out of his way to perform acts of hospitality and grace. A Franj woman once came to him devastated because bandits had kidnapped her daughter and she didn't know where to turn for help. Saladin sent his soldiers out to look for the girl. They found her in the slave market, bought her, and brought her back to her mother, and the two went back to the Franj encampment.

In his personal habits Saladin was just as ascetic and demanding of himself as Nuruddin had been, but he was less demanding of others. He was religious but lacked a streak of dogmatism that had marred Nuruddin's personality.

The Assassins tried hard to kill Saladin. Twice they penetrated right to his bedside while he was sleeping. Once they wounded him in the head but he was wearing a leather neck-guard and a metal helmet under his turban. After these two attempts, Saladin decided to smash the Assassins once and for all. He set siege to their fortress in Syria, but then—

Something happened. To this day, no one knows what. Some say that Sinon, the Syrian head of the Assassins, sent a letter to Saladin's maternal uncle promising to have every member of the family killed unless the siege was lifted. The Assassins' own sources say that in the middle of the night, after having surrounded himself with guards and every other possible precaution against assassination, Saladin woke up to see a shadow passing through his tent wall and to find a piece of paper pinned to his pillow bearing the message, "You are in our power." That story is surely apocryphal, but the fact that people believed it gives an idea of the power the Assassins had acquired in the popular imagination. This time, however, the usual Assassin tactic backfired, for having tried and failed twice to kill him, the Assassins succeeded only in adding to the legend of Saladin's invincibility.

Saladin moved carefully, letting his reputation unite his people and soften his enemies. He retook most of the Crusaders' holdings bloodlessly through encirclement, economic pressure, and negotiation. In 1187, when he finally moved on Jerusalem, he began by sending in a proposal that the Franj relinquish this city peacefully as well. In exchange, Christians who wanted to leave could take their property and depart, Christians who wanted to stay could do so and practice their religion unmolested, Christian places of worship would be protected, and pilgrims would be welcome to come and go. The Franj indignantly rejected giving up Jerusalem, their main prize and the whole point of these Crusades, so Saladin encircled the city, took it by force, and then dealt with it as Khalifa Omar had done: no massacres, no plundering, and all prisoners set free upon payment of a ransom.

Despite the gentility of it, Saladin's recapture of Jerusalem did fully reverse the gains of the First Crusade, arousing new consternation in Europe and leading the continent's three most important monarchs to organize the famous Third Crusade. One was the German Frederick Barbarossa, who fell off his horse in a few inches of water and drowned on the way to the Holy Lands. One was French monarch Phillip II of France, who made it to the Holy Lands, took part in the conquest of the port of Acre, and then went home exhausted. That left only the English king Richard I, known to his countrymen as the Lionheart. Richard was a formidable warrior, but scarcely deserved the reputation he enjoyed back home as a paragon of chivalry. He broke promises lightly and did whatever it took to win battles. He and Saladin danced around each other for about a year, and Richard won the main battle they fought, but by the time he laid siege to Jerusalem in June of 1192, illness had reduced his strength and the heat had him panting. Saladin sympathetically sent him fresh fruit and cool snow and waited for Richard to realize that he didn't have the men to retake Jerusalem. Finally, Richard agreed to terms with Saladin, which were roughly as follows: Muslims would keep Jerusalem but protect Christian places of worship, let Christians live in the city and practice their faith without harassment, and let Christian pilgrims come and go as they pleased. Richard then headed home, preceded by the news that he had won a sort of victory at Jerusalem: he had forced Saladin to be nice. In fact, he had secured exactly the terms Saladin had offered from the start.

After this Third Crusade nothing of much significance happened, unless you count the Fourth Crusade of 1206 in which the Crusaders never even made it to the Holy Land because along the way they got preoccupied with conquering and sacking Constantinople and defiling its churches. By the mid-thirteenth century the whole crusading impulse had grown feeble in Europe and at last it just died away.

Historians traditionally count eight Crusades over the course of two hundred years, but really there was at least a trickle of crusaders arriving and leaving at any given time during those years. So it's probably more accurate to say that the Crusades lasted about two hundred years, with eight periods during which the traffic swelled, usually because some monarch or coalition of monarchs organized a campaign. Over these two centuries, "crusading" simply became an ongoing activity for Europeans, with some families sending one or two sons off to the wars in every generation, these sons departing when they came of age, not when "the next crusade" was leaving.

The first wave of European knights took a handful of cities and established four quasi-permanent "Crusader kingdoms," after which would-be crusaders from England or France or Germany always had a place to land and an army to join if they headed east. Some Christians of western European stock were of course born in these kingdoms and lived and died there, but many came east for a few years, did some fighting for the cause, acquired some booty if they were lucky, and went home. The Crusaders built impressive stone fortresses, but their sojourn in the east always had a temporary feel to it.

Some modern-day Islamist radicals (and a smattering of Western pundits) describe the Crusades as a great clash of civilizations foreshadowing the troubles of today. They trace the roots of modern Muslim rage to that era and those events. But reports from the Arab side don't show Muslims of the time thinking this way, at least at the start. No one seemed to cast the wars as an epic struggle between Islam and Christendom—that was the story line the Crusaders saw. Instead of a clash between two civilizations, Muslims saw simply a calamity falling upon . . . civilization. For one thing, when they looked at the Franj, they saw no evidence of civilization. An Arab prince named Usamah ibn Munqidh described the Franks as being like "beasts, superior in courage and in fighting ardor, but in nothing else, just as animals are superior in strength and aggression."[6] The Crusaders so disgusted the Muslims that they came to appreciate the Byzantines by contrast. Once they understood the political and religious motives of the Crusaders, they made a distinction between "al Rum" (Rome—i.e., the Byzantines) and "al-Ifranj." Instead of "the Crusades," Muslims called this period of violence the Franj Wars.

In areas under attack, Muslims did, of course, feel threatened by the Franj, even horrified by them, but they didn't see in these attacks any intellectual challenge to their ideas and beliefs. And although the Crusades were certainly a serious matter for Muslims living along the eastern Mediterranean coast, the Crusaders never penetrated deeply into the Muslim world. For example, no real army ever reached Mecca and Medina, only a small raiding party led by a renegade whom even other Franj regarded as a despicable rogue. The Crusaders never laid siege to Baghdad nor did they penetrate historic Persia. People in Khorasan and Bactria and the Indus Valley remained completely unaffected by the incursion and largely unaware of it.

What's more, the Crusades stimulated no particular curiosity in the Muslim world about Western Europe. No one expended much energy wondering where these Franj had come from, or what their life was like back home, or what they believed. In the early 1300s, Rashid al-Din Fazlullah, a Jewish convert to Islam, wrote an epic *Collection of All Histories*, which included the history of China, India, the Turks, the Jews, the pre-Islamic Persians, Mohammed, the khalifas, and the Franj, but even at this late date, the part about the Franks was perfunctory and undocumented.[7] In short, the Crusades brought virtually no European cultural viruses into the Islamic world. The influence ran almost entirely the other way.

And what flowed the other way? Well, the Crusaders opened up opportunities for European merchants in the Levant and Egypt. During the Franj wars, trade between western Europe and the Middle World increased. As a result, people in places like England, France, and Germany obtained exotic goods available in the East, products such as nutmeg, cloves, black pepper, and other spices, as well as silk, satin, and a fabric made from a wonderful plant called cotton.

European merchants, pilgrims, and Crusaders (the categories were not always distinct) returning to Europe reported on the riches of the Muslim world and told tales about even more distant lands, places such as India, and the near-mythic islands of "the Indies." These stories aroused appetites in Europe that kept growing over the years and were to have tremendous consequences later on.

In the Middle World, however, just as the calamity of the Crusades was subsiding, a second and far more catastrophic assault broke out.

ASSAULT FROM THE EAST

The Mongols originated in the steppes of Central Asia, a vast treeless grassland with hard soil and few rivers. The landscape precluded agriculture but it was perfect for herding sheep and grazing horses, so the Mongols lived on mutton, milk, and cheese, burned dung for fuel, got drunk on fermented mare's milk, and used oxen to pull their carts. They had no cities or permanent encampments but lived on the move, sleeping in felt huts called *gers* (known elsewhere as yurts), which they could easily dismantle and transport.

The Mongols were closely related to the Turks ethnically, linguistically, and culturally, and historians often group them together as the Turko-Mongol tribes. To the extent that they can be considered separately, however, the Turks generally lived further west and the Mongols further east. Where they overlapped, they intermingled somewhat.

Over the centuries a number of nomadic empires had formed and dissolved on the steppes, tribal confederacies that had no core principle of unity to hold them together. In the days of the Roman republic, a group of Turko-Mongol tribes called the Hsiung-nu congealed into a force so fearsome that the first emperor of a united China put about a million men to work building the Great Wall to keep them out. Once they couldn't raid eastward, the Hsiung-nu turned west and by the time they got to Europe these steppe nomads were known as the Huns. Under Attila they swept all the way to Rome before they dissolved.

In the early days of Islam, a series of ill-defined Turkish confederacies dominated the steppes, but once they moved south they morphed into Muslim dynasties, such as the Ghaznavids and the Seljuks.

The Mongols had raided the Chinese world for many centuries, and a succession of Chinese dynasties had kept them in check by giving them subsidies to stay away, by pitting Mongol chieftains against one another, and by funding upstarts against established chieftains. In this way they had kept the Mongols divided, although truth to tell, the Mongols, like tribal nomads generally, didn't need much outside help to stay divided.

Then around 560 AH (1165 CE) the brilliant and charismatic Temujin was born. History knows him as Chengez Khan (in the West, Genghis Khan), which means "universal ruler," a title he did not take on until he was about forty years old.

Chengez's father was a chieftain among the Mongols but was murdered when Chengez was nine. His supporters drifted away, and the family fell upon hard times. For several years, Chengez, his mother, and his younger siblings were forced to live on berries and small game, such as marmots and field mice. Even so his father's killers felt they would be safer if the son never grew up, so they hunted him throughout his teenage years, and even captured him once, but the boy escaped and did grow up, and lived to make his father's enemies sorry.

Along the way, he attracted a posse of close companions called *nokars*. In Persian-speaking lands, the word later came to mean "hired help," but in Chengez's day it meant "comrade in arms." Significantly, Chengez's nokars did not belong to any single clan or tribe. What held them together as a group was one man's charisma, so Chengez had, in his nokars, the seeds of an organization that transcended tribal loyalty and eventually helped him unite the Mongols into a single nation under his rule.

In 607 AH (1211 CE), Chengez's Mongols attacked China's decrepit old Sung Empire and cut through it like a knife into warm cheese. Seven years later, in 614 (1218 CE), the Mongols entered the history of the Middle World.

What sort of world did they come upon? Well, after the Seljuks conquered the Muslim world, other Turkish tribes followed them, gnawing away at the earlier Turkish victors' holdings, and carving out frontier kingdoms of their own. One such kingdom had just started to emerge in Transoxiana, and was looking very much like the next big thing in the region. It was the kingdom of the Khwarazm-Shahs. Their king Alaudin Mohammed considered himself quite the military mastermind, and in his arrogance decided to teach the Mongols a lesson. He started by intercepting 450 merchants traveling through his kingdom under Mongol protection. Accusing these poor merchants of spying for the Mongols, he had them killed and took their goods, but he quite deliberately let one man escape so that he would take news of the massacre back to Chengez. He was looking for trouble.

The Mongol lord sent three envoys west to demand reparations. It was probably the last time Chengez would show himself so forbearing. And now, Alaudin Mohammed made his really big mistake. He executed one of the envoys and sent the other two home with their beards plucked out. In this region, one could offer a man no more grievous insult than to pluck out his beard. Alaudin knew this full well, but he *wanted* to give offense, because he was spoiling for a fight—and he got one. In 615 AH (1219 CE) the great catastrophe began.

We often hear about the Mongol "hordes," a word that evokes pictures of howling savages swarming over the horizon by the millions to overwhelm their victims with sheer numbers. In fact, *horde* is simply the Turkic word for "military camp." The Mongols did not actually field incomparably huge armies. They won battles with strategy, ferocity, and, yes, technology. For example, when they attacked fortified cities, they employed sophisticated siege machinery acquired from the Chinese. They had "composite" bows made of several layers of wood glued together, which could shoot harder and further than the bows used in the "civilized" world. They fought on horseback, and their riding skills were such that some of their victims thought the Mongols were some new species of half-human, half-horse creature previously unknown to civilization. Their horses were hardy and fast but rather small, so a Mongol warrior could grip his horse with his legs, hang off on one side, and fire his arrows from under the horse's belly, thus using the body of the beast itself as a shield. Mongols could ride their horses for days and nights on end, sleeping in the saddle and taking nourishment from veins they opened on their horse's necks, so that after sacking one city they might suddenly appear at some distant other city so fast they seemed almost to have supernatural powers. Sometimes, the Mongols did bring along extra horses with dummies mounted on them to convey an impression of overwhelming numbers: it was just one more of their many military tricks.

In 615 AH (1219 CE) Alaudin Mohammed commanded far more troops than Chengez, but his immense army did him no good. Chengez smashed it and sent Alaudin fleeing for his life. Fragments of the Khwarazmi Turkish armies turned into gangs of thugs who rolled west, disrupting law and order, and even helped dislodge the last Crusaders from their fortresses, a foretaste of things to come. Chengez scorched Transoxiana, the lands on either side of the Oxus River and destroyed famous cities such as Bokhara, where the renaissance of Persian literature had begun two centuries earlier. He razed the legendary old city of Balkh, known to the ancients as "the Mother of Cities," dumping its library into the Oxus River, hundreds of thousands of handwritten volumes swept away.

Then he marched on Khorasan and Persia, and here the Mongols attempted genocide. No other word really seems appropriate. Writing shortly after the events in question, the Muslim historian Sayfi Heravi said the Mongols killed 1,747,000 when they sacked the city of Naishapur, killing everything down to the cats and dogs. At the city of Herat, he put the toll at 1,600,000. Another Persian historian, Juzjani, claimed that 2,400,000 died in Herat. Obviously these number are inflated. Herat and Naishapur could not possibly have had anywhere near this number of inhabitants in the 1220s.[8]

Yet the numbers might not be quite as inflated as they may seem at first because when the Mongols came down upon the Islamic world, people fled from their depredations—they had to. The Mongols burned fields, destroyed crops, stripped peasants of their livelihood, and promoted tales of their murderous fury as a strategy of war. They intended for the news and fear of their deeds to travel fast and far so that subsequent cities they attacked would not put up any fight.

One city they attacked in northern Afghanistan was called— well, I don't even know what it was called originally. Today, it's called Shari Gholghola—the City of Shrieking, and all you see there now is a heap of rubble and mud and stones. So it's quite possible that by the time the Mongols attacked any major city such as Herat, it was swollen by refugees from hundreds of miles around. It may be that when these cities finally fell, it wasn't just their original population but the population of the entire region that perished.

No one could really know how many died. Surely no one actually went out to the battlefields and counted the dead. But even if these numbers aren't really statistics, they function as impressions of scale, as expressions of how it felt to be alive in the shadow of such massacres, such horror. Nobody told any such stories about the Seljuks or the other earlier Turks. The Mongol invasion was clearly a disaster on a different scale.

Whatever the numbers were based on, there must have been some truth to them. Two histories completed around 658 AH (1260 CE), one in Baghdad, one in Delhi, gave almost exactly similar accounts of these

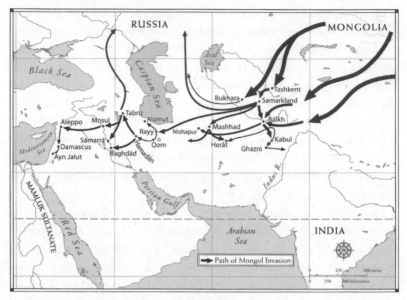

THE MONGOL INVASIONS OF THE ISLAMIC WORLD

horrors, roughly the same statistics for the casualties. The two historians could not have known each other, and they were writing more or less simultaneously, so neither one could have used the other as his source. Both then were recounting what was in the air, what people were saying from Delhi to Baghdad.

When the Mongols attacked Persia, they destroyed, among other things, the *qanat*, ancient underground canal works that were, to an agricultural society in a riverless land, life's blood itself. Some of the qanats were destroyed outright and some filled up with sand and vanished just as surely as if they had been deliberately destroyed because no one was left to repair them. When the Arab geographer Yaqut al-Hamawi wrote a description of western Iran, northern Afghanistan, and the republics north of the Oxus River a few years before the Mongol invasion, he described a fertile, flourishing province. A few years after the invasion, it was a desert. It still is.

Chengez did not live to carry out all the destruction wrought by the Mongols. He died in 624 AH (1227 CE), but after his death his empire was divided among his various sons and grandsons, who continued the holocaust. The core of the Muslim world fell into the hands of Chengez's grandson Hulagu, and since not all of this territory had been conquered yet, Hulagu took up where his grandfather had left off.

A curious footnote to the Mongol holocaust occurred in 653 AH (1256 CE), when Hulagu was passing through Persia. A Muslim jurist near Alamut complained to the Mongol khan that he had to wear armor under his clothes all the time for fear of the Assassins headquartered nearby. A short time later, two Fedayeen (suicidal Assassin agents) disguised as monks tried to kill Hulagu—and failed. They might as well have tried to pluck out the man's beard. The cult that could kill *anyone* met the army that could kill *everyone*. Hulagu took time out from his westward drive to storm Alamut. He then did to the Assassins what the Mongols had done and would do to many others: he destroyed them physically; he destroyed their stronghold; he destroyed their records, libraries, and papers—in that moment, the menace of the Assassins came to an end.[9]

After Hulagu had annihilated the Assassins, he marched on to Baghdad. There, he posted a threatening letter to the last Abassid khalifa, in which, according to the historian Rashid al-Din Fazlullah, he said, "The past is over. Destroy your ramparts, fill in your moats, turn the kingdom over to your son, and come to us. . . . If you do not heed our advice . . . get ready. When I lead my troops in wrath against Baghdad even if you hide in the sky or in the earth, I shall bring you down. I shall not leave one person alive in your realm, and I shall put your city and country to the torch. If you desire to have mercy on your ancient family's heads, heed my advice."

The Abbasid khalifate, however, had been showing signs of life recently, and an occasional khalifa had even bid for real power, at the head of actual troops. The khalifa in place at this moment was one of the cocky ones. In his pride, this khalifa wrote back to Hulagu: "Young man, you have just come of age and have expectations of living forever. You . . . think your command is absolute. . . . You come with strategy, troops, and lasso, but how are you going to capture a star? Does the prince not know that from the east to the west, from king to beggar, from old to young, all who are God-fearing and God worshipping are servants of this court and soldiers in my army? When I motion for all those who are dispersed to come together, I will deal first with Iran and then turn my attention to Turan, and I will put everything in its proper place."[10]

The attack on Baghdad began on February 3, 1258. By February 20, Baghdad was not just conquered. It was pretty much gone. The Mongols had a proscription against shedding royal blood; it ran against their traditions; they just didn't do that sort of thing. So they wrapped the khalifa and members of his family in carpets and kicked them to death. As for the citizens of Baghdad, Hulagu's Mongols killed virtually every one of them. The only ambiguity about how many people the Mongols killed at Baghdad has to do with how many there were to kill. Muslim sources put the toll at eight hundred thousand. Hulagu himself was more modest. In a letter to the king of France, he claimed he had killed only two hundred thousand. Whichever the case might be, the city itself was burned down, for Hulagu kept his promises. All the libraries and schools and hospitals, all of the city's archives and records, all the artifacts of civilization enshrined there, all the testimonials to the great surge of Islamic civilization in its golden age, perished utterly.

Only one power managed to hold the line against the Mongols and that was Egypt. No one else ever dealt the Mongols a straight-up military defeat, not here, not anywhere.

Saladin's descendants still ruled this region when the Mongol onslaught began, but by 1253 they were exhibiting the typical ailments of aging dynasties: pampered weaklings occupied the throne and predatory rivals circled round it. One day the king died, leaving no obvious heir. His wife Shajar al-Durr briefly took over as sultan, but then the mamluks, that corps of elite slave soldiers, got together and chose one of their own number to marry the sultan, whereupon he became the de facto sultan.

Hulagu was destroying Baghdad right about then. When he finished, he started south, following the well-traveled route of conquerors. But Egypt's greatest mamluk general, Zahir Baybars, confronted Hulagu at Ayn Jalut, which means "Goliath's spring." In biblical times, according to legends, David had defeated Goliath at this spot. Now, in 1260 CE, Baybars was the new David and Hulagu the new Goliath.[11]

David won again. (Incidentally, the Muslims used a new type of weapon in this battle: the hand cannon, or as we now call it, the gun. This might have been the first battle in which guns were used to any significant effect.)

Back in Cairo, meanwhile, Shajar al-Durr and her husband somehow killed each other in the bath—the sordid details remain murky. Baybars, covered with glory from his victory at Ayn Jalut, came marching into the confusion and took control, founding the so-called Mamluk dynasty.

A mamluk, as I mentioned, was a slave, usually Turkish, brought to the palace as a young boy and trained in all the military arts. Quite often in the history of the middle world, a mamluk had overthrown his master and launched a dynasty of his own. The one that Baybars founded, however, was different.

It wasn't a true "dynasty" because the principle of succession wasn't from father to son. Instead, each time a sultan died, his inner circle of most powerful mamluks chose one of their own number to be the new sultan. In the meantime, new mamluks kept rising through the ranks on merit, ascending into the circle of most-powerful mamluks, a position from which any of them might become the *next* sultan. Egypt, therefore, was not ruled by a family, but by a military corporation constantly refreshing its ranks with new mamluks. It was a meritocracy, and the system worked. Under the mamluks, Egypt became the leading nation in the Arab world, a status it has never really relinquished.

Although the Mongols conquered the Islamic world in a roaring flash, the Muslims ended up reconquering the Mongols, not by taking territories back through war, but by co-opting them through conversion. The first conversion occurred in 1257 CE, a khan named Berke. One of Hulagu's successors, Tode Mongke, not only converted but declared himself a Sufi. After that the Mongol ruling house of Persia produced more rulers with Muslim names. In 1295, Mahmoud Ghazan inherited the Persian throne. He had been a Buddhist but converted to Shi'ite Islam, and his nobles soon converted as well; his descendants went on to rule Persia as the Muslim Il-Khan dynasty.

After his conversion, Ghazan told his Mongol nobles to let up on the locals. "I am not protecting the Persian peasantry," he assured them. "If it is expedient, then let me pillage them all—there is no one with more power to do so than I. Let us rob them together! But—if you commit extortion against the peasants, take their oxen and seed, and cause their crops to be consumed—what will you do in the future? You must think, too, when you beat and torture their wives and children, that just as our wives and children are dear to our hearts, so are theirs to them. They are human beings, just as we are."[12] That doesn't sound like something Hulagu or Chengez would have said. Ghazan's words were one small sign that in the wake of the Mongol holocaust, Islam and civilization were going to come back to life after all.

10

Rebirth

661–1008 AH
1263–1600 CE

THE MONGOL HOLOCAUST wasn't like the Dark Ages of Europe. It didn't set in slowly and lift gradually. It was a terrible but brief explosion, like the Black Death that swept Europe in the fourteenth century, or the World Wars that wracked the globe in the twentieth.

Princeton historian Bernard Lewis, among others, has taken this to mean that the Mongols weren't really so bad. Yes, they destroyed whole cities, but look on the bright side: they left whole cities intact. Lewis has even said that "by modern standards," the destruction wrought by the Mongols was "trivial." His argument rests partly on the fact that within the Muslim world, Islamic civilization rapidly absorbed the Mongols. The ones who ended up in charge of Persia soon evolved into the benign Shi'ite Il-Khan dynasty. In converting to their subjects' religion, the Mongols even brought a fresh breeze, a new spirit, a cluster of new ideas into the Islamic world.

This is all very true, but it's a bit like saying the World Wars of the twentieth century were, in the final analysis, "trivial" because even though millions were killed, millions weren't, and even though countries such as Russia, Germany, France, and Great Britain were devastated, they quickly rebuilt and look at them now.

Some admiration has even accrued to Genghis Khan and his immediate successors based on the fact that they conducted mass-murder as a canny battle strategy and not out of sheer cruelty, destroying some cities utterly in order to make other cities give in without a fight. Reading such analyses, one might almost suppose the Mongols did their best to avoid needless bloodshed!

It is true that the most famous Mongol conquerors from Genghis to Hulagu look almost good in comparison to their descendant Timur-i-lang (Tamerlane, to the west) who emerged from Central Asia at the end of the fourteenth century and went on a bloody rampage that claimed countless further lives. Timur represented a last burst of the horror that began with Chengez Khan, rather like one of those movie monsters that twitches its tail after it seems dead and with that one final twitch cuts a sickening swath of new destruction.

For Timur, bloodshed was not just a canny battle strategy. He seemed to relish it for its own sake. It was he (not Chengez) who took pleasure in piling up pyramids of severed heads outside the gates of cities he had plundered. It was he, too, who executed captives by dropping them, still living, into tall, windowless towers until he had filled the towers to the brim. Timur banged and slaughtered his way to Asia Minor and then banged and slaughtered his way back again to India, where he left so many corpses rotting on the roads to Delhi that he made the whole region uninhabitable for months. His rampage was too horrific to go entirely unmentioned in any world history, but it doesn't deserve long consideration because it was essentially meaningless: he came, he saw, he killed, and then he died and his vast empire crumbled at once and no one remembers much about him anymore except that he was scary.

So yes, as an embodiment of pure savagery, Chengez Khan looks good compared to his descendant Timur (at least Timur claimed Chengez as an ancestor, though the line of descent remains obscure). But the original Mongol conquests had greater impact: they altered the trajectory of history.

First of all, they sparked a crisis for Muslim theology, and some responses to that crisis had ramifications that we are still wrestling with today. The crisis was rooted in the fact that Muslim theologians and scholars, and indeed Muslims in general, had long felt that Islam's military success proved its revelations true. Well, if victory meant the revelations were true, what did defeat mean?

Muslims had never before experienced such sweeping defeats, not anywhere in the world, not even in their nightmares. The historian Ibn al-Athir called the Mongol onslaught "a tremendous disaster" the likes of which the world might never experience again "from now until its end." Another major Muslim historian speculated that the coming of the Mongols portended the end of the world. According to yet another, the Mongol victories showed that God had abandoned Muslims. [1]

The Crusaders had at least been Christians, but the Mongols? They weren't even "people of the book." Their victories posed an agonizing puzzle for theologians and tested the faith of the masses in some pervasive way that many people probably felt but didn't intellectualize. Especially in post-Crusader Mesopotamia, after the sack of Baghdad, where the Muslim community had suffered its most devastating setback, any thinking person who subscribed to the premise that universalizing the Muslim community was the purpose of history might well have asked, "What went wrong?"

The hardest-hitting response was delivered by the Syrian jurist Ibn Taymiyah. His family originated in Harran, a town near the intersection of present-day Syria, Iraq, and Turkey, right in the path of the Mongol invasion. They fled the wrath of Hulagu with nothing but their books, ending up in Damascus, where Ibn Taymiyah grew up. He studied the standard Islamic disciplines with unusual brilliance and earned, at an early age, the standing to issue *fatwas,* religious rulings.

Intense horrors tend to spawn extreme opinions, and Ibn Taymiyah was rooted in his times. No doubt the anxiety of his uprooted family gave him an emotional stake in puzzling out the meaning of the Mongol catastrophe, or perhaps his personality would have inclined him to the views he propounded no matter when or where he was born—who can tell? But in a Syria so recently crushed by the Mongols and still suffering the residue of the Crusades, Ibn Taymiyah at least found a ready audience for his thoughts. If he had never been born, the audience that embraced him might well have found someone else to express those same ideas.

Ibn Taymiyah propounded three main points. First, he said there was nothing wrong with Islam, nothing false about the revelations, and nothing bogus about seeing Muslim victories as proof of them. The problem, he proposed, lay with Muslims: they had stopped practicing "true" Islam, and God therefore had made them weak. To get back to their victorious ways, Muslims had to go back to the book and purge Islam of all new ideas, interpretations, and innovations: they must go back to the religious ways of Mohammed and his companions, back to those values and ideals, back to the material details of their everyday lives: the earliest rulings were the best rulings. That was the core of his judicial creed.

Second, Ibn Taymiyah asserted that jihad was a core obligation of every Muslim, right in there with praying, fasting, abjuring deceit, and other sacramental practices; and when Ibn Taymiyah said "jihad" he meant "strap on a sword." The Umma, he said, was special because they were martial. No previous recipients of revelations from God had "enjoined *all* people with *all* that is right, nor did they prohibit *all* that is wrong to *all* people." Some of them did not "take up armed struggle at all," while others struggled merely "for the purpose of driving their enemy from their land, or as any oppressed people struggles against their oppressor." To Ibn Taymiyah, this limited, defensive idea of jihad was inaccurate: jihad meant actively struggling, fighting even, not just to defend one's life, home, and property but to expand the community of those who obeyed Allah.

Ibn Taymiyah went to war himself, against some Mongols. The Mongols he was fighting had converted to Islam by this time, which raised a question about Muslims fighting Muslims. But fighting these Muslims was legitimate jihad, Ibn Taymiyah expounded, because they were not real Muslims. He also opposed Christians, Jews, Sufis, and Muslims of other sects than his own—chiefly Shi'is. He once overheard a Christian making derogatory comments about the Prophet, and that night, he and a friend tracked down that Christian and beat him up.

You can see why his aggressive stance might have resonated for some of his contemporaries. Basically, he was saying, "We can't roll over for pagan Mongols and Crusaders; let's come together and fight back, finding strength in unity and unity in singleness of doctrine!" This sort of rallying cry has inevitable appeal in societies under attack by outsiders, and by this time the Islamic world had been under fearsome attack for over a century.

Ibn Taymiyah expanded the list of those against whom jihad was valid to include not just non-Muslims but heretics, apostates, and schismatics. In these categories he included Muslims who attempted to amend Islam or promoted division by interpreting the Qur'an and hadith in ways that departed from what the texts literally stated.

Ibn Taymiyah never conceded that he was pressing for his interpretation versus some other interpretation. He maintained that he was trying to stamp out unwarranted interpretation per se and urging Muslims to go back to the book, implying that the Qur'an (and hadith) existed in some absolute form, free of human interpretation.

Some would say that singling out heretics and schismatics had not been the spirit of early Islam. Arguments about the succession, yes; even bloody arguments. But Mohammed himself and the early Muslims in general tended to accept that people who wanted to be Muslims *were* Muslims. ("Hypocrites"—traitors pretending to be Muslims in order to undermine the community from within—were obviously a different case.) With all would-be Muslims accepted into the group, the group could sort out disagreements about what "Muslim" meant. Ibn Taymiyah, however, insisted that there was one way to be a Muslim, and the main Muslim duty was to ascertain that one way and then follow it. Interpretation did not come into it, since everything a person needed to know about Islam was right there in the book in black and white.

Ibn Taymiyah mythologized the perfection of life in that first community, referring to Mohammed's companions as *al-saluf al-salihin*, "the pious (or pristine) originals." Versions of his doctrines eventually reemerged in India and North Africa as the movement called Salafism, which is with us to this day. The word comes up often in news stories about "Islamists." It started here, in the shadow of the Mongol holocaust.

In his own day, Ibn Taymiyah built up only a moderate following. The masses didn't care for him much, probably because he punished Muslims for folk practices they had incorporated into their idea of Islam and also for visiting shrines. Ibn Taymiyah claimed that showing reverence for human beings, even great ones, went against the precepts of the Pious Originals.

The authorities liked him even less because he denounced rulings they accepted as established. When called before a panel of ulama to defend his rulings, he rejected their authority, charging that they had lost their legitimacy by succumbing to innovations and interpretations. On one disputed doctrine after another, Ibn Taymiyah would not go along to get along. The actual points disputed will strike non-Muslims as minutely technical: for example, was a divorce uttered three times merely final or *irrevocably* final? The establishment said it was irrevocable; Ibn Taymiyah said final but not irrevocable. In this instance, the authorities settled the argument by clapping Ibn Taymiyah in prison. He spent a lot of time in prison. In fact, he died there.

Ibn Taymiyah does not sum up what Islam is, nor even what it was in the thirteenth century—there are so many schools of thought, so many approaches—but the very attitudes that made so many clerics and officials angry with Ibn Taymiyah led many others to admire him. Ibn Taymiyah belonged to the school of Muslim jurisprudence founded by Ibn Hanbal, that Abbasid-era scholar who took a bulldog stand against the primacy and sufficiency of reason. Ibn Hanbal had favored the most literal reading of the Qur'an and the most literalist methods for applying it, for the most part rejecting even analogical reasoning as a way of expanding the doctrines, and so did Ibn Taymiyah. Both men had flinty, combative, unbending temperaments. The fact that both went to prison for their ideas tended to ennoble their legacy quite apart from whatever intellectual merits their ideas may have had.

The identification of courage with truth pops up often in history, even in our day: talk-show host Bill Maher was kicked off network TV for suggesting that the suicide hijackers of 9/11 were brave. Common decency demands that no positive character traits be associated with someone whose actions and ideas are vicious. Unfortunately, this equation enables people to validate questionable ideas by defending them with courage, as if a coward cannot say something that is true or a brave man something that is false. Ibn Hanbal had benefited from this syndrome and, now, so did Ibn Taymiyah.

Ibn Taymiyah reputedly wrote about four thousand pamphlets and five hundred books. With these, he planted a seed. The seed didn't flourish at once, but it never died out, either. It just lay there, under the surface of Islamic culture, ready to bud if circumstances should ever favor it. Four and a half centuries later, circumstances did.

There was another response to the centuries of breakdown that climaxed with the Mongol holocaust, a more popular and gentler response than

Salafism, and this was the efflorescence of Sufism, which was as broad-minded and undogmatic as Ibn Taymiyah's ideology was literalist and restrictive. Indeed, ecstatic Sufism (as opposed to "sober Sufism") disturbed Ibn Taymiyah almost as much as pagan invaders, because to him infidels were merely the enemy outside, assaulting Islam, whereas Sufism was the enemy within, insidiously weakening the Umma by enlarging and blurring the singleness of the doctrine that defined it.

Sufism was that characteristically Islamic type of mysticism which had some ideas and impulses in common with Buddhism and Hindu mysticism. Sufis were individuals who, dissatisfied with the bureaucratization of religion, turned inward and sought methods of achieving mystical union with God.

All Sufis had pretty much the same idea about where they were going, but diverse ideas about how to get there, so different Sufis espoused different spiritual techniques. Every time a Sufi seemed to break through, the word spread and other seekers flocked to the enlightened soul for guidance, hoping that direct contact with his or her charisma would fuel their own quest for transcendence. In this way, "Sufi brotherhoods" formed around prominent individual Sufis: groups of seekers who lived, worked, and practiced their devotions together under the guidance of a master called a *sheikh* or *pir* (both words mean "old man," the one in Arabic, the other in Persian).

Typically, a few of a sheikh's closest disciples earned recognition as Sufi masters in their own right. When a sheikh died, one of these disciples would inherit his authority and continue guiding his community. Some others might go off and form new communities, still expounding their master's mystical method but attracting disciples of their own. Sufi brotherhoods thus evolved into Sufi orders, traditions of mystical methodology passed down directly from master to initiate, down through the years and the decades and the centuries.

Successful Sufi orders might boast of many enlightened sheikhs at any given time, living in different places, often with their *mureeds* (spiritual apprentices), in lodges called *khanqas,* where they also offered sustenance to travelers and comfort to strangers. In a way, then, Sufi brotherhoods became an Islamic equivalent of Christianity's monastic orders which, in medieval times, built monasteries and nunneries throughout Europe, places where people retired to make spiritual effort their main occupation.

Yet Sufi brotherhoods also differed in crucial ways from monastic orders. For one thing, every monastic order had a set of strict rules that monks or nuns had to follow, under the direction of an abbot or abbess. Sufi brotherhoods were much looser and more informal, more about companionship and less about externally imposed discipline.

Furthermore, taking the vows of any of the Christian monastic orders meant renunciation of the world and some commitment to "mortification of the flesh." That's because Christianity focused essentially on personal salvation, and saw salvation as something people needed because they were born guilty of "original sin," the discovery of sexuality in the Garden of Eden. For this sin, humanity had been sentenced to imprisonment in bodies that lived (and died) in the material world.

Monks or nuns joined an order specifically to separate themselves from the world, the emblem of man's fallen state. Their devotions were aimed at punishing their bodies, because the body was the problem. They practiced celibacy as a matter of course, because Christianity saw spirituality as the remedy for sexuality.

In Islam, however, the emphasis was not on the personal salvation of the isolated soul but on construction of the perfect community. People were not sinners to be saved but servants enjoined to obedience. They were born innocent and capable of ascent to the highest nobility but also of descent to the lowest depravity.[2] The mureeds in a Sufi order joined up not to be saved but to attain a higher state; their rituals were aimed not at punishing their bodies but at focusing their energies on Allah alone; if they fasted, for instance, it was not to mortify their flesh but to strengthen their self-discipline. They saw no equation between celibacy and spirituality and did not separate from the world. Sufis and would-be Sufis usually plied trades, bought and sold, married, reared children, and went to war.

In fact, some Sufi brotherhoods evolved into bands of mystical knights, espousing an ethos called *futuwwah,* which resembled the European code of knightly valor, courtly love, and chivalric honor. Whether the influence ran from west to east, or vice versa, or both ways is a dispute I won't get into.

In any case, Sufis illustrated futuwwah ideals through mytho-poetic anecdotes about Muslim heroes of the first community. One such story, for example, told of a young traveler arrested for killing an old man. The victim's sons brought this young man before Khalifa Omar. The traveler admitted his deed. Extenuating circumstances existed, but he refused to plead them; he had taken a life and so must forfeit his own. He did make one request, however: could the execution be delayed for three days while he went home and took care of a bit of business? He had an orphan in his care back there, he had buried this child's inheritance in a spot no one knew about, and if he didn't dig it up before he died, the child would be left penniless. It wasn't fair that the child suffer for his guardian's crime. "If you let me go today," the murderer said, "I promise I'll come back three days from now and submit to execution."

The khalifa said, "Well, okay, but only if you name someone to act as your proxy, someone who will agree to suffer the penalty in your stead if you don't come back."

Well, that stumped the young traveler. He had no friends or relatives in these parts. What stranger would trust him enough to risk execution in his place?

At that moment, Abu Dharr, one of the Prophet's companions, declared that he would be the young man's proxy. And so the murderer departed.

Three days later he had not returned. No one was surprised but they did weep for poor Abu Dharr who faithfully set his head on the chopping block. The executioner was just oiling his ax and getting ready to chop when the young man came galloping up on a dusty horse, all covered with sweat. "I'm sorry, I'm sorry, I was delayed," he said, "but here I am now. Let's proceed with the execution."

The spectators were amazed. "You were free; you had totally escaped. No one could have found you and brought you back. Why did you return?"

"Because I said I would, and I am a Muslim," the young man replied. "How could I give the world cause to say that Muslims no longer keep their promises?"

The crowd turned to Abu Dharr. "Did you know this young man? Did you know of his noble character? Is this why you agreed to be his proxy?"

"No," said Abu Dharr, "I never met him before in my life, but how could I be the one to let the world say Muslims are no longer compassionate?"

The victim's relatives now dropped to their knees. "Don't execute him," they pleaded. "How can we be the ones to make the world say there is no forgiveness in Islam?"

Many proponents of Sufi chivalry traced their lineage back to Ali, not necessarily because they were Shi'i but because Ali enjoyed legendary renown as the perfect knight, the ideal combination of strength, courage, piety, and honor. It was said, for example, that in one of those iconic battles of early Islam, a young man came toward Ali, swinging a sword. Ali said, "Don't you know who I am, you foolhardy youngster? I'm Ali! You can't beat me. I'll kill you. Why are you attacking me?"

"Because I am in love," said the young fellow, "and my sweetheart says that if I kill you, she'll be mine."

"But if we fight, I am more likely to kill *you*," Ali pointed out.

"What's better than dying for love?" the young man said.

Upon hearing those words, Ali took off his helmet and stretched out his neck. "Strike right here."

Seeing Ali's willingness to die for love, however, set that young man's heart ablaze and turned his love for a woman into something higher—love of Allah. In a single moment, Ali transformed an ordinary young man into an enlightened Sufi.[3] Such were the legends that inspired these Muslim knights.

THE OTTOMANS (ABOUT 700 TO 1341 AH)

Although Sufi orders proliferated through the Muslim world, they had the most profound consequences in Asia Minor, also known as Anatolia, the territory that constitutes modern Turkey. It was here that the post-Mongol recovery of Islam began.

In Asia Minor, Sufi orders linked up with merchants' and artisans' guilds called *akhi* (the Turkish word for futuwwah). These outfits cushioned ordinary folks against the uncertainties of the time. Certainly, people needed some cushioning. Asia Minor had long been the frontier between Turkish Muslims and European Christians. The Seljuks and Byzantines had torn the land up, fighting over it. One Seljuk prince had forged a fairly stable sovereign state here called the Sultanate of Rum (*Rum* being the Arabization of *Rome*) but then armies of Crusaders crisscrossing the land had disrupted order, and Seljuks fighting among themselves had eroded stability further.

By the time the Crusades were winding down, various Turkish princes more or less controlled eastern Asia Minor, but only more or less; the Byzantine more or less controlled the western parts, but only more or less; and no claim went undisputed by the other. Asia Minor had become a lawless no-man's land, inhabited by both Christians and Turks and ruled by no one.

The Mongol eruptions drove fresh hordes of Turkish pastoral nomads out of Central Asia. They drifted until they reached Asia Minor, but here finally they felt at home. Why here? Because pastoral nomads tended to like this sort of lawless environment. As autonomous self-ruling clans, they had their own leaders and laws and just felt crimped by the sort of law and order governments imposed. In a disputed frontier zone they could roam where they wanted, graze their herds where they wished, and supplement their needs by raiding settled folks according to the time-tested traditions of the steppes they had once called home.

Christians still lived in this anarchic zone, small towns and villages endured, but no government guaranteed the safety of the roads, no police came to the aid of anyone whose store got robbed, and no agency rushed to help in cases of fire, flood, or other catastrophe. The public sphere had eroded, so one had nobody to turn to in times of trouble except one's clan, one's friends and—one's Sufi brothers.

As the new Sufism proliferated through this region, itinerant mystics began to roam the land. Some came from Persia and further east; some emerged locally. Many were *dervishes*, men who embraced voluntary poverty as a spiritual exercise. They didn't work but lived on alms in order that they might free up all their time to contemplate God.

Many of these mystic vagabonds were also eccentrics; if you were living on alms, there was probably some advantage to standing out from the crowd. Kalendar, one of the earliest of these mystic vagabonds, wandered from town to town with bands of followers, all beating drums, chanting, singing, shouting, ranting, wildly exhorting people to come to Allah and urging them also to fight the infidels, fight them, fight! He and his followers had unkempt hair, they dressed in rags, and they disturbed the peace, but they excited fervid passions and strange ideas, and wherever Kalendar went, Kalendari brotherhoods sprouted in his wake.

Almost as a defense against wild men like Kalendar, more respectable people embraced another mystic named Bektash, an austere ascetic. For all his clerical sobriety, Bektash had a disturbing intensity about him, but at least he didn't shout. He became the favorite Sufi of the ulama.

Then there were the Mevlevi dervishes, darlings of the intellectuals and cognoscenti. They sprang up around a poet named Jalaludin, who was born in Balkh, for which reason, in Afghanistan, he is known as Jalaludin-i Balkhi. He was a boy when Mongol power began to coalesce around Genghis Khan. His father smelled trouble coming and moved the family west to what was left of the sultanate of Rum, for which reason most of the world knows this poet as Jalaludin-i Rumi ("Jalaludin the Roman.")

Rumi's learned father founded a school, and Rumi began teaching there once he came of age, for he acquired his own reputation for learning. He wrote conventional religious treatises that gained him great respect and attracted numerous students, who crowded into his lectures and hung on his every word.

The key moment in Rumi's legendary biography occurred one day when a ragged stranger came into his classroom. The stranger sat in the back but he wouldn't keep his mouth shut. He kept bursting into song, disrupting the lecture—he seemed crazy. The stories about this stranger remind one of the young Jack Kerouac ceaselessly shouting "Go!" from the back of the room when Alan Ginsberg was reading *Howl* for the first time in public. Rumi's students grabbed hold of the beggar and tried to throw him out of the room, but their professor made them stop and asked the man who he was and what he wanted.

"I am Shams-i Tabrez," the stranger said, "and I have come for you."

To the astonishment of his students, Rumi closed his book, cast off his scholar's cloak, and said, "My teaching days are over. This is my master." He walked out of the classroom with Shams, never to return.

Jalaludin and the beggar became inseparable. These two bonded passionately but on a purely spiritual level, bonded so utterly that Rumi began to sign his poetry with his master's name: his lyrics from this period have been collected as *The Works of Shams-i Tabrez*. Before Rumi met Shams, he was a respected writer whose work might have been read for a hundred years. After he met Shams, he became one of the greatest mystic poets in the history of literature.

After a number of years, Shams mysteriously disappeared, and Rumi went on to compose a single thousand-page poem called *Mathnawi Ma'nawi* (*The Spiritual Manuscript*). In the famous opening passage, Rumi poses a question: why is the melody of the flute so piercingly sad? Then he answers his own question: because the flute started out as a reed, growing by the river bank, rooted in soil. When it was made into a flute, it was severed from its roots. The sorrow keening in its song is the reed's wistful memory of its lost connection to the source. In the next thirty thousand couplets, Rumi delivers hundreds of stories in a language thrumming with eroticized religiosity, illustrating how we human flutes can recover our connection to the source. Rumi remains influential, even in the English-speaking world, where translations of his work outsell those of every other poet.[4]

In short, Sufism had something for every taste and class. Sufis converted the pastoral nomads to Islam, so these tribes imbibed the passions of Islam before absorbing its doctrines. Sufi orders intertwined with artisans' guilds, with merchants associations, with the peasantry, with aristocratic military groups—like a web, Sufism connected all the disparate groups in this atomized world.

Some Sufi brotherhoods devoted to futuwwah ideals developed into ghazi corporations. The word *ghazi* meant something like "warrior saint." Ghazis were reminiscent of the Knights Templar and other Christian military orders spawned during the Crusades, except that no one ordained them, Islam having no pope-like figure to do the ordaining. Instead, ghazis ordained themselves, forming around some masterful knight and taking inspiration from some charismatic sheikh. They adopted special headgear and cloaks and other accessories as badges of membership in their group. They had initiation rituals involving vows, pledges, iconic artifacts and arcane relics, much the same sorts of things boys cook up when they form "secret clubs."

Members of ghazi orders centered their lives around campaigns into Christian territory to perform great deeds of valor for the advancement of the one true faith. They were very much like an Islamic version of the knights of Arthurian legend.

Hundreds of these ghazi group sprang up, big ones and little ones. In search of fame and fortune, these knights sallied into the frontier "marches," that ever-growing belt of territory that the Byzantines still officially claimed but where their authority had grown dubious. Once in a while some ghazi chieftain secured enough territory to claim a little state of his own, whereupon he promptly declared himself an amir (also *emir*) and his little state an emirate. "Amir" was an Islamic title that had once meant "commander" but now meant something more like "prince."

With eastern Anatolia crystallizing into numerous little ghazi emirates, Byzantine power shrank and the lawless frontier zone receded westward—which posed an ironic contradiction: the frontier marches were mother's milk to the ghazi states. As the disputed zone moved, so did the ghazi knights; they leaked away from the established emirates and off into the wild west, where a man could still prove himself in battle and incidentally score some plunder.

At a certain point, however, the wild west stopped receding because the frontier was close enough to Constantinople that the Byzantines could make a stand. Ghazi knights draining from the east began to accumulate in these frontline states situated nose to nose with Byzantine power. Knights could find employment here for at least fifty years after fighting had faded out in the rest of Anatolia. The frontline states accordingly grew ever stronger while the eastern emirates grew ever weaker. It was here on this militarized frontier, therefore, that a new world empire was born.[5]

In 1258 CE, the very year Hulagu destroyed Baghdad, a boy named Othman was born to a leading ghazi family in Anatolia. Othman's descendants were called the Othmanlis, or Ottomans, as people in the West pronounced it, and they ended up building a mighty empire.

Not that Othman himself built an empire; he only managed to construct the toughest little ghazi emirate in Anatolia. His recent ancestors had been pastoral nomads out of Central Asia, a clan of about four hundred fleeing the Mongols, and he had not moved far from his roots. His palace was his horse, his throne his saddle, and his office his saddlebag. His capital was wherever he camped for the night. All he really bequeathed to his successors was a process. In the fighting season, he would lead his men into the frontier provinces and accumulate booty by fighting Christians. In the "off-season," he collected taxes from any productive settled folks he found in areas he controlled.

As the Ottomans grew stronger, they began to absorb other ghazi states, sometimes by conquering them, sometimes by out-and-out buying them. Ghazi chieftains who had been sovereign emirs became feudal aristocrats, still powerful in their own right but subservient to an even greater power, the head of the Ottoman dynasty.

The Ottomans profited from the single most crucial bit of luck that makes the difference between success and failure for a family dynasty: it had a series of long-lived rulers, all of them pretty capable. One of them, Murat I, sailed across the Black Sea and began adding bits of Europe to his conquests. By his era (1350–1389 CE) the Ottoman dynasty no longer ruled from horseback but had an urban capital, a palace, a government bureaucracy, a tax policy, a treasury. Ottoman rulers adopted a veneer of high Islamic civilization, not to mention some of the rituals, pomp, and ceremonials of the Byzantine court.

Another Ottoman ruler, Bayazid I (1389–1402) launched a program called the *devshirme*, which consisted of bringing captured boys from Christian Europe back to his palace, raising them as Muslims, and developing them into crack soldiers. These were really just the familiar mamluks of Islamic history by another name; mamluks were Turkish boys growing up in Arab or Persian courts, these were Christian boys growing up in a Turkish court. The soldiers developed by the devshirme were called *janissaries*, a corruption of the Turkish phrase *Yeni Ceri*, which means "new troops."

Bayazid's janissaries liberated him from his own feudal lieges, those recently sovereign aristocratic ghazis who traced their descent back to Central Asia. Their troops still provided Bayazid with foot soldiers, but the janissaries gave him a professional corps of officers to lead them.

Bayazid's raids reached ever deeper into Europe. The kings of France and Hungary got together and organized a force to check him, but Bayazid demolished their joint army in 1396, at Nicopolis, a town in present-day Bulgaria. Now the amir of the Ottomans truly ruled an empire. In fact, Bayazid had outgrown the title of amir. He called himself the sultan, thereby declaring himself the chief executive of Dar al-Islam, a secular version of the khalifa. His military adventures became full-blown campaigns, and every year he launched a new one, striking west one year, heading east the next year to absorb more ghazi emirates and extend his rule into the old Muslim heartland. Back and forth he scuttled, moving at such speed that people began to call him the Thunderbolt. Bayazid acquired the swagger of a Caesar.

Then it all came crashing down. On one of his forays east, Bayazid ran into a warrior tougher than himself—the dreaded Timur-i-lang. Bayazid's own feudal lieges had called Timur into Anatolia. They resented having lost sovereignty to the Ottomans, and so they sent a message to Timur, complaining that Bayazid was spending so much time in Europe, he was turning into a Christian. Well, Timur-i-lang would have none of that, for along with being a ruthless savage of unparalleled cruelty, Timur was also a Muslim who fancied himself a patron of the high arts, a scholar in his own right, and a devout defender of Islam.

In 1402, near the city of Ankara, these two civilized patrons of the arts set niceties aside and went at each other blade to axe, and may the worst man win. Timur-i-lang proved himself the more brutal of the two. He crushed the Ottoman army, took Emperor Bayazid himself prisoner, clapped him in a cage like some zoo animal, and hauled him back to his jewel-encrusted lair in Central Asia, the city of Samarqand. Despair and humiliation so overwhelmed Bayazid that he committed suicide. Out west, Bayazid's sons began to war with each other over the truncated remains of his one-time empire.

It looked like the end of the Ottomans. It looked like they would end up having been just another of the many meteoric Turkish kingdoms that flashed and fizzled. But in fact, this kingdom was different. From Othman to Bayazid, the Ottomans had not just conquered; they had woven a new social order (which I will describe a few pages further on). For now, suffice to say that in the aftermath of Timur's depredations, they had deep social resources to draw upon. Timur died within decades, his empire tattered quickly down to a small (but culturally brilliant) kingdom in western Afghanistan. The Ottoman Empire, by contrast, not only recovered, it began to rise.

In 1452 it jumped to a higher level, a stage that began when a new emperor named Sultan Mehmet took the throne. Mehmet inherited an empire in good shape, but he brought one problem to the throne. He was only twenty-one and tougher, older men circled him hungrily, each one thinking that an older, tougher, hungrier man (like himself) might make a better sultan. Mehmet knew he had to do something spectacular to back down potential rivals and cement his grip on power.

So he decided to conquer Constantinople.

Constantinople no longer represented a really important military prize. The Ottomans had already skirted it, pushing into eastern Europe. Constantinople was more of a psychological prize: the city had immense symbolic significance for both east and west.

To the west, an unbroken line ran from Constantinople back to the Rome of Augustus and Julius Caesar. To Christians, this was still the capital of the Roman Empire, which Constantine had infused with Christianity. It was only later historians who looked at this eastern phase of Roman history and called it by a new name. The Byzantines themselves called themselves Romans, and thought of their city as the new Rome.

As for Muslims, Prophet Mohammed himself had once said that the final victory of Islam would be at hand when Muslims took Constantinople. In the third century of Islam, the Arab philosopher al-Kindi had speculated that the Muslim who took Constantinople would renew Islam and go on to rule the world. Many scholars said the conqueror of Constantinople would be the Mahdi, "the Expected One," the mystical figure whom many Muslims expected to see when history approached its endpoint. Mehmet therefore had good reason to believe that taking Constantinople would be a public relations coup that would make the whole world look at him differently.

The many technical experts now working for the Ottomans included a Hungarian engineer named Urban, who specialized in building cannons, still a relatively new type of weapon. Sultan Mehmet asked Urban to build him something special along these lines. Urban set up a foundry about 150 miles from Constantinople and poured out artillery. His masterpiece was a cannon twenty-seven feet long and so big around that a man could crawl down inside it. The so-called Basilic could fire a twelve-hundred-pound granite stone a mile.

It took ninety oxen and about four hundred men to transport this monstrous gun to the battlefield. As it turned out, the Basilic was *too* big: it took more than three hours to load, and each time it fired it recoiled so hard it tended to kill more people behind it than in front of it. Besides, at a distance of a mile, it was so inaccurate it actually missed the whole city of Constantinople; but this didn't matter. The big gun wasn't an important military asset so much as an important symbolic asset—announcing to the world that *this* was the sort of weapon the Ottomans brought to the field. In addition to the Basilic they had, of course, many smaller cannons. They were the best armed and most technologically advanced army of their time.

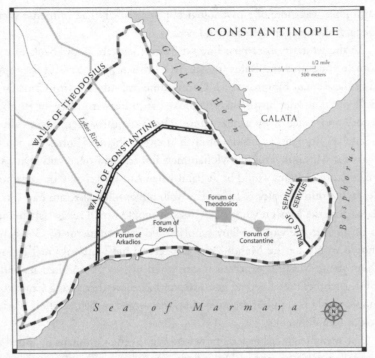

CONSTANTINOPLE: THE WORLD'S MOST IMPREGNABLE CITY

The siege of Constantinople lasted fifty-four days, the city being all but impregnable. Located on a triangular spit of land shaped like a rhinoceros horn, it faced the Bosporus Straits on one side and the Sea of Marmara on another. On these sides it had high sea walls and promontories commanding the narrow straits, from which the Byzantines could bombard any ships approaching the city. On the land side, it had a series of stone walls that stretched across the whole peninsula from sea to sea, each wall with its own moat. Each moat was broader and deeper and each wall thicker and taller than the one before. The innermost wall stood ninety feet high and was more than thirty feet thick; no one could get past that barrier, especially since the Byzantines had a secret weapon called Byzantine fire, a glutinous burning substance that was launched from catapults and splashed when it landed, sticking to flesh. It could not be doused with water—in fact, it was probably some primitive form of napalm.

The Ottomans persisted, however. The cannons kept booming, the janissaries kept charging, the immense besieging army made up of recruits from many different tribes and populations including Arabs, Persians, and even European Christians kept storming the ramparts, but in the end, the battle turned on the fact that someone forgot to close one small door in one corner of the third and most impregnable wall. A few Turks forced their way in through there, secured the sector, opened a larger gate to their compatriots, and suddenly the most enduring capital of the western world's longest lasting empire was going down in flames.

Mehmet gave his troops permission to loot Constantinople for three days but not one minute longer. He wanted his troops to preserve the city, not destroy it, because he meant to use it as his own capital. From this time on, the city came to be known informally as Istanbul (the formal name change would not occur until centuries later) and the victorious sultan was henceforth called Mehmet the Conqueror.

Imagine for a moment what might have happened if Muslims had taken Constantinople during the prime of Islam's expansion, if Constantinople rather than Baghdad had been the capital of the Abbasids: straddling the waters linking the Black Sea to the Mediterranean, possessing all the ports they needed to launch navies across the Aegean and Mediterranean to Greece and Italy and on to Spain and the French Coast and through the Straits of Gibraltar up the Atlantic coast to England and Scandinavia, combined with their proven prowess in land warfare—all of Europe might well have been absorbed into the Islamic empire.

But seven hundred years had passed since the prime of the khalifate. Europe was no longer a wretched continent eking out a meager existence in squalid poverty. It was a continent on the rise. On the Iberian peninsula, Catholic monarchs were busy driving the last embattled Muslims back to Africa and funding sailors like Columbus to go explore the world. Belgium had developed into a banking capital, the Dutch were busy cooking up an awesome business expertise, the continent of Italy was muscling up into the Renaissance, and England and France were coalescing into nation-states. Constantinople (Istanbul) gave the Ottomans a peerless base of operations, but Christian Europe was no longer any pushover. At the time, however, no one knew who was on the rise and who on the decline, and with the Ottoman triumph, Islam certainly looked resurgent to the Muslim world at large.

Istanbul had only about seventy thousand people at the time of the conquest, so Mehmet the Conqueror launched a set of policies such as tax concessions and property giveaways to repopulate his new capital. Mehmet also reestablished the classical Islamic principles of conquest: non-Muslims were accorded religious freedom and left in possession of their land and property but had to pay the *jizya*. People of every religion and ethnicity came flowing in, making Istanbul a microcosm of an empire pulsing with diversity.[6]

Now the Ottomans ruled an empire that straddled Europe and Asia with substantial territory in both continents. The greatest city in the world was theirs. Their greatest achievement, however, wasn't conquest. Somehow, in the course of their fifteen decades of rule, they had brought a unique new social order into being. Somehow, that anarchic soup of nomads, peasants, tribal warriors, mystics, knights, artisans, merchants, and miscellaneous others populating Anatolia had coalesced into a society of clockwork complexity full of interlocking parts that balanced one another, each acting as a spur and check on the others. Nothing like it had been seen before, and nothing like it has been seen again. Only contemporary American society offers an adequate analogy to the complexity of Ottoman society—but only to the complexity. The devil is in the details, and our world differs from that of the Ottomans in just about every detail.

Broadly speaking, the Ottoman world was divided horizontally between a ruling class that taxed, organized, issued orders, and fought, and a subject class that produced and paid taxes. But it was also organized vertically by Sufi orders and brotherhoods. So people separated by their classes might find themselves united in reverence to the same sheikh.

On the other hand, Ottoman society as a whole was compartmentalized into the major religious communities, each with its own vertical and horizontal divisions, and each a semi-autonomous nation or *millet,* in charge of its own religious rites, education, justice, charities, and social services.

The Jews, for example, were one millet, headed by the grand rabbi in Istanbul, a considerable community because Jews came flocking into the Ottoman world throughout the fourteenth and fifteenth centuries, fleeing from persecution in western Europe—England had expelled them during the Crusades, they had endured pogroms in eastern Europe, they were facing the Spanish Inquisition in Iberia, and discrimination hounded them just about everywhere.

The Eastern Orthodox community was another millet, headed by the patriarch of Constantinople (as Christians still called it), and he had authority over all Slavic Christians in the empire, a number that kept increasing as the Ottomans extended their conquests in Europe.

Then there was the Armenian millet, another Christian community but separate from the Greeks because the Greek and Armenian churches considered one another's doctrines heretical.

The leader of each millet represented his people at court and answered directly to the sultan. In a sense, the Muslims were just another of these millets, and they too had a top leader, the Sheikh al-Islam, or "Old Man of Islam," a position created by Bayazid shortly before he was crushed by Timur-i-lang. The Sheikh al-Islam legislated according to the shari'a and presided over an army of muftis who interpreted the law, judges who applied the law, and mullahs who inducted youngsters into the religion, provided basic religious education, and administrated rites in local neighborhoods and villages.

The shari'a, however, was not the only law in the land. There was also the sultan's code, a parallel legal system that dealt with administrative matters, taxation, interaction between millets, and relationships among the various classes, especially the subject class and the ruling class.

Don't try to follow this complexity: the complexity of the Ottoman system defies a quick description. I just want to give you a flavor of it. This whole parallel legal system, including the lawyers, bureaucrats, and judges who shaped and applied it, was under the authority of the grand vizier, who headed up the palace bureaucracy (another whole world in itself). This vizier was the empire's second most powerful figure, after the sultan.

Or was he third? After all, the Sheikh al-Islam had the right to review every piece of secular legislation and veto it if he thought it conflicted with the shari'a, or send it back for modification.

On the other hand, the Sheikh al-Islam served at the pleasure of the sultan, and it was the sultan's code the grand vizier was administering. So if the grand vizier and the Sheikh al-Islam came into conflict . . . guess who backed down. Or did he?

You see how it was: check, balance, check, balance. . . .

Another set of checks and balances built into Ottoman society involved the devshirme instituted by Bayazid. At first, as I mentioned, this was just the mamluk system by another name. Like the mamluks, the janissaries were trained to serve as the ruler's bodyguards—at first. But then the janissaries' function expanded.

For one thing, they didn't all end up as soldiers anymore. Some were taught administrative skills. Others received cultural training. The sultan began appointing janissaries to top posts in his government as well as his armies and navies. He put janissaries in charge of important cultural institutions as well. Sinon, the Ottoman architect most responsible for establishing that characteristic style of Ottoman mosque—a solid edifice capped with one big dome and many smaller mushroom domes and four pencil-tin minarets at the corners—was a janissary.

Originally, the devshirme took boys only from Christian families in newly conquered territory. But Mehmet the Conqueror instituted another crucial innovation: he extended the devshirme into the empire itself. Henceforth, any family under Ottoman rule, Muslim or non-Muslim, high or low, might see some of its sons sucked into this special form of "slavery," which was, paradoxically, a route to the highest strata of Ottoman society.

Through the devshirme, the Ottomans crafted a brand new power elite for their society. Unlike the elite of other societies, however, the janissaries were forbidden to marry or have (legitimate) children. They could not, therefore, become a hereditary elite. In fact, the devshirme was a mechanism for constantly turning the social soil. It sought out promising youngsters from all sectors of society, gave them the most rigorous possible intellectual and physical training, and then charged them with running the empire. Naturally, they sucked a good deal of power away from the old, traditional, military, Turkish aristocracy, those families whose ancestral roots went back to central Asia, which was all to the good as far as the Ottomans were concerned. It weakened their potential rivals.

And yet the Ottomans did not eliminate these potential rivals, even though they could have. No, the Ottoman genius for checks and balances kept the old aristocratic families in place and left them some power to serve as a check on the janissaries should *the latter* ever get any big ideas.

What power was left to the old nobility? Well, for one thing, they remained the biggest landowners in the empire and the major taxpayers.

"Landowner" is a bit of a misnomer, however, because officially the sultan owned every scrap of soil in his empire. He only leased out parcels of it to favored people as "tax farms" (*timars* in Turkish). A timar was a rural property from whose inhabitants the timar holder was allowed to collect taxes. Those inhabitants were, of course, mostly peasant cultivators living on the land. Tax farmers had permission to collect as much as they wanted from these people. In exchange for the privilege, they had to pay the government a fixed fee every year. Whatever they collected beyond that sum was theirs to keep; and there was no limit on how they were allowed to collect. The government's share did not depend on how much the tax farmer collected but on how much land was in the "farmer's" care. It was a tax on land, not a tax on income. If a property produced beyond all expectations, the tax farmer benefited, not the government. If a timar did poorly, the tax farmer took the hit. If he could not pay his tax for a number of years in a row, the timar was taken away from him and given to someone else.

After a successful campaign, the sultan might reward his best generals by giving them timars. Typically, of course, except in newly conquered areas, the sultan had to take a timar away from one person in order to reward another. The fact that people could lose their timars meant that the landed aristocracy was only semi-hereditary. Here then was another mechanism that promoted social fluidity and kept the Ottoman world in flux.

You might suppose that this timar system encouraged Ottoman aristocrats to wring peasants dry. After all, they got to keep whatever they extracted after paying the government fee. But the timar holders were not, in fact, free to do as they wished, because the peasants could appeal to the shari'a courts for justice, and these were a whole separate institution, a separate power base in society, controlled and staffed by the ulama. The nobility had no shortcut into it. If a family wanted to "place" a son in this legal system, the son had to go through the same long process as anyone else for joining the ulama, such a long process, in fact, that by the time he made it, his social ties would mostly be with other ulama. So his interests would be aligned with theirs and shaped by the ancient doctrine more than by his clan or family roots.

Despite its pervasive power, however, the clerical establishment did not own the religious life of Muslims in the Ottoman empire. Sufism continued to prosper as the religion of the masses, with most people claiming at least nominal affiliation with one or another of the Sufi orders and a great many actively belonging to some brotherhood. This is not to say that all (or very many) of the common folks in the Ottoman Empire were practicing mystics. It's more to say that Sufism, for most people, had come to mean folklore, superstitions, shrines, amulets, remedies, spells, and the veneration of Sufi "saints" alleged to possess supernatural abilities.

Besides, these Sufi orders were intertwined with the akhis, the associations of craftsmen and merchants I mentioned earlier. The akhi guilds had their own autonomous status as social organizations. They set standards for their members, licensed new businesses, collected dues, extended credit, paid out old-age pensions, took care of funeral expenses, offered health care, operated shelters and soup kitchens, gave out scholarships, and also organized fairs, festivals, processions, and other public entertainments. Every guild had its own masters, councils, sheikhs, and internal political processes. Members with complaints could go to guild officials the way modern industrial workers go to their union reps (where unions still exist). If necessary, guild officials represented their members in lawsuits and petitioned the state on members' behalf. By the same token, the state regulated the guilds, imposing standards of its own and controlling prices in the public interest.

Every craftsman belonged to a guild, and many guild members also belonged to some Sufi brotherhood that might cut across guild lines. The brotherhoods generally had lodges where members could gather to socialize, not just with one another, but also with merchants and other travelers passing through, for the akhi-Sufi lodges actively served as traveler's aid societies and hospitality centers.

This glimpse into the Ottoman social clockwork does not begin to exhaust its fractal intricacy: look closer and deeper into Ottoman society and you'll see the same order of complexity at every level. Everything was connected to everything else and connected in many ways, which was fine when all the connections balanced out and all of the parts were working. Centuries later, when the empire entered its decrepitude, all the intertwining parts and intermeshing institutions became a peculiarly Ottoman liability; their intricacy meant that trouble in one place or sphere translated mysteriously to trouble in a dozen other places or spheres—but that came later. In the sixteenth century, the Ottoman Empire was an awesomely well-functioning machine.

The Ottoman's eastward expansion did get blocked by another rising power, the Safavids (about whom more later), but the Ottomans simply headed south at that point and conquered the old Arab heartland from the Indian Ocean to the Mediterranean, then conquered Egypt, eliminating the mamluk dynasty from history, and then went on expanding west along the North African coast.

At their apogee, during the reign of the sixteenth century Suleiman the Magnificent (the title Europeans gave him—among his own he usually wore the honorific of Suleiman the Lawgiver) the Ottoman empire probably ranked as the world greatest power. It straddled Europe and Asia, it possessed both Rome (i.e., Constantinople) and Mecca, not to mention Cairo; and its monarch ruled over more people and more territory than any other. No wonder the Ottoman ruler began to call himself khalifa. No one disputed the title. Of course, that's partly because no one thought it worth disputing. The title had only ceremonial significance by this time, but still it's worth noting that the Ottoman emperor claimed the two most important titles of universal authority in Islam: for the first time in history khalifa and sultan were the same man. For the ordinary Muslim citizen, this meant that surely history was moving forward again: the Umma was back on track to becoming the global community.

THE SAFAVIDS (906–1138 AH)

"Khalifa" and "sultan" were not, however, the *only* titles of universal authority in Islam: there was also "imam," as understood by that other sect of Muslims, the Shi'i—which brings us to the Safavids of Persia, the ones who blocked Ottoman expansion eastward.

The Safavids came to power in a most unusual way. Their roots go back to a Sufi brotherhood that took shape just after the Mongol eruption. The order coalesced in northern Persia around a spiritual master named Sheikh Safi al-Din and came to be known as the Safavids.

For three generations, this brotherhood functioned pretty much like any other Sufi order of the time: it was a peaceful, apolitical group that offered spiritual companionship and a refuge from the turmoil of the world. But then the order began to change. For one thing, when the third sheikh died, his son became the new sheikh, and when he died, his son, and after that his son, and so on. In short, leadership of the group became hereditary.

Second, somewhere along the way, these sheikhs developed political ambitions. They enlisted chosen initiates into an elite corps who not only learned techniques for refining their spiritual devotions but also learned martial arts. They became the sheikh's bodyguards, then his enforcers, and then they grew into a serious military caste.

As an emblem of membership in the Safavid guard, these soldier-mystics wore special red hats, and so they were called the Qizilbash, Turkish for "the redheads." The hat they wore had a distinctive twelve-fold design, which reflected the third and most important change in the Safavid order: their switch to Shi'ism.

The twelve folds stood for the twelve imams of mainstream Shi'ism. As I mentioned earlier, Shi'i felt that absolute and hereditary religious authority belonged to a figure called the imam, who was God's representative on Earth. There was always one imam in the world; there were never two; and the true imam of the age was always descended from Prophet Mohammed through his daughter Fatima and her husband Ali.

Whenever an imam had more than one son, his death opened up the possibility of disagreement about which of his progeny was truly the next imam. Just such a disagreement over the fifth imam gave birth to a minority sect called the Zaidis (or Fivers.) Another disagreement over the seventh imam had spawned the Isma'ilis (or Seveners).

The remaining Shi'i agreed on the imam all the way to the twelfth generation down from Ali, but the twelfth imam disappeared when he was a little boy. Non-Shi'i assume he was murdered. Shi'i, however, believe he never died but went into "occultation," a concept peculiar to Shi'ism: occultation meant he could (can) no longer be seen by ordinary people.

Mainstream Shi'i (or Twelvers) call this twelfth imam the "hidden imam." Shi'ite doctrine holds that the Hidden Imam is and always will be alive, that he is still in direct communication with God and is still guiding the world in some unseen way. The doctrine doesn't say exactly how the Hidden Imam remains hidden. It doesn't say whether he has become invisible, donned a disguise, changed form, gone to ground in some cave, or what. Instrumental explanations like these belong to the world of science; occultation is a mystical concept to which instrumental explanations are irrelevant.

Shi'ite doctrine declares that the twelfth imam will reveal himself at the end of history, sparking the perfection of Allah's community and inaugurating the final Age of Justice, the endpoint sought by all good Muslims. Upon reaching its endpoint, history will end, the dead will be resurrected, and Allah's judgment will sort all who have ever lived into heaven or hell according to their just desserts. Because of this expectation that the Hidden Imam will appear again at the end of days, Shi'i sometimes refer to him as the Mahdi "the expected one" (a concept that exists in Sunni Islam too, but less vividly.) Most of today's Iranians adhere to this branch of Shi'ism, making the Twelvers the mainstream Shi'i of modern times.

In the mid-fifteenth century, the Safavids embraced this complex of beliefs. The twelve folds on the red hats worn by the Qizilbash symbolized the twelve imams. By this time the Safavids were a cultlike group headed by an ambitious sheikh with a growing army of soldiers at his command. The soldiers saw him not just as their commander in chief but as their lifeline to heaven.

These politicized Safavids were operating in a context of social chaos. The Persian world, smashed once by Genghis Khan and smashed again by Timur-i-lang, was fragmented into many little principalities ruled by diverse Turkish chieftains. The Turkish chieftains were all resolute Sunnis. Shi'ism, by contrast, had long been identified with Persian resistance to invasive aliens, a pattern that began in the days of Arab dominance and picked up again once Turks took over. Now, in the wake of the Mongol catastrophe, this militant Shi'ite cult known as the Safavids easily linked up with all the antistate, revolutionary activity going on. No wonder the Safavids made local princes uneasy.

In 1488, one of these princes decided to take action. He had the head of the Safavid order killed. Then for good measure he had the man's eldest son murdered as well. He probably would have done away with his younger son too, a two-year-old boy by the name of Ismail, except that the Qizilbash whisked this little fellow into hiding, just a few steps ahead of the state-paid killers.

Over the next ten years, the Safavids hardened into a formidable secret society. Ismail grew up in hiding, hustled constantly from safe house to safe house. The whole time, the Qizilbash regarded him as the head of their order, and not just a figurehead. They revered the boy and believed he had the spark of divinity in him. Imagine how he must have seen the world (and himself) by the time he reached adolescence, having spent his whole life in secrecy, imbued with a sense of mortal danger, and surrounded, even in his earliest memories, by a shadowy corps of men in red hats who bowed to him, hung on his words, and obeyed his every whim. By chance, the boy bred to such a sense of self-importance, happened to be brilliant and tough.

Around the age of twelve, Ismail came out of hiding with his force of Qizilbash. He disposed quickly of the prince who had killed his father. Other princes rushed to smash him, thinking, how hard could it be to defeat a twelve-year-old boy? Very hard, it turned out.

In 1502, at the age of fifteen, Ismail declared himself Shahanshah of Iran. Shahanshah meant "king of kings." It was the title the Sassanid monarchs had used, and the ancient Persian monarchs before them. In rejecting the titles of "khalifa" and "sultan," Ismail was rejecting Arab and Turkish historical tradition in favor of a nativist Persian identity. In calling his realm Iran, he was invoking the ancestral king named in Firdausi's epic of the Persian people, *The Book of Kings*. In fact, Ismail's propagandists said he was related by blood to the Sassanid kings of yore.

Ismail also separated himself from his neighbor by declaring Twelver Shi'ism the state religion. He had his henchman publicly curse the first three khalifas of Islam: Abu Bakr, Omar, and Othman. The state declared that Ali was the Prophet's only legitimate successor and the imams descended from him the only religious authorities. Ismail's propagandists spread the news that in addition to being descended from the Sassanids, Ismail was also descended from Ali. They suggested that he was even in direct communication with the Hidden Imam (who was, of course, in direct communication with God). In fact, Ismail came pretty close to declaring that he himself *was* the Hidden Imam and may well have believed this of himself—how could he not, given his upbringing? Some people say he even thought he was God.

Fortified by his sense of destiny, Ismail sent preachers into the Ottoman Empire to spread his religious message. His agents called upon Ottoman subjects to convert to Shi'ism and accept Ismail as their sole divinely guided leader. He also set to work vigorously persecuting Sunnis under his power. Some saw signs of madness in the king's conduct and immigrated hastily into the Ottoman empire. Of those who stayed, many were imprisoned or killed.

Well, wouldn't you know it: the Ottoman sultan Selim the Grim retaliated by locking up or executing Shi'is living in his realm. Inevitably, as Sunnis fled west into Anatolia, Shi'is fled east into Persia. The whole process led to an ever greater concentration of Shi'ism in the Safavid empire (and Sunnism in the Ottoman) and the Safavids did everything they could to promote this trend as well as to fuse Shi'ism with Persian culture. This fusion of Shi'ism and Persian nationalism became the ideological foundation of their new empire, the core of which later became the modern nation of Iran.

As part of this campaign, the Safavids elevated the *Tazieh* into a national ritual drama. The Tazieh was a cycle of Shi'ite passion plays recounting the martyrdom of Hussein at Karbala. The plays came out of a mourning ritual conducted in special buildings called *takiah khanas*. Traditionally, on the tenth day of the month of Muharam (the day of Hussein's martyrdom) Shi'i got together in these places to mourn communally: the custom had been going on for centuries. During the mourning, anyone who felt an urge to tell a piece of the story would jump up and do so in order to arouse and stoke the grief. Shi'i became thoroughly familiar with every detail of the martyrdom and every story that could possibly be told about it. For the telling of these plays they developed a distinctive style of oration designed to trigger lamentation. The collection of all these stories constituted the Tazieh (many pieces were written down, but there was no single written version) and every year, on the Tenth of Muharram, now that the Safavids held power, Shi'i through the empire took to the streets (not just to takiah khanas) for a cathartic outburst of public lamentation and then made their way to state-funded theaters where government-funded professionals enacted the ritual on stage.

When Ismail was twenty-seven years old, he discovered that he wasn't God after all. The Ottomans dealt him this lesson by invading his realm. Spoiling for a fight, Ismail rushed to meet them. The two armies clashed on the plains of Chaldiran, near the city of Tabrez. The Ottomans had firearms, but the Safavids thought they had something better: old-fashioned religious fervor and a divinely guided leader. This time, firearms proved more useful. Selim crushed Ismail's forces, almost killed Ismail, and took his capital of Tabrez.

The battle of Chaldiran was as seminal as the Battle of Hastings, which marked the birth of England as a nation-state. Historians usually score

Chaldiran as a victory for the Ottomans, but overall it was more of a draw, because Selim could not hold Tabrez. With winter coming, he fell back to more secure bases deeper inside Anatolia, and by the following year the Persians had reoccupied Tabrez and inoculated it with a scorched-earth campaign that left nothing for invaders to feed on if they wanted to attack again. So the battle of Chaldiran actually ended up defining the frontier between the Ottoman and Safavid realms, which hardened eventually into the border between the successor states, Iran and Turkey, and remains the border between those countries to this day.

Ismail went home from Chaldiran a sad and broken man. Losing a battle made him rethink his identity. He spent his remaining years more or less in seclusion, pondering the cosmos and writing religious poetry. Ismail's empire not only survived his dejection but prospered, in part because it enjoyed a succession of gifted and long-lived rulers.

With the border more or less firmed up, hostilities between the Ottoman and Safavid empires went into remission and trade began flowing in both directions to the benefit of both societies. The Safavid Empire was always smaller than the Ottomans' and never quite as powerful, but with its single state religion and its single dominant ethnic group, it was culturally more unified.

This no-doubt-about-it Persian Empire peaked under Ismail's great grandson Shah Abbas the Great, who died in 1629 after a forty-two-year reign. Abbas equipped his armies with firearms and cannons, and in his era Iran developed booming state-supported textile, ceramics, garment, and carpet industries, which exported goods to places as distant as western Europe, Africa, and India.

The art of painting, and particularly of the "Persian miniature"— exquisitely detailed scenes surrounded by floral and geometric borders— climaxed in Safavid Persia. Calligraphy, regarded as a major art form in the Islamic world due to Muslim reverence for the written Qur'an, also reached perfection here. The two arts came together in illuminated books, the highest artistic products of the age, and the culminating work in this form was a *Book of Kings*, Firdausi's epic, produced for a Safavid monarch: it had 258 paintings and sixty thousand lines of calligraphy by various artists—essentially, an entire museum between two covers.

Safavid creativity climaxed in architecture. For example, unlike the monumental Ottoman mosques—those somber mounds of domes bracketed by minarets—the Safavids built airy structures that shimmered with glazed mosaic tiles and seemed almost to float, so that even gigantic mosques looked like they were made of lace and light.

And if architecture was the highest art form of Safavid Persia, then city building was its meta-art. The Safavids kept moving their capital (seeking safety from the ever-looming Ottomans) and every time they adopted a new city as their home, they remade it aesthetically. In 1598, after choosing Isfahan as his new capital, Shah Abbas launched a building program that transformed the entire city into a single integrated jewel: by the time he was done, it abounded in public squares, gardens, mosques, mansions, pools, palaces, and public buildings interlaced with handsome boulevards. Awestruck visitors coined the phrase *Isfahan Nisfi-Jahan*, "Isfahan, half the world" (their point being that if you hadn't seen Isfahan, you'd missed half of all there was to see in the world).

The Ottoman and Safavid worlds had distinctive differences and yet, for all the hostility between the governments, a sort of civilizational unity ran between them. They were no more different than, say, England and France, and perhaps less so. A traveler going from Istanbul to Isfahan or vice versa would have felt on more or less familiar ground in either place. It's quite remarkable that two such powerful and distinctive empires could emerge in exactly the same period side by side. What's even more amazing is that yet another enormous, distinctive, grandiose, and powerful Muslim empire coalesced in just about this same period: the empire of the Moghuls, which eventually stretched from Burma, across India, to the middle of Afghanistan where it butted right up against the Safavid frontier.

THE MOGHULS (ROUGHLY 900 TO 1273 AH)

The Moghuls were every bit the equal of the Ottomans in wealth and strength. About 20 percent of the world's current population lives in the territory they once ruled, including all or part of five modern countries, Afghanistan, Pakistan, India, Bangladesh, and Burma. The man who founded this gigantic empire was an almost exact contemporary of Shah

Ismail's named Babur, which means "tiger," and in some ways, he was even more remarkable than the prodigious Safavid teenager.

Babur claimed descent from both Timur-i-lang and Chengez Khan. What the blood ties really were, who knows, but Babur took his genealogy seriously; it give him a lifelong sense of mission. His father ruled a little kingdom called Farghana, just north of today's Afghanistan, and when he died in 1495, Babur inherited this throne. He was twelve years old.

Within a year he had lost his kingdom, which is hardly surprising: he was only *twelve*, after all! But he regrouped and conquered legendary Samarqand, Timur's one-time capital—then lost it. He went back to Farghana and took that again. But his enemies won it back. Then he conquered Samarqand a second time, this time with just 240 men—but could not hold it. By the time he was eighteen, Babur had gained and lost two kingdoms twice apiece and found himself on the run through the mountains of Afghanistan with his mother and sisters and a few hundred followers. For three years, he and his band roamed the wilds, looking for a new kingdom: kinging was all he knew, and king was the only job title he was seeking.

I dare say any teenager who holds together a band of adult warriors over many years of homeless exile must have something going for him; and Babur was certainly an intimidating physical specimen. The stories say he could jump across a stream holding a full-grown man tucked under each arm. (They don't say what the full-grown men thought of this exercise.) Unlike most tough guys, however, Babur was sensitive, artistic, and romantic. He kept a diary throughout his adventures, and late in life penned an autobiography that became a classic of Turkish literature. After his grandson had it translated into the more prestigious Persian, the book achieved a high place in that canon as well. In his book, Babur reveals himself with extraordinary honesty. After a crucial military loss, for example, he tells us he could not help "crying a great deal." What kind of tough guy admits such a thing? Later he reports on his arranged marriage and his failure to work up any enthusiasm for his wife, despite his earnest efforts. He visits her only every week or two, he says, and then only because his mother nags at him. Then he falls in love—with a boy he sees in the bazaar. "In that frothing up of desire and passions and under the stress of youthful folly, I used to wander bare-headed, bare-footed, through street and lane, orchard and vineyard; I showed civility neither to friend nor stranger, took no care for myself or others. . . ."[7] Thus does the future emperor expose his vulnerable adolescent passions to us—and yet this is the fellow who has, twice already, conquered and lost Samarqand.

In the course of his wandering, Babur and his band came over a rise in the hills and saw a charming city tucked into a crack of a valley below. Babur fell in love again, this time with Kabul. And Kabul, he tells us, returned his affection: the citizens hated their own ruler and begged Babur to be their king instead. Does this sound like a conqueror's implausible propaganda? Maybe so, but I can tell you that Kabul's affection for Babur lingers to this day. The public gardens he built overlooking the city remain a favorite park, and his grave up there is still a beloved shrine.

Babur was crowned king of Kabul in 1504, and now he had a base. He considered and rejected another attempt on Samarqand. He and his advisers decided to head south, instead, as so many other Turko-Mongol conquerors had done before. Babur entered India with ten thousand men and the sultan of Delhi met him on the plains of Panipat with one hundred thousand. Ten to one odds—the stuff of legends! What's more, the sultan had a thousand elephants, but Babur had an advantage too: firearms. The new technology trumped the old biology as Babur routed the sultan and took possession of Delhi. Like the Ottomans and the Safavids, the Moghuls overwhelmed their enemies because they were fighting spears and arrows with bullets and cannonballs. The third of the three great Muslim "gunpowder" empires was now on the map.

The Moghuls, even more than the Safavids, benefited from a series of long-lived and brilliant rulers. Just six men saw the empire through its first two hundred years. Most were passionate, romantic, and artistic. At least three were military geniuses. One was a poor administrator, but his wife Nur Jahan ruled from behind the throne, and she was the fiery equal of the best Moghuls—a savvy businesswoman, a poet and patron of the arts, an extraordinary sportswoman, and one of the most cunning politicians of her age.

Only one of the six was a dud, and that was Babur's son. It took this drunkard ten years to lose the entire empire his father had built. While he was on the run through the mountains of Afghanistan, however, his beloved wife gave birth to a boy who would become Akbar the Great, the most remarkable monarch of his age, a contemporary and equal of England's Queen Elizabeth. His father managed to win his throne back just in time for Akbar to celebrate his twelfth birthday as a prince. Shortly after that, his father heard the call to prayer when he was standing at the top of a staircase in his library and had a sudden inspiration to reform his life. He hustled down to start living as a saint but on the way down tripped and broke his neck, which put his teenaged son on the throne.

Akbar consolidated his grandfather's conquests, extended them, and set his whole empire in order. These achievements alone would have made him an important monarch, but Akbar was much more than a conqueror.

Early on, he recognized his empire's key weakness: a small group of Muslims was attempting to rule a vast population of Hindus, whom Muslims had been sacking, pillaging, looting, and killing since the days of Sultan Mahmud the Ghaznavid, some five centuries earlier. Akbar attacked this flaw with a principle he called *sulahkul*, "universal tolerance." To prove his sincerity, he married a Hindu princess and declared her first son his heir.

Akbar opened all government positions to Hindus on equal terms with Muslims. He abolished a punitive tax Muslim rulers of this region had long imposed on pilgrims visiting Hindu shrines. Akbar also eliminated the jizya, the Qur'anic tax on non-Muslims. He replaced both with a land tax that applied uniformly to all citizens, high and low. Virtually no other state in the world at this time taxed the nobility, but Akbar broke the mold. He also ordered his troops to protect the shrines and holy places of all religions, not just Islam.

This great Moghul emperor abolished the standing military aristocracy on which his predecessors had depended and set up an administrative system in which every official was appointed and could hold office for only a specified period, after which he had to move on to a new job in another place. Essentially, Akbar pioneered the concept of term limits, interrupting a process that had produced all too many troublemaking regional warlords in the past.

Born and raised a Muslim, Akbar certainly considered himself a Muslim monarch, but he was deeply curious about other religions. He called leading Hindus, Muslims, Christians, Jains, Zoroastrians, Buddhists, and others to his court to explain and debate their views while the emperor listened. Finally Akbar decided every religion had some truth in it and no religion had the whole truth, so he decided to take the best from each and blend them into a single new religion he called *Din-i Illahi*, "the God Religion." The doctrines of this new religion included, first, that God was a single, all-powerful unity; second, that the universe was a single integrated whole reflecting its creator; third, that every person's first religious obligation was to do no harm to others; and fourth, that people could and should model themselves on Perfect Lives, of which many examples existed—Mohammed provided such a model, said Akbar, and so did the Shi'i imams. Akbar went on to suggest modestly that he himself provided yet another.

Ablaze with fervor for his new religion, Akbar built a whole new city dedicated to it. Constructed of red sandstone, Fatehpur Sikri rose in the desert around the grave and shrine of Akbar's favorite Sufi mystic. The main building here was the private-audience hall, a single large room that had a high domed ceiling and only one element of furniture: a tall pillar connected by catwalks to balconies along the walls. Akbar sat atop this pillar. People who wanted to petition the emperor addressed him from the balconies. Courtiers and other interested parties listened from the floor below.

It's a testament to Akbar's charm and majesty that no one revolted against him for trying to promulgate his new religion, but the religion did not take. It wasn't Muslim enough for Muslims or Hindu enough for Hindus. Fatehpur Sikri didn't last, either: its water sources dried up and the city withered.

But Akbar's ideas had not sprung full-blown out of nothing. Movements to blend the best of Islam and Hinduism had been percolating on the subcontinent since Babur's days, with mysticism providing the point of intersection. In 1499, for example, a man named Nanak had a religious experience that led him to declare, "There is no Hindu, there is no Muslim." Although born Hindu, he reached toward Sufism and devoted his life to rejecting and repudiating the caste system. He launched a tradition of spiritual techniques transmitted directly from master to initiate, echoing both Hindu masters and Sufi saints. Guru Nanak's followers ended up calling themselves Sikhs, a new religion.

A contemporary of Guru Nanak's, the illiterate poet Kabir, was born of a widowed Hindu mother but raised by a family of Muslim weavers. He began spouting lyrics celebrating love in a spirit that smacked of both Sufism and Hinduism, and scribes recorded his utterances. The lyrics have survived to this day.

While folk mystics in Moghul India were producing passionate lyrics rooted in oral traditions, court poets were elaborating a complex metaphysical style of Persian-language poetry. At the same time, Moghul artists were developing their own more robust version of the painted "Persian" miniatures and illuminated books.

Moghul creativity reached its apogee in architecture, which managed to combine the solid majesty of Ottoman styles with the airy lightness of the Safavid. The fifth Moghul monarch Shah Jahan was himself a genius in this field. In his time, he was called the Just King, but few today remember his many political or military achievements: what they remember about him is his consuming love for his wife Mumtaz Mahal, "ornament of the palace," who died shortly after Shah Jahan began his reign. The grieving emperor devoted the next twenty years to building a mausoleum for her: the Taj Mahal. Often called the most beautiful building in the world, the Taj Mahal is a masterpiece as singular and universally famous as the Da Vinci's *Mona Lisa* or Michelangelo's Sistine Chapel. What's astounding is that the artist responsible for this tour de force had a day job running an empire, for while many architects and designers contributed to the Taj Mahal, it was the emperor who oversaw every detail of its construction: his was the master eye.[8]

Shah Jahan's son Aurangzeb, the last of the great Moghuls, had no artistic leanings. Music, poetry, and painting left him cold. His passion was religion, and nothing irritated him more than the tradition of tolerance his family had pioneered in the subcontinent. Toward the end of his father's reign, he went to war with Shah Jahan and seized power. He had the old man clapped in a stone fortress, where the old emperor lived out his life in a one-room cell with a single window too high for him to see through. After his death, however, his jailers found a small mirror affixed to one wall. In that mirror, it turned out, from his bed, Shah Jahan could view the outside world and the only thing he could see out there through that one high window was the Taj Mahal.

Restoring orthodox Islam to a position of privilege in the Moghul empire was Aurangzeb's obsession. He was a military genius equal to his great grandfather Akbar, and like Akbar he ruled for forty-nine years, so he had time and power to work deep changes in the subcontinent.

The changes he sought and wrought were exactly the opposite of those promoted by his great-grandfather Akbar the Great. He reinstated the jizya. He reimposed special taxes on Hindus. He had his security forces demolish all new Hindu shrines. He expelled Hindus from government positions and went to war with the Rajputs, semiautonomous Hindu rulers in the south, in order to bring them more firmly under the power of his Moghul government and the Muslim clerical establishment, India's ulama.

Aurangzeb also tried to exterminate the Sikhs. Guru Nanak had been a resolute pacifist, but Aurangzeb's persecution transformed the Sikhs into a warrior sect whose sacred ritual objects ever since have included a long, curved knife carried by every pious Sikh man.

Even though the last of the Moghul titans was a grim zealot, this dynasty cut a fiery swath through history, and at its peak, around the year 1600, it was surely one of the world's three greatest and most powerful empires.

Indeed, in the year 1600, a traveler could sail from the islands of Indonesia to Bengal, cross India, go over the Hindu Kush to the steppes north of the Oxus River and back down through Persia, Mesopotamia, and Asia Minor to the Balkans, and then back across or around the Black Sea through the Caucusus region and south through Arabia into Egypt and then west to Morocco, and always find himself in a generally familiar world permeated by a single coherent civilization—in much the same way that a modern traveler roaming from San Francisco to London and all across Europe would find himself in a generally familiar civilization with a German flavor here, a Swedish flavor there, a Spanish, British, or Dutch flavor somewhere else.

Yes, that seventeenth-century traveler through the Muslim world would encounter diverse local customs and come across a variety of languages, and yes, he would cross borders and present paperwork to officials working for different sovereign powers, but everywhere he went, he would find certain common elements as well.

In all three of the great Muslim empires and their satellite regions, for example, he would find that Turks generally held political and military power. (Even in Safavid Persia, the ruling family was actually ethnically

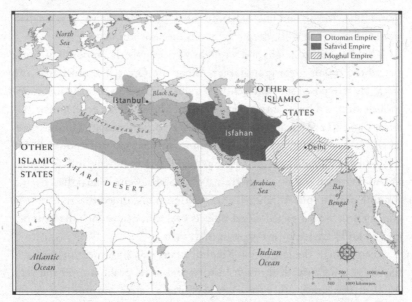

THE THREE ISLAMIC EMPIRES OF THE SEVENTEENTH CENTURY

Turkish and so were many of the Qizilbash.) Throughout this world, the traveler would find that the educated literati tended to know Persian and the classic literature written in that language. Everywhere, he would hear the *azan*, the call to prayer, chanted in Arabic at certain times of day from numerous minarets, and he would hear Arabic again whenever people performed religious rites of any kind.

Everywhere he went, not just in the three empires but in the outlying frontier zones such as Indonesia and Morocco, society would be permeated with a web of rules and recommendations that shaded up into law and down into the practices and rituals of everyday life with no border between the two. And every society would have its ulama, that powerful, self-regenerating, unelected class of scholars, and they would have an influential grip on daily life. Everywhere, the traveler would come across Sufism and Sufi orders as well. Merchants and traders would have an elevated status, but it would be lower than that of bureaucrats and officials connected to the court, itself a distinct and significant class in society.

Passing through the public realm, the traveler would see very few women. Throughout this world stretching from Indonesia to Morocco, he would have found society divided to a greater or lesser extent into public and private realms, and women would have been sequestered in the private world, while men exercised near total possession of the public realm.

What women the traveler did see in the public world—shopping, for example, or going from one house to another on a visit—would probably have a garment of some kind at least obscuring and perhaps covering their faces. If he saw women with uncovered faces, he would know that they belonged to the lower classes: they might be peasants, for example, or servants, or laborers of some kind. Whatever the women might be wearing, it would not expose their arms, legs, or cleavage, and they would wear a head covering of some kind.

Men's clothing styles would differ from place to place, but everywhere the traveler went, men's heads, too, would be covered, their garments would be loose rather than form fitting, and they would wear something that would not permit their crotches to show when they prostrated themselves in the prayer ritual.

Throughout this world, calligraphy would have prestige as an art form, representational (as opposed to abstract and decorative) art would be rare except in illuminated books, and the spoken and written word would be honored.

Every city the traveler passed through would be like a collection of villages without many big through-streets; none would be set up on the checkerboard pattern of Hellenic cities. Every neighborhood would have its own bazaar, every city its spectacular mosques, and the mosques would always feature domes and minarets and would very commonly be decorated with glazed mosaic tiles.

If the traveler struck up a conversation with some stranger in this world, he would find that he and this stranger shared certain mythological references: both would know the leading personalities of the Abrahamic tradition—Adam, David, Moses, Noah, and so on; both would also know not just all about Mohammed but also Abu Bakr, Omar, Ali and Othman, and they would have impressions of and opinions about these personalities. They would share knowledge of major events in history as well; they would know, for example, about the Abbasids and the Golden Age over which they presumably presided, and they would know about the Mongols and the devastation they wrought.

In 1600, in fact, ordinary folks anywhere in this world would have assumed that the Muslim empires and their adjacent frontier territories were in fact "the world." Or, to quote University of Chicago historian Marshall Hodgson, "In the sixteenth century of our era, a visitor from Mars might well have supposed that the human world was on the verge of becoming Muslim."[9]

The Martian would have been mistaken, of course; the course of history had already tipped, because of developments in Europe since the Crusades.

I I

Meanwhile in Europe

689–1008 AH
1291–1600 CE

T HE LAST CRUSADERS fled the Islamic world in 1291, driven out by
Egypt's mamluks, but in Europe residues of the Crusades persisted for
years to come. Some of the blowback came from those military religious orders spawned by the Church of Rome. The Templars, for example, became
influential international bankers. The Knights Hospitaller took over the island of Rhodes, then moved their headquarters to Malta, from which place
they operated more or less as pirates, looting Muslim shipping in the
Mediterranean. The Teutonic Knights actually conquered enough of Prus-
sia to establish a state that lasted into the fifteenth century.

Meanwhile, Europeans kept trying to launch new campaigns into the
Muslim world too, but these were ever more feeble, and some dissipated
along the way, while others veered off on tangents. The so-called Northern
Crusade ended up targeting the pagan Slavs of the Baltic region. Many little wars against "heretical" sects within Europe, whipped up by the pope
and conducted by this or that monarch, were also labeled "crusades." In
France, for example, there was a long "crusade" against a Christian sect
called the Albigensians. Then there was Iberia, where Christians kept on
crusading until 1492, when they overran Granada finally and drove the
last of the Muslims out of the peninsula.

The crusading spirit persisted in part because over the course of the real crusades, a new motivation had entered the drive to the east: an appetite for trade goods coming from places like India and the islands beyond them, which Europeans called the Indies. One of many desirable goods to be found in India was an amazing product called sugar. From Malaysia and Indonesia came pepper, nutmeg, and many other spices. Chefs of the High Middle Ages put spices in everything they cooked—often the same spices in savories and desserts; they just liked spices![1]

The trouble was, the Crusades stoked an appetite for the goods but also separated European merchants from those goods by creating a belt of anti-Christian hostility that stretched from Egypt to Azerbaijan. European businessmen couldn't get past that wall to trade directly with the source: they had to deal with Muslim middleman. It's true that Marco Polo traveled to China in this period, but he and his group were just one anomalous band, and Europeans were amazed that they had made it all the way there and back. Most, in fact, didn't believe he had really done it: they called Marco Polo's book about his adventures "The Millions," referring to the number of lies they thought he had packed into it. Muslims owned the eastern shores of the Black Sea, they owned the Caucasus mountains, they owned the Caspian coastline. They possessed the Red Sea and all approaches to it. Europeans were forced to get the products of India and the Indies from Muslim merchants in Syria and Egypt, who no doubt jacked the prices up as high as the market would bear, especially for their European Christian customers, given the ill will from all that happened during the Crusades, not to mention the fact that the Farangi Christians had aligned themselves with the Mongols.

What were western Europeans traders to do?

This is where the crusading spirit bled into the exploring impulse. Muslims straddled the tangle of the land routes that connected the world's important ancient markets, but over the centuries, unnoticed by Muslim potentates and peoples, western Europeans had been developing tremendous seafaring prowess. For one thing, Europeans of the post-Crusades era included Vikings, those invading mariners from the north who were so good at seafaring, they had even crossed the North Atlantic to Greenland in their dragon boats. One wave invaded England where the word *Northmen* slurred into *Norman*. A few of these then moved to the coast of France, where the region they inhabited came to be known as Normandy.

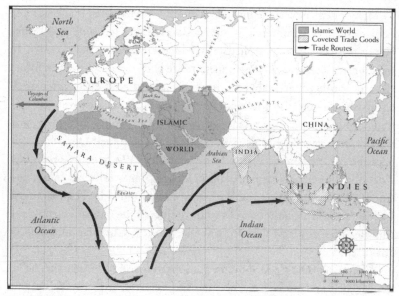

THE EUROPEAN QUEST FOR A SEA ROUTE TO THE INDIES

But it wasn't just the Vikings. Everyone who sailed regularly between Scandinavia and southern Europe had to develop rugged ships and learn how to manage them in the big storms and high seas of the North Atlantic; western Europeans, therefore, ended up very much at home on the water. With such accomplished mariners amongst their subjects, some ambitious monarchs began to dream of finding a way to skirt the whole land mass between Europe and east Asia and with it the whole Muslim problem: in short, they got interested in finding a way to get to India and the islands further east entirely by sea.

One aristocrat who poured serious support into this enterprise was Prince Henry of Portugal (called "Henry the Navigator" even though he never went on any of the expeditions he sponsored). Prince Henry was closely connected to the king of Portugal, but more important, he was one of the richest men in western Europe. He funded sea captains to sail south along the coast of Africa looking for a way around it. Henry's letters and proclamations show that he originally saw himself as a crusader, out to prove himself a great Christian monarch by scoring victories against the Moors and finding new souls to save for the one true faith.[2]

Many of the new souls his sailors found were living in black-skinned bodies and had commercial value as slaves, it turned out, and Prince Henry the Navigator morphed into Prince Henry the Slave Trader. In addition to slaves, as the Portuguese made their way south, they found all sorts of other marketable commodities such as gold dust, salt, ostrich eggs, fish oil—the list goes on and on. The constant discovery of new trade goods infused the crusader's dream with an economic motive, and the Crusades gave way to what Europeans call the Age of Discovery. Perhaps the most dramatic discovery occurred in 1492, when Christopher Columbus sailed across the Atlantic, looking for a route to India, and stumbled across the Americas. His voyage was funded by Ferdinand and Isabella, the Christian monarchs who completed the Crusade against the Muslims of Iberia and founded a single, unified, Christian kingdom of Spain.

When Columbus landed on the Caribbean island of Hispaniola, he famously believed he had reached the Indies. After his mistake became known, the islands east of India were called the East Indies, and these islands in the Caribbean the West Indies. Most Muslims were only vaguely aware of this momentous discovery. Ottoman sources mention Columbus's voyage in passing, although by the 1570s, a few Ottoman cartographers were creating fairly accurate maps of the world showing the two Americas right where they are in fact located. By then, Spain had built the rudiments of a new empire in Mexico and the English, French, and others had planted settlements further north.

Meanwhile, at the eastern end of the Middle World, Muslims had already discovered what the Europeans were originally seeking: Muslim traders had been sailing to Malaysia and Indonesia for centuries. Many Muslim traders who plied these waters belonged to Sufi orders, and through them Islam had taken root in the (east) Indies long before the first Europeans arrived.

Even before the Portuguese, Spaniards, English, Dutch, and other northern Europeans caught the exploring fever, southern Europeans were already making their clout known at sea, for their civilization had emerged out of seafaring, and their sailing prowess went back to the Romans, the Greeks, the Mycenaeans before them, and the Cretans and Phoenicians before that.

By the fourteenth century CE, the Genovese and the Venetians were competing for the Mediterranean trade in some of the biggest, sturdiest fleets around, and on the water, these Italians could fight. Venetians did vigorous business in Constantinople, and after the Ottomans took over they boldly opened commercial offices at Istanbul.

The Mediterranean trade drew tremendous wealth into Italy and spawned booming city-states, not just Venice and Genoa, but also Florence, Milan, and others. Here in Italy, money supplanted land as the chief marker of wealth and status. Merchants became the new power elite; families like the Medicis of Florence and the Sforzas of Milan supplanted the old military aristocracy of feudal landowners. All the money, all that entrepreneurial energy, all that urban diversity, all those sovereign entities in such close proximity competing for grandeur, eminence, and reputation generated a dynamism unprecedented in history. Any talented artist or craftsman with a skill to sell could have a field day in the Italy of this era because he could get so many patrons bidding against one another for his services. Dukes and cardinals and even the pope competed to lure artists such as Michelangelo and Leonardo da Vinci to their courts because their works were not only beautiful but represented great status symbols. Italy began to overflow with the art, invention, creativity, and achievement that was later labeled "the Italian Renaissance."

Books, meanwhile, were coming back into fashion. During the Dark Ages, hardly anyone in Europe knew how to read except clerics, and clerics learned the skill just to read the Bible and conduct services. Among Germanic Christians, in Charlemagne's time for example, clerics revered Latin, the language in which Christian services were performed, because they thought of it as the language God spoke. They worried that if their Latin deteriorated, God would not understand their prayers, so they preserved and studied a few ancient books written by pagans such as Cicero purely as an aid to mastering the grammar and structure and pronunciation of the old tongue. They wanted to ensure that they would be able to continue sounding out syllables that would reach God. When reading writers such as Cicero, they tried assiduously to ignore what they were saying and focus only on their style so as not to be contaminated by their pagan sensibilities. Their efforts to preserve Latin petrified it into a dead language suitable only for ritual and incantatory purposes, incapable of serving as a vehicle for discussion and thought.[3] Nonetheless, their reverence for books as artifacts meant that some churches and monasteries kept books tucked away in basements and back rooms.

Then, in the twelfth century, Christian scholars visiting Muslim Andalusia stumbled across Latin translations of Arabic translations of Greek texts by thinkers such as Aristotle and Plato. Most of these works were generated in Toledo, where a bustling translation industry had developed. From Toledo, the books filtered into western Europe proper, finding their way at last into church and monastery libraries.

The Arabic works found in Andalusia included a great deal of commentary by Muslim philosophers such as Ibn Sina (Avicenna to the Europeans) and Ibn Rushd (Averroes). Their writings focused on reconciling Greek philosophy with Muslim revelations. Christians took no interest in that achievement, so they stripped away whatever Muslims had added to Aristotle and the others and set to work exploring how Greek philosophy could be reconciled with *Christian* revelations. Out of this struggle came the epic "scholastic" philosophies of thinkers such as Thomas Aquinas, Duns Scotus, and others. The Muslim connection to the ancient Greek works was erased from European cultural memory.

European scholars began gravitating to monasteries that had libraries because the books were there. Then, would-be students began gravitating to monasteries with libraries because the scholars were there. While pursuing their studies, penniless scholars eked out a living teaching classes. Learning communities formed around the monasteries and these ripened into Europe's first universities. One of the earliest emerged around Notre Dame cathedral in Paris. Another very early learning community became the University of Naples. Then a university developed at Oxford, England. When a fight broke out among the scholars there, the dissident group migrated to Cambridge in a huff and started a learning community of its own.

The scholars in these protouniversities came to realize that most would-be students didn't know enough to even begin studying, so they developed a set of standard courses designed to get students ready to begin, courses in rhetoric, grammar, logic, and arithmetic, for example, that were designed to teach students merely how to read, write, and think. Students who successfully completed this basic course were called baccalaureates, Latin for "beginners"; now they could *begin* to learn some actual subject such as theology, philosophy, medicine, or law. Today, of course, the baccalaureate is the degree one gets for graduating from a four-year liberal arts college.

As wealth accumulated in Europe, a few people were able to spend all their time studying, reading, writing, and making art. With Greek thought back in the mix, a set of new ideas filtered into the imagination of learned Europeans. The Greeks had said, "Man is the measure of all things," and their pagan pantheon had represented "God" as a collection of deities with human personalities who interacted with one another and with humanity in dramatic ways. The Greeks had taken a penetrating interest in the natural world and the human here-and-now. They had made great strides in discerning patterns among natural events as a first step toward explaining them. People who read and discussed the ancient Greek texts got interested, therefore, in unraveling the mysteries of life on earth, an orientation quite at odds with the attitudes fostered by the church since the fall of Rome, for in the Christendom of the Middle Ages, the prevailing doctrine declared the material world to be evil. The only point of being here was to get out of here, and so the only subject worth studying was the hereafter and the only texts worth consulting were the scriptures and scriptural commentaries. The new humanists did not think of themselves as competing with Christianity; they were hardly godless atheists; but Church officials saw a threat in the new forms of thought. They could feel where all this was going.

Christianity grew within the framework of a dying Rome. It developed a hierarchy that resembled and shadowed the administrative hierarchy of Rome. As the imperial structure crumbled, the Christian structure took its place by default, becoming the framework that continued to support civilized life. The Byzantine emperor, always the head of the imperial hierarchy, automatically evolved into the head of this Christian hierarchy. The various bishops were subservient to him as the head of the Church, just as the governors had been (and were still) subservient to him as the head of the empire. The doctrines of the Christian religion were formulated by bishops at councils convened by the emperor and updated periodically at similar councils, with the emperor always having the final say.

So closely did Christianity intertwine with Rome that when the empire split in two, the church divided too. In the east, the emperor remained the head of the church. In the west, the very title of "emperor" dropped out of existence. Politically, the continent fragmented into small realms ruled, essentially, by warlords. In this context, the Church emerged as the single source of cultural coherence and unity in western Europe, the cultural medium through which people who spoke different languages and served different sovereigns could still interact or travel through one another's realms. To serve this function, the doctrines of the Church had to be uniform, universally understood, and universally accepted, so the Church developed a ferocious propensity for spotting and stamping out heresies.

By the time of the Crusades, church officials in western Europe were regularly executing heretics—anyone whose publicly stated convictions departed from the prevailing doctrine—by tying them to stakes and lighting bonfires under them.

As the Church tightened its grip on daily life, the bishop of Rome became the preeminent figure in western Europe. People called him *il pape,* the pope, because they considered him the "father" of the Christian community. In the east, the patriarch of Constantinople was the leading religious figure, but there were many patriarchs and he was only the first among equals. In the west, the pope acquired an authority transcending that of all other bishops. Around the time of the Crusades, Catholics began to propound the doctrine that the pope was infallible.

Meanwhile, the church was extending its reach across the continent and down into every cranny. Every rural village, every town, every neighborhood in every city had its parish priest and its local church and every priest was administering exactly the same rites in the same way and in the same language. The hierarchy became fully rationalized and embedded: every priest answered to a higher bishop, every bishop to an archbishop, archbishops to cardinals, and cardinals to the pope.

But then, as the Crusades died away, this hegemony began to crack. Here and there, reformers began to question the authority of the church. In the late fourteenth century, an Oxford professor named John Wycliffe shocked church officials by translating the Bible into that most vulgar of languages, common English. And why? So that common, ordinary folks could read and understand what the Bible said for themselves. Church officials couldn't fathom why ordinary folks would need to understand the Bible for themselves when they had priests to do the understanding for them.

Wycliffe went further. He suggested that clerics should all be poor, like the apostles, and that land should be taken away from churches and monasteries and put to secular uses, which offended the church deeply. Wycliffe had powerful political protectors, so he managed to live out his natural life span, but four decades after his death, a pope had his bones dug up, crushed into powder, and scattered over a river: the rage, it seemed, persisted.

It persisted in part because Wycliffe's ideas would not die out. In the generation after his, for example, the Bohemian priest Johann Huss embraced Wycliffe's idea that all people had a right to a Bible in their own language. He commenced a great translation project. When church officials quoted canon law at him to show that his actions were wrong, he quoted scripture back at them and declared that the Bible trumped church councils. This was too much. The church arrested Huss and burnt him at the stake in a fire fueled with copies of the vulgate Bibles he had been promoting. In short, Christianity did to its first reformers what Islam had done to the proto–Sufi Hallaj.

Killing reformers, however, could not kill the hunger for reform. Wycliffe, Huss, and others of their ilk had scratched through to something smoldering dangerously among the people: an unrequited desire for real religious experience.

The bureaucratization of religion had made the church powerful and given Europe cultural unity, but the religious bureaucracy eventually couldn't deliver the core experience that was its raison d'etre. German theology professor Martin Luther put his finger most precisely on the dysfunction. Luther was a man tormented by guilt. No matter what he did, he felt like a sinner headed for hell. The Christian rites were supposed to alleviate this guilt by washing him clean of sin, but for Luther the rites weren't working. He tried everything—fasting, self-flagellation, daily communion, endless penances, but at the end of it all, when the priest told him he was pure now, Luther didn't believe him. He had only to look into his heart to see that he was still impure. He knew because he still felt the guilt.

Then one day, a great insight hit Luther. He could not have salvation until he believed himself saved. If he lacked this belief, it didn't matter what the priest said or did. If he had this belief, it didn't matter what the priest said or did. Which raised a big, big question: of what use was the priest? Why was he even in the mix?

In fact, the conviction gripped Luther that salvation could not be earned, like a pension. It was a gift, which could only be received, and then only through faith, an inner process, never through "works," external deeds and doings.

Armed with this insight, Luther looked around and saw a world full of people pursuing salvation through "works," and to make it all worse, works prescribed by a vast, wealthy, well-organized bureaucracy, the Church of Rome. It filled him with horror, for if his insight was true, all these "works" were for naught!

Of all the "works" prescribed by the Church, the one that most alarmed and offended Luther was the granting of indulgences. An indulgence was a remission of punishment for certain sins, which the Church proclaimed itself empowered to give, in exchange for good and valuable considerations. The practice went back to the Crusades, when the pope offered indulgences to those who signed up to fight the heathen Turk. Later, as crusading opportunities faded out, the Church began to grant indulgences in exchange for cash contributions. Given the petty corruption that inevitably infests any far-flung bureaucratic system, some clerics here and there—let's face it—probably handed out indulgences in exchange for cash contributions to, well, themselves. Any way you look at it, by Martin Luther's time, the whole practice of granting indulgences had come to mean that people could supposedly buy their way out of purgatory and fast-track their way into heaven.

Making people pay to get into heaven was bad enough. But to Luther the practice smacked of something worse. If salvation was a direct, personal interaction between each individual and God, then the Church was extorting bribes to let people through a gate *they had no actual power to open or keep shut*. It wasn't just corruption. It was thievery and deception of the worst sort!

On Halloween night, 1517, Luther nailed an inflammatory document to the door of a church in Wittenberg in which he set forth ninety-five "theses," ninety-five objections to the Church and its doings. Luther's paper was an overnight sensation, and it sparked the Protestant Reformation.

The Protestant Reformation was no single thing. Once Luther opened the gates, the passion spread in numerous directions with numerous reformers launching separate movements and many new sects springing up, each with its own idiosyncratic creed; but generally they had four tenets in common:

- Salvation could be a palpable, right-here/right-now experience.
- Salvation could be achieved through faith alone.
- No person needed an intermediary to connect with God.
- People could get everything they needed to know about religion from the Bible; they didn't need to know Latin or the conclusions of church councils or the pronouncements of priests and scholars.

In some ways, the Protestant Reformation came out of the same sorts of dissatisfactions and hungers that had given birth to Sufism. In the West, however, no Ghazali appeared to synthesize orthodox dogmas with the quest for personal religious breakthrough.

In other regards, the Protestant Reformation resembled the movements of Ibn Hanbal and Ibn Taymiyah—the exact opposite of Sufism. Like those Muslim theologians, Protestant reformers sought to delegitimize all later accretions of doctrine and go back to the original source: the Bible. The Book.

But ultimately, the Protestant Reformation was nothing like anything that had happened in Islam. Protestant Reformers rebelled against the Church and the pope, but in Islam, there was no church or pope to rebel against. In the West, the religious reformers who broke the hegemony of the Catholic Church didn't do so to raise up some monolithic new church but to empower the individual. Such a quest in no way pitted them against Christianity itself, because Christianity was inherently about the individual: a plan for the salvation of each person. Islam, however, was a plan for how a community should work; any reform movement that sought to secure for each individual the right to practice the religion as he or she thought best would inherently go up against the core doctrines of Islam itself.

By empowering the individual, the Protestant Reformation had conse-quences that went far beyond religion. At some level, breaking the hold of "the Church" amounted to breaking the hold of *any* church. It's true that the Protestant reformers of the sixteenth and seventeenth century were talking only about religious strivings, and it's true that each sect had a pretty definite and limited idea of a person's proper relationship to God.

Probably none of the reformers thought they were encouraging people to think outside the box on matters of faith. And yet, calling the quest for salvation the province of the individual legitimized the authority of each individual to think what he or she wanted about God, no matter what the reformers intended. And legitimizing the authority of individuals to think what they wanted about God implicitly legitimized their authority to think what they wanted about *anything*.

It was this aspect of the Reformation that cross-fertilized with the European rediscovery of ancient Greek thought, the renewal of interest in pagan Latin writers, and the trickling influence of Arab thinkers. Individuals who felt they could seek salvation on their own terms were naturally going to speculate freely on the nature of God and the world and with all these interesting ideas floating around, some people inevitably were going to start playing with new ways to put together the pieces of the puzzle they saw around them.

If the Church had still been ubiquitous and all-powerful, every idea would have required that an addendum be accounted for: how does it relate to the faith? If one were thinking, "I wonder why everything falls down instead of up," the voice of the church inside one's conscience would immediately ask, "and how will the explanation help me to be a better Christian?" There's only so far and so fast a mind can roam if it's dragging around this baggage all the time.

Liberated from this baggage, Copernicus could posit that the Earth went around the sun. This simple and daring hypothesis explained everything about the motion of the stars and planets except for why God would make the universe revolve around something other than His most precious creation. If you didn't have to deal with that second part, you could much more easily work out an answer to the first part. A lot of nature's puzzles were like that: they became much easier to explain if you didn't have to square your explanation with the dictates of the faith.

For most thinkers, this didn't mean contradicting the faith; it just meant that faith was one thing and explaining nature was another: they were two separate fields of inquiry and never did the twain have to meet. Separating inquiries about nature from the framework of faith enabled Europeans to come up with a dazzling array of scientific concepts and discoveries in the two centuries following the Reformation.

Francis Bacon and René Descartes, for example, overturned the Aristotelian method of inquiry and elaborated the scientific method in its stead. They and others also helped establish the mechanistic model of the universe, which held that every physical event had a purely physical cause. Galileo, Descartes, and others went on to dismantle the Aristotelian idea that everything is made of earth, air, water, and fire, replacing it with the atomic theory of matter, which laid the basis for modern chemistry.

Andreas Vesalius mapped the anatomy of the human body for the first time, and William Harvey discovered the circulation of blood. Together, they and others laid the basis for modern medicine. Antonie Van Leeuwenhoek discovered the world of microorganisms, which eventually led to Pasteur's powerful germ theory of disease.

Robert Boyle began the process that led to formulating the four laws of thermodynamics, just four laws that govern the transformation of energy into work in any system from a rabbit's digestive tract to the birth of the universe.

And let us not forget to mention the greatest scientist of them all, Isaac Newton, who invented differential calculus, explained the motion of all objects in the universe from pebbles to planets with three simple formulas, and discovered the laws of gravitation, thereby definitively explaining the motion of all heavenly bodies, the work begun by Copernicus and Galileo. Just for a capper, he described the particle nature of light and discovered the spectrum. No scientist had ever done so much and none has equaled his achievements since. It's ironic, therefore, that he himself felt his proudest accomplishment was remaining celibate all his life.

But here's the really interesting mystery to think about. Muslim scientists had come right to the threshold of virtually all these discoveries long before the West arrived there. In the tenth century, for example, al-Razi refuted Galen's theory of four humors as a basis for medical treatment. In the eleventh century, Ibn Sina analyzed motion mathematically, as Newton was to do so fruitfully six centuries later. In the thirteenth century, about three hundred years before Vesalius, Ibn al-Nafis described how blood circulated in the body. Ibn al-Haytham, who died in 1039, discovered the spectrum, described the scientific method, and established quantification and experiment as the basis for scientific exploration: he pretty much pre-Newtoned Newton and pre-Descarted Descartes. Muslims had already elaborated the atomic view of matter, which they took from Indian scientists, and some had elaborated the mechanistic model of the universe, which they had gotten from the Chinese.

The momentous thing was not so much the discoveries themselves as the fact that in the West they persisted, they accumulated, and they reinforced one another until they brought about a complete and coherent new way to view and approach the world, the scientific view, which enabled the West's later explosive advances in technology. Why did all this happen in the West but not in the East?

Possibly because Muslims made their great scientific discoveries just as their social order started crumbling, whereas the West made its great scientific discoveries just as its long-crumbled social order was starting to recover and in the wake of a religious reformation that broke the grip of church dogma on human thought, empowering individuals to speculate freely.

The Protestant Reformation was thus a key to the resurgence of Europe. But the Reformation also intertwined with another European development of tremendous consequence, the emergence of the nation-state as a form of political organization. The two were intertwined because when Luther and the others defied the Church, they took refuge with one or another of the monarchs of Europe, monarchs who had variously been struggling with the pope for some time now over who had final power in any given locale, the religious establishment or the secular one. The Reformation triggered an outburst of violence throughout Europe that ended with the Peace of Augsburg (1555). There the contending forces agreed on a landmark principle: that each monarch would have the authority to say whether his state, big or little, would stay with the Church of Rome or adopt one of the new Christian sects. Augsburg was only a ceasefire, it turned out. The pressure burst out again as the Thirty Years' War, a kind of civil war that raged all over Europe, basically over the issue of which religion was to prevail. When the conflict wound down finally, and a treaty was signed at Westphalia, in 1648, the principle established at Augsburg was confirmed. So along with empowering individualism, the Reformation ended up dismantling a Europe-wide ideology in favor of a system in which church and state reinforced each other to promote nationalism.

Some of the first germs of nation-states formed in England and France, whose monarchs had fought the sporadic Hundred Years' War from 1337 to 1453. It wasn't actually one continuous war, of course, but a series of campaigns interrupted by periods of peace. Before the war, there really was no such thing as "England" and "France." There was just territory, controlled by various nobles, who had various affiliations with other nobles. Empires, such as that of the medieval Carolingians, had been collections of territories. Being the emperor of these territories meant possessing the right and power to collect taxes there and draft soldiers from among its people. Emperors could mix and match and shuffle their collections of territory, trading or fighting over patches with other monarchs the way children fight over toys or exchange baseball cards. The people of two territories owned by the same emperor did not feel any sense of common peoplehood on that account. They weren't united in a feeling of kinship just because they both belonged to Charles the Bald.

A sense of shared peoplehood did, however, begin to develop over the course of the Hundred Years' War. For one thing, it became more distinctly the case that people in France spoke French and people in England spoke English. The French began to feel ever more united with others who spoke their language and lived in the same invaded territory and ever more distinct from the English-speaking armies who kept coming amongst them. Meanwhile, English soldiers, thrown together with one another over long campaigns that might recapitulate a campaign their fathers had been on, and which their sons might go on, felt ever more united with each other in a team-spirit kind of way. Over this period the "king" developed into something more than just the biggest nobleman: the idea of "king" as embodiment of "nation" began to form.

The Hundred Years' War began as a war between big-shot nobles and their knights, with yeomen who came along to carry the baggage and sometimes shoot their silly bows at other yeoman, those arrows being completely ineffectual against the real warriors, the men in metal suits. Partway through the Hundred Years' War, however, the English longbow was invented, a bow that could shoot harder and further than previous bows and whose arrows could pierce armor. Suddenly, a team of archers standing far behind the lines, could bring down a row of knights before they even got off their lists.

From that moment on, knights no longer determined the outcomes of battles, which meant that knights were obsolete. Feudal political organizations consisted of networks of personal connections. As feudalism faded, people who controlled money could organize large impersonal forces for war and eventually for work too. On the one hand, this transformed the king as a power figure in his country: he was the one person best situated to organize funding for large-scale military campaigns. But on the other hand, kings had to organize their fundraising through their nobles. In England, the organization of nobles whom the king had to call together to ratify a new military campaign was called "parliament." The English monarch's dependence on parliament to legitimize taxation eventually led to the development of democratic institutions in England—but that was still far down the line. In 1400, the transcendent grandeur of a king was big news all by itself.

Before nation-states emerged, the strongest forms of political organization were loose collections of territory with quasi-independent authority vested in many figures, at many levels. The overall leader had to operate through many intermediaries. Any order he gave was likely to be modified by every authority figure through whom it passed, not to mention distorted as it was translated into various languages, not to mention altered as it was made to fit local customs, not to mention lost entirely as people at the final, most local levels forgot (or refused) to pass it on. The greatest roar of the greatest emperor was likely to dissipate into a faint noise by the time it reached the smallest villages in the most outlying provinces. But in a nation-state, where everyone spoke more or less the same language, where a single network of officials administered the rules from top to bottom, where everyone was more or less on the same page, the king's policies traveled without much distortion to every cranny and corner of his realm.

That's not to say that England or France was that kind of nation-state in 1350 or 1400, but both were heading that way, and so were some of the principalities in northern Europe. The emergence of the nation-state enabled a single coherent government to set policies that affected all aspects of the lives of all the people living in its realm of control, people who still thought of themselves as subjects but were on their way to becoming citizens. So later, when the West went east, it was a case of nation-states, hard and sharp as knives, cutting into empires, loose and soft as bread.

The European quest for a sea route to the Indies, a direct aftermath of the Crusades, came to a head just as nation-states were emerging in Europe, just as the Protestant Reformation was turning the individual into a major actor on the historical stage, and just as the synergy between individualism and resurgent classical learning was giving rise to modern science.

In 1488, the Portuguese explorer Bartholomew Diaz rounded the Cape of Good Hope, proving at last that a ship could sail from the Atlantic Coast to the Indian Ocean. A stream of traffic followed his route. In 1492, Christopher Columbus sailed west across the Atlantic and discovered two big continents hitherto unknown to Europeans. A stream of traffic was soon going back and forth to the Americas.

Because Spain financed Columbus, Spain got first crack at the wealth of the Americas. This good fortune made Spain the richest nation in Europe for a while. Spain sucked so much gold out of the Americas, and spent it so freely at home, that the European gold market crashed. Ironically, that crash destroyed the Spanish economy, and Spain ended up as one of the poorest European nations.

The gold of the Americas, however, also washed through the whole economy of Europe. This happened just around the time that western Europe was firming up into nation-states, and nation-states have such coherence that they tend to operate as if they were individual persons. Before the nation-state emerged, it wasn't possible for some guy in England to hope that "England" would get richer, and to take personal satisfaction and pride in this happening. He might want wealth to flow to his area; he might want his town to get richer, or his family, or even his king, but England? What was England? Now, however, in areas where the people thought of themselves collectively as "a nation" it was easy and inevitable for people to think in terms of policies that would benefit the nation. One such policy was mercantilism.

Mercantilism was quite a simple concept, really. It was based on the notion that the economy of nations was like that of individual people. An individual person who earns a lot of money and spends very little becomes rich: guaranteed. For any individual person, the most desirable form that (incoming) money can take is gold. Accumulate lots of gold and you're set. So people in western Europe easily fell into thinking that the wealth of their nations depended on bringing in as much gold as they could and letting out as little as possible. And they saw how this could be done: by selling lots of products to their friends and neighbors for gold and buying—ideally—nothing.

To sell a lot you have to make a lot. To buy nothing, you have to be self-sufficient. But how could a nation sell and sell and never buy? Where would the raw materials come from? This is where mercantilism, which was intertwined with nationalism, which was intertwined with the Protestant Reformation, which was intertwined with the ethos of individualism, which was intertwined with Renaissance humanism—intersected with European sea prowess and the urge to explore the world—which came right out of the Crusades.

All these synergistic, cross-fertilizing developments were beginning to peak in Europe just around 1600. At that moment, Europeans were master mariners. They were rapidly getting organized as compact nation-states. They were rethinking the world in scientific terms. They had the gold of the Americas burning holes in their pockets. And they were economically energized by protocapitalist entrepreneurs armed with a new ethos of individualism.

Incredibly enough, all of this development went virtually unnoticed by the Muslim world where, at that very moment, Moghul civilization was peaking in India, Safavid culture was peaking in Persia, and the Ottoman empire was only just past its peak period of efflorescence in Asia Minor, Mesopotamia, the Levant, the Hijaz, Egypt, and North Africa.

And then the two worlds began to intermingle.

12

∽

West Comes East

905-1266 AH
1500-1850 CE

B ETWEEN 1500 AND 1800 CE, western Europeans sailed pretty much all over the world and colonized pretty much everything. In some lands, they simply took possession, entirely supplanting the original inhabitants: North America and Australia suffered this fate, ending up as virtual extensions of Europe.

In other areas, they left the original inhabitants in place but moved in above them as a ruling elite in control of all-important resources. Some portion of the original population ended up as their servants or slaves while the rest went on living as best they could in constricted circumstances. Such was the fate of the people in most of South America and sub-Saharan Africa.

In some places, however—most notably China and the Islamic heartland—Europeans came up against well-organized, wealthy, technologically advanced societies seemingly quite able to hold their own, and here the interaction between newcomers and natives took a subtler course. The Islamic world presented a particularly complex psychosocial drama, first, because western Europeans had a tangled history with Muslims already, and second, because they started trickling into the Muslim world just as

217

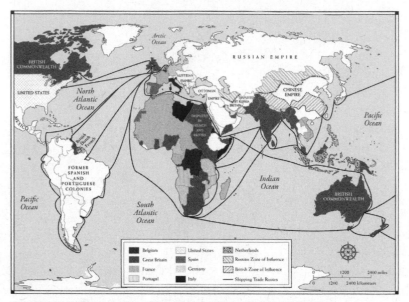

WESTERN IMPERIALISM: THE GLOBAL REACH OF SEA POWER

the three great Islamic empires were rising toward their peak of power and brilliance.

Let's be clear about one thing: the European penetration of the Muslim world never amounted to a clash of civilizations (to use a term coined in the 1990s). In this period of colonization, "European civilization" never went to war with "Islamic civilization," and that's one key to understanding all that followed. In fact, after 1500, western Europeans arrived in the eastern Islamic world mainly as traders. What could be less threatening? Trade is what people do *instead* of making war. Trade—why, it's practically a synonym for peace!

Nor did the Europeans come in great numbers. The first European expedition to reach India by sea was led by Portuguese aristocrat Vasco da Gama and consisted of four ships and a total crew of 171 men. They arrived at Calicut on the west coast of India in 1498 and asked the local Hindu ruler if they might set up a trading post along the coast there and do a little buying, maybe a little selling. The ruler said sure. Why wouldn't he? If these strangers wanted to buy cloth, or raw cotton, or sugar or whatever, why would he say no? His people had businesses to run! You don't make money by refusing to sell your products.

The Europeans did encounter a flash of hostility from Muslims thereabouts a bit later, but the Muslims were interlopers themselves that far south and so the Portuguese got local Hindu support to build a little town and fort at a place called Goa. They had nothing very remarkable to trade, but they did have money to buy, and as the years went by more of them were coming along with more and more money to spend, as the gold of the Americas flooded the European economy. Goa became a permanent Portuguese implant in India.

Then more traders came along from other parts of western Europe. The French set up a "trading post" at Pondicherry and the British set up one at Madras.[1] The Dutch sailed by and looked in as well. These European communities started fighting among themselves for business advantages, but the Indians paid little notice. Why should they care who won? Babur and his descendents were just establishing the Moghul empire up north, and they were the big story of the time, much bigger than a few obscure traders building little forts along the coast. And so the sixteenth century passed without Europeans making much of an impact on the Islamic world.

Then again, not all Europeans came to the Muslim world as traders. Some came as business advisers or technical consultants. In 1598, a pair of English brothers, Robert and Anthony Sherley, found their way to Persia, which was well into its "golden age" under the greatest of the Safavid monarchs, Shah Abbas. The Englishmen said they came in peace with an interesting proposition for the Persian king: they wanted to sell him cannons and firearms and they could promise technical support to back up their products—they would have their people come in and train the Shah's people in the new weapons, teach military strategy to go with them, plus how to fix the weapons if they broke, things like that.

Shah Abbas liked what he heard. Safavid Persia lagged behind its neighbors in military technology. The Qizilbash didn't like firearms; they were still fighting mostly with spears and swords and bows; this deficit had cost the Safavids the battle of Chaldiran, and now the hated Ottomans were trying to stop weapons shipments to Persia. Getting weapons and consultants from some distant, insignificant speck of an island west of Europe seemed like a perfect solution. The Englishmen knew their stuff, and a few of them from so far away couldn't possibly do much harm, it seemed. And so it began: the practice of giving European advisers commanding positions in the Persian army.

It's true, however, that not all interactions between westerners and Muslims were peaceful. The Ottoman Turks had been fighting with Christian Europeans for centuries; their western border was the frontier between the two worlds, and here the friction showed. Between battles, however, and even while pitched battles were raging in some places, a lot of trading was going on in other places, because this was not a World War II–type total-war situation. Battles were geographically contained. At the very moment that two armies were clashing one place, business-as-usual might well be going on just a few miles away. The friction had an ideological dimension left over from the Crusades, to be sure—Christianity versus Islam—but in any practical sense the battles were outbursts of professional violence between monarchs over territory. Lots of Christians and Jews lived within the Ottoman empire, after all, and some of them were in the Ottoman armies, fighting for that side, not out of patriotic fervor for the House of Othman but because it was a job, and they needed the money. This kind of fighting certainly allowed for other people to be going back and forth, buying and selling.

By the seventeenth century, it wasn't just Venetians but also French, English, German, Dutch, and other European traders who were traveling into the Muslim world armed not with gold but with guns. These businessmen contributed to a process that slowly and inexorably transformed the mighty Ottoman Empire into the lumbering monstrosity that Europeans called the Sick Man of Europe, or sometimes—more gently but in some ways even more condescendingly—"the Eastern question." The process was so slow, however, and so pervasive and so complex that it was hard for anyone going through the history of it all day by day to make a connection between the European encroachment and the burgeoning decay.

The first thing to note about the process is what *didn't* happen. The Ottoman Empire did not go down in flames to conquering armies. Long after the empire was totally moribund, long after it was little more than a virtual carcass for vultures to pick over, the Ottomans could still muster damaging military strength.

Historians identify two seminal military defeats that spelled the beginning of the end for the Ottomans, though both went more or less unnoticed by the Turks at the time. One was the battle of Lepanto, which took place in 1571. In this naval engagement, the Venetians and their allies destroyed virtually the entire Ottoman Mediterranean fleet. In Europe, the battle was hailed as a thrilling sign that the heathen Turk was finally, finally going down.

In Istanbul, however, the grand vizier compared the loss of the fleet to the shaving of a man's beard: it would only make the new beard grow in thicker. Indeed, within one year, the Ottomans replaced the whole lost fleet with an even bigger and more modern fleet, featuring eight of the largest ships ever to ply the Mediterranean. Within six months after *that*, the Ottomans won back the eastern Mediterranean, conquered Cyprus, and began to harass Sicily. Small wonder that contemporary Ottoman analysts didn't see the battle of Lepanto as any big turning point at the time. It would take at least another century before European naval dominance would become fully evident and the significance of that dominance unmistakable.

The other seminal military event took place a bit earlier with a followup much later. The earlier bracket was Suleiman the Magnificent's failure to take Vienna. Ottoman forces had never stopped pushing steadily west, and in 1529 they reached the gates of Vienna, but the sultan set siege to the famous Austrian city too late in the season. With winter coming on, he decided to let Vienna go this time and conquer it the next time around. But there was no next time for Suleiman, because other issues cropped up and he got distracted—the empire was so big, after all, and its borders so long, that distractions were constantly sprouting up on those borders *somewhere*. The sultan never made another attempt on Vienna but his contemporaries saw no sign of weakness in this. "Conquer Vienna" remained on his to-do list always; it's just that the man was *busy*. He was fighting and winning other battles, and his rule was so successful that only a blithering idiot would have suggested that the Ottomans were in decline in his day just because they had not taken Vienna. It wasn't a military defeat, after all, just a failure to score the usual crushing victory.

And yet historians looking back can see quite clearly that Suleiman's failure to take Vienna marked a watershed. At that moment the empire had reached its greatest extent. After that moment, it was no longer expanding. This was less than obvious at the time because the empire was still fighting someone somewhere all the time, and the news from the battlefield was often good. Maybe the Ottomans were losing battles here and there, but they were also winning battles here and there. Were they losing more than they were winning? Were they losing the big ones and winning only the little ones? That was the real question, and the answer was yes, but that was hard to gauge for people swimming through the historical moment. How does one weigh the significance of a battle? Some people raised alarmist cries, but some people always do. After all, in 1600, the empire certainly was not shrinking.

Unfortunately, however, not shrinking was not good enough for the Ottoman Empire. In truth, this empire was built on the *premise* of permanent expansion. It needed a constant and generally successful war on its borders for all of its complicated internal mechanisms to work.

First of all, expansion was a source of revenue, which the empire could ill afford to lose.

Second, war served as a safety valve, which vented all internal pressures outward. For example, peasants who were forced off the land for one reason or another didn't hang around hungry and hopeless, turning into a surly rabble. They could always join the army, go on a campaign, score some booty, and then come home and start a little business. . . .

Once expansion stopped, however, all those pressures began to press inward. Those who could no longer make a living off the land for any reason now drifted to the cities. Even if they had a skill, they might not be able to ply it. The guilds controlled all manufacturing and they could absorb only so many new members. A good many of the drifters ended up unemployed and disgruntled. And there were lots of other little consequences like this, generated by no longer expanding.

Third, the classic *devshirme* depended on the constant conquest of new territories out of which "slaves" could be drafted for the institutes that produced the empire's elite. The *janissary* had originally labored under one important restriction: they were not allowed to marry and produce heirs, a device designed to keep new blood flowing into the administration. But once the expansion stopped, the devshirme began to stagnate. And then the janissaries began to marry. And then they did what people do for their children: swing their clout to get the kids the best possible educational and employment opportunities. It was perfectly natural, but it did mean the janissaries encrusted into a permanent, hereditary elite, which reduced the vigor of the empire because it meant the experts and specialists who ran the empire were no longer drawn exclusively from those who showed early promise but also included dullards with rich and important parents.

No one linked these stagnations to the fact that Suleiman had failed to conquer Vienna decades ago. How could they? The consequences were so distantly and so indirectly related to their causes that for the general public they registered merely as some sort of indefinable social malaise that was hard to explain, the sort of thing that makes religious conservatives rail about the moral fabric of society and the importance of restoring old-fashioned values like discipline and respect for elders.

Then came the follow-up to Suleiman's failure. In 1683, the Ottomans tried again to take Vienna and they failed again, just as they had 154 years earlier, but this time they were routed by a coalition of European forces. Technically this second battle for Vienna was also merely a failure to score a victory, but the Ottoman elite knew they had been trounced and something had gone very wrong.

It made them doggedly determined to pump up their military strength. Too easily did they assume that the might and vigor of their empire depended on troops and weapons. Against the formless forces eroding the empire, they thought to fling up a military bulwark. Pouring resources into their military, however, only imposed more expenses on a government that was already overburdened.

It was overburdened in part because European traders entering the economy had upset the delicate checks and balances in the Ottoman system. Forget the battle of Lepanto. Forget the failed siege of Vienna. Ultimately, it was traders, not soldiers, who took down the Ottoman Empire.

Let me trace some of the details. In the Ottoman Empire, guilds (intertwined with Sufi orders) controlled all manufacturing and they protected their members by locking out competition. One guild had a monopoly on producing soap, for example, while another had a monopoly on making shoes. . . . The guilds couldn't exploit their monopoly positions to jack up prices, because the state imposed limits on how much they could charge. The state protected the public and the guilds protected their members; everything balanced, everything worked.

Then westerners came into the system. They didn't compete with the guilds by trying to sell soap or shoes—the state wouldn't let them. No, they came looking for stuff to buy, raw materials mainly, such as wool, meat, leather, wood, oil, metals, and the like—whatever they could get their hands on. Suppliers were happy to sell to them, and even the state smiled on this trade, because it brought gold into the empire, and how could that be a bad thing? Unfortunately, the Europeans were after the same materials the guilds needed to make their products. And the Europeans could outbid the guilds because they had the gold of the Americas in their satchels, while the guilds had only their profits, which were limited by government price controls. They could not make up the difference with volume—by producing and selling more goods, that is—because they just couldn't get enough raw materials to increase production. With foreigners sucking those out of Ottoman territories and shipping them to Europe, artisans in the Ottoman world felt the pinch: domestic production began to fall.

Ottoman officials saw the problem and dealt with it by banning the export of strategic raw materials needed by domestic industries. But laws of this type only opened up contraband opportunities: when exporting wool is a crime, only criminals will export wool. A black market economy began to thrive; a whole class of nouveau riche black-market entrepreneurs emerged; and since they were breaking the law to make money, they had to bribe various officials to look the other way, which opened up opportunities for corruption, which spawned another class of nouveau riche "entrepreneurs": bribe-battened bureaucrats.

So now a lot of folks had illegal cash to spend that didn't come out of any increased productivity. It was cash funneled into the Ottoman economy by free-spending Europeans drawing down on the gold of the Americas. But what could the newly rich Ottoman citizens spend their money on? Investing in aboveboard industries was out: it would attract unwelcome attention from the state. So they did what drug dealers do in modern American society. They spent freely on extravagant luxury items. In the Ottoman world, these included consumer goods from the West, which could be had for cash paid under the table. The very trends undermining Ottoman ability to manufacture goods were providing a market for European industry and incidentally draining the gold back to Europe.

Outside cash coming into the Ottoman system just as production was falling generated inflation: that's what happens when you have more money chasing fewer goods. I've seen the same pattern in certain rural counties in northern California, where a few people are getting fabulously rich from growing marijuana. In an area with no apparent economy, you see people driving BMWs, ordinary houses start selling for a million dollars, and even bread finally costs more in suddenly gentrified grocery stores.

Whom does inflation hurt? It hurts people on fixed incomes. These days, we tend to equate "fixed income" with "small income"; we think of pensioners living on social security or welfare. In Ottoman society, there was no welfare system. Families and communities took care of their own elderly and sick. No, in Ottoman society, the people on "fixed incomes" were the salaried government bureaucrats and more particularly the salaried officials of the court—that bloated, wholly nonproductive upper class. Those "fixed income" folks were rich beyond the dreams of Croesus, but even the richest of the rich somehow feel threatened when their buying power goes down. In 1929, when the U.S. stock market crashed, some of those bankers who famously jumped out of high-rise windows were still worth a million dollars when they hit the sidewalk. How much they *had* didn't matter: it was how much *less* they had that got to them. Similarly, in Ottoman society, inflation made rich courtiers living on fixed salaries feel like they had to tighten their belts and this they didn't like. They began to supplement their incomes by wielding the only instrument they controlled.

What do courtiers (and bureaucrats) control? Access to the administrative and legal workings of the state. When people have no role except to provide access, however, they have no power except to *deny* access. Courtiers and bureaucrats in the Ottoman Empire began to prevent instead of facilitate—unless they were given bribes. The Ottoman Empire became a paperwork nightmare. To negotiate one's way through it, a person needed to bribe people who knew people who knew people who could bribe people who could bribe other people who knew people.

To combat this gumming up of the works, the state raised salaries, so that courtiers and bureaucrats wouldn't feel the *need* to take bribes. But the state didn't have any source of extra funds based in real productivity, especially since, with the empire no longer expanding, the state did not have the revenue that traditionally flowed into its coffers from conquest. In order to raise salaries, pensions, and soldiers' wages, therefore, the empire had to simply print money.

Printing money spurs inflation—which puts us back where we started! Everything the Ottoman government did to stem corruption and promote efficiency only aggravated the problem it was trying to solve. Eventually, government officials gave up and decided to hire some consultants to come in and help them set things in order. The advisers they hired were management consultants and technical experts from the continent that seemed to know how: western Europe.

Perhaps some brilliant executive could have done something about the unraveling that led the Ottoman elite to this sorry state; but the very success of the empire, and the very might of its ruling family, had transformed its imperial culture and the life of its royal family in ways that pretty much precluded any new Mehmet the Conquerors or Suleiman the Magnificents from emerging. Specifically, the court had grown ever bigger, heavier, and less productive until it was like some giant deformity that the whole society was carrying on its back.

The archetypal symbol of this deformity was, perhaps, the so-called Grand Seraglio, the Sultan's harem in Istanbul. Earlier dynasties around the Muslim world had harems, of course, but in Ottoman society, this grim institution grew to proportions never seen before, except perhaps in China under the Ming dynasty.

Thousands of women from every conquered population lived in the labyrinthine Grand Seraglio. Although steeped in an overall atmosphere of wealth and luxury, most of these women lived in cubicles within the maze. The women of the harem were supplied with cosmetics and all other supplies useful to enhancing their adornments and had no other occupation except for self-adornment: no useful work to do, no opportunity to study, no call to produce anything, nothing to rescue them from a life of meaningless boredom. They were prisoners in gem-crusted cells.

The sequestration of women had been hundreds of years in the making in the Islamic world, but even at this point, it didn't run through the whole society, only through the upper classes. In rural areas, the casual traveler might still see peasant women working in the fields or driving animals along the roads. In urban areas, lower class women went about their business in the public bazaars, shopping for their households or hawking their handicrafts. Among the middle classes, some women owned property, managed businesses, and directed employees. But the public visibility of these women denoted the humble status of their men.

Privileged men showed off their status by keeping their womenfolk out of public life and hidden from view in the private quarters of their households. The psychology underlying this custom was (I think) the feeling that a man's honor—which really means his ability to hold his head high among his fellow men—depended on his ability to keep any women associated with him from becoming the objects of other men's sexual fantasies. In the end, this is what the sequestration of women boiled down to, and in such a cultural milieu, even men in the lower strata of society felt a pressure to keep their women out of sight, so they wouldn't look bad to other men.

In the sultan's harem, this syndrome had magnified to a staggering level. In ordinary usage, especially among western Orientalists, the word *harem* has a lascivious connotation to it, as if everyday life in a harem consisted of sexual frolicking from dawn to dusk; but how could this possibly have been the case? The sultan was just one man, and no other man ever even saw the women of the imperial harem except the guards, and the guards were all eunuchs. And the sultan, some may be surprised to learn, didn't spend his leisure hours hanging around the harem, playing around with the women. One of the eunuchs had the specific job of choosing one woman for the sultan to sleep with each night, and this eunuch would escort the chosen woman secretively and properly bundled, under cover of night, to the sultan's chamber. Sexual license and sexual repression were weirdly intertwined in this institution.[2]

Eunuchs could move freely between the harem and the world, and so acted as the women's eyes and ears and hands, their means of learning about the outside world, their instruments for effecting changes out there. The sultan's children, including his sons, grew up in the harem until they were twelve, never mingling with ordinary people or taking part in the rough-and-tumble of ordinary life until adolescence. By the time such a prince mounted the throne he was quite typically a socially dysfunctional creature whose main skill consisted of the ability to maneuver through the maze of harem intrigue.

And very high-stakes, high-intensity intrigue it was, because even though one prince may have been the heir-designate, the mothers of the many other princes did not necessarily abandon hope that their own boy would somehow achieve the throne (which would make mother a power-figure in the empire.) So the women and their progeny plotted and conspired and attempted (and sometimes succeeded at) assassinations of potential rivals until the reigning sultan died, whereupon the struggle for power moved from back-room intrigue to front-room fisticuffs. The prince who came out victorious won the throne not just for himself but for some whole faction of women and eunuchs within the harem. An Ottoman princeling growing up in this environment knew he had some small chance of ending up as the supreme master of the universe and a much larger chance of ending up dead before he reached maturity.

This system ended up producing a long line of weak, idiotic, and eccentric sultans. But this fact in itself did not account for the decline and fall of the Ottoman Empire, because by the time the system ripened into its corrupt maturity, the sultan no longer ran the state. The executive powers of his position had begun to decay shortly after Suleiman the Magnificent died. In the Ottoman system, grand vizier became the power position.

Yet the ungainly court with its enormous harem did hamper the Ottoman Empire, because it *cost* so much and produced so little—produced in fact nothing, not even decisions. The vizier and other officials had to run the empire while carrying this court on their shoulders and keeping the damn thing fed, which made the whole operation ungainly and slow.

Between 1600 and 1800, Safavid Persia was unraveling too. The Europeans were on hand to exploit what happened, but it was the kingdom's own internal contradictions that pulled it apart. First of all, the usual dynastic rot set in. Princes raised in too much luxury were coming to the throne dissolute and lazy. Every time one of these flawed kings died, a power struggle erupted among his survivors; whoever won the throne took over a realm debilitated by war and was generally too idle or incompetent to repair the damage, so the golden age turned to silver, the silver to bronze, and the bronze to mud.

When the Safavids first came to power they had created a distinctly Persian Islam by making Shi'ism the state religion. This was useful to the state at first, because it promoted a national coherence that made Persia strong for its size. But it alienated Sunnis within the borders, and as the throne weakened, these Sunnis turned rebellious and began to pull away.

Making Shi'ism the official state religion had another downside, as well. It gave the Shi'i religious scholars a dangerous sense of self-importance, especially the *mujtahids,* a title that meant "scholars so learned they have a right to make original judgments" (later these worthies were called ayatollahs). These Shi'i ulama began to claim that if Persia was *really* a Shi'i state, kings could rule only with their approval, because only they spoke for the Hidden Imam. Ominously, the ulama had strong links among peasants and among the merchants who made up the urban middle class. Safavid kings therefore found themselves facing a Hobson's choice. If they sought the approval of the ulama they would be conceding ultimate authority to the ayatollahs; if they asserted their own authority as supreme, they would have to forego the ulama's approval and in that case rule without popular legitimacy.

They opted for the latter; but kings who lack legitimacy need some other source of power to give them authority, and what could the Safavids tap? They had nothing to turn to but their armies—and by this time their armies were armed and trained and "advised" by European military experts. In short, Persia ended up with European Christians helping Safavid kings clamp down on Muslim religious scholars who were closely tied to the masses: obviously a formula for trouble.

As the eighteenth century waned, succession struggles over the throne grew ever more ferocious. Contending factions began recruiting more European military consultants and importing more European arms to gain the edge on their rivals. A time came when the power struggles failed to produce single winners. Different contenders took possession of different areas. And as Persia came apart, Sunni provinces broke away from the kingdom, and Sunni neighbors such as the Uzbeks and the Afghans broke into the kingdom to wreak terrible havoc.

When the smoke cleared the Safavids were gone. In their place, stood a new family monarchy. Nominally, this so-called Qajar dynasty ruled the shrinking country of Iran for the next 131 years. (It was still "Persia" to Europeans, but locals generally were calling the country Iran by this point, although the name did not switch at any one moment: both names go back to ancient times.) Under the Qajar kings, the disturbing trends of Safavid times became the ordinary, accepted order of things. The national armies were riddled with European advisers and officers. The ulama were chronically at odds with the throne. Repelled by foreign influences at court, these ulama set themselves up as guardians of traditional Islamic culture, to which the lower and middle classes were still wedded. The kings were generally lazy, rapacious, shortsighted, and weak. Europeans pulled the strings that made these puppets jerk and squeak in a most lifelike manner.

Europeans never invaded Persia, never made concerted war on it. They just came to sell, to buy, to work, to "help." But there they were when things came apart. And like opportunistic viruses that lurk in the body unnoticed but flourish into illness when the immune system breaks down, the Europeans flowed into whatever cracks opened up in the fragmenting society, growing ever more powerful as the cracks grew wider, until at last they were in command.

Europeans pretty much failed to notice they were taking over Persia; and that's partly because there was no "they." Westerners came to Persia from various European countries, and Persians were not the enemy to them but the backdrop. The enemy, for each group of Europeans, was another group of Europeans. The British, the French, the Russians, the Dutch and others kept moving into power vacuums in Persia not so much to conquer Persia as to block other Europeans from conquering Persia. The rivalry eventually boiled down to Russia versus Great Britain, and to understand this competition, one must factor in the thunderous events happening further east, in the last of those three big Islamic Empires, the land of the Moghuls.

In the Moghul empire the core contradiction had always been Hindus versus Muslims. Akbar the Great had worked out a sort of accommodation,

but his great-grandson Aurangzeb reversed all his policies, enforcing orthodox Islam rigidly, restoring discrimination against Hindus, squashing
smaller religious groups such as the Sikhs, and generally replacing tolerance with repression. And yet, say what you will about the man's narrow-
minded zealotry, Aurangzeb was a titanic talent, so he not only held his
empire together but extended it. The whole time, however, he was sowing
the discord and tension that would erupt to ruin the empire as soon as a
less capable ruler took charge.

This less capable ruler was the very next one after Aurangzeb—and the
next one after him and the next one after that and so on down. In its first
two hundred years, the Moghul empire had just six emperors; in its next
fifty years it had eight. Of the first six, five were world historical geniuses;
of the last eight, all were midgets.

During the fifty-year era of those midgets, Hindu kings called the
Marathas surged again in the south. The Sikhs became a militant force.
Nawabs, Muslim provincial governors, began to ignore orders from the
capital and rule as independent princes. In fact, India broke up into
smaller states and each state dissolved into turmoil as clashes broke out between Hindus and Muslims and others, making life uncertain for all.

Throughout this fragmentation, the Portuguese, the Dutch, the
French, and the English were hovering on the edges, doing business from
their trading posts along the coast. At first the Portuguese had dominated this trade. Then the Dutch had outflanked them, planting forts
and trading posts in both Southeast Asia and Persia, and beating the Portuguese at sea with better ships and bigger guns. Then the French came
in and held their own, and so did the English, who built a fort at Madras
in 1639, acquired Bombay (now called Mumbai) a bit later when their
king married a Portuguese princess (Bombay came with her as part of her
dowry) and then planting a colony on the Bay of Bengal, which grew
into Calcutta.

The Europeans who came to East Asia in this era represented something new and unprecedented in world history. They weren't generals or
soldiers, they didn't come as the envoys of kings, they didn't represent
governments. They were employees of private companies, but companies
of a new kind: joint stock-holding companies or, as we now call them,
corporations.

The first such company was born in 1553, when forty English merchants ponied up twenty-five pounds apiece to finance a search for a sea route to India. The expedition they funded found Moscow instead of India (don't ask), but it brought home a tidy profit and when this news spread, other people clamored to buy into "the Russia Company." Those who paid the subscription fee got slips of paper entitling them to a proportional cut of any profits the company's future ventures earned, slips of paper they could sell to speculators if they wished (and thus the institution of the stock market was born).

Around 1600, three gigantic national versions of that first corporation were created in Europe: they were the English, the Dutch, and the French "East India Companies." Each was a limited liability corporation with private shareholders. Each was founded for the sole aim of turning a profit on trade in East Asia in order to enrich its shareholders. Each was run by a board of directors. Each was chartered by its national government, and in each case the government in question gave its company a national monopoly on doing business in the Islamic east. The actual entities jockeying for advantage in Persia, India, and Southeast Asia, then, were these corporations.

Over the course of two centuries in India, these European corporations altered the texture of the Indian economy in ways reminiscent of what was happening in the Ottoman world. In Bengal, where the British elbowed out all other Europeans, the East India Company pretty much destroyed the Bengali crafts industry, but hardly noticed itself doing so. It was simply buying up lots of raw material at very good prices. People found more profit in selling raw material to the British than in using those materials to make their own goods. As the native economy went bust, indigenous Bengalis became ever more dependant on the British and finally subservient to them.

When the corporations first arrived in India, they competed to earn the favor of the Moghul emperor, but as the empire broke down, the favor of the central government mattered less and less. The Europeans came to realize they had better align themselves with various local rulers rising up. But they had to pick the right ones of these, because some turned out to be losers and got churned under. Guessing wrong about the subcontinent's internal politics would cost the company money. It was tempting, therefore, to take the guesswork out of it and try to control the outcomes of local power struggles. To this end, the companies brought in private armies to help their allies. Here, as in Persia, the enemy, for each group of Europeans, was not the local population but other Europeans. In supporting their Indian allies, the European corporations were actually fighting proxy wars against one another. The Portuguese lost out early, the Dutch were eliminated next (from India, anyway—they remained dominant in Southeast Asia) and the contest for India finally came down to the British versus the French.

As it happened, the French and the British were also the finalists in the contest for North America, halfway around the world. There, a skirmish between a few dozen Europeans kicked off a chain of events that ended up making all of India a British colony. It started in the spring of 1754, when a British army major named George Washington was leading a surveying party up the Ohio River and stumbled across a French scouting party. Shots were fired, one Virginian and ten Frenchmen died, and a global conflict erupted between Great Britain and France, with most of the other European powers jumping in quickly. In North America the conflict was called the French and Indian War, in Europe the Seven Years' War, and in India the Third Carnatic War. [3]

As the name implies, the European rivals in India had already fought two proxy wars in the Carnatic region north of modern-day Madras, trying to seat their respective allies on minor thrones. The fighting, in each case, was conducted by the East India Companies of Britain and France. In 1756, the nawab of Bengal, Siraj al-Dawlah, overran the British fort at Calcutta. On a sweltering June night, someone (not the nawab; he knew nothing about it) locked up sixty-four British citizens in an airless underground prison cell. "Someone" was supposed to process them out that night and send them home, but signals got crossed and the prisoners were left in the dungeon overnight. By morning, forty-three of them were dead.

The report swiftly made its way to England. The press went crazy. They titled the nawab's dungeon "the black hole of Calcutta." In each retelling of the story, the dimensions of the cell shrank and the number of prisoners burgeoned, finally reaching 146, while the number of dead rose to 123. The story outraged the British public. In India, a one-time company clerk named Robert Clive, now a captain in the company's private army, marched to Calcutta to extract revenge. He deposed the nawab, and installed the nawab's uncle in his place. (The so-called battle of Plassey, which effected this change, consisted of Clive bribing the nawab's body-guards to go home and then arresting and executing the abandoned nawab.)

Even then, the British did not name themselves rulers, not even of this one provincial piece of India. Officially, Bengal remained a Moghul possession and its government remained Bengali. Clive appointed him-self a mere employee of this provincial government, setting his own salary at thirty thousand pounds a year. The East India Company en-shrined itself as the Bengali government's "advisers," nothing more. For the sake of efficiency, the company decided to go ahead and collect taxes on behalf of the Moghul government. And again, for efficiency's sake, they decided to go ahead and spend the money themselves, directly, locally: what was the point of sending it to the capital and having it come back again? Oh, and henceforth the company's private army would take care of security and maintain law and order. But the company insisted that it was not now governing Bengal: it was just providing needed services for a fee.

The first few years of British rule worked out poorly for Bengalis. The company left day-to-day administration in local hands and focused only on matters relevant to its business interests. In practice, this meant the (powerless) "government" was responsible for solving all problems while the (powerful) company was entitled to reap all benefits but disavowed any responsibility for the welfare of the people; after all, it was not the govern-ment. Rapacious company officials bled Bengal dry, but those who com-plained were referred to "the government." The plundering of the province resulted in a famine that killed about a third of the population in just two years—we're talking about an estimated ten million people here.[4] The famine damaged the company's interests too, however, just as a parasite suffers when the plant on which it is feeding wilts.

At this point, the British government decided to step in. Parliament ap-pointed a governor-general for India, brought the East India Company under control, and sent troops to the subcontinent. For the next hundred years, there were *two* British armies in India: so-called "John company" troops who worked for the corporation and "Queen's company" troops, who worked for the British crown. It should be noted, however, that only the officers were European. The grunts who carried the rifles and took the bullets were local recruits or draftees known as sepoys.

In Bengal, Clive set a precedent that would soon be repeated in many other states. He established that Britain had the power and right to appoint and depose rulers in any part of India where the East India Company had business interests. After 1763, this was every part of India, because France lost the Seven Years' War and had to abandon the subcontinent.

Britain soon decreed that whenever an Indian ruler died without a male heir, the British crown inherited his territory. In this way, Great Britain gradually took direct control of many states. In others, it installed a proxy who ruled in accordance with British wishes and interests. India became a patchwork of states ruled directly or indirectly by the British, the East India Company gradually emerging as the top power in the subcontinent and the true successor of the Moghuls.

Great Britain lost its North American colonies at almost exactly the same time that it was gaining control of India. General Cornwallis, well known to American-history buffs as the man whom George Washington beat at Yorktown, was the second governor general of India and the one who really consolidated British control there. Seen only in the context of American history, Cornwallis was a loser, but the chances are that he died proud of his life's accomplishments, because India became "the jewel in the British crown," the country's most precious colonial possession, and the key to its dominance around the world.

With the vast resources of the subcontinent on tap, Great Britain could finance further colonial adventures in Africa and elsewhere around the globe. Naturally, therefore, it was very touchy about any threats to its jewel. And just such a threat did begin to emerge as the eighteenth century gave way to the nineteenth: the threat posed by an expanding Russia.

When the Turks conquered Constantinople, they plunged Orthodox Christianity into a crisis. Constantinople had been "the New Rome" and the heart of the (Orthodox) Christian world. Without a heart, how could the faith live on? The grand duke of Moscow stepped into the breach. This man, Ivan the Third, declared his capital "the Third Rome," the new heart of Orthodox Christianity. His grandson Ivan the Terrible took on the title of Caesar, thereby claiming the imperial tradition of ancient Rome. (In

Russian, of course, his title was pronounced "czar.") Between 1682 and 1725, one of the czars, Peter the Great, built a formidable army and began carving out an empire east of Moscow. By 1762, when Catherine the Great of the Romanoff dynasty came to power, this empire extended way beyond the Caspian Sea, beyond the Ural Mountains even, deep into Siberia, stretching across all the lands north of India, Persia, Mesopotamia, and Asia Minor.

Catherine soon gave notice that Russia would not only push east; it might push south as well. Catherine's armies engaged the Ottomans in a bid to take the Black Sea coast and drive the Turks out of Europe. Fighting the Ottomans was all very well, but the British could not have the Russians coming south into Persia or worse, down into the mountains inhabited by the Afghan tribes, for that would put the Russians within striking distance of the jewel in the British crown. For many centuries, in fact, the Hindu Kush mountains and the Persian highlands had served as a staging area for conquests of India. British leaders decided they must block Russian advances everywhere along this front. And so the Great Game began.

"The Great Game" was the term invented by British novelist Rudyard Kipling for the struggle between Great Britain and Russia to control the territory stretching between the Russian Empire in the north and the British Empire in the south. Everything that had once been Safavid Persia, everything that is now Afghanistan, much of what is now Pakistan, and all the territories covered by the former Soviet republics of Turkmenistan, Uzbekistan, Kyrghizistan, and Tajikistan—all of this was the arena in which the Great Game was "played."

It wasn't really a game, of course, and "play" is a misnomer. But it wasn't really a war, either. Occasional battles broke out, and a few massacres, an atrocity here and there, but the Great Game consisted mostly of plotting, pushing, conspiring, maneuvering, manipulating, politicking, bribing, and corrupting people in the region mentioned. The adversaries were the two great European powers, and the people who lived in these lands, virtually all of them Muslims, were merely the chess pieces, the game tokens.

In Iran, the Qajar kings entertained a hope of reempowering their country by importing European technology and know-how. But whom

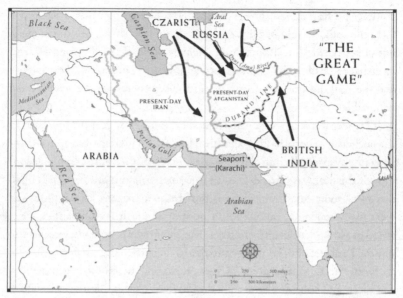

"THE GREAT GAME"

should they get it from? They had such a choice of Europeans! Russian envoys were pressing in eagerly here, British envoys and businessmen were pressing there. The French, the Germans, the Swedes, and others were in there too. The Qajars had little power versus the Europeans, by whom they were wholly owned. They might have carved out some independence by playing one set of Europeans off against another but the kings of Iran saw different opportunities here, opportunities to enrich themselves by selling monopoly contracts to the Europeans and pocketing kickbacks. Essentially, they auctioned off their economy to foreigners.

One particularly audacious concession gave German-born British citizen Baron Julius de Reuters the exclusive right to build streetcar lines and railroads in all of Iran, the exclusive right to mine its minerals and log its forests, and the right to build and operate the country's national bank. He got all this in exchange for a cash payment to the shah and the promise of some small future royalties paid to the national treasury. A storm of opposition erupted, which might have made no difference in itself except that Russia lined up with this opposition for reasons of its own. Under this pressure the shah buckled and canceled the deal. By the terms of the contract he had signed, however, Iran now had to pay Baron Reuters a forty-thousand-pound penalty. Fortunately (for the shah), this didn't come out of his pocket but out of the Iranian treasury. Thus, the country (and its taxpayers) had to pay a British lord an immense sum to build nothing—and the deal did leave him with a controlling interest in the new Iranian national bank.[5]

This sort of thing happened again and again, each deal putting cash in the pockets of a corrupt king and his relatives and giving a European company or government control over some aspect or other of the Iranian economy. If the deal was rescinded as it sometimes was, this always cost Iranian taxpayers some huge sum in penalties. Iranian citizens knew quite well what was happening, but could do nothing about it. Weak as they were, the Qajar kings had plenty of power over their own people: they could still put their subjects in prison, torture them, execute them.

From the European point of view, however, the country being sliced and diced and consumed was only the spoils: the great question was which European country would get to do the consuming and which would end up with a strategic advantage for further exploitation. Since the two chief adversaries were pretty evenly matched, Britain and Russia eventually divided Iran up into zones of influences, with Russia securing the right to dominate and plunder the north and Great Britain the right to do the same in the south. This agreement more or less solidified the country's northern and southern borders and marked a line east of which all bets were off, a line that became Iran's border with Afghanistan.

Meanwhile, the Great Game was playing out in that wild territory to the east as well, the Hindu Kush mountains and the plains north of them. Here, in the early eighteenth century, a tribal chieftain named Ahmad Shah Baba had united the unruly Afghan tribes and carved out one of those sprawling empires that unfurled periodically into India. Ahmad Shah's empire was to be the last of these, however, because his successors had to deal with a new reality: the two mighty European imperial powers pressing in from north and south. The Russians kept sending spies and agents into Afghan territory to press for alliances with the king or with any of the rival chieftains who might overthrow him. The British did the same.

Twice, Great Britain invaded and tried to occupy Afghanistan, in order to block out the Russians, but each time the Afghans drove the British back out. The first Anglo-Afghan war ended in 1841 with the Afghans massacring the entire British community and its army as it tried to flee the country. (A British army came back briefly, however, to set fire to the Grand Bazaar in Kabul and burn up everyone in it.)

The British were still licking the wounds they had suffered from their first invasion of Afghanistan when a conflagration erupted in India. It began in 1857 with a revolt among the foot soldiers known as sepoys. British officers had ordered these men to grease their bullets with a mixture of beef tallow and pig lard, and the order didn't sit well. The vast majority of sepoys were either Hindus or Muslims. To the Hindus, cows were sacred so greasing bullets with their tallow felt like sacrilege. To the Muslims, pigs were ritually unclean beasts, and greasing bullets with *their* fat felt repulsive.

One day a whole regiment of sepoys refused to load their guns. The officer in charge took decisive action: he put the whole lot of them in prison, whereupon riots exploded all over town. Apparently, it never occurred to the British that issuing bullet grease made of beef and pig fat might offend their sepoys. This cluelessness reflected the cultural gulf between the British officers and their foot soldiers, a gulf that had not existed before Europeans arrived, even though Indian armies were frequently composed of many different ethnic and religious groups jammed together, Muslim Turks fighting alongside Muslim Persians fighting alongside Hindi-speaking Hindus and others. These groups quarreled and bristled at each other, but each knew who the others were: they interacted. In Moghul military camps, their languages blended into Urdu, a single new language derived from Hindi, Persian, and Turkish (Urdu literally means something like "soldier-camp lingo" in Turkish). In the British-led Indian army, no new language emerged. English didn't blend with any of the local languages because the British officers and their men moved in separate strata.

With their bullet-grease gaffe, the British achieved the goal that had eluded Akbar the Great: they united the Muslims and Hindus. The sepoy rebellion expanded into the Great Indian Mutiny of 1857–1858, during which both Hindus and Muslims attacked British settlements all over India. Muslim activists called the mutiny a jihad, and their well-organized assaults suggested that the bullet-grease issue had merely been the spark: a great deal of preparation had gone into the mutiny.

A great deal of preparation and yet not nearly enough, because British troops crushed the rebellion quickly and then went on a rampage of their own, plundering Indian cities for about a month, hauling frightened locals out of their homes and massacring them in the streets. In at least one case, they had native prisoners line up along a pit and shot them in groups of ten so that when they died they would fall conveniently into the hole, which made burying them easier.[6] British historian Sir Charles Crosthwaite depicted the victorious campaign as a British *Iliad,* calling it the "epic of the Race."

Once the mutiny had been totally quelled, the British abandoned all pretense, sent the pitiful last Moghul monarch into exile, and relegated the East India Company to private status. The crown took charge of India directly. The ninety-year period of direct British rule that ensued was called "the Raj."

British leaders regarded India as the "jewel in Queen Victoria's crown" and guarded it even more jealously than before. In 1878, detecting new Russian interest in Afghanistan, they tried to occupy Kabul again. Once again, however, they miscalculated the difficulties of occupying a mountainous territory inhabited by so many hostile and mutually antagonistic tribes. It wasn't that the land was hard to "conquer," as Europeans understood the term *conquest.* Great Britain easily marched into the capital, put its own compliant nominee on the throne, and appointed an "envoy" to direct him. In most contexts, this would have been conquest. But the British found that bending Afghan leaders to their will did them little good. The leaders they bent simply broke off in their hands and ended up as their dependents, not their tools, while the tribal people they were supposedly the rulers of operated in the hills as leaderless guerillas. The second Anglo-Afghan War took a nasty turn when the British envoy Cavagnari was killed and ruinous urban battles broke out; in the end the British were forced to pull back to the subcontinent again.

In the wake of this second Anglo-Afghan war, the Russians and British decided the territory ruled by the Afghan tribes cost too much to occupy and agreed to make the whole place a buffer zone between their empires: the Russians would not come south of the Oxus River, if the British would agree not to push north of an arbitrary line in the desert drawn by British diplomat Mortimer Durand. The territory between these lines became

Afghanistan. Afghan kings, who might have conquered widely in the past, now focused on conquering deeply instead—conquering each tribe, each little valley, until this no-man's-land gradually came under the tenuous control of a central government headquartered in Kabul.

But of course, the Russians never really abandoned their hope of pushing on down to a port on the warm waters of the Indian Ocean; and the British never dropped their suspicion of Russian intentions; so the "Great Game" went on.

West of the Great Game, another drama unfolded throughout the nineteenth century, another extension of European politics playing out in the Muslim world. Here, the major players were Great Britain and France and the tokens they fought over were the provinces of the crumbling Ottoman Empire. To the Europeans, the core narrative was the struggle for power in Europe among the developed nation-states there. What happened in Mesopotamia, the Levant, Egypt, and the rest of North Africa was just the relatively unimportant eastern part of the greater drama—just . . . "the Eastern question."

The Eastern question gained particular urgency in the wake of the French Revolution, a revolution that frightened all the royal families of Europe, since its ideas denied the legitimacy of them all. The monarchies therefore united to crush the revolutionaries. They assumed this would be easy since the revolution had thrown France into such turmoil, but to the shock of all concerned, revolutionary France proved about as easy to conquer as a nest of angry hornets.

To make matters worse, out of the revolution came Napoleon Bonaparte, whose leadership instantly vaulted France to world-conquering might. Great Britain led the forces arrayed against Napoleon, and one episode of the struggle between these two sides took place in Egypt.

Western histories report that Napoleon went to Egypt in 1798 with an army of thirty-four thousand, Lord Nelson followed him there, the French lost a naval battle to the British in the Nile, Napoleon abandoned his army and sneaked home to stage a coup d'etat that made him the sole ruler of France and stronger than ever; and the war went on.

But what about the Egyptians? Who were they? What part did they play? Did they welcome Napoleon? Help him? Did he have to conquer them? Did they play any part in the battle between France and Britain? Who did they side with? What happened after the Europeans left? Western histories don't address these questions much, focusing mainly on the clash of Britain and France. It's almost as if the Egyptians weren't there.

But of course they *were* there. When Napoleon arrived, Egypt was nominally still a province of the Ottoman Empire. Napoleon, however, engaged the main Egyptian armies in the shadow of the pyramids and destroyed them in less than a day! All the rest was mop-up until the British arrived, whereupon the real battles began—and they were between Europeans. The British fleet sank most of Napoleon's ships in the Nile. He held on as "ruler" of Egypt for a year, but the plague ravaged his troops and order dissolved in the country he ruled as rebels attacked not so much French troops as any local authority. The British sent in more expeditions and convinced the Turks to attack Egypt too. Napoleon responded by sweeping into Syria and massacring thousands of people in the city of Jaffa. Finally he went back to Europe, but Egypt was a shambles by then. An Ottoman army officer soon took advantage of the turmoil to seize power. This man Mohammed Ali, a Turk born in Albania, declared himself "governor" of Egypt, as if he were acting only on behalf of the sultan in Istanbul. Everyone knew, however, that he was no governor but an independent power, a new king whom no one could deny.

Mohammed Ali saw how easily Napoleon cut his way into Egypt, and he was impressed. He decided he had better bring Egypt into line with whatever Europeans and especially the French were doing so that no new Napoleon and no new Lord Nelson could march in like a bunch of gang-bangers and treat Egypt like a grade-school playground.

But what was Napoleon's secret? Well, Ali knew that Napoleon had stripped the French clergy of power, shut down church schools, and built a secular school system to replace it. Mohammed Ali decided to do the same thing in Egypt. He cut state funding for the ulama. He cut funding for the charitable foundations, the religious schools, and the mosques. He ordered all religious foundations to produce titles for the lands they owned, and of course they couldn't do it, since their ownership went back to early medieval times, three or four empires ago. So Ali's state took their lands. Egypt still had a class of elite mamluks entrenched as the country's tax farmers, but Ali saw that in Europe the state collected taxes directly. So

Mohammed Ali invited the leading tax-farming mamluks to dinner and had them massacred. Then he launched a crash program to build modern roads, modern schools, and the like. This was all a foretaste of a pattern that was to be repeated many times in the next century.

All this sudden development bankrupted Egypt, and Mohammed Ali had to borrow money to keep his government afloat. He borrowed it from European bankers, of course, who insisted that European financial advisers be allowed to monitor the various agencies of Mohammed Ali's government, just to oversee the work and make sure the money was not being misused.

Meanwhile, the Ottomans were getting nervous about Mohammed Ali, who was asserting some claims to Syria. They were already too weak to curb him on their own, so they asked the British for help. The British said they would lend a hand if the Ottomans would only sign a treaty allowing Europeans certain privileges on Turkish soil. They organized a consortium of European nations to come in on the treaty, a coalition of the willing, so to speak, and when the dust settled, Mohammed Ali was safely confined to Egypt, but Europeans were powerful players throughout the Levant. Now, only "the Eastern question" remained to resolve, the question being: which European nation would be responsible for "protecting" which part of the eastern Mediterranean?

Egypt was the richest prize, so both France and Britain cozied up to rulers here. Mohammed Ali legally established his family as dynastic rulers of Egypt, power passing to his sons, grandsons, and so on down, and in the next few decades, these governor-kings of Egypt, these *khedives* as they were called, gave Britain a concession to build a railroad in Egypt; then mollified France with a rich contract to build the Suez canal; then placated the indignant British by giving them the right to build and own the Egyptian national bank, squeezing kickbacks out of each transaction for themselves—you see where this is going.

Meanwhile, Mohammed Ali's descendants decided Egypt's future lay in cotton. Textile manufacturing was the first enterprise to be industrialized in Europe, so the market for cotton became voracious, and the Nile Valley grew excellent cotton. Around 1860, the price of cotton on the world market suddenly soared. The khedive of that moment, a spendthrift playboy of the Eastern world named Ismail, got starry-eyed with dreams of wealth for himself and his country. He borrowed enormous sums of money from European bankers to industrialize Egypt's cotton industry overnight: he bought cotton gins and other such machinery at enormous expense, money he figured Egypt could easily repay since it would be selling cotton forever.

But the rise in cotton prices was a mere blip caused by the outbreak of the U.S. Civil War, which choked off cotton exports from the southern states there and forced English textile factories to look elsewhere for thread. As soon as the U.S. Civil War ended, the price of cotton dropped and Egypt was ruined. Now, the bankers and financial advisers flooded into the country in earnest. Every Egyptian government official ended up with a European adviser of his very own. The Eastern questions still remained—both France and Britain stood poised to achieve total dominance in Egypt.

Britain seemed to have the edge, however, which made France all the more determined not to lose the edge it had further west. In the period of France's revolutionary turmoil, two Algerian Jewish families had sold 8 million francs' worth of grain to France to feed its armies. When Napoleon fell and France reverted to monarchy, France disavowed that debt. The Ottoman governor of this province met with the French consul, Pierre Duval, to demand an explanation. Duval told him France did not discuss money with Arabs. The governor slapped Duval in the face with . . . a fly swatter. What a blow to French honor! *L'Affaire de Mouche-Swatter* (the "affair of the fly swatter") made it into the French press, and nobody laughed. More insults were exchanged and tensions went on rising. As it happened, there was a struggle under way in France just then between monarchists and liberals. The monarchists who held power saw domestic political advantage in a quick, successful military adventure. Napoleon had proven how easily Arabs could be defeated in Egypt, and so, in 1830, France invaded Algeria.[7]

The venture proved as quick and successful as any Frenchman might have hoped. The governor fled to Naples, leaving his fortune behind and his country leaderless. France hauled about 100 million francs out of Algeria, about half of which made it to the French treasury. The rest disappeared into the pockets of the soldiers and officers who invaded the country.

With its government gone, Algeria was a power vacuum, and you know how nature abhors those things. Instead of setting up a proxy or puppet, France decided to incorporate Algeria into its national structure as three new provinces. In other words, the French treated Algeria not as a colony but as part of France. A "joint stock" company was set up to sell land to French citizens who would immigrate to these new provinces and help "develop" them.

Even here in Algeria, which France out and out invaded, the foreigners flooding in as immigrants didn't fight a war with the natives. They just bought up 80 percent of the land, fair and square, and set up a whole new economy that didn't compete with the native economy so much as ignore it. Algerian Arabs remained free to plant what they wanted on whatever land they retained, ship what they grew to Algerian ports if they could afford the freight charges, and sell their products in world market if they could find any buyers, which they couldn't. Or if they preferred, they could leave the land and move to the cities and start businesses, if they had the capital—which they didn't—and if they could get a business license from French officials, which for various good and legal reasons, they often couldn't.

So the Arabs of Algeria ended up buying and selling to each other in the old traditional ways while the bulk of the country, absorbed as it was into the European and world markets, did business in streamlined, super-productive modern ways.

If any Algerian had been asked whether he opposed or supported selling 80 percent of the country to French buyers, he would surely have said he opposed it. If anyone had been faced with *that* decision, he would almost certainly have decided no. But no one ever had a chance to decide whether to sell off 80 percent of the country. Each landowner who sold property to "the French" was only deciding whether to sell his one piece of land to this one buyer. It was quite possible to oppose selling 80 percent of the country to foreigners while seeing persuasive reasons to sell one particular bit of it to one particular foreigner.

Over the next century, the French community in Algeria grew to seven hundred thousand French citizens. They came to own most of the land and considered themselves native Algerians, since they were born on Algerian soil and most were the children of parents born there. Inconveniently, some

5 million Arabs happened to be living there as well and no one could fathom where they had come from or what they were doing there. They didn't seem to have any function, and whatever they subsisted on, it was an almost completely separate economy from the one the French Algerians were involved in.

By 1850, Europeans controlled every part of the world that had once called itself Dar al-Islam. They lived in these countries as an upper class, they ruled them directly or decided who would rule, they controlled the resources, they dictated the policies, and they circumscribed the daily lives of their people. In places such as Egypt, Iran, and India, there were clubs that the native people could not enter because they were Egyptian or Iranian or Indian. Europeans had achieved this dominance without any grand war or broadscale assault. The Europeans were scarcely even aware that there had been a struggle and that they had won. But Muslims noticed, because it's always harder to ignore a rock you're under than a rock you're on.

13

∞

The Reform Movements

1150–1336 AH
1737–1918 CE

AT THE SAME TIME as these political developments, a crucial story was
unfolding in the intellectual arena as well. This story began before
1800 and continued long after, with consequences that shake the world to
this very day: it consisted of revival and reform movements that surged up
throughout the Muslim world at the same time that Europeans were overwhelming these lands.

The two stories are related, though not identical. Some sort of sweeping challenge to the Muslim status quo was going to take place around this
time with or without the Europeans. Why? Because in the Muslim world,
by 1700 or so, religious institutions had bureaucratized spirituality in
much the same way that the Catholic Church had bureaucratized Christianity in late medieval Europe. The whole system of Muslim law had been
worked out so fully that there was no creative work left for any new en-
thusiast to do. The application of shari'a to every dot and detail of personal
and social life was a done deal. The power of the ulama had grown encrusted. The Sufi orders had been institutionalized, and authorities at
every level agreed that "the gates of ijtihad were closed."

Ijtihad, remember, means "free and independent thinking based on reason." It can't depart from scripture, but it consists of thinking through the
implications of scripture creatively. Muslim scholars had once allowed that
ijtihad might be exercised on issues not explicitly settled by Qur'an; then
by Qur'an and hadith; then by Qur'an, hadith, and the work of previous
authoritative scholars. . . . And so by the eighteenth century, important
scholars generally agreed that no unsettled issues existed. Everything had
been covered, everything worked out; ordinary people no longer needed to
exercise free and independent thought. There was nothing left for them to
do but follow the rules.

Following the rules, however, does not provide the spiritual fulfillment
people seek from religion. The bureaucratization of Islam created much
the same stultifications and discontents that in Christendom had provoked
the Protestant Reformation. And indeed, by the middle of the eighteenth
century, reform movements were beginning to sprout throughout the
Muslim world.

But there never was a Muslim version of Europe's Protestant Reformation, and thus none of the consequences that followed from the Reformation: no doctrine of individualism emerged here, no coupling of religion to
nationalism (except in a sense in Iran), no separation of church and state,
no conceptual division of the world into secular and religious realms, no
sudden development of enlightenment-style liberalism, and so no democratic, scientific, or industrial revolutions.

Why not?

Well, for one thing, some of the issues that fueled the Reformation
could not arise in Islam. Protestant reformers rebelled against the Church;
Islam had no church. Protestant reformers attacked the authority of the
pope; Islam had no pope. Protestants said priests could not mediate between man and God; Islam never had a priesthood (the ulama were more
like lawyers than priests.) The Protestant reformers insisted on a direct,
personal interaction between the individual worshipper and God. The
Muslim prayer ritual had always been just that.

But the Europeans were certainly a factor too. Without them in the
picture, the Muslim reform movements might well have taken a different
course. European religious reform took shape in a purely European context. That is, when Protestant reformers challenged Catholic practices and

doctrines, they were addressing issues internal to their own society, not steeling Christianity against some external cultural challenge. In 1517, few western Christians worried that Muslims might have a more convincing message to offer than Christianity or that Christian youth might start converting to Islam. The Turks were at the gate, it's true, but they weren't in the living room, and they certainly weren't in the bedroom. The Turks posed a threat to the physical health of Christians, but not to the spiritual health of Christianity.

Muslims were in a different boat. Almost from the start, as I've discussed, Islam had offered its political and military successes as an argument for its doctrines and a proof of its revelations. The process began with those iconic early battles at Badr and Uhud, when the outcome of battle was shown to have theological meaning. The miracle of expansion and the linkage of victory with truth continued for hundreds of years.

Then came the Mongol holocaust, which forced Muslim theologians to reexamine their assumptions. That process spawned such reformers as Ibn Taymiyah. Vis-à-vis the Mongols, however, the weakness of Muslims was concrete and easy to understand. The Mongols had greater killing power, but they came without an ideology. When the bloodshed wound down and the human hunger for meaning bubbled up, as it always does, they had nothing to offer. In fact, they themselves converted. Islam won in the end, absorbing the Mongols as it had absorbed the Turks before them and the Persians before that.

Conversion to Islam made the Mongols no less bloody (as Timur-i-lang proved), but at least, under the aegis of the converted rulers, the old quest could begin again, albeit starting over from the smoking rubble of a ruined world—the quest to build and universalize the community of Allah.

The same could not be said for the new overlords. The Europeans came wrapped in certainty about their way of life and peddling their own ideas of ultimate truth. They didn't challenge Islam so much as ignore it, unless they were missionaries, in which case they simply tried to convert the Muslims. If they noticed Islam, they didn't bother to debate it (missionaries are not in the debating business) but only smiled at it as one would at the toys of a child or the quaint relics of a more primitive people. How maddening for Muslim cognoscenti! And yet, what could Muslims do about it?

Even if Muslim and Christian scholars had found some forum in which to exchange views, it would have been irrelevant to the conundrum facing Muslims because by the nineteenth century, the challenge to Islam came not so much from Christianity as from a secular, humanistic world-view that evolved out of the Reformation, the mélange now often called "modernity."

The source of Muslim weakness and European strength was not obvious. It wasn't strictly a question of military advantage. For the most part, the foreigners weren't torturing and killing. For the most part, the new overlords didn't even set themselves up as rulers, quite. Officially, most Muslims still had their own native monarchs, still had their own government buildings where Muslim officials still stamped documents, and somewhere in every Muslim state was still a capital dating back to ancient days of bygone splendor, and in that capital was a palace and in that palace a throne and on that throne usually a shah, sultan, nawab, khan, khedive, or what you will, some native ruler whose wealth and pomp made him all but indistinguishable from the potentates of old.

In Iran, the foreigners roamed the corridors of power merely as advisers. In Turkey, there they were, collecting salaries as consultants. In Egypt and the Levant, they stood by as "protectors." Even in India, which had a governor-general appointed by the British parliament, the military and police forces that "kept order" consisted mostly of Muslims, Hindus, Sikhs, Parsees, and other locals. How could Muslims claim that they were not still ruling themselves?

And yet by the end of the eighteenth century, Muslims looked around and saw with dawning horror that they had been conquered: from Bengal to Istanbul, they were subservient to foreigners in every aspect of their lives, in their own cities and towns and neighborhoods and in their very homes. And not just foreigners like the ones next door, but people who spoke a whole different set of languages, practiced different religious rituals, wore different kinds of clothes and different kinds of headgear (or, shockingly, none at all!), built different kinds of houses, formed different kinds of groupings. These foreigners ate pork, they drank liquor, their women moved about in public with their faces showing, they laughed at jokes that weren't funny and failed to see the humor in things that were hilarious, ate weird-tasting food, listened to music that sounded more like noise, and spent their leisure time in puzzling and pointless activities such as cricket and quadrilles.

So the question arose now, as it had in the wake of the Mongol holocaust: if the triumphant expansion of the Muslim project proved the truth of the revelation, what did the impotence of Muslims in the face of these new foreigners signify about the faith?

With this question looming over the Muslim world, movements to revive Islam could not be extricated from the need to resurrect Muslim power. Reformers could not merely offer proposals for achieving more authentic religious experiences. They had to expound how the authenticity they proposed would get history back on course, how their proposals would restore the dignity and splendor of the Umma, how they would get Muslims moving again toward the proper endpoint of history: perfecting the community of justice and compassion that flourished in Medina in the original golden moment and enlarging it until it included all the world.

Many reformers emerged and many movements bubbled up, but all of them can be sorted into three general sorts of responses to the troubling question.

One response was to say that what needed changing was not Islam but Muslims. Innovations, alterations, and accretions had corrupted the faith, so that no one was practicing true Islam anymore. What Muslims needed to do was to shut out Western influence and restore Islam to its pristine, original form.

Another response was to say that the West was right. Muslims had gotten mired in obsolete religious ideas; they had ceded control of Islam to ignorant clerics who were out of touch with changing times; they needed to modernize their faith along Western lines by clearing out superstition, renouncing magical thinking, and rethinking Islam as an ethical system compatible with science and secular activities.

A third response was to declare Islam the true religion but concede that Muslims had certain things to learn from the West. In this view, Muslims needed to rediscover and strengthen the essence of their own faith, history, and traditions, but absorb Western learning in the fields of science and technology. According to this river of reform, Muslims needed to modernize but could do so in a distinctively Muslim way: science was compatible with the Muslim faith and modernization did not have to mean Westernization.

These three answers to the challenge of modernity were well-embodied in three seminal reformers of the eighteenth and nineteenth centuries: Abdul Wahhab of the Arabian peninsula, Sayyid Ahmad of Aligarh, India, and Sayyid Jamaluddin-i-Afghan, whose birthplace is disputed and whose presence was felt everywhere. By no means were they the only reformers. Their ideas were not always mutually exclusive. They sometimes straddled two different currents of reformism. Their contemporaries and students often borrowed from each other. But still, these three men represent three distinctively different approaches to reforming and reviving Islam.

WAHHABISM

Abdul Wahhab was born around 1703 in the Nejd, that desert of yellow sand dunes that many of us picture reflexively when we think of Arabia. He grew up in a small oasis town, the son of a judge. When he showed promise as a Qur'anic student, he was sent to Medina for further schooling. There, one of his teachers introduced him to the works of Ibn Taymiyah, the austere Syrian theologian who, in the wake of the Mongol holocaust taught that God had abandoned Muslims and that Muslims must return to the exact ways of the First Community if they were ever to regain His favor. These teachings resonated for the young Wahhab.

From Medina the youngster made his way to the cosmopolitan city of Basra on the Persian Gulf, and what this ultimate country boy saw in Basra—the clamorous diversity of opinion, the many schools of thought, the numerous interpretations of the Holy Word, the crowds, the lights, the noise—appalled him. This, he decided, was the sort of excrescence that was making Islam weak.

He returned, then, to the stark simplicity of his hometown in the desert and began to preach religious revival through restoration of Islam to its original form. There was only one God, he thundered, and everyone must worship the one God exactly as instructed in the Holy Book. Everyone must obey the laws laid down by the revelations. Everyone must live exactly as the Pure Originals of Medina in Mohammed's time, and anyone who blocked the restoration of the original and holy community must be eliminated.

The Ottomans considered all of Arabia their possession, but they had no real authority among the small Bedouin tribes who inhabited this arid landscape, living in scattered oases and eking out a thin survival as traders and herders. Wahhab attracted some followers among his fellow Bedouins, and he led his group around the countryside destroying shrines because they were objects of improper reverence, and Abdul Wahhab preached that reverence for anything or anyone except God was idolatry. Eventually, Wahhab achieved the position of judge and began to apply Hanbali law as he saw it with uncompromising zeal. One day, he had a well-known woman of the town stoned to death as an adulteress. The locals had seen enough. A mob gathered to demand that Abdul Wahhab be ousted from his post; there was even talk of lynching. Wahhab fled that town and made his way to another oasis called Dariyah.

There, the local ruler Mohammed ibn Saud welcomed him warmly. Ibn Saud was a minor tribal chieftain with very big ambitions: to "unite" the Arabian Peninsula. By "unite," of course, he meant "conquer." In the single-minded preacher Abdul Wahhab he saw just the ally he needed; Wahhab saw the same when he looked at Ibn Saud. The two men made a pact. The chieftain agreed to recognize Wahhab as the top religious authority of the Muslim community and do all he could to implement his vision; the preacher, for his part, agreed to recognize Ibn Saud as the political head of the Muslim community, its amir, and to instruct his followers to fight for him.

The pact produced fruit. Over the next few decades, these two men "united" all the bedouin tribes of the Arabian Peninsula under Saudi-Wahhabi rule. Each time they confronted another recalcitrant tribe, they began by called on them to convert. "Convert! Convert! Convert!" they yelled three times. If the warning was ignored three times (as it generally was) Wahhab told the soldiers they could go ahead and kill the people they were confronting; Allah permitted it, because these were infidels.

The call to convert confused the tribes they were attacking at this point because all of these tribes considered themselves devout Muslims already. But when Abdul Wahhab said "Convert!" he meant to the vision of Islam he was preaching. He did not call it Wahhabism because, like Ibn Taymiyah before him, he maintained that he was simply calling Muslims back to pristine, original Islam, stripped of all accretions and washed of all corruptions. He was not an innovator; in fact, he was the anti-innovator.

People unconvinced of his views, however, saw his vision as a particular interpretation of Islam, not Islam itself; and they had no trouble labeling his ideology Wahhabism, a term that came into use even among some who endorsed his views.

In 1766, Ibn Saud was assassinated but his son Abdul Aziz took over and continued his father's campaign to unite Arabia under the banner of Abdul Wahhab's theology. Then in 1792, Wahhab himself died, leaving behind twenty widows and countless children. His life had spanned virtually the entire eighteenth century. While he was imposing his vision of pristine Islam in Arabia, England and Scotland melded into Great Britain, the United States of America was born, the French Revolution issued the Declaration of the Rights of Man, Mozart wrote his entire corpus of music, and James Watt invented the steam engine.

Upon Wahhab's death, Aziz ibn Saud declared himself his successor. Already the amir, the new Ibn Saud now anointed himself the chief religious authority as well. In 1802, Aziz ibn Saud attacked the city of Karbala, where the Prophet's grandson Hussein had been martyred. This city was central to Shi'i devotions, and many of them had gathered just then to commemorate Hussein's martyrdom. But Shi'is ranked high on Wahhab's list of those who had altered and corrupted pristine original Islam, and so, upon conquering the city, Aziz ibn Saud had some two thousand of its Shi'i inhabitants put to death.

In 1804, Aziz ibn Saud conquered Medina, where he had his army promptly destroy the tombs of Mohammed's companions. From Medina, the Saudi-Wahhabi armies went on to Mecca, where they wrecked a shrine that supposedly marked Prophet Mohammed's birthplace (so that no one would fall into idolatrous worship of Mohammed). As long as he was in the city, Ibn Saud took advantage of the opportunity to humbly perform the rites of pilgrimage in the Ka'ba.

Then in 1811, the Saudi-Wahhabi alliance began to organize a new campaign, this time to Asia Minor, the heart of the Ottoman Empire. Now at last the sultan took notice of the Wahhabi movement. To grapple with these surging Bedouins, he called on Mohammed Ali, khedive of Egypt, to help him out. Mohammed Ali took his disciplined modern army into Arabia, and in 1815—the same year that Napoleon's career was ending at Waterloo—he crushed Ibn Saud, restored Ottoman control over

Mecca and Medina, and opened the Holy City up again to Muslim pilgrims of every stripe. Then he sent Aziz ibn Saud's son and successor to Istanbul to be paraded before derisive crowds and then beheaded.

Little more was heard of the Saudi-Wahhabi alliance for about a century, but the alliance did not die. The executed chieftain had a son who took over the collapsed remnants of the Saudi confederacy. Now he was just a minor tribal chieftain again, but he was still a chieftain, and he was still a Wahhabi, and wherever he could still impose his authority, Wahhabi ulama presided and prospered. Wahhab was dead, but Wahhabism lived on.

What were its tenets?

You can look long and hard through the actual writings of Abdul Wahhab and not find Wahhabism as it is defined today. That's largely because Abdul Wahhab didn't write political tracts; he wrote Qur'anic commentary and wrote it strictly in the vocabulary of his doctrine. His single-minded focus on details of Muslim doctrine, law, and practice might strike outsiders as obsessive. His major work, *Kitab-al-Tawhid* (*The Book of Unity*) has sixty-six chapters, each of which presents one or more quotes from the Qur'an, unpacks each quote, lists lessons to be learned from the quote, and then explains how this quote relates to Wahhab's core creed. There is no talk here of East or West, nothing about Western influence or Muslim weakness, nothing recognizably political at all. To read Wahhab's words is to realize that he looked at the world through purely religious spectacles. In his own view, his entire theology boiled down to two tenets: first, the importance of *tawhid*, or "unity," that is, the singleness and unity of God; and second, the fallacy of *shirk*, the idea that anyone or anything shared in God's divinity to even the smallest degree.

Marx once said "I am not a Marxist," and if Abdul Wahhab were alive today, he might well say, "I am not a Wahhabi," but nonetheless, Wahhabism exists, and it now includes many further tenets that derive from Wahhab's preachings by implication or that developed historically from its application by Saudi chieftains. This expanded Wahhabism told Muslims that the Law was Islam and Islam was the Law: getting it right, knowing it fully, and following it exactly was the whole of the faith.

The Law was all right there in the Qur'an, according to Wahhab and his followers. The sunna—the life of the Prophet as revealed through hadith—amounted to a commentary on the Law. The Qur'an did not prescribe principles to guide human behavior but actual acts Muslims were to perform. It revealed not just the form but the content of human life. In the life of Prophet Mohammed, it gave a stencil for every Muslim to follow.

Medina in the time of Mohammed and the first *three* khalifas was the ideal community, the one time and place when everybody knew the law, got the law and followed it fully. That was why the First Community was able to flourish and expand so miraculously. That Medina was the stencil for every Muslim community to recreate.

The purpose of life was to follow the Law. The purpose of social and political life was to build the community in which the Law could be reified. All who hindered the great task of building that ideal community were enemies of Islam. The obligations of a Muslim included participation in jihad, the struggle to defeat the enemies of Islam. Jihad was right up there with prayer, fasting, alms, pilgrimage, and attesting to the unity of God as a religious obligation.

And who were the enemies of Islam?

According to Wahhab's doctrines, those who did not believe in Islam were, of course, potential enemies but not the most crucial offenders. If they agreed to live peacefully under Muslim rule, they could be tolerated. The enemies of real concern were slackards, apostates, hypocrites, and innovators.

Slackards were Muslims who talked the talk but didn't really walk the walk. They espoused the creed, but when it was time to pray, you found them playing cards or taking naps. They had to be punished so they would not corrupt other Muslims. Apostates were those who were born into or had converted to Islam but had then renounced it. They were to be killed. Hypocrites were those who said they were Muslims but weren't really. They mouthed the words but in their hearts their allegiance went to some other faith. They were inherently a fifth column working against the community and could commit disastrous betrayal in a crisis. Hypocrites were to be killed as soon as they were unmasked. And finally, perhaps the worst offenders of all were the innovators: Muslims who were corrupting Islam by adding to or altering any aspects of the pristine original Law. People who performed the rituals differently than the Pious Originals, or who performed rituals the Prophet and his companions never practiced, or who advocated ideas not found in the Qur'an were innovators. Both the Shi'i and the Sufis belonged to this group. Jihad against them was not only legitimate but obligatory, according to Wahhabism as it developed in historical practice.

Wahhabi attitudes and enthusiasms spread far beyond Arabia. Wahhabism found particularly fertile ground at the other end of the Muslim world, in the subcontinent of India. In practice, various people who called themselves Wahhabis emphasized various aspects of the creed the Saudi tribe preached. In India, for example, some so-called Wahhabis rejected jihad as an obligation. Others said apostates should be engaged in debate not battle. Some thought slackards should be reeducated rather than punished or that hypocrites should be chastened rather than killed, or some other variation. But all who called themselves Wahhabis looked at the Law as the core of Islam, even the whole of Islam. All tended to look back to a golden era that provided a stencil for Muslim life and tended to believe that restoring the First Community of Mohammed's Medina would restore Muslims to favor in Allah's eyes, thereby restoring the vigor and power the Umma enjoyed under the first four khalifas.

Outside the Islamic world, the Saudi-Wahhabi alliance may have seemed like some brief anomaly that flared and vanished; but in fact it went on smoldering in the deserts of Arabia, and the world was to hear a great deal more about the alliance in the twentieth century, after the British agent remembered as Lawrence of Arabia found his way to that desert.

THE ALIGARH MOVEMENT: SECULAR MODERNISM

Sayyid Ahmad, or Sir Sayyid Ahmad of Aligarh, as he liked to be called later in life, represents an attitude of thought that sprang up independently in many parts of the Muslim world in the nineteenth century. He and others began exploring ways to rethink Islam as an ethical system that would stay true to its own traditions and spirit but make it compatible with a secular world dominated by Europeans.

Sayyid Ahmad was born in 1817 to a prominent Muslim family in Delhi. His forebears had been important officials under the Moghuls, back when the Moghuls ruled this part of the world. Now, the British grip on the subcontinent had been deepening for many generations and Sayyid

Ahmed's family had adapted to the new order. His grandfather served the East India Company in positions of responsibility, once running a school for them and another time traveling to Iran as a British envoy. Twice he had worked for the Moghul emperor as his prime minister, but the "emperor" at this point was just another British pensioner and his prime minister's chief duties were to fill out the appropriate forms to keep his pension flowing. Sayyid Ahmad's father worked for the company too, and his brother started one of India's first Urdu newspapers. In short, Sayyid Ahmad hailed from a high-status, modernist, Western-oriented family, and he knew something about British life.

His mother, however, was a devout Muslim of legendary piety, respected for her scholarship. She made the boy go to madrassa, and she equaled his grandfather as an influence on this life, so Sayyid Ahmad grew to manhood with these two dueling currents in his personality: a heartfelt allegiance to his own Muslim community and a high regard for British culture and a longing for the respect of those colonials.

Unfortunately, his family sank into financial trouble after his father's untimely death. Sayyid Ahmad had to quit school and go to work. He hired on with the East India Company as a clerk and eventually earned promotion to subjudge, handling small claims, but this was a minor post in the company's judicial system: really not much more than a glorified clerk. He couldn't rise higher because he had never completed his formal education; he was largely self-taught.

Still he read avidly, all the science and English-language literature he could get his hands on. He formed reading groups and discussion clubs with his Indian Muslim friends and organized lecture series on scientific topics. During the Indian Mutiny of 1857, he sided with the British; but afterwards he wrote a pamphlet called *The Causes of the Indian Revolt* in which he reproached the British administrators for their errors and oversights, a pamphlet he sent to government officials in Calcutta and London. He followed up with *An Account of the Loyal Mohammedans of India*, which was translated into English by a British colonel. In this little book, he tried to resurrect his coreligionists in British eyes by depicting Indian Muslims as the Queen's most loyal subjects. He also argued that Muslims could have no jihadist sentiments toward the British and ought not to have, quoting scholarly religious sources to prove that jihad against the

British was not permissible since the British did not restrict or interfere with Muslim devotions.

Finally, in 1874, he decided to see England for himself. It was the first time Sayyid Ahmad had traveled beyond the confines of India. In London, where his writings had earned him some affection, he lived beyond his means, attending fashionable parties and hobnobbing with intellectuals, artists, and aristocrats. He cut a striking figure in this milieu, resolutely clad in Muslim robes, sporting a large beard, and wearing a small pillbox-shaped religious cap, looking every inch the old-school Muslim gentleman of Moghul high society. The queen herself awarded him a ribbon, making him a "Companion of the Star of India," which led him ever afterward to call himself *Sir* Sayyid Ahmad Khan.

Then one day, there in London, he ran across a derogatory biography of Prophet Mohammed written by some Englishman. He was devastated. He dropped all his other concerns and began writing his own biography of the Prophet to refute the one by the Englishman. He wrote in Urdu, because it was his mother tongue, but he was aiming his book at a European public, so he paid to have it translated, chapter by chapter, as he was writing it, into English, French, German, and Latin. The job proved too immense; he had to scale down his ambitions, in the end going for a collection of essays about Mohammed. He ran out of money before he could finish even that, and seventeen months after leaving India he dragged himself home again, penniless and exhausted.

England had impressed him deeply, however—too deeply, said his critics. In comparison to England, he found his homeland painfully backward. "Without flattering the English," he wrote, "I can truly say that the natives of India, high and low, merchants and petty shopkeepers, educated and illiterate, when contrasted with the English in education, manners, and uprightness, are like a dirty animal is to an able and handsome man."

But what made his fellow Muslims so backward? What could he do to elevate his community? Sayyid Ahmad decided that the problem lay partly in the way Muslims were interpreting Islam. They were mired in magical thinking, they were clinging to superstition and calling it Islam. Sir Sayyid Ahmed Khan began elaborating a doctrine that offended his contemporaries among the Indian ulama. Religion, he suggested, was a natural field of human inquiry and achievement. It was integral to human life. It evolved with the human community in the natural course of things—just like art, agriculture, and technology—growing ever more sophisticated as man grew more civilized.

Early humans had a limited capacity to explore moral and ethical issues intellectually, Sayyid Ahmad speculated. They needed revealed religion to help them overcome their passions and guide them to moral judgments and conduct: rulings from a higher power, delivered by prophets with the charismatic authority to persuade without explanation. But the moral and ethical injunctions of all great, true religions are not fundamentally irrational. They are reasonable, and reason can discover them, once people have developed the intellectual capacity to do so.

That's why Mohammed announced that he was the last of the prophets— he didn't mean that his rulings about issues in the Mecca and Medina of his day were to be the final word on human conduct throughout the ages. He meant that he had brought the last tools people needed to proceed on the quest for a moral community on their own, without unexplained rulings from God. Islam was the last of the revealed religions because it was the beginning of the age of reason-based religions. Rational people could achieve moral excellence by reasoning correctly from sound fundamental principles. What Islam brought were sound fundamental principles. They were the same as those found in Christianity and all the other great revealed religions with the one caveat that Islam also enjoined rationality. It would have liberated humanity from blind obedience to superstition and dogma had not Muslims misinterpreted the meaning of the Qur'anic revelations and gone off course.

Sayyid Ahmad was suggesting implicitly that Muslims disconnect from obsessing about heaven and hell and miraculous interventions by God in history and rethink their faith as an ethical system. In this approach, good Muslims would not necessarily be those who read the Qur'an in Arabic for many hours every day, or dressed a certain way, or prayed just so. Good Muslims would be defined as those who didn't lie, or cheat, or steal, or kill, those who developed their own best capacities assiduously and behaved fairly toward others, those who sought justice in society, behaved responsibly in their communities, and exercised mercy, compassion, and charity as best they could.

Before he went to England, Sayyid Ahmad had founded an organization called the Scientific Society, in the northern Indian town of Aligarh. This organization produced lectures and made advanced European learning accessible to Indian Muslims by translating and publishing the important books of Western cultures into Urdu and Persian. After his return from England, Sir Sayyid Ahmad developed the Scientific Society into a university, which he hoped to make into the "Cambridge of the Muslim World." In addition to the "religious sciences" and other traditional subjects of Islamic learning, the curriculum at Aligarh University offered courses in physics, chemistry, biology, and other "modern" subjects.

Even though many of the Indian ulama attacked Sayyid Ahmad's views, the university prospered and attracted students. Aligarh University students and faculty formed the seeds of a secular movement which, in the twentieth century, lobbied for Muslims to separate from India and build a nation-state of their own, a movement that finally resulted in the birth of Pakistan.

Sayyid Ahmad's specific ideas failed to create any widespread movement associated with his name, but modernist intellectuals in other Muslim lands were exploring similar ideas and coming up with similar conclusions. In Iran, a prime minister working for the Qajar Shahs established a school called Dar al-Funun, which offered instruction in all the sciences and in the arts, literature, and philosophies of the West. Graduates of that school began to seed Iranian society with modernists who sought to reshape their society along European lines.

Similar modernists were active at the heart of the Ottoman Empire. In the later nineteenth century, the modernist faction in the Ottoman government promoted policies called Tanzimat, or "reforms," which included setting up European-style schools, adopting European techniques of administration in the government bureaucracies, reorganizing the army along European lines, dressing the soldiers in European style uniforms, encouraging European-style clothes for government officials, and so on.

ISLAMIST MODERNISM

We come now to the dominant Muslim reformer of the nineteenth century, a volcanic force named Sayyid Jamaluddin-i-Afghan. Afghans believe he was born in Afghanistan, in 1836, about fifty miles east of Kabul, in a town called Asadabad, the capital of Kunar province. His family was connected to Afghanistan's ruling clan through marriage but did something to offend the royal and had to move to Iran in a hurry when Jamaluddin was a little boy.

Confusingly enough, they settled close to an Iranian town also called Asadabad, which has given rise to a long-standing dispute about where Jamaluddin-i-Afghan was actually born and which country, Afghanistan or Iran, can claim him as its native son. Afghans point out that he always called himself Jamaluddin-i-*Afghan*—"Jamaluddin the Afghan"—and on this basis consider the matter closed. Iranian historians say he only called himself "the Afghan" to hide the fact that he was Iranian and allude to documentary evidence that they say settles the question quite definitively. On the other hand, when I was growing up in Afghanistan, lots of people in Kabul seemed to know his family and relatives, who still had land in Kunar at that time. To me, *that* seems to settle the matter, but maybe that's just because I'm Afghan.

One thing is certain. Today, many Muslim governments see Sayyid Jamaluddin as a prize to claim. In his day, however, every Muslim government eventually came to see this fellow as a troublemaking pest and threw him out. Let me present a brief outline of his amazing, peripatetic career.

Wherever he may have grown up, no one disputes that he went to India when he was about eighteen years old. Anti-British sentiment was rising to a fever pitch in India just then, and Jamaluddin may have met some Muslims who were cooking up anti-British plots. He happened to be in Mecca on pilgrimage when the Great Indian Mutiny broke out, but he was back in time to witness the British reprisals that shocked the Muslim east so deeply. It was during that first journey to India that Jamaluddin probably developed a lifelong hatred of the British and a lasting antipathy to European colonialism in general. In any case, from India, he went to . . .

- **Afghanistan.** There he gained the confidence of the king whom the British had tried unsuccessfully to unseat. The king hired Jamaluddin to tutor his eldest son, Azam. Jamaluddin was already formulating ideas about the need to reform and modernize Islam as a way of restoring Muslim power and pride, and he saw the job of tutoring the country's heir apparent as an opportunity to shape a ruler who would implement his vision. He steeped Prince Azam Khan in his reformist ideas and trained him to lead Afghanistan into the modern age. Unfortunately, Azam succeeded his father only briefly. One of his cousins quickly overthrew him, with British backing. The British probably moved to unseat Azam in part because they didn't want any protégé of Jamaluddin's on the Afghan throne. They sensed what he was up to. In any case, Azam moved to Iran, where he died in exile. Jamaluddin was forced to flee as well, so he made his way to . . .

- **Asia Minor.** There he began to deliver speeches at Constantinople University. He declared that Muslims needed to learn all about modern science but at the same time ground their children more firmly in Islamic values, tradition, and history. Modernization, he said, didn't have to mean Westernization: Muslims could perfectly well seek the ingredients of a distinctively Islamic modernization in Islam itself. This message proved popular with both the masses and the upper classes. Sayyid Jamaluddin was well situated now to claim a high position in Ottoman Turkey and live his life out as an honored and richly compensated spokesperson for Islam. Instead, he began to teach that people should have the freedom to interpret the Qur'an for themselves, without oppressive "guidance" from the ulama, whom he blamed for the retardation of scientific learning in Islamic civilization. Naturally, this turned the powerful clerical establishment against him and they had the man expelled, so in 1871 he moved to . . .

- **Egypt,** where he started teaching classes and delivering lectures at the famous Al Azhar University. He continued to expound his vision of modernization on Islamic terms. (In this period, he also wrote a history of Afghanistan, perhaps just another sly ploy to make people think he was from Afghanistan and not Iran.) In Egypt, however, where the dynasty founded by Mehmet Ali had rotted into a despotic ruling class in bed with British and French interests, he began to criticize the corruption of the rich and powerful. He said the country's rulers ought to adopt modest lifestyles and live among the people, just as leaders of the early Muslim community had done. He also started calling for parliamentary democracy. Again, however, he insisted that democratization didn't have to mean Westernization. He found a basis for an Islamic style of democracy in two Islamic concepts: *shura* and *ijma.*

Shura means something like "advisory council." It was the mechanism through which early Muslim leaders sought the advice and consent of the community. The first shura was that small group Khalifa Omar appointed to pick his successor. That shura had to present its nominee to the Muslims of Medina and get their approval. Of course that community numbered in the low thousands and its leading members could all fit in the main mosque and its surrounding courtyard, so shura democracy was the direct democracy of the town hall meeting. How that model could be applied to a whole huge country such as Egypt was another question.

Ijma means "consensus." This concept originated in a saying attributed to the Prophet: "My community will never agree on an error." The ulama used the saying as a justification for asserting that when *they* all agreed on a doctrinal point, the point lay beyond further questioning or dispute. In short, they co-opted ijma to mean consensus among themselves. Jamaluddin, however, reinterpreted the two concepts and expanded their application. From shura and ijma, he argued that in Islam, rulers had no legitimacy without the support of their people.

His ideas about democracy made the king of Egypt nervous, and his harangues about the decadence of the upper classes offended everyone above a certain income level. In 1879, Jamaluddin was evicted from Egypt, at which point he backtracked to . . .

- **India**. There, the "liberal" Aligarh movement, founded and led by Sir Sayyid Ahmad, had evolved into a force to be reckoned with. But Jamaluddin saw Sir Sayyid Ahmad as a fawning British lapdog, and said so in his only full-scale book, *Refutation of the Materialists*. The British, however, liked Sayyid Ahmad's ideas. When a rebellion broke out in Egypt, British authorities claimed that Jamaluddin had incited the eruption through his followers and they put him in prison for a few months. When the rebellion died down, they released him but expelled him from India, and so, in 1882 he went to . . .

- **Paris**, where he wrote articles for various publications in English, Persian, Arabic, Urdu, and French (in all of which languages he was not merely fluent but articulate and even capable of eloquence). In his articles he developed the idea that Islam was at core a rational religion and that Islam had pioneered the scientific revolution. He went on insisting that Muslim ulama and despots had retarded scientific progress in the Muslim world but said cler-

ics and despots had done the same in other religions too, including Christianity. In France, at this time, a philosopher named
Ernest Renan was writing that Muslims were inherently incapable
of scientific thinking (Renan also said that the Chinese were a
"race with wonderful manual dexterity but no sense of honor,"
that Jews were "incomplete," that "Negroes" were happiest tilling
soil, that Europeans were natural masters and soldiers, and that if
everyone would just do what they were "made for" all would be
well with the world.[1]) Jamaluddin engaged Renan in a famous debate at the Sorbonne (famous among Muslims, at least) in which
he argued that Islam only seemed less "scientific" than Christianity because it was founded later and was therefore in a somewhat
earlier stage of its development.

Here in Paris, Jamaluddin and one of his Egyptian protégés, Mohammed Abduh, started a seminal journal called *The Firmest Bond*.
They published only eighteen issues before they ran out of money
and into other difficulties and had to shut the journal down, but in
those eighteen issues, Jamaluddin established the core of the credo
now called pan-Islamism. He declared that all the apparently local
struggles between diverse Muslim and European powers over various specific issues—between the Iranians and Russia over Azerbaijan, between the Ottomans and Russia over Crimea, between the
British and Egyptians over bank loans, between the French and Algerians over grain sales, between the British and the people of India
and Afghanistan over borders etc., etc. were not actually many different struggles over many different issues but one great struggle
over one great issue between just two global entities: Islam and the
West. He was the first to use these two words as coterminous and
of course historically conflicting categories. Sometime during this
period Jamaluddin also, it would seem, visited . . .

- **the United States,** but little is known about his activities there,
  and he certainly dipped in and out of . . .
- **London** a few times, where he argued with Randolph Churchill,
  the father of Winston Churchill, and with other British leaders
  about British policies in Egypt. He also traveled in Germany, as
  well as spending some time in Saint Petersburg, the capital of

Russia. Once his journal folded, he had nothing to keep him in Europe anymore, so he moved to . . .

- **Uzbekistan.** There, he talked czarist authorities into letting him publish and disseminate the Qur'an to Muslims under czarist rule, and to translate, publish, and disseminate other Islamic literature, which had been unavailable in Central Asia for decades. His efforts led to a revival of Islam throughout the region. Here, Jamaluddin also fleshed out an idea he had long been pushing, that Muslim countries needed to use the rivalry among European powers to carve out a zone of independence for themselves, by aligning with Russia against British power, with Germany against Russian power, with Britain and France against Russian power, and so on. These ideas would emerge as core strategies of the global "non-aligned movement" of the twentieth century. In 1884 he moved to . . .

- **Iran** where he worked to reform the judiciary. This brought him head to head with the local ulama. Things got hot and he had to return to Central Asia in a hurry. In 1888, however, Iran's King Nasiruddin invited him back to the country as its prime minister. Nasiruddin was locked in a power struggle with his country's ulama, and he thought Jamaluddin's "modernism" would help his cause. Jamaluddin did move to Iran, not as its prime minister but as a special adviser to the king. This time, however, instead of attacking the ulama, he attacked the king and his practice of selling economic "concessions" to colonialist powers. The most striking example of this during Jamaluddin's stay in Iran was the no-bid tobacco concession awarded to British companies, which gave British interests control over every aspect of tobacco production and sale in Iran.[2] Jamaluddin called for a tobacco boycott, a strategy later taken up in many lands by many other political activists, including the Indian anticolonialist leader Mahatma Gandhi (who famously called on Indians to boycott English cotton and instead spin their own). Jamaluddin's oratory filled the streets of Iran with demonstrators protesting against the Shah, who was probably sorry he had ever set eyes on the Afghan (Iranian?) reformer. Jamaluddin even talked one of the grand ayatollahs into declaring the tobacco concession un-Islamic. Well, that finally snapped the shah's patience. He sent troops to roust Jamaluddin out of his house and escort him to the border. Thus, in 1891, Jamaluddin the Afghan returned to . . .

• **Istanbul**, where the Ottoman emperor Sultan Hamid gave him a house and a stipend. The Sultan thought Jamaluddin's pan-Islamist ideas would somehow pay political dividends to him. Jamaluddin went on teaching, writing, and giving speeches. Intellectuals and activists came to visit him from every corner of the Muslim world. The great reformer told them that *ijtihad*, "free thinking," was a primary principle of Islam: but freethinking, he said, had to proceed from first principles rooted in Qur'an and hadith. Every Muslim had the right to his or her own interpretation of the scriptures and revelations, but Muslims as a community had to school themselves in those first principles embedded in the revelations. The great error of Muslims, the reason for their weakness, said Jamaluddin, was that they had turned their backs on Western science while embracing Western education and social mores. They should have done exactly the opposite: they should have embraced western science but closed their gates to Western social mores and educational systems.

In 1895, unfortunately, an Iranian student assassinated King Nasiruddin. The Iranian government immediately blamed Jamaluddin for it and demanded that he be extradited to Iran for punishment. Sultan Hamid refused the demand but he put the great reformer under house arrest. Later that year, Jamaluddin contracted cancer of the mouth and requested that he be allowed to travel to Vienna for medical treatment but the sultan turned him down. Instead, he sent his personal physician over to treat him. The court physician treated Jamaluddin's cancer by removing his lower jaw. Jamaluddin-i-Afghan died that year and was buried in Asia Minor. Later his body was transported to Afghanistan for reburial. Wherever he had started out, he certainly ended up in Afghanistan: his grave is situated at the heart of the campus of Kabul University.

It's interesting to remember that Sayyid Jamaluddin Afghan had no official leadership title or position. He didn't run a country. He didn't have

an army. He had no official position in any government. He never founded
a political party or headed up a movement. He had no employees, no
subordinates, no one to whom he gave orders. What's more he didn't leave
behind some body of books or even one book encapsulating a coherent political philosophy, no Islamist *Das Capital*. This man was purely a gadfly,
rabble-rouser, and rebel—that's what he was.

Yet he had a tremendous impact on the Muslim world. How? Through
his "disciples." Sayyid Jamaluddin-i-Afghan operated like a prophet, in a
way. His charismatic intensity lit sparks everywhere he went. His protégé
Mohammed Abduh became the head of Al Azhar University and the top
religious scholar in Egypt. He did write books elaborating on and system-
atizing Jamaluddin's modernist ideas.

Another of Jamaluddin's disciples, Zaghlul, did found a political party,
the Wafd, which evolved into the nationalist movement for Egyptian independence. Yet another of his disciples was the religious leader in the
Sudan who erupted against the British as "the Mahdi." In Iran, the Tobacco Boycott that he inspired spawned the generation of activists who
forged the constitutionalist movement in the twentieth century.

Jamaluddin inspired an Afghan intellectual named Tarzi living in
Turkey who returned to Afghanistan and, following in Jamaluddin's footsteps, tutored Prince Amanullah, Afghanistan's heir apparent. Tarzi shaped
the prince into a modernist king who won full Afghan independence from
the British and declared Afghanistan a sovereign nation just twenty-two
years after the death of Jamaluddin.

And his students had students. The credo and the message changed as
it was handed down. Some strands of it grew more radically political, some
grew more nationalist, some more developmentalist—that is, obsessed
with developing industry and technology in Muslim countries by whatever
means. Mohammed Abduh's student, the Syrian theologian Rashid Rida,
elaborated ways for Islam to serve as the basis for a state. Another of Jamaluddin's intellectual descendants was Hassan al-Banna, who founded
the Muslim Brotherhood; more about him later. In short, the influence of
this intense, mercurial figure echoes in every corner of the Muslim world
he roamed so restlessly.

14

⌘

Industry, Constitutions, and Nationalism

1163–1336 AH
1750–1918 CE

ABDUL WAHHAB, Sayyid Jamaluddin-i-Afghan, and Sayyid Ahmed of Aligarh—each of these men typified a different idea of what went wrong with the Islamic world and how to fix it. Throughout the nineteenth century, numerous permutations of these three currents evolved and spread. Of them all, it was secular modernism, the direction championed by Sayyid Ahmad of Aligarh, that acquired political power most overtly. This is not to say that Sayyid Ahmad fathered some mighty movement himself. He was just one of many secular reformists across the Islamic world who came up with roughly similar ideas. What made these ideas so persuasive was a trio of phenomena spilling into the Islamic heartland just then, from Europe: industrialization, constitutionalism, and nationalism.

The most consequential of the three was probably industrialization, the seductions of which affected every part of the world. In Europe, the Industrial Revolution came out of a great flurry of inventions straddling the year 1800 CE, beginning with the steam engine. Often, we speak of great inventions as if they make their own case merely by existing, but in fact, people don't start building and using a device simply because it's clever. The technological breakthrough represented by an invention is only one ingredient in its success. The social context is what really determines whether it will "take."

The steam engine provides a case in point. What could be more useful? What could be more obviously world-changing? Yet the steam engine was invented in the Muslim world over three centuries before it popped up in the West, and in the Muslim world it didn't change much of anything. The steam engine invented there was used to power a spit so that a whole sheep might be roasted efficiently at a rich man's banquet. (A description of this device appears in a 1551 book by the Turkish engineer Taqi al-Din.) After the spit, however, no other application for the device occurred to anyone, so it was forgotten.

Another case in point: the ancient Chinese had all the technology they needed by the tenth century to mechanize production and mass produce goods, but they didn't use it that way. They used geared machinery to make toys. They used a water-driven turbine to power a big clock. If they had used these technologies to build labor-saving machinery of the type that spawned factories in nineteenth-century Europe, the Industrial Revolution would almost certainly have started in China.

So why didn't it? Why did these inventions fail to "take" until they were invented in the West? The answer has less to do with the inventions themselves than it does with the social context into which the inventions were born.

When the Chinese invented geared machinery, theirs was an efficient, highly centralized state in which an imperial bureaucracy managed the entire society. The main function of this bureaucracy aside from record-keeping and defense was to organize public works. The genius of Chinese political culture was its ability to soak up surplus labor with massive construction projects useful to the public good. The first emperor, for example, put about a million people to work building the Great Wall. A later emperor employed even more workers to dig the Grand Canal, which connected the country's two major river systems. Yes, China had the technology to build labor-saving machinery, but who was going to build it? Only the imperial bureacracy had the capacity, and why would it bother to save something it already had too much of? China was overpopulated and labor was cheap. If a lot of laborers were left at loose ends, whose job would it be to deal with the resulting social disruptions? The bureacracy. The one institution capable of industrializing China had no motive to undertake it.

Likewise, Muslim inventors didn't think of using steam power to make devices that would mass-produce consumer goods, because they lived in a society already overflowing with an abundance of consumer goods, handcrafted by millions of artisans and distributed by efficient trade networks. Besides, the inventors worked for an idle class of elite folks who had all the goods they could consume and whose lot in life did not call upon them to produce—much less mass-produce—anything.

It wasn't some dysfunction in these societies that generated their indifference to potentially world-changing technologies, quite the opposite. It was something working too well that led them into "a high-level equilibrium trap" (to borrow a phrase from historian Mark Elvin.[1]) Necessity, it turns out, isn't really the mother of invention; it's the mother of the process that turns an invention into a product, and in late-eighteenth-century Europe, that mother was ready.

Steam engines evolved out of steam-powered pumps used by private mine owners to keep their mine shafts free of water. These same mine owners had another business problem they urgently desired to solve: getting their ore as quickly as possible from the mine to a river or seaport, so they could beat their competitors to market. Traditionally, they hauled the ore in horse-drawn carts that rolled along on parallel wooden tracks called tramways. One day, George Stephenson, an illiterate English mining manager, figured out that a steam pump could be bolted to a cart and made to turn the wheels, with appropriate gearing. The locomotive was born.

England at this point brimmed with private business owners competing to move products and materials to markets ahead of one another. Anyone with access to a railroad could get an edge on all the others, unless they too shipped by train; so everyone started using railroads, whereupon everyone who had the means to build a railroad, did so.

Likewise, after James Watt perfected the steam engine in the late eighteenth century, clever European inventors figured out how to mechanize textile looms. Anyone who possessed a power loom could now outproduce rival cloth makers and drive them out of business—unless the rivals acquired power looms too; so they all did.

But anyone who had the capital to acquire *two* power looms, ten looms, a hundred, could drive out many many many many competitors and grow rich, rich, rich! All the money to be made got clever tinkerers wondering what else could be manufactured by fuel-driven geared machinery. Shoes? Yes. Furniture? Yes. Spoons? Absolutely. In fact, once people got started, they came to find that almost every item in common use could be made by some fuel-driven machine faster, cheaper, and in much greater quantities than by hand. And who wouldn't want to be a shoe tycoon? Or a spoon tycoon or any kind of tycoon?

Of course, this process left countless artisans and craftspeople out of work, but this is where nineteenth-century Europe differed from tenth-century China. In Europe, those who had the means to install industrial machinery had no particular responsibility for those whose livelihood would be destroyed by a sudden abundance of cheap, machine-made goods. Nor were the folks they affected downstream their kinfolk or fellow tribesmen, just strangers whom they had never met and would never know by name. What's more, it was somebody else's job to deal with the social disruptions caused by widespread unemployment, not theirs. Going ahead with industrialization didn't signify some moral flaw in them; it merely reflected the way this particular society was compartmentalized.

The Industrial Revolution could take place only where certain social preconditions existed, and in Europe at that time they happened to exist. The Industrial Revolution also had inevitable social consequences and in Europe, at that point, turning production over to machinery did change societies, daily life, and Europeans themselves. Let us count (some of) the ways:

- Rural areas emptied into exploding new cities.
- Animals vanished from daily life for most people.
- Clock and calendar time became more important than natural time markers such as the sun and the moon.
- Large family networks dissolved, and the nuclear family—one man, one woman, and their children—became the universally accepted default unit of the industrial age.

- The connection between people and place weakened as new economic realities demanded mobility: people had to go where the work was, and suddenly the work could be anywhere.
- The connection between generations weakened, as most individuals no longer had any useful work skills to learn from their parents and little of value to pass on to their kids. The best parents could do for their children was to make sure they had the basic skills needed to flex, learn, and adapt. Thus, more broadly than ever before, reading, writing, and arithmetic became the indispensable skills of functional individuals.
- And finally, psychological adaptability—an ability to constantly relinquish old values and ideas and embrace new ones—became a competitive asset.

All these changes generated anxiety, but it was not catastrophic anxiety, because Europeans (and Americans even more) had already evolved a complex of attitudes enabling them to cope, and the core of this complex was individualism, an orientation that had taken centuries to develop in the West.

When Europeans came to the Islamic world, they brought along goods that were the end products of the Industrial Revolution, but not the evolutionary processes that made those goods possible. Muslims wanted the products, of course, as who wouldn't: the cheap cloth, the machine-made shoes, the packaged dried goods and whatnot, and saw no reason why they should not have them. They could buy and operate any machine the West could make. They could take the machines apart, study how they were built, and make similar machines themselves. Nothing in the manufacturing process lay beyond their comprehension.

But the social underpinnings were a different matter. The preconditions of industrialization could not be instantly imported. The social consequences could not be so easily absorbed in societies structured so differently from those of western Europe.

In the Ottoman world, for example, manufacturing had long been in the hands of guilds, which were interwoven with Sufi orders, which were interwoven with the machinery of the Ottoman state and society, which was interlinked with the fact that every person had numerous tribal affiliations, which was interwoven with a universal assumption that the public realm belonged exclusively to men and that women were properly kept sequestered in a private world, cut off from politics and production.

And yet, all across the world, in Europe as much as in the Islamic world, before industrialization, a great deal of manufacturing was actually in the hands of women, since almost everything of value was produced in or near the home. Women wove the cloth and made the garments. Women had a big role in animal husbandry. Women transformed the raw products of flocks and fields into useful products, and they practiced many other handicrafts as well. When these processes were mechanized, "cottage industries" went under and left countless women out of work.

In Europe, large numbers of these women then went to work in factories, shops, and eventually offices. Given the European social structure, they could do so: it caused some social and psychological disruption, to be sure, but women had already won access to the public realm, and so they could go to work outside the home, and they did, and out of this great movement, which was going to happen anyway, came the philosophical musings, political theorizing, and social activism known today as feminism, a movement premised on the existence and sanctity of individual rights. (Only after a concept of "the individual" exists can one say, "Every individual has rights" and once that assertion is accepted, one can entertain the notion that women might have the same rights as men, since both are individuals.)

In the Islamic world, the pervasively embedded division of the world into a masculine public realm and a feminine private one made the move from cottage industries to industrial production much more problematic and produced social dislocations that were much more wrenching. It required, first of all, overturning that whole divided social system, which struck at the core of family life for every family and left unsettled questions of identity for both men and women at the deepest level of conscious and even subconscious life, as became most evident by the late twentieth century.

But also, replacing guilds with factories meant severing the connection between manufacturing and Sufi orders, which at some level implied severing the connection between spirituality and work. What's more, moving production into factories required that people start living a life regulated by clocks; yet the fundamental core of Muslim life, the prayer ritual that must be performed five times daily, is situated in a framework of natural time markers: the position of the sun was what determined the times of prayer. Here, then, was another way in which industrialization pitted production against spiritual practice. (Europe would have faced the same contradiction had industrialization emerged in feudal times when events such as matins and vespers framed people's schedules.)

Besides all this, industrialization required that a society organized universally as large networks of interconnected clans with tribal loyalties superseding most other affiliations rethink itself overnight as a universe of atomized individuals, each one making independent economic decisions based on rational self-interest and responsible only to a nuclear family. It wasn't going to happen; not easily. And it couldn't happen suddenly. It asserted a crosscurrent against the whole river of Islamic civilization since the 700s. Muslim societies needed time to let the social preconditions of industrialization evolve in their world. But that wasn't going to happen either; even less so. For one thing, no one thought in terms of developing "social preconditions." They thought in terms of acquiring products, technologies and their underlying scientific principles.

That is, no one looking at machine-made consumer goods said, "Gee, we, too, should have a Reformation and develop a cult of individualism and then undergo a long period of letting reason erode the authority of faith while developing political insitutions that encourage free inquiry so that we can happen onto the ideas of modern science while at the same time evolving an economic system built on competition among private businesses so that when our science spawns new technologies we can jump on them and thus, in a few hundred years, quite independently of Europe, make these same sorts of goods ourselves." No, people said, "Nice goods, where can we get some?" Because it's pointless to reinvent the wheel when the wheel is already sitting on the shelf, priced to move.

Marx and Engels, among others, documented that industrialization had some undesirable side effects in the West, but it caused even greater social and psychological disruption in the Islamic world. Yet the mere existence of industrially produced consumer goods made an argument that no pamphlet could refute and no religious harangue undercut. "We're nice stuff; you should get some," they whispered, triggering a widespread sense that something had to change, that people living in Iran or Afghanistan or Asia Minor or Egypt or Morocco had to become in some way . . . more Western. Thus, as awareness of the Industrial Revolution seeped through the Muslim world, secular reform ideas gained ground in Islamic countries.

In Iran, after the 1840s, an extremely energetic prime minister named Mirza Taqi, also called Amir Kabir, "the Great Leader," launched a crash program to "modernize" the country. By "modernize," he meant "industrialize," but he understood this to be a complicated process. He knew Iran couldn't just acquire industrial goods. To really match up to the Western powers devouring their country, Iranians had to acquire some aspects of Western culture. But what aspects? The key, Amir Kabir decided, was education.

He built a network of secular public schools across the country. Just outside Tehran, he established the university mentioned earlier, Dar al-Funun or "house of wisdom," where students could study foreign languages, science, technical subjects, and the history of Western cultures. Iran started sending students abroad, as well, to countries such as Germany and France. Not surprisingly, these students hailed largely from privileged urban families assocated with the court and government bureacracy—not from rural peasant stock, merchant families, or high-status religious families. And so, the new educational program expanded social divisions that already existed in this society.

Graduates pouring out of the secular education system were tapped to staff a "modernized" government bureacracy and army. (*Modern* in this context meant "more like you would see in Europe.") Thus, the Iranian response to industrialism generated a new social class in Iran consisting of educated civil servants, army officers, university students, teachers, technicians, professionals, anyone who had graduated from Dar al-Funun, anyone who had studied in Europe. . . . This burgeoning class developed an ever more secular outlook and grew ever more receptive to thinking of Islam as a system of rational, ethical values rather than a revelation-based manual for getting into heaven.

Constitutionalism, a second phenomenon born in Europe, now began to have an impact in Iran, largely because this new class was open to it. Constitutionalism is not quite the same as democratic idealism, since even totalitarian dictatorships can have constitutions, but a constitution is certainly a necessary precondition to democracy. It asserts that a society operates within a stable framework of stated laws binding ruler as well as ruled. Absolute monarchies, the system long in place throughout the Muslim world, gave rulers de facto power to decide the rules as they pleased at any given moment. It's important to realize that in absolute monarchies this pattern doesn't apply just to the top ruler; it is reified throughout society, each man having arbitary power over those below him and subject to the arbitrary whims of those above. (Similarly, democracy doesn't just mean top leaders gaining office through election; it means that some sort of interactive participatory process goes on at every level: elections are not equivalent to democracy; they are only a sign that democracy exists.)

Constitutionalism made headway in Iran in part because, out of the rising class of educated secular modernists, a new intelligentsia emerged. They announced their modernity not just in their ideas but in the very language they used to express their ideas. New writers began to eschew the diction of classical Persian literature, which was so full of ornate rhetorical flourishes and devices, and developed instead a simple, muscular prose, which they used to write, not epic poems and mystical lyrics, but satirical novels, political plays, and the like.

Literary scholar Hamid Dabashi notes the curious case of the English language novel *The Adventures of Hajji Baba of Ispahan,* written by a traveler named James Morier, who pretended he had merely translated a Persian original. Morier used a ridiculous diction in his novel to lampoon Persian speech and depicted Iranians as dishonest scoundrels and buffoons.

Then, in the 1880s, an astounding thing happened. Iranian grammarian Mirza Habib translated *Hajji Baba* into Persian. Remarkably, what in English was offensive racist trash became, in translation, a literary masterpiece that laid the groundwork for a modernist Persian literary voice and "a seminal text in the course of the constitutional movement." The ridicule that Morier directed against Iranians in an Orientalist manner, the translator redirected against clerical and courtly corruption in Iranian society, thereby transforming *Hajji Baba* into an incendiary political critique.[2]

With the emergence of a secular modernist intelligentsia, the classics of Persian literature, poetry by the likes of Rumi and Sa'di and Hafez, began to gather dust while readers instead devoured, not just the new Iranian writing, but also books by European thinkers such as Charles Montesquieu and Auguste Comte, philosophers who theorized that societies evolved through successively higher stages. Montesquieu categorized and ranked political systems, declaring that republics were the next higher stage after monarchies and despotisms. Comte said that as people grew more civilized they evolved from religious to metaphysical to scientific consciousness.[3]

Iranian modernist intellectuals decided their country needed to evolve. Their discontent focused on the Qajar monarchs, now into their second century of rule. These kings had pretty much been treating the country like a private possession. One Qajar after another had been selling off the national economy bit by bit to foreigners, to fund their own luxuries and amusements, including expensive excursions to Europe.

Resentment among secular modernists came to a head with the Tobacco Boycott, the movement so passionately promoted by Jamaluddin-i-Afghan. As it happens, Jamaluddin also drew the Shi'i clerical establishment into the Tobacco Boycott, and it was this alliance that forced the shah to back down. But once the shah nullified the British monopoly on tobacco sales in Iran, the clerics felt they had won and retired from the field.

The remaining activists held together, however, and crafted new demands. They called for a constitution that would limit the powers of the king and give the people a voice in running the country. Cheered on from afar by Jamaluddin (deported to Asia Minor by this time), these secular modernists began to discuss building a parliamentary democracy. The clerics totally opposed them. A constitution would be un-Islamic, they said, because Iran already had a constitution: it was called the Shari'a. They derided the idea of democracy, too: only dynastic rule was permitted by Islam, they declared. By the early years of the twentieth century, the long struggle in Iran between clerics and crown had turned into a complicated three-way struggle among clerics, crown, and secular modernist intelligentsia, a struggle in which any two factions might pair up against the third. In the matter of the constitution, clerics and crown stood united against the modernists.

But the modernist tide was running high. In 1906, Qajar king Muzaffar al-din yielded, finally. He accepted a consitution that limited his powers severely and allowed a parliament to be formed, the Majlis, as it was called. The king died a week after the Majlis first convened, and his son Mohammad Ali Shah took over. It wasn't clear what powers the parliament really had—it didn't have an army and didn't command a police force—yet within two years the Majlis had passed a host of laws that laid the basis for free speech, a free press, and a full range of civil liberties in Iran.

Before the third year was up, however, the king pointed cannons at the parliament building and blew it down, his way of saying: "Let's give the old ways another chance." The ulama and all the other traditional groups cheered him on; and this is where matters stood in Iran as World War I approached.

Meanwhile, a third European phenomenon was seducing minds and hearts across the Islamic world: nationalism. Iran provided the least fertile soil for this ideology, perhaps because it was already pretty much a nation-state, or at least closer to one than any other part of the Islamic heartland. In India, nationalism began transforming Aligarh modernism into a movement that would finally give birth to Pakistan. But it was in the Ottoman Empire and in territories that had once been part of this empire that nationalism really caught on.

When I say nationalism, I don't mean the nation-state per se. A nation-state is a concrete geographical fact: a territory with definite borders, a single central government, a single set of laws enforced by that single government, a single currency, an army, a police force, and so on. Nation-states such as France and England developed spontaneously out of historical circumstances and not because nationalists conceived of them and then built them.

The nationalism I'm speaking of was (is) an idea. It didn't develop where nation-states had formed, but where they *hadn't*. It didn't describe what was but what (supposedly) ought to be. The German-speaking people came into the nineteenth century as a multitude of principalities and kingdoms. Italy was similarly divided, and so was the whole of Europe east of Germany. Nationalism sprouted in these areas.

The seeds of the idea go back to the eighteenth-century German philosopher Johann Herder, who criticized "enlightenment" philosophers such as Immanuel Kant. The enlightenment philosophers taught that man is essentially a rational being and that moral values must ultimately be based on reason. Since the rules of reason are the same for everyone, at all times, in all places, civilized people who subdue their passions and let themselves be guided solely by reason must eventually progress toward a single universal set of laws and value judgments.

Herder, however, argued that there was no such thing as universal values, either moral or aesthetic: rather, he said, the world was composed of various cultural entities, which he called *volks*: or "people." Each of these entities had a *volksgeist*, a spiritual essence possessed in common by the given people. Shared language, traditions, customs, history—ties like these bound a group of people together as a volk. Although a true volk was a purely social entity, its "groupness" wasn't just a social contract or some sort of agreement among its members to team up, any more than a multitude of cells agree to come together and be an organism. Nations had a unified singleness that made them as real as butterflies or mountains: that's the sort of thing Herder meant by volk. And when Herder spoke of volksgeist, he meant something like what religious people mean by soul or what psychologists mean when they speak of "the self." Every nation, to Herder, had some such unified spiritual essence.

Herder's argument implied that no moral or aesthetic judgment was universally valid or objectively true. If humanity was not reducible to a capacity for reason, then values were not the same at all times for all people. In aesthetics, for example, an Indian and a German might disagree about what was beautiful, but this didn't mean one side was right and the other wrong. Each judgment reflected a volksgeist and was true only insofar as it truly expressed the volksgeist. A value judgment could rise no higher than the level of the nation.

Herder wasn't saying one nation was better than another, just that they were different, and that one nation couldn't be judged by the values of another. But a slightly younger philosopher, Johann Gottlieb Fichte, took Herder's ideas a step further and shifted their import. Fichte agreed that humanity clumped together as discrete nations, each one bound together by a common spirit; but he suggested that some volks might actually be superior to others. Specifically, he suggested that Germans had a great inherant capacity for liberty, theirs being a vigorous living language as contrasted to the French language, which was dead. (The French no doubt disagreed.)

Fichte died in 1814: his career, therefore, peaked in the period when Napoleon was conquering Europe and dominating the Germans, which is probably one key to Fichte's influence. Many Germans chafing under French rule felt that, yes, they could tell: French and German really were two different spirits; and they liked hearing that even though the French might be dominant, the Germans might be somehow "higher". . .

Fast-forward five decades from the fall of Napoleon Bonaparte to the year 1870. Prussian Chancellor Otto von Bismarck had just forged a single nation out of the many little German states. France, as it happened, was now ruled by Napoleon's buffoonish great-nephew Napoleon III, who was twice as pompous and half as talented as Napoleon the First. Bismarck goaded this Napoleon into declaring war on him, then overwhelmed France with a lightning strike, conquered Paris within months, and imposed humiliating terms upon the French, as well as wresting two resource-rich border provinces away from France.

German nationalism, born out of defeat and resentment, now had victory to batten on. A triumphalist vision of a German nation with a mythic destiny took wing. Artists sought the sources of the German volksgeist in ancient Teutonic myths. Wagner expressed the German nationalist passion in bombastic operas. Historians began spinning a mythological narrative tracing German origins back to the primal Indo-Europeans, the Aryan tribes of the Caucasus mountains.

German nationalism especially captivated professors at the Gymnasium, which was then Germany's most prestigious institution of higher education. Here, philosophers such as Heinrich von Treitschke began teaching that nations were the most authentic social entities in the world and the highest expression of human life. They rhapsodized about a pan-German nation that would rule all territories in which German speakers lived. They spoke of the heroic destiny that justified "great" nations imposing their will on barbaric lands. (In other words, colonialism was noble.) Their pupils, laden with these passions, moved into society as engineers, bankers, teachers, or whatnot, and infected the German masses with this virus of pan-German nationalism.

In Italy, meanwhile, a revolutionary named Joseph Mazzini was adding further and perhaps the final pieces to nationalism as a political ideology. Mazzini was mainly interested in rescuing Italy from foreign rulers such as the Austrians and saw unificiation as the only means for achieving this goal. His politics led him to propound that individuals could act only as collective units, and should relinquish their individual personalities to their nation. "Say not *I* but *we*," he harangued his fellow revolutionaries in his pamphlet *On the Duties of Man.* "Let each man among you strive to incarnate his country in himself."[4] Mazzini went on to assert a theory of collective rights based on nationalism. Every nation had "a right" to a territory of its own, a "right" to leaders from amongst its own, a "right" to defined borders, a "right" to extend those borders as far as necessary to encompass all the people who comprised the nation, and a "right" to complete sovereignty within those borders. It was only right, natural, and noble, he said, for the people of a nation to live within one geographically continuous state, so that none of them would have to live among strangers.

In the last half of the nineteenth century, movements fueled by nationalism spawned first Germany and then Italy, but the virus spread beyond these countries, into eastern Europe, where a multitude of disparate communities speaking many languages, claiming different ethnic origins, and telling diverse stories about their origins rattled around as indigestible parts of two ramshackle empires, the Ottoman and the Austro-Hungarian. The government of both empires tried to squelch all nationalists within their borders, but succeeded only in driving them underground, where they went on seething in secrecy. European cartoonists imagined these revolutionaries as stout little bearded men carrying bombs shaped like bowling balls under bulky overcoats: an amusing image. The real anarchist and terrorist movements spawned by European nationalism were not so amusing. And it was from here that nationalism rolled east into the Islamic heartlands.

Before leaving Europe, however, let me mention two other nationalist movements of consequence that matured in the West. One had immediate relevance for the Ottoman Empire; the other would signify later. The latter one took shape in North America where a new country formed. Technically, this country was born when thirteen small colonies of British settlers revolted against their home government and launched independent destinies, but in many ways the confederation they put together didn't actually become a nation-state until the Civil War of 1861 to 1865. Before that war, people in the United States spoke of their country as "these united states." After the war, they called it "*the* United States."[5] The issue of slavery triggered the war, but President Lincoln frankly put preserving the union at the center of his arguments for the justice and necessity of the war. In his Gettysburg Address, he said the war was being fought to test whether a nation "conceived in liberty" and a government of, by, and for the people could endure. He and others who forged the United States—politicians, historians, philosophers, writers, thinkers, and citizens in general—asserted a nationalist idea quite distinct from the ideologies spawned in Europe. Instead of seeking nationhood in a common religion, history, traditions, customs, race, or ethnic identity, they proposed that multitudes of individuals could become "a people" by virtue of shared principles and shared allegiance to a process. It was a nationalism based on ideas, a nationalism that anyone could embrace because, in theory, it was a nation any person could become a member of, not just those who worn born into it.

During that same Civil War, the emerging country gave notice of its potential power. The American Civil War was the first in which a single man at one point commanded an army of a million, the first in which nearly a quarter of a million soldiers clashed on a single battlefield, and the first in which industrial technology from railroads to submarines to proto–machine guns, played a decisive role. It's true that in this war the (dis)united states were fighting each other and posed, therefore, no military threat to anyone else, but anyone could imagine what a formidable power would emerge once the two sides melted back into a single state.

The other European nationalist movement of world-historical consequence and immediate relevance for the Muslim world was Zionism. This bundle of passion and ideas was just like all the other nineteenth-century European nationalisms in its arguments and appeals. It agreed with Herder that people who share a language, culture, and history were a nation. It agreed with Mazzini that a nation had a right to its own self-ruling state situated securely in a territory of its own. It agreed with the likes of Treitschke that a nation-state had a right (even a destiny) to include all of its own people within its borders and a right to exclude all others if necessary. If the Germans were a nation and had such rights, said the founders of political Zionism, if the Italians were a nation, if the French were a nation, then by God the Jews were a nation too.

There was, however, one key difference between Zionism and other nineteenth-century European nationalisms. The Italians, Germans, Serbians, and others claimed a nationalist right to the territory they inhabited. The Jewish people had no territory. They had been scattered around the globe for two millenia and were now living as landless minorities in other people's states. Throughout their two thousand years in Diaspora, however, Jews had held together, maintaining a sense of peoplehood built around a Judaism that was as much cultural and historical as it was religious: in nineteenth-century Europe, it was perfectly possible to be Jewish without being a practicing or even a "believing" Jew. Still, a core element of the Jewish religious-historical narrative asserted that God had promised the land of Canaan to the original Hebrews—Abraham and his tribal descendants—in exchange for their worshipping no other and obeying only His commandments. According to this narrative, the Jewish people had kept their side of the bargain and had thus earned the right to reclaim "their" land, the territory called Palestine, which was now inhabited by Arabs and ruled by the Ottoman Turks. Many nineteenth-century European Zionists were secular but this tenet about a Promised Land nonetheless made its way into the argument for a Jewish nation-state along the eastern Mediterannean coast.

In 1897, an Austrian journalist, Theodor Herzl, founded the first official organ of political Zionism, the World Zionist Congress, but Zionism already existed and its ideas went back to the early 1800s. It was amid all the other nationalist murmurings of that era that Jewish intellectuals in Europe began to speak of moving to Palestine. Some German proto-nationalists agreed with these proto-Zionists, and not in a friendly way. Fichte, for example, held that Jews could never assimilate into German culture, even if they were German-speaking from birth. If they stayed in Germany, they would always be a state within a state, and therefore, he suggested, they should seek their national destiny in Palestine.

Palestine had never been without an indigenous Jewish population, but in 1800 that population formed a miniscule fraction of the total—about 2.5 percent as opposed to the more than 97 percent who were Arabs. By the 1880s, when Jewish immigration from Europe to Palestine began in earnest, the ratio of Jews to Arabs had climbed to roughly 6 percent of the total. About thirty thousand moved to Palestine in the first aliyah, as waves of Jewish immigration to Palestine were called, and the ratio changed again. The first immigrants, however, were idealistic urban intellectuals who pictured themselves as Palestinian farmers, even though they didn't know a shovel from a hoe. Most of them returned to Europe, and the first aliyah petered out. That is where matters stood as World War I approached.

When these three phenomena from Europe—constitutionalism, nationalism, and industrialism—seeped into the Ottoman world they had a particularly corrosive effect, in part because the Ottoman "world" was shrinking throughout the nineteenth century, which was engendering much restless anxiety. Algeria was absorbed into France. Great Britain took over Egypt in all but name. Technically, the Mediterranean coast north of Egypt belonged to the Ottoman empire, as did the whole Arabian peninsula and most of what is now Iraq, but even here the Ottomans gradually found themselves bowing to Europeans. Meanwhile, the Ottoman hold on its European territories kept weakening. The whole of this ancient empire, so recently the world's greatest, was like some colossal creature whose extremities had fallen away and whose body was rotting, but was somehow still breathing, still alive.

It was alive, but Western business forces, backed by the power of their governments, operated freely here. Through the first half of the nineteenth century, their interaction with the Ottomans could be summed up in one word: *capitulations*.

Capitulations: it sounds like another word for "humiliating concessions." That, however, is not what the word meant at first.

The capitulations began when the empire was at its height, and the term simply referred to permissions granted by mighty Ottoman sultans to petty petitioners from Europe pleading to do business in the empire. The capitulations merely listed what these folks were permitted to do in Ottoman territory. Anything not listed was forbidden. Why call them "capitulations"? Because in Latin, the word simply means "categorize by headings." So the capitulations were lists of permitted business activities for Europeans, organized by category.

Since no single great war reversed the balance of power between the Ottomans and the Europeans, there was no single moment when *capitulations* stopped meaning "permissions doled out haughtily by mighty Ottoman lords" and started meaning "humiliating concessions wrung out triumphantly from Ottoman officials (by haughty European bosses)." But that's certainly what they meant by 1838, when the Ottomans signed the Treaty of Balta Liman with a consortium of European powers (to secure their aid against Mohammed Ali), a treaty establishing unequal terms between Ottomans and Europeans on Ottoman soil. The treaty placed low tariffs, for example, on European products coming into the empire but imposed high tariffs on Ottoman products flowing out. It forbade Ottoman subjects to establish monopolies but permitted and eased the way for Europeans to do exactly that. *These* capitulations had but one purpose: to ensure that Ottomans would be unable to compete with European businessmen on their own soil.

In the few decades after the Treaty of Balta Liman, the Ottoman government shook its aging limbs and promulgated a series of new rules to revamp Ottoman society so that it could match up to the Europeans—exactly the sort of thing that was going on in Iran around this same time. In the Ottoman Empire, these modernizing moves were called Tanzimat or "reorganization measures." They began with an 1839 proclamation grandiosely titled "The Noble Edict of the Rose Chamber." In 1856 came another document, "The Imperial Edict." Then in 1860 came a third set of reform measures.

Here are a few things the Tanzimat established:

- a new national government bureaucracy modeled along French lines;
- secular state courts superseding the traditional Shari'a courts;
- a new code of criminal justice based on France's "Napoleonic" code;
- new commercial rules favoring "free trade," which essentially gave Europeans a free hand to set business rules in the Ottoman empire;
- a conscripted army modeled on the Prussian system, to replace the devshirme;
- public schools with a secular curriculum similar to what was taught in British schools, bypassing the traditional school system run by Muslim clerics;
- one single empire-wide state-run tax collection agency (rather like the IRS in today's United States), replacing the traditional Ottoman "tax farmers" (who were, essentially, freelance tax collectors working on commission);

- guarantees that the "honor, life, and property" of all Ottoman subjects were inviolable and would be secured, regardless of race or religion.

On paper these reforms may look good, especially that one about guaranteeing the life and safety of all citizens, regardless of ethnic origin: who could be against ending discrimination? It's practically European.

But put yourself in the shoes of an average Turkish Muslim citizen of the empire in the nineteenth century: the inherent merits of such reforms would be hard to separate from the fact that they were dictated to Ottoman officials by Europeans—literally, according to historian James L. Gelvin: apparently the Imperial Edict was written out verbatim by British ambassador Stratford Canning and handed to Ottoman officials with instructions to translate it and proclaim it publicly.[6] Noble Edict of the Rose Chamber indeed! To many Ottoman Muslims, these smelled less like reforms and more like fresh evidence of alien power over their lives.

Not all Ottoman Muslims felt this way. A growing movement of reformists in Asia Minor, a Turkish version of movements in India, Afghanistan, and Iran, embraced and promoted the *Tanzimat*. They thought the only way to defeat European imperialism was to beat the Europeans at their own game, which would necessitate, first of all, adopting whatever European ideas accounted for European strength.

But the ulama were still around. The Tanzimat worked directly against their interests. Taking education out of clerical hands . . . replacing Shari'ah courts with secular courts . . . substituting French laws for Islamic law—such reforms not only stripped the ulama of power but robbed them of a reason to exist. Of course they were going to resist; and the ulama still had a lot of moral authority among the ordinary people. They still wielded clout at court too.

The sultan and his advisers, therefore, soon found themselves caught between the clamor of secular modernists and the yammer of an Islamic old guard. Tugged and yanked from both sides, the court tilted now this way, now that. As the secular modernists argued ever more stridently for European-style reforms, the traditionalists dug in ever more stubbornly to reactionary dicta. When the modernists called for mechanized state-run

factories, the ulama railed against Ottoman officials using typewriters—
Prophet Mohammed never used one, they argued.

For a moment, the modernists gained the upper hand. In 1876, they
forced the sultan to adopt a constitution, a momentous victory widely celebrated as the "French Revolution of the East." For just a few years there,
the crumbling empire was a constitutional monarchy like Great Britain (in
form). In that brief period, modernizing activists of every ethnic and religious stripe interacted companionably in a heady atmosphere of progressive enthusiasm: Turkish Muslims, Arab Muslims, Jews, Orthodox
Christians, Armenians, all rubbed shoulders as members of a single broad
movement to build a new world.

But the old guard retrenched, outmaneuvered the modernists, and rebuilt the sultan's power, until he was strong enough to abolish the constitution and rule as an absolute monarch again. The pendulum swung back,
in part, because the reforms were not working. Turkish Muslims of Asia
Minor saw their standard of living sinking, their autonomy shrinking.
They felt ever more powerless against the enormous forces of Europe
pressing from outside.

But they did have what they regarded as one fragment of that outside
world within their borders and completely in their power. That fragment
was the Armenian community. In reality, of course, the Armenians were no
more European than the Turks. They lived right where they had been living since time immemorial. They had their own non-European language,
traditions, and history. They didn't come from anywhere else and were, in
fact, more indigenous than the Turks.

They were, however, a Christian minority surrounded by a Muslim majority, and what's more, in that period of ever more humiliating capitulations, when business interests from western Europe acquired the power to
march into the Ottoman Empire and establish profitable business operations at the expense of the locals, the Armenians found themselves in a
paradoxical position. For Ottoman citizens, the only way to prosper at this
point was to work for, do business with, or best of all form partnerships
with European businesses. But when Europeans sought business partners
in the empire, they gravitated quite naturally towards those with whom
they felt kinship, and if they had a choice, they chose Armenian Christians
over Muslim Turks, so the favorable terms extracted by foreigners seemed

to benefit the Armenian community within the empire, or such at least was the perception among resentful Muslims slipping into poverty.

The Armenians had lived peacefully in the Ottoman world up to this time; as non-Turks, however, they had been shut out of the military-aristocratic ruling caste. They had also been cut off, to some extent, from big-time land ownership and "tax farming." Many therefore, had turned to business and finance to make a living.

Finance—that's what used to be called moneylending. It was frowned upon pretty widely in early times. Charging interest on a loan was explicitly forbidden in the Qur'an, just as it was in Medieval Christian Europe where the term *usury* in canon law didn't mean "charging *exorbitant* interest" but "charging *any* interest." Why did moneylending have this odor? I suppose it's because ordinary folks saw the lending of money in the context of charity, not of business: it was something one did when a neighbor got into trouble and needed help. Seen in that framework, charging interest on a loan smacked of exploiting somebody's misery to get rich. Yet the need to borrow money came up constantly, even in the most primitive feudal economy, often in the wake of crisis: a blacksmith's workshop burned down; a famous cleric died unexpectedly leaving his family to host an expensive funeral; someone wanted to get married without having saved up a dowry; someone fell catastrophically ill. . . . People went to moneylenders at moments when they felt particularly vulnerable and raw, yet they went with a culturally implanted feeling that any decent person would give them a loan for nothing. The desperation that forced them to accept a banker's terms only added a further dollop of resentment. When the borrower and the moneylender belonged to the same community, other sentiments such as kinship or loyalty might temper the resentment, but when people went to moneylenders whom they already saw as the Other, the dynamics of the interaction tended to exacerbate any existing communal hostility. The worst possible case, then, was for moneylending to become the exclusive province of a distinct cultural minority surrounded by a vast majority. In Europe, this dynamic made victims of the Jews. In the Ottoman Empire, it was the Armenians who fell afoul of it.

As tension built up, it was easy to forget that Turks and Armenians had lived together peacefully, not even three generations back; the hostility seemed like an age-old feature of the two communities' relationship. The Ottoman policy of dividing the population into self-governing communities was originally a way of conferring upon each a measure of cultural sovereignty. It reflected tolerance. It functioned as an instrument of harmony. Now, this same policy became a deficiency, a liability, a crucial key to the coming troubles, because it worked to separate, isolate, and spotlight the unfortunate Armenians. In fact, the *millet* system became a mechanism for exacerbating existing fault lines in Ottoman society.

Between 1894 and 1896, in eastern Anatolia, a series of anti-Armenian pogroms broke out. Turkish villagers began to massacre Armenians, much as Jews were being massacred in eastern Europe and Russia, but on an even larger scale. As many as three hundred thousand Armenians died before the madness subsided, and it subsided then only because Europeans put pressure on the Ottoman government to do something. Since the power of Europeans to dictate to Ottoman officials was a factor in the resentment vented upon the Armenians, this authority ending the violence only exacerbated the original psychosocial sources of the violence. It was like parents stepping in to protect a little boy from neighborhood bullies and then going off about their business: once the little boy is alone with the bullies again, he's in worse trouble than before.

Meanwhile, even though the sultan had scuttled the constitution, power remained divided between old guard and new bucks. The political struggle kept raging on and the balance inexorably tipped back to the new guys, for here, as in Iran, the tide was with the modernists. By 1900, a whole new generation of activists were calling for the constitution to be restored. They wanted their parents' French Revolution back.

Politically it was an exhilarating but confusing time. It wasn't like one group of agitators were nationalists, another group secular modernists, some other one liberal constitutionalists. Many ideologies and movements were intertwined and interacting. Any single person might espouse a bit of this and a bit of that. There had not yet been time enough to sort out which ideas went together and which were incompatible. All who set themselves against the old guard thought themselves Ottoman citizens with a common stake in reshaping the empire. All felt like young people in the know aligned against clueless elders, comrades-in-arms merely because they all fiercely favored the "modern," whatever that was.

This new generation of activists called themselves the Young Turks. They used the name in part because they actually *were* young, in their twenties, mostly, but also in part as a way of thumbing their noses at the old guard, for among traditional Muslims, older was always regarded as better—respectful titles such as *shiekh* and *pir* literally meant "old man." What the fuddy-duddies derided as a shortcoming, the Young Turks flaunted with pride: they were *young!*

Although they had many incipient disagreements, the Young Turks held together long enough to overwhelm the last Ottoman sultan, a weak and silly man named Abdul Hamid II. In 1908, they forced him to reinstate the constitution, reducing himself to a figurehead.

No sooner had they wrestled the sultan to the mat, however, then the Young Turks realized they were not one group but several. One faction, for example, favored decentralizing the empire, securing rights for minorities, and giving the people a bigger voice in the government. They were quickly squeezed out of the government altogether. Another faction embraced Turkish nationalism. Founded around 1902 by six medical students, it coalesced into a tightly organized, militaristic party called the Committee for Union and Progress.

The CUP found ever-increasing support for its views. Many anti-imperial Turks, many younger Turks, many educated civil servants, university students, intelligentsia and children of the intelligentsia, many literati who had read the nationalist arguments of the European philosophers and knew all about the successful strivings of German and Italian nationalists, began to see nationalism as their road to salvation from imperialism. Get rid of the cumbersome, old-fashioned, multicultural, Ottoman idea of empire and replace it with a lean, clean, mean, specifically Turkish state machine: this was the idea. The Arab provinces would have to be cut loose, of course, they no longer fit, but these new Turkish nationalists dreamed of linking up Anatolia with those central Asian territories that formed the ancestral homeland of the Turkish people. They dreamed of a Turkish nation-state that would stretch from the Bosporus to places like Kazakhstan.

Turkish nationalist intellectuals began to argue that Christian minorities, especially the Armenians, were a privileged aristocracy in Turkey, inherant internal enemies of the state, in league with the Russians, in league with the western Europeans, in league with the breakaway Slavic territories of Eastern Europe.

This new generation of Turkish nationalists said the nation superseded all smaller identities and suggested that the national "soul" might be vested in some single colossal personality, an idea that came straight from the German nationalist philosophers. The writer Ziya Gökalp declared that except for heroes and geniuses, individuals had no value. He urged his fellow Turks never to speak of "rights." There were no rights, he said, only duties: the duty to hear the voice of the nation and follow its demands.[7]

Trouble for the empire tended to confer glamour upon such militaristic nationalism. And trouble did keep coming. It had been coming for a long, long time. Bulgaria wrenched free. Bosnia and Herzegovina left the Ottoman fold to be annexed by the Habsurgs into their Austro-Hungarian empire. About a million Muslims, forced into exile by these changes, streamed into Anatolia looking for new homes in the dying, dysfunctional, and already-crowded empire. Then the Ottomans lost Crete. Nearly half the population of that island were Muslims, nearly all of whom migrated east. All this social dislocation generated a pervasive atmosphere of free-floating anxiety.

Amid the uproar, nationalism began heating up among other groups. Arab nationalism began to bubble, for one. And after all the horrors they had suffered at the hands of their fellow Turks, Armenian activists too declared a need and right to carve out a sovereign nation-state of Armenia. These were exactly the same nationalist impulses stirring among so many self-identified nationalities in eastern Europe at this time.

In 1912, a war in the Balkans stripped the empire of Albania, of Macedonia, of its last European holdings outside Istanbul, a military defeat that triggered a final spasm of anxiety, resentment, and confusion in Asia Minor. Turmoil like this favors the most tightly organized group, whatever its popular support may be; the Bolsheviks proved as much in Russia five years later. In Istanbul, the most tightly organized group just then was the ultranationalist Committee for Union and Progress. On January 23, 1913, the CUP seized control in a coup d'etat, assassinated the incumbent vizier, deposed the last Ottoman sultan, ousted all other leaders from the government, declared all other parties illegal, and turned Ottoman Turkey into a one-party state. A triumverate of men emerged as spearheads of this single party: Talaat Pasha, Enver Pasha, and Djemal Pasha, and it was these "three Pashas" who happened to be ruling the truncated remains of the Ottoman empire in 1914, when the long-anticipated European civil war broke out.

In Europe, it was called the Great War; to the Middle World, however, it looked like a European civil war at first: Germany and Austria lined up against France, Britain, and Russia, and most other European countries soon jumped in or got dragged in unwillingly.

Muslims had no dog in this fight, but CUP leaders thought that they might reap big benefits by joining the winning side before the fighting ended. Like most people, they assumed the war would last no more than a few months, because the great powers of Europe had been stockpiling "advanced" technological weapons for decades, fearsome firepower against which nobody and nothing could possibly stand for long, so it looked as if the war could only be a sudden bloody shootout from which the first to fire and the last to run out of ammo would emerge as winner.

CUP strategists decided this winner would be Germany. After all, Germany was the continent's mightiest industrial power, it had already squashed the French, and it held central Europe, which meant that it could move troops and war machines through its own territory on its superb rail network to every battlefront. Besides, by siding with Germany, the Turks would be fighting two of its enduring foes, Russia and Great Britain.

Eight months into the war, with Russian troops already threatening the northern border of their empire, CUP leaders ordered the infamous Deportation Act. Officially, this order was supposed to "relocate" the Armenians living near Russia to sites deeper within the empire where they wouldn't be able to make common cause with the Russians. To this day, the Turkish government insists that the Deportation Act was purely a security measure necessitated by war. They admit that, yes, some killing did take place, but a civil war was raging, so what can you expect, and besides the violence went both ways—such is the official position from which no Turkish government has yet budged.

And the fact is, there *was* a war on, the Russian *were* coming, some Armenians *were* collaborating with the Russians, some Armenians *did* kill some Turks, and some of the violence of 1915 early on was, it seems, a continuation of that unstructured hatred that burst out in the 1890s as pogroms and ethnic cleansing. (The United Nations defines "ethnic cleansing" as the attempt to enforce ethnic homogeneity in a given territory by driving out or killing unwanted groups, often by committing atrocities that frighten them in into fleeing.)

Outside of Turkey, however, few scholars doubt that in 1915 something much worse than ethnic cleansing took place, reprehensible as that alone would have been. The Deportation Act was the beginning of an organized attempt by Talaat Pasha, and perhaps Enver Pasha, and possibly other nameless leaders in the anonymous secret core of the CUP, to exterminate the Armenians, as a people—not just from Asia Minor or Turkish-designated areas but from the very Earth. Those who were being "relocated" were actually force-marched and brutalized to death; it was, in short, attempted genocide (defined by the United Nations as any attempt to erase a targeted ethnic group not just from a given area but altogether). The exact toll remains a matter of dispute but it exceeded a million. Talaat Pasha presided over this horror as minister of the Interior and then prime minister of Ottoman Turkey, a post he held until the end of World War I.

Turkish revisionist historian Taner Akçam quotes a doctor affiliated with the CUP at the time of the massacres explaining that, "Your nationality comes before everything else. . . . The Armenians of the East were so excited against us that if they remained in their land, not a single Turk, not a single Muslim could stay alive. . . . Thus, I told myself: oh, Dr. Rechid, there are only two options. Either they will cleanse the Turks or they will be cleansed by the Turks. I could not remain undecided between these two alternatives. My Turkishness overcame my condition as a doctor. I told myself: 'instead of being exterminated by them, we should exterminate them.'"[8]

But the CUP had thoroughly miscalculated. For one thing, the war did not end quickly. Instead of one big blast of offensive destruction, the western-European theater ground down to a bizarre defensive struggle between armies of millions, lined up for hundreds of miles, in trenches separated by desolate killing fields that were littered with explosives and barbed wire. Battles kept breaking out along these lines, and sometimes they killed tens of thousands in the course of a few hours but the territory won or lost in these battles was often measurable in mere inches. This was the European theater.

To break the deadlock, the British decide to attack the Axis powers from behind, by coming at them through Asia Minor. Doing this required first crippling the Ottomans. The Allies landed troops on the peninsula of Gallipoli, from which they hoped to storm Istanbul, but this assault failed and Allied troops were massacred.

Meanwhile, the British were already busy trying to exploit another Ottoman weakness: rebellion was percolating throughout the empire's Arab provinces, stemming from many sources. Nationalist movements sought Arab independence from Turks. Ancient tribal alignments chafed at Ottoman administrative rules. Various powerful Arab families sought to establish themselves as sovereign local dynasties. In all this discontent, the British smelled an opportunity.

Among the dynastic contenders, two families stood out: the house of Ibn Saud, which was still allied with Wahhabi clerics, and the Hashimite family, which ruled Mecca, the spiritual center of Islam.

The Saudi-Wahhabi realm had shrunk down to a Bedouin tribal state in central Arabia but was still headed by a direct descendant of that ancestral eighteenth-century Saudi chieftain Mohammed Ibn Saud, the one who had struck a deal with the radically conservative cleric Ibn Wahhab. Over the decades, the two men's families had intermarried extensively; the Saudi sheikh was now the religious head of the Wahhabi establishment, and Ibn Wahhab's descendents still constituted the leading ulama of Saudi-ruled territories. British agents dispatched by the Anglo-Indian foreign office visited the Saudi chief, looking to cut a deal. They did what they could to excite his ambitions and offered him money and arms to attack the Ottomans. Ibn Saud responded cautiously but the interaction gave him good reason to believe that he would be rewarded after the war for any damage he could do to the Turks.

The Hashimite patriarch was named Hussein Ibn Ali. He was caretaker of the Ka'ba, Islam's holiest shrine, and he was known by the title of Sharif, which meant he was descended from the Prophet's own clan, the Banu Hashim. Remember that the ninth-century revolutionaries who had brought the Abbasids to power called themselves the Hashimites: the name had an ancient and revered lineage and now a family by this name was ruling again in Mecca.

But Mecca was not enough for Sharif Hussein. He dreamed of an Arab kingdom stretching from Mesopotamia to the Arabian Sea, and he thought

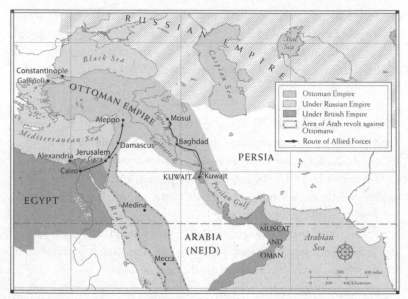

WORLD WAR I AND THE ARAB REVOLT

the British might help him forge it. The British gladly let him think they could and would. They sent a flamboyant military intelligence officer to work with him, a one-time archeologist named Colonel Thomas Edward Lawrence, who spoke Arabic and liked to dress in Bedouin tribal dress, a practice that eventually earned him the nickname "Lawrence of Arabia."

Looking back, it's easy to see what a pot of trouble the British were mixing up here. The Hashimites and the Saudis were the two strongest tribal groups in the Arabian peninsula; both hoped to break the Ottoman hold on Arabia, and each saw the other as its deadly rival. The British were sending agents into both camps, making promises to both families, and leading both to believe that the British would help them establish their own kingdom in roughly the same territory, if only they would fight the Ottomans. The British didn't actually care which of the two ruled this region: they just wanted immediate help undermining Ottoman power, so they could beat the Germans back home.

As it turned out, the Hashimites led the way in helping the British. They fomented the Arab Revolt. Two of Hussein's sons, working with Lawrence, drove the Turks out of the region, clearing the way for the

THE SYKES-PICOT AGREEMENT

British to take Damascus and Baghdad. From there, the British could put pressure on the Ottomans.

At the very time that British agents were making promises to the two Arab families, however, two European diplomats, Mark Sykes and Francois George-Picot, were meeting secretly with a map and a pencil, over a civilized cup of tea, to decide how the region should be carved up among the victorious *European* powers after the war. They agreed which part should go to Sykes's Britain, which part to Picot's France, and where a nod to Russian interests might be appropriate. Which part the Arabs should get went curiously unmentioned.

All these ingredients portended trouble enough, but wait, as they say on late-night-TV infomercials, there was more! Arab nationalism was starting to bubble in Palestine and adjacent Arab-inhabited territories, including Egypt, and this had nothing to do with the dynastic aspirations of the Hashimites and Saudis. It was the secular modernists who embraced this new nationalism, all those professionals, government workers, and emerging urban bourgeoisie for whom constitutionalism and industrialism also had great appeal. In Palestine and Syria, these Arab nationalists not only demanded independence from the Ottomans and Europeans but also from the Hashimites and Saudis.

Then there was one last problematic ingredient, perhaps the most intractable of them all: Jewish immigration from Europe to Palestine. European anti-Semitism, which had helped give rise to Zionism, had continued to intensify as the continent moved toward war, making life ever more untenable for Jews throughout Europe. As a result, the Jewish population of Palestine swelled from 4 percent in 1883 to 8 percent by the start of World War I to nearly 13 percent by the time the war ended.

In 1917, the British foreign minister Arthur James Balfour wrote a letter to Lord Lionel Rothschild, a British banker and a leading Zionist, a man who had supported Jewish immigration to the Levant generously out of his own private funds. Balfour told Rothschild that the British government would "view with favor the establishment in Palestine of a national home for the Jewish people, and will use their best endeavors to facilitate the achievement of this object."

Balfour also insisted that "nothing shall be done which may prejudice the civil and religious right of existing non-Jewish communities in Palestine," but how Britain planned to accommodate both Jewish and Arab nationalism in the same territory, Balfour didn't say.

To recap—it's worth a recap: Britain essentially promised the same territory to the Hashimites, the Saudis, and the Zionists of Europe, territory *actually* inhabited by still another Arab people with rapidly developing nationalist aspirations of their own—while in fact Britain and France had already secretly agreed to carve up the whole promised territory between themselves. Despite the many quibbles, qualifiers, and disclaimers offered over the years about who agreed to what and what was promised to whom, that's the gist of the situation, and it guaranteed an explosion in the future.

But the good thing about the future was that it lay in the future. In the present a war was raging, and what the British and French cooked up for the short term worked wonderfully: the CUP lost everything the Ottomans had ever owned outside of Asia Minor. They ceded Palestine, Greater Syria, and Mesopotamia to the British. And the war was going badly for their friends in Europe, as well. In 1918, Germany surrendered unconditionally to the Allies, and the three Pashas knew they were in big trouble. All three of them, Talaat, Enver, and Djemal, fled Istanbul inches ahead of arrest warrants. Talaat went to Berlin, where an Armenian assassinated him in 1921. Djemal went to Georgia, where an Armenian assassinated him in 1922. Enver went to Central Asia to stir up rebellion against the Bolsheviks. A Red Army detachment commanded by an Armenian Bolshevik killed him there in 1922.

So ended the Committee for Union and Progress, a bad government to be sure, but with its demise, the carcass of the "Ottoman Empire" was left with no government at all.

15

Rise of the
Secular Modernists

1336–1357 AH
1918–1939 CE

B Y 1919, ASIA MINOR was crawling with French and Italian troops. Greek armies led by Greek nationalists dreaming of a Greater Greece were forging deep into the Ottoman heartland. Istanbul itself was occupied by British troops. Resistance movements bubbled up throughout Anatolia, coalescing around a hawk-faced general with piercing eyes. He was Mustafa Kemal, later known as Atatürk—Father of the Turks. His forces drove out all the foreigners and in 1923 he declared the birth of a new nation-state: Turkey.

Turkey was not to be the Ottoman Empire reinvented. Atatürk repudiated the Ottoman past; he repudiated empire. He claimed nothing outside Asia Minor because he sought a coherent territory that made sense as a *country*. Henceforth, Turkey was to be a state with clear and immutable borders within which the majority of people would be ethnic Turks and the language would be Turkish. In this new country, Islam would be excluded from any role in public policy and demoted to the private sphere where it might go on thriving as a religion like any other, so long as its adherents didn't bother the neighbors.

Turkey was thus the first Muslim-majority country to declare itself secular and to make the separation of politics and religion an official policy. Having demoted Islam, however, Atatürk needed some other principle to unify his new country, so he elaborated an ideology that sanctified six isms: nationalism, secularism, reformism, statism, populism, and republicanism. Turks still call this creed Kemalism, and some of version of it, usually emphasizing the first four isms, spread to or sprang up throughout the Islamic world after World War I.

Atatürk's nationalism was not to be confused with the hardcore militarism of the Committee for Union and Progress. The roots of both went back to the Young Turks, but "Young Turkism" was a broad movement spanning a gamut from liberal constitutionalism to fascism, and Atatürk's was a flexible, cultural nationalism that grew out of the liberal end.

It was cultural nationalism that led Atatürk to discard the many languages spoken in the Ottoman Empire in favor of one national language, Turkish. The many dialects and variants of Turkish spoken in the old empire gave way to a single standard dialect, and not the literary Turkish of the old court but a purified form of the street Turkish spoken by the masses. Some enthusiasts then wanted to ban all words that had crept into Turkish from other languages, but Atatürk disarmed this agitation with a simple narrative: Turkish, he said, was the mother of all the languages, so words borrowed from other languages were simply Turkish words coming home. The Arabic script, however, the one in which Turkish had long been written, was replaced by a new *Latin* alphabet.

A modernist to the core, Atatürk did not declare himself king or sultan. He had a new constitution written, set up a parliament, and established a republican form of government with himself as president. The parliamentary democracy he built endures to this day, but let's be frank: another leader could not have replaced Atatürk through the ballot box in his lifetime—hey, he was Father of the Turks! One does not vote one's *father* out of office! And although he was no military dictator and his ruling circle was not a junta (he established and abided by the rule of law), Atatürk did come up through the military and he valued discipline; so he herded his people toward his vision for the country with a military man's direct, iron-handed resolve.

What was his vision? To break the authority of the ulama in Turkey, unseat Islam as the arbiter of social life, and authorize a secular approach to the management of society. In the Western context, this makes him a "moderate." In the Islamic context, it made him a breathtakingly radical extremist.

First up on his agenda: opening the public sphere to women. Toward this end, he promulgated new laws that gave women the right to vote, hold public office, and own property. He had polygamy outlawed, discouraged dowries, frowned on traditional marriage customs, and sponsored new rules for divorce based on the Swiss civil code, not the Qur'an and hadith.

He also banned veils and head scarves, part of a new state-sanctioned dress code that applied to men as well as women—for example, the fez was banned too. Turbans and beards were strongly discouraged. Derby hats were okay, though, and so were bowlers, baseball caps, and berets. Atatürk himself wore suits and ties and urged his fellow Turks to do the same.

The religious establishment was shocked when ballroom dancing was introduced as official entertainment at state functions, but there was nothing they could do about it. Atatürk meant business, and he had the power and prestige to get it done. His parliament backed him to the hilt when he proposed a law requiring that public readings of the Qur'an henceforth be conducted in Turkish, not Arabic—blasphemy to the devout. Parliament backed him again when he moved the workers' day off from Friday to Sunday—to *Sunday!* Atatürk's government went on to close religious schools, shut down the Sufi brotherhoods, and abolish the waqfs—those ancient religion-based charitable foundations—in favor of state-dispensed social services. In 1925, Atatürk capped his secular modernist revolution with a truly jolting declaration: he declared the khalifate dead.

This wasn't actually breaking news, of course. For all practical purposes, the khalifate had been dead for centuries, but in the world between Istanbul and the Indus, the khalifate held a special place in the public imagination roughly analogous to that of ancient Rome in the West: it embodied the lingering dream of a universal community. In the West, the ghost of Rome persisted right to the end of World War I, visible in such traces as the Austro-Hungarian Empire, which was really just the final form of "the Holy Roman Empire," and in the titles of the last German and Russian rulers before World War I—*kaiser* and *czar* were both variations on *Caesar*. Rome had been dead for centuries, but the Roman ideal of a universal state did not fully wink out until the end of World War I. The same was true of the khalifate. When Atatürk abolished the khalifate, he was abolishing an idea, and that's what jolted the Muslim world.

Or at least it jolted traditionalists, but who cared what they thought? They were no longer in power. In fact, Atatürk would turn out to be the prototypical Muslim leader of the half-century to come. Iran generated its own version of the prototype. After the war, the last Qajar king faced the "Jungle Revolution," a guerilla insurgency launched by admirers of Sayyid Jamaluddin-i-Afghan. The king's forces consisted of two armies, one commanded by Swedish officers, one by Russian mercenaries.[1] Little did the king realize that the real threat to his rule lay not in the jungle but among the foreigners propping him up. When Bolsheviks began joining the jungle revolutionaries, the British got nervous. Lenin had just seized power in Russia and they didn't want this sort of thing to spread. The British decided the king wasn't tough enough to squelch Bolsheviks, so they helped an Iranian colonel overthrow him.

This colonel, Reza Pahlavi, was a secular modernist in the Atatürk mold, except that he had no use for democracy (few secular modernist leaders did). In 1925, the colonel declared himself king, becoming Reza *Shah* Pahlavi, founder of a new Iranian dynasty. From the throne, he launched the same sorts of reforms as Atatürk, especially in the matter of a dress code. Head scarves, veils, turbans, beards—these were banned for ordinary citizens. Registered clerics could still wear turbans in the new Iran, but they had to have a license certifying that they really were clerics (and how could they meet this irksome proviso, given that Islam never had a formal institution for "certifying" clerics?). Still, anyone caught wearing a turban without a license could be beaten on the street and hauled off to prison.

Much the same thing was happening in Afghanistan, where, an impetuous young man named Amanullah inherited the throne in 1919. An ardent admirer of the Young Turks, this moon-faced fellow with a Hercule Poirot moustache gave Afghanistan a liberal constitution, declared women liberated, funded a nascent secular school system lavishly, and, yes, declared the usual dress code: no veils, no beards, no turbans, etc.

What I find interesting about this dress-code policy is that radical Islamists did exactly the same thing fifty years later when they came back into power in Iran and Afghanistan, except that their dress code was the opposite: suddenly, women were *forced* to wear head scarves and men were beaten for appearing in public *without* beards. But the principle of beating and imprisoning people for their clothes and grooming—this principle, both sides embraced.

The three rulers between Istanbul and the Hindu Kush could use state power to push the secular modernist agenda. Other parts of Dar al-Islam still lived under imperial rule but had vigorous independence movements, which were also led by secular modernists. In India, for example, the most prominent Muslim leader was the suave, British-educated attorney named Mohammed Ali Jinnah.

In short, secular modernism surged up throughout the Muslim world in the 1920s, one society after another falling under the sway of this new political creed. I will call it secular modernism, even though the term is inadequate, because secular-modernist-nationalist-statist-developmentalist is too cumbersome and even then doesn't cover the entire movement. Suffice to say, this was a broad river of attitude and opinion that drew upon ideas explored earlier by the likes of Sayyid Ahmad of Aligarh, Amir Kabir of Iran, the Young Turks of Istanbul, and countless other intellectuals, educated workers, professionals, writers, and activists from the middle classes that had been emerging in the Middle World for a century. Suddenly, Muslim societies knew where they were going: the same way as the West. They were behind, of course, they would have to play desperate catch-up, but that was all the more reason to hurry, all the more reason to steamroll over nuances and niceties like democracy and get the crash program underway—the core of which crash program was "development."

In Afghanistan and Iran, the state clamped down on citizens, but did so in pursuit of a "progressive" agenda. Monarchs in both countries set out to build roads, dams, power plants, factories, hospitals, and office buildings. Both established airline companies, set up state-run (and state-censored) newspapers, and built national radio stations. Both countries continued to grow their secular public schools. Iran already had a national university and Afghanistan founded one now. Both governments promulgated policies to liberate women and draw them into the public realm. Both were eager to make their countries more "Western" but saw no connection between this and expanding their subjects' freedom. What they promised was not freedom but prosperity and self-respect.

It would be quite plausible to say that at this point, Islam as a world-historical narrative came to an end. Wrong but plausible. The Western cross-current had disrupted Muslim societies, creating the deepest angst and the most agonizing doubts. The secular modernists proposed to settle the spiritual turmoil by realigning their societies with the Western current. Make no mistake, most of these leaders still thought of themselves as Muslims; they just adopted a new idea of what "Muslim" meant. Most still worked to break the grip of specific Western powers over their specific people; they just did so as revolutionary anticolonialists rather than as zealous Muslims committed to promoting Islam as one big community on a mission from God. These elites sought to make gains by holding the West to its own standards and ideals and in doing this they implicitly validated the Western framework of assumptions.

They were not without popular support. Throughout the Middle World, traditional, religious Islam was quiescent now: beaten and subdued. Educated people tended to see the old-fashioned scholars and clerics as quaint. The ulama, the scriptural literalists, the miracle merchants, the orthodox "believers"—all these had dominated Dar al-Islam for centuries, and what had they created? Threadbare societies that couldn't build a car or invent an airplane, much less stand up to Western might. Their failure discredited their outlook, and a sizable public was ready to give someone else a turn. The future belonged to the secular modernists.

Or so it seemed.

But secular modernism was not the only reformist current to come out of the nineteenth-century Muslim world. What of the other currents? What of the Wahhabis, for example? What of Sayyid Jamaluddin's disciples? These movements should not be confused with orthodox Islam or old-fashioned religious conservatism. They were just as new-fangled as secular modernism, just as intent on smashing the status quo.

Even the Wahhabis, by their very appeal to a mythic moment in the distant past, were rejecting the petrified present (and the twelve centuries that led up to it). And they still breathed in the Arabian Peninsula. In fact, they seized state power there, with the founding of Saudi Arabia, about which more later. Outside Arabia, the Wahhabis could not gain much purchase among the educated elite or the new middle classes but they preached away in rural mosques to ill-educated and impoverished villagers.

For that audience their message had resonance, especially in India. When they spoke of a glorious past, revivable only by a return to the ways of the First Community, the poor and dispossessed knew whom they were talking about. They could see their own elites drifting away from the Muslim way of life, and boasting about it! They were to blame for Muslim weakness. In fact, if the Wahhabi narrative held water, the poverty of the rural poor was the fault of the urban rich.

In 1867, a group of puritanical Indian Wahhabis had built a religious seminary in a town called Deoband. For fifty years, missionaries pouring out of this seminary had been spreading through the subcontinent preaching Indian Wahhabism. In the late 1920s, these Deobandis gave a glimmer of their strength in Afghanistan.

King Amanullah, upon coming to the throne, had dazzled his country by declaring full independence from the British and sending troops to the border. The battles were inconclusive but he won Afghanistan's independence at the bargaining table, making him the first and only Muslim monarch to win a direct confrontation with a major European power. Indian Wahhabis exultantly proclaimed him the new khalifa; but Amanullah was not the kind of man to accept that mantle. In fact, he "betrayed" the Deobandis by launching the full array of Atatürkist initiatives mentioned earlier. The Indian Wahhabis swore to bring the apostate down.

And they did it, but not by themselves. They got help from Great Britain. This may seem odd, because Amanullah was culturally so much more in tune with British values than the Deobandis were. European ideals were his ideals. But perhaps the British recognized him as a threat for that very reason. They knew what an anti-imperialist revolutionary was; they had seen Lenin. They didn't know what a Deobandi was. Bearded preachers swathed in turbans no doubt struck them as picturesque primitives who might serve a purpose. Britain therefore fed funds and guns into the Deobandi campaign against Amanullah and soon, with further help from radical local clerics, the Deobandis set Afghanistan ablaze. In 1929, they managed to drive Amanullah into tragic exile.

Amid the uproar, a *really* primitive bandit, colorfully nicknamed the Water Carrier's Son, seized the Afghan capital. The bandit ruled for nine riotous months, during which time he not only imposed "pure" Islamic rule but undid all of Amanullah's reforms, wrecked the city, and drained the treasury. Anyone who knows what the Taliban did in Afghanistan at the end of the century will recognize an eerily precise preview of their carnage in the career of the Water Carrier's Son. By the time he was finished, Afghans were so sick of chaos, they were eager to accept a strongman. The British obliged them by helping a more compliant member of the old royal clan claim the Afghan throne, a grim despot named Nadir Shah.

This new king was a secular modernist too, but a chastened one. He guided his country back toward the Atatürkist road but very, very slowly, taking care not to offend the British, and placating his hometown Deobandis by clamping down on Afghanistan socially and culturally.

So much for Wahhabism. What of the reformist current embodied by Sayyid Jamaluddin? Was that one dead? Not at all. Intellectually, Jamaluddin's work was carried forward by his chief disciple, Mohammed Abduh, who taught at Egypt's prestigious thousand-year-old Al Azhar University. Abduh pulled the Master's patchwork of ideas together into a coherent Islamic modernist doctrine. Abduh's own disciple and friend Rashid Rida went on to explore how a modern state might actually be administered on Islamic principles.

Then came Hassan al-Banna, perhaps the most important of Sayyid Jamaluddin's intellectual progeny. This Egyptian schoolteacher was more activist than philosopher. In 1928, he founded a club called the Muslim Brotherhood, originally something like a Muslim version of the Boy Scouts. This was a seminal event for Islamism, but one that went virtually unnoticed at the time.

Banna lived and taught in the Suez Canal Zone, where he could feel the scrape of West against East every day. Virtually all trade between Europe and the eastern colonies passed through this canal, which was the most boomingly modern structure in Egypt, and every cargo ship had to pay a steep toll. A European firm owned by British and French interests operated the canal and took 93 percent of the rich revenue it generated. Foreign technicians therefore abounded in the Canal Zone, making this little strip of land the starkest embodiment of two worlds intersecting. One whole infrastructure of shops, restaurants, cafés, dance halls, bars, and other services catered to the European community. Another whole infrastructure consisted of markets, coffeehouses, and whatnot frequented by Egyptians of the humbler classes: two worlds interwoven but entirely distinct.

Hassan Banna saw his fellow Egyptians earnestly struggling to learn European languages and manners, trying slavishly to acquire enough Westernized polish to enter the Western world, even if only as workers of the lowest strata. The sight of all this Egyptian envy and subservience offended his pride. He founded the Muslim Brotherhood to help Muslim boys interact healthily with one another, learn about their own culture, and acquire some self respect. Boys dropped into the Brotherhood center after school to play sports, at which time they also received lessons in Islam and Muslim history from Banna and his instructors.

Eventually the boys' fathers and older brothers started dropping in as well, so the Brotherhood began offering evening programs for adults, which were so popular that new centers were opened up. By the mid-1930s, the brotherhood had outgrown its origins as a club for boys and become a fraternal organization for men.

From this, it slowly morphed into a political movement, a movement that declared secular Islam and Egypt's own "Westernized" elite to be the country's chief enemies. The Muslim Brothers opposed nationalism, the impulse to secure sovereignty for small separate states such as Syria, Libya, or Egypt. They called on Muslims to resurrect instead the one big transnational Umma, a new khalifate embodying the unity of all Muslims. Like Sayyid Jamaluddin, they preached pan-Islamic modernization without Westernization.

The Muslim Brotherhood was taking shape around the same time the United States was struggling with the Great Depression. In this same period, the Nazis were taking over Germany, and Stalin was consolidating his grip on the Soviet Union. Outside of Egypt, no one knew much about the brotherhood, not because it was secretive (at first) but because it had few adherents among the Egyptian elite and held little interest for foreign journalists. Even Egyptian newspapers published few stories about its activities and the Western press none at all. Why would they? This was mostly a movement of the urban working poor, and the foreigners who came and went through Egypt hardly noticed those hordes moving like shadows through the streets, doing the heavy lifting and loading, providing services, and begging for "baksheesh," as tips were called (prompting the writer S. J. Perlman to quip of Egypt, "It's not the heat, it's the cupidity").

As Westernization and industrialization proceeded, Egypt's urban working poor kept proliferating. With the expansion of this class, the brotherhood outgrew even its identity as a political movement and became more of a pandemic low-level insurgency—seething against secularism and Western influence, seething against its own modernist elite, against its own government, against all nationalist governments in Muslim countries, even against the apparatus of democracy to the extent that this reflected Western values.

By the late thirties, then, secular leaders throughout the Muslim world, whether they held state power or spearheaded independence movements, found themselves squeezed between two sets of forces: European imperialists still pressed down on them from above; meanwhile, Islamist insurgents were pushing up from below. What was a leader to do?

Under this kind of pressure, politicians typically try to associate themselves with some popular passion to shore up support; and often the passion they tap into for this purpose is religion. But religion was the one passion secular modernists could not appeal to, because it was the very thing they were trying to move their societies away from. So they waved two other banners instead. One was "development" and the material prosperity it would bring; and the other was nationalism, which they claimed to represent. In Iran, for example, the Pahlavi regime tried to invoke a connection to pre-Islamic Persia. In Afghanistan, the Nadir Shah regime insisted on declaring Pushto a national language, even though only a minority spoke it at home. Everywhere, the glories of the nation, the splendor of its culture, and the proud history of its people were trumpeted.

Nationalist sentiment was not in short supply; lots of *that* was sloshing around in the Middle World at this time. The trouble was, most of the new nation-states were rather artificial. Afghanistan, for example, had been created by Russia and Britain. Iran, until recently, had been a loose conglomeration of disparate parts, an empire, not a country. Turkey was a nation-state because Atatürk said so. As for India, where does one even begin?

But the most problematic region for nationalism was the Arab heartland. Here's why.

After World War I, the victors had met at Versailles, France, to reshape the world. As a prelude to that conference, U.S. president Woodrow Wilson had given a speech to the U.S. Congress laying out a "fourteen point" vision of a new world order that most colonized people found inspiring. To Arabs, the most thrilling of Wilson's Fourteen Points was his declaration that every people's right to self-rule must be respected and accommodated. Wilson had also suggested creating a neutral "League of Nations" to adjudicate international issues, such as the fate of Arab-inhabited lands formerly ruled by the Ottomans. At Versailles, the "peacemakers" had set up just such a body.

But stunningly enough, the United States refused to join this body! And once the League set to work, the European victors of World War I quickly turned it into an instrument of their will. In principle, for example, the League endorsed the idea of self-rule in the Arab world, but in practice, it implemented the Sykes-Picot agreement, dividing the area into zones called "mandates," which were awarded to Britain and France. The document setting up these mandates called them territories "inhabited by peoples not yet able to stand by themselves under the strenuous conditions of the modern world" and said "the tutelage of such peoples should be entrusted to advanced nations who by reason of their . . . experience . . . can best undertake this responsibility." In short, it spoke of Arabs as children and of Europeans as grown-ups who would take care of them until they could do grown-up things like feed themselves—such was the language directed at a people who, if the Muslim narrative were still in play, would have been honored as the progenitors of civilization itself—and who still retained some such sense of themselves.[2]

France got Syria for its mandate, and Great Britain got pretty much everything else in the "Middle East." France divided its mandated territory into two countries, Syria and Lebanon, the latter an artificial state with borders gerrymandered to ensure a demographic majority for the Maronite Christians, whom France regarded as its special clients in the region.

Great Britain had clients to satisfy as well, beginning with the Hashimites who had led that helpful Arab Revolt, so the British bundled together three former Ottoman provinces to create a new country called Iraq and made one of their Hashimite clients king of it. The lucky man was Faisal, second son of the sheikh of Mecca.

Faisal, however, had an older brother named Abdullah, and it wasn't seemly for a younger brother to have a country while his older brother had none, so another country was carved out of the British mandate and given to Abdullah, and this was Jordan.

Unfortunately, the boys' father ended up with nothing at all, because in 1924 that other British client in the region, Aziz ibn Saud, attacked Mecca with a band of religious troops, took the holy city, and ousted the

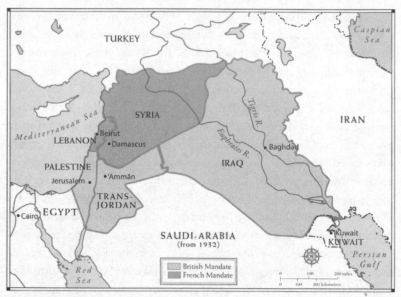

DIVISION OF THE ARAB WORLD: THE MANDATES PLAN

Hashemite patriarch. Ibn Saud went on to conquer 80 percent of the Arabian Peninsula. Only Yemen, Oman, and a few sliver-sized coastal emirates remained outside his grasp. The European powers did nothing to stop him because he too held some IOUs. In 1932, Ibn Saud declared his holdings a sovereign new country called Saudi Arabia.

In Egypt, meanwhile, Great Britain succumbed to its own pieties and declared the country independent, sovereign, and free—with a few caveats. First, Egyptians could not change their form of government; they must remain a monarchy. Second, Egyptians could not replace their actual rulers; they must retain their existing royal family. Third, the Egyptians must accept the continued presence of British military forces and bases on their soil. Fourth, the Egyptians must leave the Suez Canal in British hands without protest. Fifth, the private company controlled by Britain and France must continue to collect all fees from that busiest of sea channels and send the bulk of it back to Europe.

Egypt *would* get an elected parliament, but this parliament's decisions must be approved by British authorities in Cairo. Beyond these few points, Egypt was to consider itself sovereign, independent, and free. Egypt quickly developed a full-fledged (secular modernist) independence move-ment, of course, which offended the British, because why would an inde-pendent country need an independence movement? Didn't they get the memo? Apparently not.

The French faced a bit of resistance too, in Syria. There, a Sorbonne-educated Christian Arab writer named Michel Aflaq was elaborating a pan-Arab nationalist ideology. He asserted the existence of a mystical Arab soul forged by a common language and a shared historical experience that gave a unified singleness to the vast body of Arabic-speaking people. Like all the other twentieth century nationalists inspired by nineteenth century European philosophers, Aflaq argued that the "Arab nation" was entitled to a single contiguous state ruled by Arabs.

Although he was Christian, Aflaq put Islam at the center of Arabism, but only as a historical relic. Islam, he said, had awakened the Arab soul at a certain moment in history and made it the spearhead of a global quest for justice and progress, so Arabs of every religion should honor Islam as a product of the Arab soul. What counted, however, was the Arab soul, and Arabs should therefore seek a rebirth of their spirit, not in Islam, but in "the Arab Nation." Aflaq was a hardcore secular modernist and in 1940 he and a friend founded a political party to pursue their vision. They called it the Ba'ath, or "rebirth" party.

Four new countries were carved out of the European mandates, a fifth one emerged independently, and Egypt acquired pseudoindependence. But one question remained unresolved: what should be done with Pales-tine? The principle of self-rule dictated that it too should become a coun-try ruled by itself, but who was its "self?" Was the natural "nation" here the Arabs, who constituted nearly 90 percent of the population and had been living here for centuries? Or was it the Jews, most of whom had come here from Europe in the last two decades but whose ancestors had lived here two thousand years ago? Hmm: tough question.

To the Arabs, the answer seemed obvious: this should be one more Arab country. To the Jewish immigrants from Europe, the answer also seemed ob-vious: whatever the exact legal arrangements, this patch of territory should become a secure Jewish homeland, because Jews were endangered everywhere else in the world and only Palestine made sense as a place they could call their own. Besides Britain's Balfour had made them that memorable promise.

Britain decided to make *no* grand decision about Palestine at all, but to deal with events de facto as they came up and just see how things went.

How on earth could secular modernist leaders use nationalism to bind together their dubious nations, especially since some of their own were calling for an Arab nation transcending existing boundaries—while at the same time Islamists and Wahhabis were saying to hell with nations; to hell with ethnic identity politics; we're all Muslims; let's rebuild the khalifate?

Ultimately, in this environment, the success of secular modernism hung on two things. First, since the secular modernists kept waving the banner of "development," they had to develop something and deliver the prosperity they evoked. Second, since they sought legitimacy through nationalism, they had to gain actual independence for their nations.

In the decades after World War I, however, they failed to achieve either goal. They failed because, despite the thrilling rhetoric of Wilson's Fourteen Points, there was never any real chance of the Western powers loosening their grip on the core of the Muslim world.

No chance of it because at this point every Western power was racing to outindustrialize every other. The Western powers were moving toward an apocalyptic showdown fueled by ideologies, communism, fascism, nazism, democracy. The stakes were absolute. Victory depended on industrial strength, industrialism now depended on petroleum, and most of the world's petroleum lay under Muslim-inhabited soil.

The first big pools of petroleum oil had been discovered in the late nineteenth century in Pennsylvania and Canada but at the time these discoveries had sparked little excitement because the only product really made from petroleum back then was kerosene, and kerosene was used only to light lamps, for which purpose most consumers preferred whale oil.

In 1901, the first of the big Middle Eastern oil fields was detected in Iran by a British prospector named William Knox D'Arcy. He promptly bought exclusive rights to all of Iran's petroleum from the Qajar king of the time, in exchange for a sum of cash stuffed immediately into that shah's pockets, and a 16 percent royalty payable to the Iranian treasury later, a royalty to be calculated on "net profits" realized from Iran's petroleum, not on the gross, which means that D'Arcy's lease made no guarantees about how much money Iran *ever* stood to make from its oil.

You might wonder what sort of king would sell his country's entire stock of *any* mineral known and unknown for cash to some vagabond wandering through and why the citizens of the country would not immediately depose such a king. The answer is, first: tradition. The Qajar kings had been doing this sort of thing for a hundred years. Second, the country had just struggled mightily to scuttle the tobacco monopoly, which their king had sold to British interests, a struggle that had left the country's activists exhausted. Third, oil didn't seem very important; it wasn't *tobacco*, for God's sake (or even whale oil). Fourth, activists were girding for a struggle that did seem more important than oil and tobacco combined: the struggle for a constitution and a parliament. The oil deal therefore went unnoticed.

At the very time that Iran was giving away its oil, however, the importance of oil was about to skyrocket, due to a new invention: the internal combustion engine. *External* combustion engines such as steam engines ran on anything that burned, which in practice meant wood or coal; but *internal* combustion engines ran strictly on refined petroleum.

In the 1880s, a German inventor had used this type of engine to power a big tricycle. That tricycle evolved into a car. By 1904, cars were becoming just popular enough in Europe and the United States that some roads were being rebuilt to accommodate them. Soon after that, trains started to run on oil. Then in 1903 the airplane was invented. Next, ocean-going ships began switching over.

World War I saw the first use of tanks, the first oil-powered navies, and the first airplanes that dropped bombs. By the time the war ended, anyone could tell that petroleum-powered war machinery would grow only more sophisticated and that whoever owned the world's oil would end up owning the world.

For Iran, that realization came too late. William D'Arcy had already sold his Iranian oil concession to a company owned by the British government (it still exists: it's now British Petroleum, or BP). By 1923, according to Winston Churchill, Great Britain had earned 40 million pounds from Iranian oil, while Iran had earned about 2 million from it.[3]

Meanwhile, that British company had joined forces with Royal Dutch Shell and certain U.S. interests to form a supercompany ("the Turkish Petroleum Company") that proposed to look for oil in the Ottoman provinces bordering the Persian Gulf. By the time the supercompany was ready to drill, the area in question was part of the British "mandate." It was then that the British created Iraq and put their Hashemite client in charge of it. The oil consortium immediately approached King Faisal for a monopoly on the country's oil resources, and he gladly accommodated them. Going into the negotiation, the Iraqis were hoping for a 20 percent equity share in the company, but they compromised at 0 percent, in exchange for a flat fee per ton of oil extracted, that sum not to be linked in any way to the price of oil or the company's profits, at least for the first twenty years of the agreement. Equity in the company was divided among the several European powers and the United States, and the only real wrangling was among them over who would get what percent. In 1927, after all these issues had been settled, the company found the first of Iraq's enormous oil fields.[4]

Nine years later, Aziz ibn Saud celebrated the discovery of oil in his realm as well. Saudi Arabia would, in fact, turn out to have the world's biggest reserves of the crucial mineral. The Saudis had barely started pumping their oil when World War II broke out and the strategic significance of oil soared even higher. During that war, U. S. president Franklin Delano Roosevelt met with Ibn Saud, and the two men reached an understanding to which both sides have adhered faithfully ever since, even though it is not enshrined in any formal public treaty. The deal ensures the U.S. unfettered access to Saudi oil; in exchange, the Saudi royal family gets as much U.S. military equipment and technology as it needs to stay in power against all comers. Indirectly, this understanding partnered the United States with the Wahhabi clerical establishment and made American military prowess the guarantor of the Wahhabi reform movement. And by the time World War II broke out, the Wahhabis, and the Islamists throughout Dar al-Islam were gathering their strength for a full assault on the secular modernists.

16

The Crisis of
Modernity

1357–1385 AH
1939–1966 CE

THE BLOODIEST OUTBURST in the history of violence started in 1939 and raged for six long years. Once again, Germany was battling France and Britain. Once again the United States came in late but decided the outcome. Parts of the configuration had changed this time, to be sure: Russia was now the Soviet Union, the Ottomans were missing, Japan had grown mighty—but in the end, this bloodbath only finished what World War I had begun. The old colonial empires suffered death blows, and the old alignments of power became obsolete. Britain came out of the war starving, France in ruins, Germany destroyed and divided. With the gunfire fading, two new superpowers stood astride the globe, and both were soon armed with thermonuclear bombs capable of destroying the human race. The next chapter of world history would be dominated by their competition.

Other narratives continued to play out, however, beneath the surface of the bipolar Cold War struggle, including the submerged narrative of Islam as a world-historical event. The hunger for independence, which had built up during the war years among virtually all colonized people, both Muslim and non-Muslim, now hit the breaking point. In Egypt, rebellion started brewing among army officers. In China, Mao's communist insurgency began to move against Chiang Kai-shek, widely seen as a Western puppet. In Vietnam, Ho Chi Minh, who had come back from thirty years of exile to organize the Viet Minh, attacked the French. In Indonesia, Sukarno declared his country independent from the Dutch. All over the world, national liberation movements were springing up like weeds, and the ones in Muslim countries were much like the ones in non-Muslim countries: whatever else might be happening, the Islamic narrative was now intertwined with a narrative Muslims shared with others.

Geographically, many of the "nations" that the liberation movements strove to liberate were defined by borders the imperialist powers had drawn: so even in their struggle for liberation they were playing out a story set in motion by Europeans. In sub-Saharan Africa, what the king of Belgium had managed to conquer became Congo (later renamed Zaire). What the Germans had conquered became Cameroon, what the British had conquered in East Africa, Kenya. A label such as "Nigeria" referred to an area inhabited by over two hundred ethnic groups speaking more than five hundred languages, many of them mutually unintelligible, but the world was now organized into countries, so this, too, became "a country," its shape and size reflecting the outcome of some long-ago competition among colonizing Europeans.

In North Africa, national liberators accepted the reality of Algeria, Tunisia, and Libya as countries, each one spawning a national liberation movement of its own. All three movements eventually succeeded, but at great cost. Algeria's eight-year war of independence from France claimed over a million Algerian lives, out of a starting population of fewer than 9 million, a staggering conflict.[1]

Issues inherited from the days of Muslim hegemony continued to echo here and there. The persistence of the Muslim narrative manifested most dramatically in the subcontinent of India, the biggest full-fledged colony to gain independence. Even before the war, as this nascent country struggled to rid itself of the British, a subnational movement had developed within the grand national movement: a demand by the Muslim minority for a separate country. At the exact moment that India was born (August 15, 1947) so was the brand-new two-part country of Pakistan, hanging like saddlebags east and west of India. The partition of the subcontinent sent tidal waves of frightened refugees across new borders to the supposed shelter of their co-religionists. In the tumult, hundreds of thousands were slaughtered within weeks, and countless more rendered homeless, yet even this mayhem failed to settle the questions raised by "the partition." Kashmir, for example, remained in play, for it had a Hindu monarch but a predominantly Muslim population. Which then should it be part of, India or Pakistan? The British decided to wait and see how things shook out. Kashmir is still shaking.

It was not only decolonization that came to a head after World War II, but "nation-statism." It's easy to forget that the organization of the world into countries is less than a century old, but in fact this process was not fully completed until this period. Between 1945 and 1975, some one hundred new countries were born, and every inch of earth finally belonged to some nation-state or other.[2]

Unfortunately, the ideology of "nationalism" and the reality of "nation-statism" matched up only approximately if at all. Many supposed countries contained stifled sub-countries within their borders, ethnic minorities who felt they ought to be separate and "self-governing." In many cases, people on two sides of a border felt like they ought to be part of the same nation. Where Syria, Iraq, and Turkey came together, for example, their borders trisected a contiguous area inhabited by a people who spoke neither Arabic nor Turkish but Kurdish, a distant variant of Persian, and these Kurds naturally felt like members of some single nation that was "none of the above."

In some places, even the separate existence of given countries remained open to question. Iraq, Lebanon, Jordan—these were still congealing. Their borders existed, they had separate governments, but did their people really think of themselves as *different nations*? Not clear.

In the Arab world, ever since Woodrow Wilson's Fourteen Points, the watchword had been self-rule, but this tricky concept presumed some definition of a collective "self" accepted by all its supposed members. Nationalists throughout Arab-inhabited lands were trying hard to consolidate discrete states: Libya, Tunisia, Syria, even Egypt . . . but the question always came up: who was the bigger collective self? Was there "really" a Syrian nation, given that the Syria seen on maps was created by Europeans? Could there be such a thing as Jordanian nationalism? Was it true that people living in Iraq were ruling themselves so long as their ruler spoke Arabic?

The most problematic single territory for the competing claims of nationalism versus nation-statism was Palestine, soon to be known as Israel. Before and during World War II, the Nazis' genocidal attempt to exterminate the Jews of Europe confirmed the worst fears of Zionists and gave their argument for a sovereign Jewish homeland overwhelming moral weight, especially since the Nazis were not the only anti-Semites in Europe, only the most extreme. The fascists of Italy visited horrors upon Italian Jews, the French puppet government set up by the Germans hunted down French Jews for their Nazi masters, the Poles and other Eastern Europeans collaborated enthusiastically in operating death camps, Great Britain had its share of anti-Semites, Spain, Belgium—no part of Europe could honestly claim innocence of the crime committed against the Jews in this period. Millions of Jews were trapped in Europe and perished there. All who could get away escaped in whatever direction lay open. Boatloads of Jewish refugees ended up drifting over the world's seas, looking for places to land. A few were able to make their way to the United States and resettle there, but even the United States imposed strict quotas on Jewish immigration, presumably because a single country could absorb only so many immigrants of any one group; but just perhaps some anti-Semitism was mixed into that policy as well.

The one place where the refugees *could* land was Palestine. There, earlier immigrants had bought land, planted settlements, and developed some infrastructure of support. Toward that slender hope of safety, therefore, the refugees headed, overcoming heroic hardships to begin building a new nation in an ancient land inhabited by their ancestors. Such was the shape of the story from the Jewish side.

From the Arab side, the story looked different. The Arabs had long been living under two layers of domination by outsiders, the first layer being the Turks, the next the Turks' European bosses. Then, in the wake of World War I, amidst all the rhetoric about "self-rule" and all the hope aroused by Wilson's Fourteen Points, their land was flooded by new settlers from Europe, whose slogan was said to be "a land without a people for a people without a land"[3]—an alarming slogan for people living in the "land without a people."

The new European immigrants didn't seize land by force; they bought the land they settled; but they bought it mostly from absentee landlords, so they ended up living among landless peasants who felt doubly dispossessed by the aliens crowding in among them. What happened just before and during World War II in Palestine resembled what happened earlier in Algeria when French immigrants bought up much of the land and planted a parallel economy there, rendering the original inhabitants irrelevant. By 1945, the Jewish population of Palestine almost equaled the Arab population. If one were to translate that influx of newcomers to the American context, it would be as if 150 million refugees flooded in within a decade. How could that not lead to turmoil?

In the context of the European narrative, the Jews were victims. In the context of the Arab narrative, they were colonizers with much the same attitudes toward the indigenous population as their fellow Europeans. As early as 1862, a German Zionist, Moses Hess, had drummed up support for political Zionism by proposing that "the state the Jews would establish in the heart of the Middle East would serve Western imperial interests and at the same time help bring Western civilization to the backward East."[4] The seminal Zionist Theodor Herzl wrote that a Jewish state in Palestine would "form a portion of the rampart of Europe against Asia, an outpost of civilization as opposed to barbarism."[5] In 1914, Chaim Weitzman wrote a letter to the Manchester *Guardian* stating that if a Jewish settlement could be established in Palestine "we could have in twenty to thirty years a million Jews out there. . . . They would develop the country, bring back civilization to it and form a very effective guard for the Suez Canal."[6] Arabs who saw the Zionist project as European colonialism in thin disguise were not inventing a fantasy out of whole cloth: Zionists saw the project that way too, or at least represented it as such to the imperialist powers whose support they needed.

In 1936, strikes and riots broke out among the Arabs of Palestine, serving notice that the situation was spiraling out of control. In a clumsy effort to placate the Arabs, Great Britain issued an order limiting further Jewish immigration to Palestine, but this order came in 1939, with World War II about to break out and the horrors of Nazism fully manifest to European Jews: there was no chance that Jewish refugees would comply with the British order; it would have been suicidal. Instead, militant organizations sprang up among the would-be Jewish settlers, and since they were a dispossessed few fighting the world-straddling British Empire, some of these militant Jewish groups resorted to the archetypal strategy of the scattered weak against the well-organized mighty: hit and run raids, sabotage, random assassinations, bombings of places frequented by civilians—in short, terrorism.

In 1946, the underground Jewish militant group Haganah bombed the King David Hotel in Jerusalem, killing ninety-one ordinary civilians, the most destructive single act of terrorism until 1988, when Libyan terrorists brought down a civilian airliner, Pan Am Flight 103, over Scotland, killing 270.

The horrors of Nazism proved the Jewish need for a secure place of refuge, but Jews did not come to Palestine pleading for refuge so much as claiming entitlement. They insisted they were not begging for a favor but coming *home* to land that was *theirs by right*. They based their claim on the fact that their ancestors had lived there until the year 135 CE and that even in diaspora they had never abandoned hope of returning. "Next year in Jerusalem" was part of the Passover service, a key cultural and religious rite in Judaism. According to Jewish doctrine, God had given the disputed land to the Hebrews and their descendants as part of His covenant with Abraham. Arabs, of course, were not persuaded by a religious doctrine that assigned the land they inhabited to another people, especially since the religion was not theirs.

In the aftermath of World War II, the United States led efforts to create new political mechanisms for keeping the peace, one of which was the United Nations. Palestine was just the sort of issue the United Nations was designed to resolve. In 1947, therefore, the United Nations crafted a proposal to end the quarrel by dividing the disputed territory and creating two new nations. Each competing party would get three patches of curiously interlocking land, and Jerusalem would be a separate international city belonging to neither side. The total territories of the proposed new nations, Israel and Palestine, would be roughly equal. Essentially, the United Nations was saying, "It doesn't matter who's right or wrong; let's just divide the land and move on." This is the sort of solution that adults typically impose on quarreling children.

But Arabs could not agree that both sides had a point and that the truth lay somewhere in the middle: they felt that a European solution was being imposed on them for a European problem, or more precisely that Arabs were being asked to sacrifice their land as compensation for a crime visited by Europeans on Europeans. The Arabs of surrounding lands sympathized with their fellows in Palestine and saw their point; the world at large did not. When the matter was put to a vote in the General Assembly of the United Nations, the vast majority of non-Muslim countries voted yes to partition.

Most Arabs had no personal stake in the actual issue: the birth of Israel would not strip an Iraqi farmer of his land or keep some Moroccan shop-

Palestine: U.N. Partition Plan (1947)
- Arab State
- Jewish State
- International Zone (Jerusalem and suburbs)

CYPRUS

Beirut
LEBANON

SYRIA
•Damascus

Mediterranean Sea

Haifa

PALESTINE

Tel Aviv
Jaffa
(Arab enclave)

•'Ammān
Jerusalem

Dead Sea

JORDAN

•Cairo

E G Y P T

SINAI PENINSULA

SAUDI ARABIA

Red Sea

ISRAEL AND PALESTINE

keeper from prospering in his business—yet most Arabs and indeed most Muslims could wax passionate about who got Palestine. Why? Because the emergence of Israel had emblematic meaning for them. It meant that Arabs (and Muslims generally) had no power, that imperialists could take any part of their territory, and that no one outside the Muslim world would side with them against a patent injustice. The existence of Israel signified European dominance over Muslims, Arab and non-Arab, and over the people of Asia and Africa generally. That's how it looked from almost any point between the Indus and Istanbul.

On May 15, 1948, Israel declared itself born. Immediately, Arab armies attacked from three sides, determined to crush the new country before it could take its first breath. But instead, Israel did the crushing, routing the armies of its three Arab adversaries, Syria, Jordan, and Egypt, and so it was Palestine, not Israel, that became the stillborn child. When the war ended, a war that Israel remembers as their War of Independence but that Arabs called the Catastrophe, some seven hundred thousand Arabs found themselves homeless and stateless, living as refugees in the neighboring Arab countries. The lands that were supposed to become Palestine were annexed (mostly by Jordan). The bulk of the Arab refugees collected on the West Bank of the Jordan River, where they seethed and stewed and sometimes staged small raids into the land that had once been theirs.

In the aftermath of the war of 1948, the Arabs lost the public relations battle even more drastically than they had lost their land. For one thing, some prominent Arabs publicly and constantly disputed Israel's "right to exist." They were speaking within the framework of the nationalist argument: Zionists wanted Israel to exist, the Arabs of Palestine wanted Palestine to exist, and since they claimed the same territory, both could not exist: the assertion of each nation's "right to exist" was inherently a denial of the other nation's "right to exist." But in the shadow of the Nazis' attempted genocide, asserting that Israel had no right to exist sounded like saying, "Jews have no right to exist."

To make matters worse, at least one Arab notable made no bones about actually endorsing Nazi anti-Semitism. This was the Mufti of Jerusalem, who had lived in Nazi Germany during the war and now spouted racism from many pulpits including his radio broadcasts. The weight of world opinion, the tone of media reporting, and the rantings of Arabs such as this mufti subtly conflated the Arab cause with Nazism in the public mind, especially in the West. Arabs not only lost the argument about the land but in the process became the Bad Guys who *deserved* to lose their land. This combination of feeling wronged and feeling vilified fed a spiraling resentment that rotted into the very anti-Semitism of which Muslims stood accused.

One man who took part in the debacle of 1948 was Egyptian army officer Gamal Abdul Nasser. Nasser was born in southern Egypt, the son of a humble postman. Even as a boy, he felt keenly wounded by his country's subservience to Europeans. At an age when most boys were starting to obsess about girls, Nasser was obsessing about his nation's "honor." His prospects for doing anything about it looked dim, however, until a sudden need for army officers opened up places for lower class boys in the country's elite military schools and Nasser rode this opportunity all the way to the rank of colonel.

The Arab defeat in 1948 deepened his sense of grievance. He blamed the country's king for it, and so he conspired with some hundred other army officers ("the Free Officers Club") to overthrow the monarchy and set up a republic. One morning in the summer of 1952, the Free Officers struck hard and fast: a nearly bloodless coup—two casualties and the monarchy was gone.

Getting rid of the king was the easy part, though. The big step was getting the British out of Egypt. For this step, however, Nasser needed serious firepower. The Cold War being in full swing at this time, almost any emerging nation-state could get arms from one of the two superpowers, so Nasser approached the Americans; but they didn't see Egypt as a key to "containing" Communism and mistrusted what this Arab fellow would do with weapons, so they turned him down. Nasser then went to the Soviets and from them got mountains of weaponry—which made the Americans sit up and take notice. In typical Cold War fashion, they decided Egypt was important after all. In a bid to win Nasser back, they offered to build him the world's biggest dam, right across the Nile River at a place called Aswan, a dam that would multiply Egypt's farmland and produce enough electricity to vault the country into the ranks of industrialized nations instantly! A breathtaking vision—the fulfillment of the secular modernist dream!

But when Nasser looked at the fine print, he saw that the aid agreement included U.S. military bases on Egyptian soil and U.S. oversight of Egypt's finances: here was the thin end of the imperialist wedge once again entering his country's heart. Nasser refused the aid, but could not stop dreaming of the Aswan Dam. But how could he finance the dam without selling his country to one of the superpowers?

Then he saw the answer: the Suez Canal, of course. The canal was pulling in about $90 million a year, and Egypt was getting only $6.3 million of it, roughly. Here was the money Egypt needed for its development, and it was mostly draining away to Europe! In 1956, Nasser suddenly poured troops into the Canal Zone and took over the canal.

A furor broke out in Europe. British politicians called Nasser another Hitler, a madman with a grandiose scheme of world conquest. The French press said Egyptians were too primitive to run the canal; they would disrupt global trade and wreck the world economy. These two European countries colluded with Israel in a complicated scheme to bomb Cairo, kill Nasser, and recover the canal.

Just in time, however, U.S. president Ike Eisenhower heard about the scheme and flew into a rage. Didn't the Europeans know there was a Cold War on? Didn't they know their little plot could deliver the whole Middle East to the Soviets? Eisenhower ordered the Europeans to give the canal back to Egypt and go home, and U.S. dominance was such that both countries (and Israel) had to obey.

Arabs saw this as a great victory for Nasser. For the next eleven heady years, Nasser was the decolonizing hero, the prophet of Arab unity, and the avatar of "Islamic Socialism," by which he meant a classless society achieved not through class warfare, as in Marxism, but through class co-operation regulated by the principles of Islam—a vigorous "socialist" re-statement of the basic secular modernist Muslim creed.

Nasser built his dam and electrified his nation. He also joined with India's Nehru, Indonesia's Sukarno, Sri Lanka's Bandaranaike, and several others to forge the Non-Aligned Movement, a bloc of neutral countries intended to counterbalance the two Cold War superpowers.

Nasser's big deeds and global stature won him countless new admirers at home, and not just in Egypt. Arabs of all classes and countries found him intoxicatingly charismatic. As a speaker, no one could touch him. When he spoke, Arabs (who heard him mostly on the radio) said they felt like he was in the room with them, addressing each person eye to eye, drawing each one into a conversation about what was to be done, as if all of them were in this thing together and every one of them mattered.

Nasser's popularity got him to dreaming of something bigger than a sovereign Egypt—a pan-Arab nation! This was exactly what the Ba'ath Party had been preaching in Syria. In fact, in 1958, Egypt and Syria tried to form one big country, the United Arab Republic, but Syria seceded three years later—a blow to Nasser's prestige.

Meanwhile, the Muslim Brotherhood was still alive. In 1952, they had helped overthrow the Egyptian king but as soon as Nasser's secular government commenced operations, they turned against *him*, even attempting to assassinate him. Nasser retaliated by putting the movements' leaders in prison, where he had them tortured.

Hassan al-Banna, the founder of the Muslim Brotherhood, had been assassinated before Nasser's day, but a nervous, brilliant, erratic, anxious intellectual zealot named Sayyid Qutb had taken charge of the Brotherhood in his place. Qutb's outlook had been shaped by a curious two-year sojourn at a teacher's college in Greeley, Colorado, where the Egyptian government had sent him to study U.S. educational methods. The materialism Qutb saw in America repelled him, the individualism disturbed him, the social freedoms unnerved him, and the sexual mores shocked him—the sight, for example, of young men and women *square dancing* together at a church social!

Qutb came home convinced that the United States was a Satanic force and had to be destroyed. He began publishing political tracts. He wrote that Islam offered a complete alternative, not just to other religions such as Christianity and Buddhism, but also to other political systems, such as communism and democracy, and he renewed the call for Muslims to rebuild one big universal Muslim community. And if that sounded like he was saying that the Muslim Brotherhood should seize power in Egypt, so be it.

Nasser clapped this man in prison: big mistake, it turned out. There in prison, garbed in the glamour of victimhood, Qutb wrote his most incendiary work, a book called *Milestones*. Here, he proposed a radical reinterpretation of Sayyid Jamaluddin's pan-Islamist modernism. He revived the ancient theoretical schema of a world divided between Dar al-Islam and Dar al-Harb, the realms of (Muslim) peace and (infidel) violence. Qutb was no ranter. His prose was cool and measured; he picked his words precisely. And in this steady, lucid, unblinking language, he called on every Muslim to embrace and practice jihad, not just against non-Muslims but against Muslims who faltered in their allegiance to Islam or collaborated with the enemy.[7] Under Qutb's leadership, the Muslim Brotherhood basically declared war against the governments of Egypt, Syria, Iraq, Jordan, and Lebanon and against all the secular modernists who supported them.

Egypt had no democratic process with which to co-opt the Brotherhood's hold on the underclass. Nasser relied instead on police power to quell demonstrations and on *secret* police to nip conspiracies in the bud.

Qutb and his brotherhood were all the more irritating to Nasser because he had plenty of other rivals assailing him, more daunting ones, he thought. The rulers of Syria, Jordan, and Iraq envied Nasser's popularity, and they were doing their best to discredit him. Ba'ath activists challenged his status among Arabs, claiming that they were the *real* pan-Arab nationalists. Then there were Egypt's communists. At the height of the Cold War, given their pipeline to Soviet support, they no doubt seemed more dangerous than some cult organizing the Muslim rabble. And finally there were the frankly antirevolutionary monarchs and the tribal dynasts who still ruled some of the Arab states, and who disapproved of everything Nasser stood for.

In 1963, Nasser blundered into a proxy war in Yemen. He sent troops in only as a gesture, to show support for a socialist party that had seized power there by ousting the tribal monarchy; but as soon as Egyptian troops arrived in Yemen, Saudi Arabia began pumping money and guns to the royalists. Suddenly Nasser found himself bogged down in a quagmire of a war that dragged on without result for years.

Meanwhile, Sayyid Qutb went on preaching his doctrines from prison. Nasser decided that, frustrated though he was on other fronts, he didn't have to put up with this gadfly. In August 1966, he did what men with too much power and too few procedural restraints often do: he had Qutb hanged—only to see him hailed as a martyr by a frighteningly far-flung network of admirers.

Just three months later, Syria and Israel got locked into a cycle of raids and counterraids back and forth across their border, which escalated for six months, growing ever more bloody. Ba'athists ruled Syria by this point. They were Nasser's main rivals in the secular modernist camp and by going toe-to-toe with Israel, they were gaining credibility at Nasser's expense, among Arabs generally and among the Palestinians in particular, those wretched refugees still mired in the camps.

So there was Nasser, hero of the Arab world, besieged by his own Arab Muslim masses, eclipsed by his Arab secular modernist rivals, bogged down in an endless war—with other Arabs. Clearly he needed to do something! And clearly it could not be directed against any other Arab country, group, or movement.

This is where matters stood in the spring of 1967, just before one of the most seminal events of modern history, at least as seen through Islamic eyes: Israel's Six Day War against her Arab neighbors.

17

⊗

The Tide Turns

1369-1421 AH
1950-2001 CE

I N MAY, 1967, Nasser began to spout martial rhetoric at Israel; to prove he meant business, he even blockaded Israel's access to the Red Sea. Actually, of course, with seventy thousand of his best troops bogged down in Yemen, Nasser could not possibly take any real military action; but a man can talk. Talk, if it's tough enough, will sometimes do the job.

And sometimes not. On June 5, without warning, Israel attacked Egypt, Jordan, and Syria simultaneously. "Without warning" should be uttered with an asterisk here: Arab-Israeli tension had been ratcheting up for months. Yet none of the Arab states were expecting a war on that June morning; and none of them were ready.

In the first twenty-four hours, Israel destroyed virtually the entire Egyptian air force on the ground. In the next five days, Israel conquered all the territories penciled in by the United Nations as the state of Palestine. These became instead the Occupied Territories, ruled by Israel but populated mostly by Palestinians. By the seventh day, the war was over, and the world would never be the same.

You might think there can be no such thing as a triumph *too* decisive. And maybe not, in a conflict between two monolithic sides. But in 1967,

when Israel won the most decisive victory in the history of modern warfare, it wasn't clashing with a monolith. The Arab side was a querulous
scramble of contradictions locked in struggle with one another.

The Six Day War humiliated Nasser, finished his career. Within four
years the man was literally dead. If Nasser had really been the leader of a
monolithic Arab bloc, his defeat might have forced "the Arabs" to come to
terms with Israel and work out some basis for eventual peace.

But there was no "the Arabs." Nasser was in fact just one contender
among several for leadership of just one current among all who called
themselves Arabs: secular modernism. When Israel attacked the Arabs, it
really attacked only this current; and when it crushed Nasser, it damaged
only this Westernizing, modernizing, secular, nationalist tendency, and not
even every expression of that. With Nasser's fall, down went "Nasserism,"
that odd mélange of secular modernism and Islamic socialism. Into the
power vacuum left by its demise flowed other, more dangerous forces,
some of them more primal, more irrational.

In the wake of the war, the Arab refugees clumped along the borders of
Israel gave up hope that any Arab state would save them and decided to
rely only on themselves henceforth. These refugees, their numbers swelled
to more than a million by the latest mayhem, could properly be called
Palestinians at this point, because their intense shared historical experience
had certainly given them a common identity and made them a "nation" in
the classic sense. *They* were now the "people without a land" and among
these Palestinians sprouted many groups dedicated to the restoration of
Palestine by any means. The biggest of them drifted into a coalition called
the Palestine Liberation Organization, which had been founded in 1964 as
a mechanism by which Arab governments could "manage" the Palestinians. After the Six Day War, Palestinians took control of this organization
and made it their own. A part-time engineer and full-time revolutionary
named Yasser Arafat emerged as its chairman[1], and with the PLO as their
quasi-government, the Palestinians dug in for a protracted war with Israel.
This was the first consequence of the Six Day War.

Second, the fall of Nasser created an opening for the other secular
Arab nationalist movement, the one founded by Michel Aflaq. His party
had joined with the Syrian Socialist Party to form the Ba'ath Socialist Party,
the ideology of which combined state-glorifying socialism with Arab-

worshipping nationalism. After the Six Day War, disgruntled army officers flooded into this new Ba'ath, giving the already unhealthy nationalist-
socialist mixture a militaristic cast. What had started out as a fairly liberal,
modernist movement, dedicated to women's rights, equality for religious
minorities, freedom of speech, civil liberty, democracy, literacy, and other
such progressive ideals, now skewed sharply toward nationalistic develop-
mentalism with totalitarian overtones. The Ba'ath credo boiled down to a
shout of, "Our *Nation*! Our *nation* must *develop* factories, industry,
bombs!" Even before the Six Day War, the Ba'ath Party had taken control
of Syria; after the Six Day War, a second branch of the party seized power
in Iraq and began to build a police state soon to be headed up by that
take-no-prisoners dictator Saddam Hussein. Both Ba'ath parties had popular support at first, because the Arab citizens of their countries were
frightened by Israel and wounded by the debacle of 1967; they were desperate for someone to restore their pride. But the glow faded as the middle-
class masses in Syria and Iraq tasted life under the boot of an ideology
that had nothing at its core but power. And this was a second consequence
of the Six Day War.

The third consequence was the most ominous. The Six Day War
marked a turning point in the general struggle between the secular modernists of the Islamic World and adherents of those other currents of Islamic thought and action coming out of the nineteenth century:
Wahhabism and the various strains of political Islamism.

In Saudi Arabia, Wahhabis already had a state of their own. Though
Egypt had a long claim to being the center of the Arab world, Saudi Arabia could bid for that status too, in part because it controlled the holy
cities of Mecca and Medina. Any weakening of Egypt added to Saudi Arabia's power—and what power it was! Oil gave the Wahhabis wealth, and
U.S. arms gave them military strength. With Egypt in disarray, Wahhabi
clerics quietly began using their resources to fund missionary activity
throughout the Muslim world, setting up religious schools, building
mosques, appointing imams, and establishing charities that extended
their reach into the lives of poor and rural Muslims everywhere, extended
south into sub-Saharan Africa and east to the southern Pushtoons of
Afghanistan, and on into Pakistan, where Wahhabi ideology already had
millions of adherents.

Then there was the Muslim Brotherhood. When Nasser lost face in the Six Day War, the Egyptian masses simply abandoned him. They turned instead to the vast anti-Nasserite movement permeating their country. And now, the Muslim Brotherhood metastasized. The organization itself thrust beyond the borders of Egypt, into Syria, into Jordan, into the Arab emirates and the rest of Arab heartland. What's more, the original movement began sprouting offshoots, each one more radical than the last. One such branch was Egypt's Islamic Jihad, founded by a man named al-Zawaheri, who in turn mentored the now-infamous Saudi jihadist Osama bin Laden.

Some ideologues inspired by Qutb began to teach that jihad was not only "an obligation" for devout Muslims but the "sixth pillar" of Islam, on a par with prayer, pilgrimage, fasting, charity, and the creed of monotheism. A few extremists, such as Abdullah Azzam, a Palestinian who fought the Soviets in Afghanistan, went even further and declared that participation in jihad was the *only* way to distinguish a Muslim from a non-Muslim: according to his doctrine, anyone who held back from armed struggle was fair game.[2] These hardcore revolutionaries should properly be called "jihadists" rather than simply "Islamists." Their ideology was plainly off the charts for the vast majority of Muslims, hardly even recognizable as Islam to most: it was a sliver of Islamism, itself a sliver of political Islam, itself one branch of Islam as a whole.

Overall then, what did the Six Day War accomplish? Israel gained the Occupied Territories. They were supposed to buffer the country against further attacks. Instead, within those same territories, Israeli authorities have faced ever-mounting insurgencies called *intifadas*, to which they have responded with ever more brutal measures. Year after year and decade after decade, this strike-and-counterstrike syndrome has drained the nation's energies and compromised its moral arguments in the world.

On the other side of the ledger, the war radicalized and "Palestinianized" the PLO, empowered the Ba'ath party, and energized the Muslim Brotherhood, which spawned Jihadist splinters as the years went by, ever more extremist zealots who mounted increasingly horrific attacks not just at innocent bystanders who got in the way—a tragic byproduct of virtually all wars—but against anyone who could be gotten and the more innocent the better, the distinctive genre of violence known today as terrorism. In short, the Six Day war was a crushing setback for world peace, a disaster for the Muslim world, and not much good in the end even for Israel.

Such was the narrative that unfolded in the Arab heartland after World War II. Let me go back now and follow another thread of narrative further east, in the Persian heartland. There too a seminal event took place, almost as world-changing as the Six Day War, because it established, in the Islamic world, an image of the United States that has proved intractable.

It was only after World War I that Muslims really started taking notice of the United States, and their first impression was highly favorable. Right through World War II, they admired America's sleek efficiency, its ability to pour out wonderful goods, its military strength, especially in light of the higher values the United States proclaimed—freedom, justice, democracy. They respected the American argument that its political system could save people of every nation from poverty and oppression. American idealists proffered democracy with something of the same ardor enjoyed by religious movements, making it a competitor to other world-organizing social ideas such as communism, fascism, and Islam. Religious Muslims may have rejected America's moral claims, but secular modernist Muslims saw great hope in it, and found no inherent contradiction between American ideals and Islam as they understood it.

When Wilson's Fourteen Points came to nothing, Muslims didn't blame the United States; they blamed the European old guard. In the last days of World War II, American president Franklin Delano Roosevelt renewed America's moral leadership by issuing (with Winston Churchill) the Atlantic Charter, a document calling for the liberation and democratization of all countries. Churchill later said he didn't mean it, but American leaders never repudiated the charter. In fact, just after the war, the United States took the lead in drafting the Universal Declaration of Human Rights, which was issued by the United Nations, more proof, if any were needed, that America was committed to supporting political freedom and democracy everywhere.

All this looked very good to Iranians. In the wake of World War II they were ready to resume a project dear to the secular modernists among them: replacing dynastic despotism with homegrown democracy. Reza Shah Pahlavi had blocked this project for decades, but he was gone, finally: the

Allies, the wonderful Allies, had removed him during the war for flirting with the Nazis. The stage was set for Iranians to restore their 1906 constitution, resurrect their parliament, and hold real elections: at last they could build the secular democracy they had dreamed about for so long.

With high hopes, then, Iranians went to the polls and voted a secular modernist named Mohammad Mosaddeq into power as their prime minister. Mosaddeq had pledged to recover total control of the country's most precious resource, its oil, and accordingly upon taking office he canceled the lease with British Petroleum and announced that he was nationalizing the Iranian oil industry.

Nice try.

The U.S. Central Intelligence Agency immediately moved to stop "this madman Mosaddeq" (as U.S. secretary of state John Foster Dulles called him). In late August of 1953, a faction of the Iranian military carried out a bloody CIA-funded coup that left thousands dead in the streets and put Iran's most popular political figure under house arrest from which he never emerged. In his place, the CIA restored the son of Reza Shah Pahlavi (also called Reza Shah Pahlavi) as the country's king. The young shah signed a treaty with the United States giving an international consortium of oil corporations the job of "managing" Iran's oil.

It would be hard to overstate the feeling of betrayal this coup embedded in Iran or the shudder of anger it sent through the Muslim world. Just three years later, Eisenhower's intervention secured the Suez Canal for Egypt, but the United States reaped no public relations benefit out of it among Muslims: Nasser got all the credit. Why? Because the damage done by the CIA coup in Iran was too deep. Across the Islamic heartland and indeed throughout the once-colonized world, the conviction took hold that the imperialist project was still alive, but with the United States at the helm now, in place of Great Britain. From the perspective of the Islamic narrative, the history unfolding in Iran still revolved around the struggle between secular and religious impulses. How best to revive Islam, how to recover Muslim strength, how to cast off the weight of the West—these were the issues that drove events. But Iran was also part of the world narrative now, and that narrative revolved around the superpower competition for control of the planet. From that perspective, what shaped events were Cold War strategic considerations and the politics of oil. The same held true throughout the Middle World, and these two sets of issues continued to intertwine throughout Dar al-Islam to the end of the century.

East of Iran, the Cold War simply looked like the Great Game revisited. The differences were only cosmetic. What had been czarist Russia was now called the Soviet Union. The role once played by Great Britain now belonged to the United States. The dynamics, however, were the same: the intrigues, the pressures, the threat of violence, and the actual bloodshed.

The scale was bigger, though. The Great Game had unfolded along the line where the Russian Empire butted against the British one. The Cold War was driven by U.S. determination to block Soviet expansion around the world; and since new nation-states were emerging everywhere, and most of them had the potential to end up as either Soviet or U.S. allies, the line of scrimmage in the Cold War could be anywhere on earth. Every potentially disputed country could receive money and guns from both superpowers, one funneling aid to the government, the other to some anti-government insurgency, depending on which way that country tilted.

The core battlefield of the Great Game had been Iran, Afghanistan, and central Asia, and this region remained in play. The Russians of the nineteenth century had wanted to push south through Afghanistan to the Persian Gulf to secure a warm water port for their navies and shipping. The Soviets had the same interest, but with added stakes: geologists were now confirming that roughly 65 percent of the world's petroleum lay under and around the Persian Gulf and in a few other Muslim countries of North Africa (and much of the rest of it, geologists would later find, lay in the Muslim countries of Central Asia, north of Afghanistan.) With global industrialization escalating off the charts, the significance of oil was still soaring.

Although oil had a huge political impact on the Muslim world, its social impact was probably even deeper. Ever since the 1930s, countries that had oil had been chipping away at the rapacious terms of those early leases. Every few years one or another of them had managed to renegotiate its agreements with foreign oil corporations and come away with incrementally better terms. By 1950, the "oil exporting" countries were generally receiving as much as 50 percent of the revenues from their oil, and from that time on considerable wealth began flowing into the region.

This sudden gush of wealth might have had a very different impact if only democratic institutions had emerged in the oil-rich nations before oil was discovered. With power distributed throughout society in these countries, with avenues of participation available to people of all classes, the wealth might have empowered the creative energies of millions and sparked a cultural renaissance.

But time and circumstances had permitted no such institutions to arise. These Muslim societies were haunted by memories of greatness lost. Their ruling elites were obsessed with developing the modern infrastructure they deemed indispensable to recovering that grandeur. They were desperate to catch up to the West and believed that only centralized states with a monopoly on power could do what needed to be done. They didn't think they could wait for the necessary infrastructure to emerge organically nor could they afford to let their people find their way to modernization at their own pace and in their own way. Islamic societies were falling behind by the minute, and they needed the full physical infrastructure of modernity right now!

With oil, they could have it just that quickly. They could sell the oil and use the money to drop the desired infrastructure into place, boom. The wealth accumulated by the ruling elite of oil-rich countries is the stuff of legends, and it's true that a tiny minority of Arabs and Iranians accumulated obscene wealth and squandered it as jetsetters frolicking in the resorts and casinos of the world, but the ruling elites of these countries did not merely pocket the money. They also directed vast sums of it into "development," true to the secular modernists creed: that's really the bigger story. In country after country, governments installed national school systems, built power plants and skyscraping office towers, established national airline companies, set up national television stations, radio stations, and newspapers. . . .

In one country after another, large scale development of this kind was carried out by the state and its functionaries, spawning a new class of educated technicians and bureaucrats to operate the machinery of the new modernism. This "technocracy," as some have called it, was a salaried employee class: its money came from the state, and the state got it from foreign corporations that were pumping and selling the country's oil. The state still collected taxes from farmers, herders, artisans, merchants, and others working in the traditional economy, but those revenues didn't amount to much. The traditional economy just wasn't that productive.

Certainly, governments could not depend on *that* tax base to fund their ambitious development programs.

Once the ruling elite stopped depending on the traditional economy for tax revenues, they no longer needed allies in that world. Even in totalitarian dictatorships, the power elite have to propitiate some domestic constituency. But in these oil-rich Muslim states, they could diverge from the masses of their people culturally without consequence. The people they did need to get along with were the agents of the world economy coming and going from their countries. Thus did "modernization" divide these "developing" societies into a "governing club" and "everyone else."

The governing club was not small. It included the technocracy, which was not a mere group but a whole social class. It also included the ruling elite who, in dynastic countries, were the royal family and its far-flung relatives and in the "republics" the ruling party and its apparatchik. Still, in any of these countries the governing club was a minority of the population as a whole, and the border between the governing classes and the masses grew ever more distinct.

People in the club were part of an exciting project, working to transform their country. Those outside the club were passive beneficiaries of a modernization that was simply happening *to* them. Suddenly a hospital might go up nearby: good, now they could get better health care. Suddenly a paved highway might appear nearby: good, now they could get to the city quicker. But people outside the governing club had no role in modernization for good or ill, no share in decision making, no voice in how the new money flowing into the country would be spent, no political participation in their country's transformation.

They also didn't get, as a by-product of modernization, enhanced power to realize their personal dreams and goals, whatever those might have been. In fact, even as oil-exporting nations got richer overall, those outside the "governing clubs" grew relatively poorer.

For most people, the only hope of claiming a stake in their own country was to go to a government school, do well, go abroad (ideally), get a degree, preferably in some technical field, and then break into the technocracy. Anyone who took this route probably ended up wearing a suit to work and living a life resembling that of people in the West. Their time was regulated by clocks, their family tended to be "nuclear," their entertainment tastes might run to alcohol, nightclubs, opera. Their children might listen to rock and roll, date members of the opposite sex, and choose their own spouses.

Anyone who didn't take this route probably ended up wearing the traditional garments of the society: *pehran-u-tumban, shalwar kameez, sari, jelabiyyah, keffiyeh*—whatever was traditional in a given country. Their daily schedule was shaped by religious rituals, and when they spoke of their family they would tend to mean a large network of relatives to whom they were bound by intricate obligations. Their spouses would probably be chosen for them by others, possibly a committee of relatives from which they themselves might be excluded.

Diplomats, businessmen, and other functionaries of the Western world would feel comfortable dealing with the folks who wore suits to work; they were culturally familiar. They might rarely interact with denizens of the other culture.

Those who wore suits to work had a good chance of living in houses with modern kitchens and bathrooms equipped with electricity and plumbing. Those who didn't, ended up in houses with kitchen and bathrooms like those of their ancestors with informal plumbing and possibly no connection to a public sewage system. As an energy source, instead of electricity, they might use charcoal, wood, or some other fuel burned directly for heat and light.

The people within the nation's governing club made money on a scale corresponding to that of the world economy. People in the left-behind, domestic economy generally had much smaller incomes, adequate perhaps to their needs in a village or an urban slum, but not enough to let them move out of poverty.

This whole dynamic was not limited to the oil-rich nations. A similar process was taking place in countries without oil, if they had strategic value as Cold War chips, and who didn't? Egypt, Afghanistan, Pakistan, and many other countries that fit this definition got torrents of money from the superpowers as "development aid" designed to tilt them toward whichever side was doing the giving. Roads and hospitals, schools and airports, armaments and police equipment, whatever the ruling elite of a country needed, they could get the money for it in the forms of grants or loans from outside. It wasn't oil money, but compared to the revenues generated by the traditional economies of these countries, it was *lots* of money. Aid like this relieved ever-more centralized states from depending on domestic taxes and their elites from having to please or appease domestic constituencies. It was money enough to spawn technocracies and divide societies into separate worlds.

The division into separate worlds was indeed so sharp that in many places it was visible to the naked eye. Every major metropolis from Casablanca to Kabul had in essence two downtowns: one was its Old City, perhaps dubbed its "casbah" or its "medina," a downtown for citizens of the left-behind economy. Everybody there dressed quite differently from people in the other downtown, the modern one, where business was transacted with the world at large. The two downtowns smelled different; they had different styles of architecture; there was a different feel to the social life. All countries once colonized by Europeans had some such division perhaps, but it may have been most palpable in Muslim countries.

Of course it's true that in Europe, too, the sudden changes wrought by the industrial revolution had divided societies into sharply separate classes. London had its sleek business center and its Cheapside, its posh neighborhoods and its slums, but there the division derived more strictly from the economic gulf: the rich ate better, dressed better, lived more comfortably, went to better schools, and used a more educated diction when they spoke, but they were just a richer version of the poor.

In the Muslim world, the difference was not just economic but cultural and therefore the gulf between the worlds fed alienation and produced a more anti-colonialist flavor of resentment, but against the nation's own elite. This resentment led to occasional civil unrest. Since these culturally divided countries had no democratic institutions to mediate disputes, governments casually resorted to force to suppress disorder. The native elites took over the role of the one-time foreign colonialists. From Morocco through Egypt to Pakistan and beyond, prisons filled up with political dissenters and malcontents. Nowhere was the cultural and political tension more palpable than in Iran. Shah Reza Pahlavi, who had profited from Mosaddeq's ouster, was a secular modernist in the Atatürk mold, but where Atatürk had been a fundamentally democratic man with an autocratic streak, the Shah of Iran was a fundamentally autocratic man with a totalitarian streak. He built a secret police outfit called SAVAK to consolidate his grip on the country, and as if just to salt his countrymen's wounds, he signed a treaty with the United States giving American citizens in Iran complete immunity from Iranian laws—an astounding giveaway of sovereignty.

The shah's tyranny energized a resistance movement that harkened back to the spirit of Sayyid Jamaluddin. Its leading theoretician, Dr. Ali Shariati was a Sorbonne-educated Muslim socialist intellectual. He crafted a vision of Islamic modernism that rejected what he called "Westoxification" and sought a basis for progressive socialism in Islamic tradition. Shariati said, for example, that Islam's insistence on the unity of God expressed the need for human unity on Earth. In the modern era, the "polytheism" forbidden by Islam was embodied in the division of society into classes by wealth and race. According to Shariati, the three idols that Muslims pelted with stones during the Hajj pilgrimage represented capitalism, despotism, and religious hypocrisy. He tapped Islamic stories and traditions as fuel for revolutionary fervor, pointing for example, to Hussein's uprising against Mu'awiya as a symbol of the human struggle for liberation, justice, and salvation: if Hussein could inspire a group of seventy-plus against a massive state, then a small underground revolutionary group of just a few hundred members had no reason to hold back from declaring war on the shah of Iran and the superpower that supported him.[3]

The Islamic socialist resistance incarnated as an underground group called the Mujahideen-e-Khalq. From the midfifties until the Iranian revolution of 1978, this small group led the struggle against the Shah and fought a secret war against SAVAK. These Mujahideen-e-Khalq (sometimes called Islamic Marxists) bore the brunt of the executions, imprisonment and torture by which the shah hoped to crush resistance, and the cruelties these men and women endured beggar description.

At the same time, however, a very different sort of religious resistance movement was gathering steam in Iran, one that came out of the orthodox religious establishment as embodied by the grim cleric Ayatollah Khomeini.

Like the Wahhabis of Sunnism, Khomeini claimed that Muslims had fallen away from "true" Islam as understood from a literal reading of the Qur'an and the traditions of the prophet and (because these were Shi'is) the imams who succeeded him. Khomeini attacked the Shah not for his despotism but for his modernism—for promoting the western dress code, favoring women's rights, allowing nightclubs to be built in Iran, and so on.

Khomeini also tapped Shi'i tradition to construct a novel political doctrine: that government power properly belonged in the hands of the world's single chosen representative of the Hidden Imam, a chosen one who could be recognized by his immense religious learning and the reverence that other learned scholars had for him. Such a man was a *faqih*, a leader with authority to legislate, and in the modern world, Khomeini suggested, *he* was that man.

The Shah deported Khomeini in 1964, but the stern cleric ended up in neighboring Iraq, from which base he directed a growing army of Iranian religious zealots loyal to *him*.

The Six Day War of 1967 had reinforced a Muslim belief that the United States headed a new imperialist assault on Muslim civilization with Israel as its beachhead. After all, Israel's strength depended on U.S. arms and support. This conclusion was underscored in 1973, when Nasser's successor, Anwar al-Sadat, started a fourth Arab-Israeli war by attacking Israel during Yom Kippur, a solemn religious holiday in Judaism. This time, Egyptian arms and troops scored sweeping early gains, but Israel received a sudden massive shipment of weapons from the United States and this turned the tide; so Israel triumphed again.

As it happened, during this Arab-Israeli War, the Organization of Petroleum Exporting Countries was meeting to conduct its routine business of coordinating production and pricing policies. OPEC was founded in 1960, and of its twelve member nations, nine were Muslim countries. At the very moment that OPEC leaders were gathering to confabulate, the masses in their countries were marching and raging about the military humiliation Israel and the United States were dealing the Arabs. OPEC had not been particularly political up to this point, but at the 1973 meeting, its members decided to use oil as a weapon for striking back. They announced an embargo on shipments to countries that supported Israel.

That move sent a shock through the industrialized world. In Oregon, where I lived at the time, gas was quasi-rationed: people could buy it only on alternate days, their turn determined by whether their license plate ended with an odd or even number. I remember getting up long before dawn every other day that winter to secure my place in line at a local gas station for a chance at the scarce commodity. Sometimes, the gas had run out by the time I got to the pump. I thought I was seeing the end of civilization, and perhaps I was getting a foretaste of it; perhaps we all were. That OPEC embargo sent the price of oil skyrocketing from $3 a barrel to $12. As I write, oil is selling for about $130 a barrel.

Media backlash soon began constructing the now-familiar stereotype of Arabs as rich, oily, evil men with long noses, conspiring to rule the world. That stereotype closely, even eerily, matches the one constructed a hundred years early by European anti-Semites as a depiction of Jews, particularly an imagined secret Jewish cult called the "elders of Zion," who were supposedly conspiring to, yes, rule the world.

The oil embargo did give the OPEC nations an intimation of their potential power. Although it lasted only a few months, it ended up increasing the oil-producing nations' mastery of their own resource. Thereupon, the elites of these nations got even richer—which only exacerbated the division of Muslim societies into separate worlds, as described earlier.

Throughout this time, secular forces in Dar al-Islam went on struggling to "modernize" their countries while coping with international forces. But the submerged, even suppressed "other" currents of Muslim revival—the political Islamists, the Salafis, the Wahhabis, the Deobandis, the jihadists, et al—continued to thrive among the excluded people of the left-behind economies. There, they went on preaching that the world was divided into two distinct, mutually exclusive parts, a realm of peace and a realm of war, a realm of Muslim brotherhood and one of violent pagan greed.

The people they were preaching to could look about and see that, yes indeed, society *was* divided into whole separate worlds; it was palpable; you'd have to be blind not to notice. And when the jihadists went on to predict that an apocalyptic showdown was coming up between those who remained faithful to the letter of the revelations received by Mohammed in seventh century Arabia and those who had joined Satan in his quest to draw people away from God, people who lived in these blatantly divided societies knew what they meant: they woke up every day to the reality of their own growing impoverishment, even as their television screens showed them people just across town but living in a whole other world, rich beyond all fantasies. They thrilled to the idea of an apocalypse coming that would give them Earth and Heaven while knocking the undeserving Godless elite off their high horses.

And yet, until the 1970s, few in the West paid much attention to this explosive underworld of growing rage. The dominant Western narrative of world history said these left-behind folks were vestigial elements of a bygone era that would gradually disappear as developing nations became developed nations, as despotisms realized the errors of their ways and became democracies, as that universal panacea called education eliminated superstition and replaced it with science, as parochial emotion gave way to dispassionate reason. According to prevailing doctrines, the problem plaguing the left-behinds of the Muslim world (and of other regions) was not the social conditions in which they lived, but the wrong ideas they had. And then—the secular modernists of the Islamic world began to fall.

Zulfikar Ali Bhutto was the first to go. He was the urbane, Berkeley-educated prime minister of Pakistan, leader of the left-flavored, secular socialist People's Party. In 1977, an Islamist general named Zia al-Haq overthrew him and imprisoned him. Soon, Pakistan's Deobandis began howling for his head. A kangaroo court tried him for vague crimes, and sentenced him. Bhutto was hanged. Sayyid Qutb had suffered exactly the same fate in Egypt, thirteen years earlier.

The next to fall was the shah of Iran. In 1978, a coalition of secular leftists, Islamic socialists, and pro-Khomeini Shi'i revolutionaries drove him out of the country and for a moment it looked as if the Mujahideen-e-Khalq and their modernist allies would construct a progressive government in Iran based on their new ideology of Islamic socialism.

But Khomeini craftily out-maneuvered all other factions of the Iranian revolution. On November 4, 1979, a band of his student followers overran the American embassy and took sixty-six Americans hostage. Khomeini exploited the year-long confrontation with America to weaken his rivals and consolidate his grip.[4] Then again, perhaps Khomeini's success can't be explained entirely by his spiderlike strategizing and political gamesmanship. Perhaps he won because he did indeed speak for the deepest impulse of the Iranian masses at that moment. Maybe that impulse wasn't to correct the course of secular modernism but to kill all movement in that direction and give the Islamic Way another try. In any case, by 1980, Khomeini had

transformed Iran into an "Islamic Republic" ruled by the most conservative clerics of Iran's orthodox Shi'i ulama.

Next to go were the secular modernists of Afghanistan. Their demise
began with a seeming triumph for an extreme version of the secularist impulse. A coup by a tiny group of Afghanistan communists smashed the dynasty Nadir Shah had founded in the 1920s. Every member of that clan
who could not escape was killed. Then the Soviet Union invaded and took
direct control of the country. But the leftward swing of the pendulum was
momentary and meaningless; it only triggered an overwhelmingly more
massive tribal and religious insurgency. The eight-year, anti-Soviet guerilla
war that followed totally empowered the country's Islamist ideologues. Not
only that but the rural Afghan resistance attracted Islamist zealots from
around the Muslim world, including jihadists from the Arab world and Deobandis from Pakistan, all of them sponsored by Wahhabi money from the
oil-rich Arab states of the Persian Gulf. Among the many who tasted first
blood in these battlefields of Afghanistan was Osama bin Laden.

In fact, in the last two decades of the twentieth century, Islam's secular
modernists saw their power erode almost everywhere. In Algeria, the secular government came under siege by the Islamic Salvation Party. In Palestine, the secular PLO gave way to the religious ideologues of Hamas.
Islamic Jihad, another militant group rooted in religious ideology, gained a
toehold in this region as well. In Lebanon, a series of devastating Israeli invasions emptied the Palestinian refugee camps along the southern border,
destroyed Beirut, and drove the PLO to new headquarters in Tunis, but
this only spawned the radical Shi'i political party Hezbollah, which ended
up as the de facto ruler of the country's southern half and proved itself just
as committed to destroying Israel as the ousted PLO.

In Syria and Iraq, the Muslim Brotherhood (and its offshoots) fought a
grim war with the Ba'ath Party, a war that went largely unnoticed in the
West. The Ba'ath governments could not eradicate these Islamist insurgents despite horrific measures such as Syrian president Hafez Assad's
1982 massacre of nearly all the people of a good-sized town called Hama.

Saddam Hussein, the ruler of Iraq, was a Sunni secular modernist and a
sworn enemy of radical religious Islamism. In 1980, directly after Khomeini took power, Hussein invaded Iran. Perhaps he considered the country
ripe for the picking due to its internal turmoil; perhaps he had his eye on

Iran's oil; perhaps he felt threatened by Khomeini—as he had good reason to be: Khomeini blatantly announced his intention to export his revolution, and secular Iraq, with its large Shi'i population, was the obvious first market for this export. Whatever Hussein's aims, his war proved catastrophic for both countries. Both lost nearly an entire generation of their young men and boys. Not since World War I had such vast armies met head to head nor had so many lives been squandered so casually for such trivial gains. And throughout this war, the United States funneled arms and funds to Iraq, bolstering its capacity to keep fighting to the last Iraqi, because the United States feared that the Soviets might gain ground in this strategic region, now that the United States had lost its foothold in Iran. Helping the Iraqis was a way to weaken Iran and possibly keep the Soviets at bay. Here again was a catastrophic intertwining of the Muslim and Western narratives, the one narrative still about secular modernism versus back-to-the-source Islamism, the other still about superpower rivalry and control of oil, though couched in rhetoric about democracy and totalitarianism.

The Iran-Iraq war ended in 1988 with no winners, unless you count Iran's mere survival as a victory. Iraq certainly ended up in ruins, its treasury exhausted by the pointless bloodshed. Saddam Hussein licked his wounds for two years, and then, in 1990, he made a bid to recoup his losses. A double-or-nothing risk-taker if ever there was one, Saddam Invaded and "annexed" neighboring Kuwait, hoping to add that country's oil to his own. Apparently, U.S. ambassador April Gillespie had given him reason to believe the United States would back him in this venture too.

Instead, the United States led a coalition of thirty-four countries against its erstwhile ally in an assault code-named Desert Storm, a short war that destroyed much of Iraq's infrastructure and culminated in the firebombing of Saddam's pathetic draftees as they were dragging themselves back toward Basra on what came to be known as the Highway of Death. This time Iraq was absolutely, totally, and unambiguously defeated—and yet the war ended with Saddam Hussein somehow still in power, somehow still in control of his core military outfit, the elite Republican Guard, and still able to crush—as he savagely did—the rebellions that erupted in the wake of his defeat by the West.

After the war, the United Nations imposed sanctions that virtually severed Iraq from the world and reduced Iraqi citizens from a European standard of living in 1990 to one that approached the most impoverished on Earth. Incomes dropped about 95 percent. Disease spread, and there was no medicine to stem it. Over two hundred thousand children—and perhaps as many as half a million—died as a direct result of the sanctions. One U.N. official, Denis Halliday, resigned because of these sanctions, claiming that "Five thousand children are dying every month. . . . I don't want to administer a program that results in figures like these."[5] Iraqis, who had suffered through so many years of deepening horror trapped in a war-mad police state, were now reduced to inconceivable squalor. The only sector of Iraqi society on whom the sanctions had little impact was the Ba'ath Party elite, Saddam Hussein and his cohorts, the very people the sanctions were intended to punish.

And in the east, the Soviets, who had invaded Afghanistan less than a year before Iraq invaded Iran, pulled out of Afghanistan less than a year after Iraq finally left Iran. The Afghan communists clung to power for another three years, but when they did at last go down, the entire Soviet Union was crumbling too, its empire unraveling in Eastern Europe, its constituent republics—even Russia—declaring independence until there was nothing left to declare independence *from.*

In America, conservative historian Francis Fukuyama wrote that the collapse of the Soviet Union marked not just the end of the Cold War but the end of history: liberal capitalist democracy had won, no ideology could challenge it anymore, and nothing remained but a little cleanup work around the edges while all the world got on board the train headed for the only truth. In fact, he offered this thesis in a book titled *The End of History and the Last Man.*

On the other side of the planet, however, jihadists and Wahhabis were drawing very different conclusions from all these thunderous events. In Iran, it seemed to them, Islam had brought down the Shah and driven out America. In Afghanistan, Muslims had not just beaten the Red Army but toppled the Soviet Union itself. Looking at all this, jihadists saw a pattern they thought they recognized. The First Community had defeated the two superpowers of its day, the Byzantine and Sassanid empires, simply by having God on its side. Modern Muslims also confronted two superpowers, and they had now brought one of them down entirely. One down, one to go was how it looked to the jihadists and the Wahhabis. History coming to an end? Hardly! As these radicals saw it, history was just getting interesting.

For years, they had been describing a world bifurcated between Dar al-Islam and Dar al-Harb. For years they had been predicting an apocalyptic showdown between good and evil, God and Satan, a great global battle to resolve all the contradictions and melt all factions into a single world, Medina universalized.

For the West, the end of the Cold War meant Afghanistan could be abandoned. There was nothing left to do there. The United States and its western European allies had pumped billions of dollars worth of arms and money into the country, but now they disengaged entirely, rejecting proposals from several sources that they sponsor some sort of conference, broker some sort of peace, help cobble together some sort of political process to help the country find its way back to civil order. CIA station chief Milton Bearden explained the reason for this sudden disengagement succinctly: "No one gives a shit about Afghanistan." The tribal armies that had battled the Soviets fell to quarrelling over the country they had won with the arms they had scored. The Soviets had already destroyed the Afghan countryside. Now, the civil war among the various guerilla armies destroyed the cities. Foreign jihadists who had fought in Afghanistan during the 1980s swarmed back to make the rubble their base of operations for a war against the West.

Step one was erecting in Afghanistan a pure version of the community they envisioned, one in which every man, woman, and child lived exactly according to the letter of God's law as they understood it or suffered the punishment. For this reason, jihadists, sponsored by Wahhabi money from Saudi sources, helped develop the Taliban, a party of primitive ideologues that emerged out of the refugee camps in that tribal belt that vaguely separates Afghanistan from Pakistan.

And eventually, some subset of the militant Jihadists holed up in the carcass of Afghanistan crafted a scheme to fly hijacked airliners into the World Trade Center in New York and Pentagon headquarters in Washington, D.C.

On that day, September 11, 2001, two world histories crashed together, and out of it came one certainty: Fukiyama was mistaken. History was not over.

AFTERWORD

Although history is not over, the period since 9/11 has not mulched down enough to enter history yet: it still belongs to journalists. It is not too soon, however, to reflect on this period as a manifestation of two great, out-of-sync narratives intersecting.

In the weeks immediately after the terrorist attacks in New York City and Washington, D.C., President Bush rallied the United States for military action with rhetoric that evoked long-standing themes of American and Western history. He said the terrorists were out to destroy freedom and democracy and that these values must be defended with blood and treasure, the same rallying cry raised against Nazism in the thirties and communism in the fifties. Since then, the United States and a coalition of largely unwilling allies have poured a great many troops into Iraq to fight a war cast rhetorically in much the same terms as the Cold War, and the twentieth century world wars, and so on back into earlier chapters of the Western world historical narrative.

But did the perpetrators of 9/11 really see themselves as striking a blow against freedom and democracy? *Is* hatred of freedom the passion that drives militantly political Islamist extremists today? If so, you won't find it in jihadist discourse, which typically focuses, not on freedom and its opposite, nor on democracy and its opposite, but on discipline versus decadence, on moral purity versus moral corruption, terms that come out of centuries of Western dominance in Islamic societies and the corresponding fragmentation of communities and families there, the erosion of Islamic social values, the proliferation of liquor, the replacement of religion with entertainment, and the secularization of the rich elite along with the ever-hardening gap between rich and poor.

One side charges, "You are decadent." The other side retorts, "We are free." These are not opposing contentions; they're nonsequiturs. Each side identifies the other as a character in its own narrative. In the 1980s, Khomeini called America "the Great Satan," and other Islamist revolutionaries have echoed his rhetoric. In 2008, Jeffrey Herf, a history professor at the University of Maryland, suggested that radical Islamists are the Nazis reborn, motivated at core by anti-Semitism and hatred of women. It's a common analysis.

Herf and others see the Islamist doctrine as boiling down to a call for cutting off heads, cutting off hands, and clamping bags over women. There's no denying that radical Islamists have done these things. Yet radical Islamists themselves see the main conflict dividing the world today as a disagreement about whether there is one God, many gods, or no God at all. All the problems of humanity would be resolved, they contend, if the world would only recognize the singleness of God (and of Mohammed's special role as his spokesperson).

Secular intellectuals in the West don't necessarily disagree about the number of gods. They just don't think that's the burning question. To them—to us—the basic human problem is finding ways to satisfy the needs and wants of all people in a manner that gives each one full participation in decision making about his or her own destiny. One God, two gods, three, none, many—whatever: people will have differing views, and it's not worth fighting about, because settling that question will not help solve hunger, poverty, war, crime, inequality, injustice, global warming, resource depletion, or any of the other ills plaguing humanity. Such is the secular position.

Yet *secular* and *Western* are not synonymous, despite what Islamists may declare. A 2001 survey by the City University of New York showed that 81 percent of Americans identified with an organized religion, 77 percent of them with Christianity. Of the rest, many called themselves "spiritual." Declared atheists were so few they didn't even register on the charts. Whatever the conflict wracking today's world, it's not between those who are and those who aren't religious.

In fact, the West has its own religious devotees who want to put God at the center of politics, most notably the Christian evangelicals who have wielded such clout in the United States since the 1970s. Tariq Ali wrote a book after 9/11 titled *The Clash of Fundamentalisms*, suggesting that this tension between Islam and the West boils down to a religious argument between fundamentalist extremists. If so, however, the two sides don't present opposing doctrines. Christian fundamentalists don't necessarily disagree about how many Gods there are; they just don't think that's the question. Their discourse revolves around accepting Jesus Christ as one's savior (whereas no Muslim would ever say "Mohammed is our savior"). So the argument between Christian and Muslim "fundamentalists" comes down to: Is there only one God or is Jesus Christ our savior? Again, that's not a point-counterpoint; that's two people talking to themselves in separate rooms.

The fact that the Muslim world and the West have come to the same events by different paths has had concrete consequences. After 2001, U.S. strategists acted on the premise that the climactic terrorist act of modern times somehow fit into the framework of power politics among nation-states. After all, that's what European wars had been about for many centuries. Even the Cold War came down to a confrontation between blocs of nations, the warring entities lined up along the ideological fault line ultimately being governments. In the immediate aftermath of 9/11, therefore, the Bush administration looked around, over, past, through, anywhere but directly at the specific terrorists of that day, in its quest to find the *government* behind those men. Reflexively, U.S. strategists—and many analysts in the Western media—sought an adversary of the same genre, the same class, the same type the country had confronted in earlier wars.

Thus it was that, after a brief initial incursion into Afghanistan and a transitory obsession with Osama bin Laden, the Bush team zeroed in Saddam Hussein as the mastermind and Iraq as the core state responsible for terrorism against Western citizens, the state whose conquest and "democratization" would put an end to this plague. But after Saddam Hussein had been captured and hanged, after Iraq had been fully occupied, if not subdued, terrorism showed no real sign of abating, whereupon U.S. government strategists shifted focus to Iran. And depending on what happens there, Syria, Libya, Saudi Arabia, Pakistan, and a host of other nations await their turn as designated chief "state sponsor" of terrorism.

With its policies deeply rooted in the Western narrative, the United States has prescribed democracy and sponsored elections to remedy local ills in Iraq and Afghanistan and other troubled regions. Upon the successful completion of such elections, the countries in question are said to have become democracies or at least to have moved closer to that happy state.

But I keep remembering the elections held in Afghanistan after the Taliban had fled the country. Across the nation, people chose delegates to represent them at a national meeting organized by the United States to forge a new democratic government, complete with parliament, constitution, president, and cabinet. That summer in Paghman, a town near Kabul, I met a man who said he had voted in the elections. I couldn't picture him in a voting booth, since he looked like the traditional rural villagers I had known in my youth, with the standard long shirt, baggy pants, turban, and beard, so I asked him to describe the voting process for me—what was the actual activity?

"Well, sir," he said, "a couple of city men came around with slips of paper and went on and on about how we were supposed to make marks on them, and we listened politely, because they had come a long way and we didn't want to be rude, but we didn't need those city fellows to tell us who our man was. We made the marks they wanted, but we always knew who would be representing us—Agha-i-Sayyaf, of course."

"And how did you settle on Sayyaf?" I asked.

"Settle on him? Sir! What do you mean? His family has lived here since the days of Dost Mohammed Khan and longer. Go over that ridge, you'll see his house across the valley—biggest one around! Every year at Eid, he comes by and gives candy to the children and inquires about our problems, and if someone needs help, why, he fetches money out of his pocket and hands it over then and there, whatever he has on him. That man is a Muslim! Did you know that my sister's husband has a cousin who is married to Sayyaf's sister-in-law? He's one of our own."

It struck me that what Western planners called "democracy" was an extraneous apparatus this man shouldered because he had to, under which load he carried on with his real life as best he could. In him flowed two streams of history that were unrelated and interconnecting awkwardly. And if this was happening an hour outside Kabul, it was happening all over the country.

From the Western side, it seems plausible (to some) to assert that funding and arming rulers amenable to Western ways in places like Pakistan,

Jordan, Iraq, Afghanistan, and Egypt helps bring democracy to those societies, not to mention the blessings of a free market. It also seems plausible (to some) to assert that Islamic social values are backward and need correction by more progressive people, even if force must needs be applied to get it done.

From the other side, however, the moral and military campaigns of recent times look like the long-familiar program to enfeeble Muslims in their own countries. Western customs, legal systems, and democracy look like a project to atomize society down to the level of individual economic units making autonomous decisions based on rational self-interest. Ultimately, it seems, this would pit every man, woman, and child against every other, in a competition of all against all for material goods.

What looks, from one side, like a campaign to secure greater rights for citizens irrespective of gender, looks from the other side, like powerful strangers inserting themselves into the private affairs of families and undercutting people's ability to maintain their *communal* selves as familial and tribal networks. In short, what looks from one side like empowering each individual looks, from the other side, like disempowering whole communities.

The conflict wracking the modern world is not, I think, best understood as a "clash of civilizations," if that proposition means we're-different-so-we-must-fight-until-there's-only-one-of-us. It's better understood as the friction generated by two mismatched world histories intersecting. Muslims were a crowd of people going somewhere. Europeans and their off-shoots were a crowd of people going somewhere. When the two crowds crossed paths, much bumping and crashing resulted, and the crashing is still going on.

Unraveling the vectors of those two crowds is the minimum precondition for sorting out the doctrinal bases of today's disputes. The unraveling will not itself produce sweetness and light, because there are actual incompatibilities here, not just "misunderstandings." When I started working on this book, I read my proposal to a group of fellow writers, two of whom declared that the conflict between the Muslim world and the West was promoted by hidden powers because "people are really the same and we all want the same things"; the conflict would fade away if only people in the West understood that Islam was actually just like Christianity. "They believe in Abraham, too," one of them offered.

This sort of well-meant simplification won't get us very far.

On the other side, I often hear liberal Muslims in the United States say that "*jihad* just means 'trying to be a good person,'" suggesting that only anti-Muslim bigots think the term has something to do with violence. But they ignore what *jihad* has meant to Muslims in the course of history dating back to the lifetime of Prophet Mohammed himself. Anyone who claims that jihad has nothing to do with violence must account for the warfare that the earliest Muslims called "jihad." Anyone who wants to say that early Muslims felt a certain way but we modern Muslims can create whole new definitions for jihad (and other aspects of Islam) must wrestle with the doctrine Muslims have fleshed out over time: that the Qur'an, Mohammed's prophetic career, and the lives, deeds, and words of his companions in the first Muslim community were the will of God revealed on Earth and no mortal human can improve on the laws and customs of that time and place. This doctrine has forced all Muslim reformers to declare that they are proposing nothing new, only restoring what was originally meant. They must deny that they are forging forward, must insist that they are going back to the pristine original. That's a trap Muslim thinkers must break out of.

The modernist Egyptian theologian Sheikh Mohammed Abduh wrote famous books showing that the Qur'an actually prescribed science and *certain* (but not other) modern social values. He cites scriptural declarations to show that in marriage the Qur'an actually favors monogamy over polygamy. His case is convincing but he clearly came to his task intending to find support for monogamy in the Qur'an. It was a conclusion he had already reached. The question is, from what other source did he derive this conclusion? Was it not rational thought applied to the deepest principles of shared human life?

The role of women in society is no doubt the starkest instance of the incompatibility between the Islamic world and the West, an issue much in need of intellectual unraveling and deconstruction. Every society in every era has understood the powerful potential of sexuality to disrupt social harmony and every society has developed social forms to check that power. On this point, the disagreement between Islamic and Western culture is not about whether women should be oppressed, as is often represented in the West. Well-meaning folk on both sides believe that no human beings should be oppressed. This is not to deny that women suffer grievously from oppressive laws in many Muslim countries. It is only to say that the principle on which Muslims stand is not the "right" to oppress women. Rather, what the Muslim world has reified over the course of history is the idea that society should be divided into a men's and a women's realm and that the point of connection between the two should only be in the private arena, so that sexuality can be eliminated as a factor in the public life of the community.

And I must say, I don't see how a single society can be constructed in which some citizens think the whole world should be divided into a women's realm and a men's realm, and others think the genders should be blended into a single social realm wherein men and women walk the same streets, shop the same shops, eat at the same restaurants, sit together in the same classrooms, and do the same jobs. It can only be one or the other. It can't be both. From where I stand, I don't see how Muslims can live in the West, under the laws and customs of Western societies, if they embrace that divided-world view, nor how Westerners can live in the Muslim world as anything but visitors, if they embrace that genders-shuffled-together view.

I don't offer one answer or another to the questions I am posing. I only say that Muslim intellectuals have to grapple with them. And they *have* been. Some of the most daring departures from orthodox Islamic doctrines emerged in Iran, during the two decades after that country expelled the United States and claimed its cultural sovereignty. There, anonymous writers proposed that every generation had the right to interpret the Shari'ah anew without reference to the accumulated code of the religious scholars. This idea and others like it were suppressed. The suppression made news in the West—it was more evidence that Iran was *not a democracy*. What struck me, however, was that such ideas were voiced at all in the Muslim world. I wondered if it could only happen in a place where Muslims were struggling with themselves and each other, not with the West.

After 9/11 the Bush administration ratcheted up the pressure on Iran, and in the face of this external threat, ideas with a Western aroma lost credibility because they smelled of collaboration: they no longer needed to be suppressed; they could gain no purchase with a public that had turned conservative, a public that chose the ultranationalist Ahmadinejad to head up their nation.

Many points for discussion, even argument, simmer between the Islamic world and the West. There can be no sensible argument, however, until both sides are using the same terms and mean the same things by those terms—until, that is, both sides share the same framework or at least understand what framework the other is assuming. Following multiple narratives of world history can contribute at least to developing such a perspective.

Everybody likes democracy, especially as it applies to themselves personally; but Islam is not the opposite of democracy; it's a whole other framework. Within that framework there can be democracy, there can be tyranny, there can be many states in between.

For that matter, Islam is not the opposite of Christianity, nor of Judaism. Taken strictly as a system of religious beliefs, it has more areas of agreement than argument with Christianity and even more so with Judaism—take a look sometime at the laws of diet, hygiene, and sexuality prescribed by orthodox religious Judaism, and you'll see almost exactly the same list as you find in orthodox, religious Islam. Indeed, as Pakistani writer Eqbal Ahmad once noted, until recent centuries, it made more sense to speak of Judeo-Muslim than of Judeo-Christian culture.

It is, however, problematically misleading to think of Islam as one item in a class whose other items are Christianity, Judaism, Hinduism, Buddhism, etc. Not inaccurate, of course: Islam *is* a religion, like those others, a distinct set of beliefs and practices related to ethics, morals, God, the cosmos, and mortality. But Islam might just as validly be considered as one item in a class whose other items include communism, parliamentary democracy, fascism, and the like, because Islam is a social project like *those* others, an idea for how politics and the economy ought to be managed, a complete system of civil and criminal law.

Then again, Islam can quite validly be seen as one item in a class whose other items include Chinese civilization, Indian civilization, Western civilization, and so on, because there is a universe of cultural artifacts from art to philosophy to architecture to handicrafts to virtually every other realm of human cultural endeavor that could properly be called Islamic.

Or, as I have tried to demonstrate, Islam can be seen as one world history among many that are unfolding simultaneously, each in some way incorporating all the others. Considered in this light, Islam is a vast narrative moving through time, anchored by the birth of that community in Mecca and Medina fourteen centuries ago. The story includes many characters who are not Muslim and many events that are not religious. Jews and Christians and Hindus are part of this story. Industrialization is an element of the plot, and so is the steam engine and the discovery of oil. When you look at it this way, Islam is a vast complex of communal purposes moving through time, driven by its own internally coherent assumptions.

And so is the West.

So which is the *real* history of the world? The philosopher Leibniz once posited the idea that the universe consists of "monads," each monad being the whole universe understood from a particular point of view, and each monad containing all the others. World history is like that: the whole story of humankind from a particular point of view, each history containing all the others, with all actual events situated somewhere with respect to a central narrative, even if that "somewhere" is in the background as part of the white noise against which the meaningful line stands out. They're all the real history of the world. The work lies in the never-ending task of compiling them in the quest to build a universal human community situated within a single shared history.

APPENDIX

The Structure of Islamic Doctrine

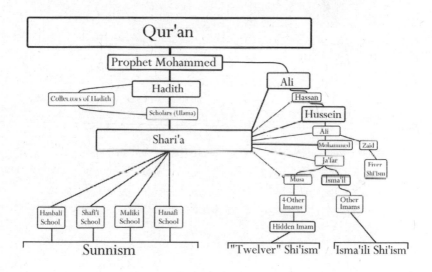

NOTES

INTRODUCTION
1. With footnotes.

CHAPTER 1
1. See Georges Roux, *Ancient Iraq* (New York: Penguin, 1980), p. 148.
2. Conan Doyle, for example, uses "Parthian shot" to mean "parting shot" in his 1886 novel *A Study in Scarlet.*
3. The eleventh-century Persian poet Firdausi drew on this vast body of Persian legends to write the *Shahnama* (The Book of Kings), an epic poem in which Kay Khosrow the Just figures largely.

CHAPTER 2
1. From a passage by Tabari, excerpted in *The Inner Journey: Views from the Islamic Tradition,* edited by William Chittick, (Sandpoint, Idaho: Morning Light Press, 2007), p. xi.
2. Akbar Ahmed's *Islam Today* (New York and London: I. B. Tauris, 1999), p. 21, for excerpts from Mohammed's last sermon.

CHAPTER 3
1. Reza Aslan, *No god but God* (New York: Random House, 2006), p. 113.
2. This is Tabari's description; an excerpt appears on page 12 of *Islam: From the Prophet Mohammed to the Capture of Constantinople,* a collection of documents edited and translated by Bernard Lewis. (New York and Oxford: Oxford University Press, 1997).
3. The core of a document purporting to be Omar's original declaration to Jerusalem appears in Hugh Kennedy's *The Great Arab Conquests* (New York: Da Capo Press, 2007), pp. 91–92.

CHAPTER 5

1. From Ibn Qutayba's ninth-century history *Uyun al-Akhbar,* excerpted in *Islam: From the Prophet Muhammed to the Capture of Constantinople* (New York and Oxford: Oxford University Press, 1987), p. 273.

2. *Nafasul Mahmum* (chapter 14), Sheikh Abbas Qummi quoting from thirteenth-century historian Sayyid Ibn Tawoos's book *Lahoof* (Qom, Iran: Ansariyan Publications, 2005).

3. G. E. von Grunebaum, *Classical Islam* (Chicago: Aldine Publishing Company, 1970), p. 70.

CHAPTER 6

1. Wiet, *Baghdad: Metropolis of the Abbasid Caliphate,* pp. 12–24.

2. From *Four Thousand Years of Urban Growth: An Historical Census* by Tertius Chandler. (Lewiston, New York: St. David's University Press, 1987).

CHAPTER 7

1. My rendering of a poem that appears in *Perfume of the Desert: Inspirations from Sufi Wisdom,* edited by A. Harvey and E. Hanut, (Wheaton, Illinois: Quest Books, 1999).

2. From Muhammad Zubayr Siddiqi, "Women Scholars of Hadith," at http://www.jannah.org/sisters/womenhadith.html.

3. Maulana Muhammad Ali, *The Early Caliphate* (1932; Lahore, Pakistan: The Ahmadiyya Anjuman Isha'at Islam, 1983), p. 119.

4. Ghazali, "On the Etiquettes of Marriage," *The Revival of the Religious Sciences* book 12 at http://www.ghazali.org/works/marriage.htm.

CHAPTER 8

1. Chaim Potok, *History of the Jews* (New York: Ballantine Books, 1978), pp. 346–347.

2. Mohammed Ali, *A Cultural History of Afghanistan, 120–123* (Kabul: Punjab Educational Press, 1964).

3. My cousin Farid Ansary quoted this line from a contemporary of Firdausi's; he couldn't recall the poet's name. However, similar (but more extensive) anti-Arab vituperations can be found at the end of Firdausi's *Shahnama.*

CHAPTER 9

1. Philip Daileader discusses the fragmentation process in medieval Europe in lectures 17–20 of his audio series *The Early Middle Ages* (Chantilly, Virginia: The Teaching Company, 2004). See also the Columbia Encyclopedia, 6th edition, entry for "knight."

2. Amin Maalouf, *The Crusades through Arab Eyes* (New York: Schocken Books, 1984), pp. 38–40.

3. Ibid., p. 46.

4. Quoted by Karen Armstrong in *Holy War: The Crusades and Their Impact on Today's World* (New York: Anchor Books, 2001), pp. 178–179.

5. Ibid., p. 73.

6. Ibid., p. 39.

7. David Morgan, *The Mongols* (Malden, Massachusetts: Blackwell, 2007), p. 17.

8. Ibid., pp. 64–71.

9. Sabbah's sect resurrected itself as the Nizari Isma'ilis, gained new converts, and rose again, but it morphed into a peaceful movement that is now one of the most progressive sects of Islam, devoted to science and education. Its leader is called the Agha Khan, and the Isma'ilis run the Agha Khan University in Pakistan, one of the brightest centers of learning in today's Islamic world: everything changes.

10. An account of the sack of Baghdad by Muslim historian Rashid al-Din Fazlullah (1247–1318) appears in *The Middle East and Islamic World Reader* (New York: Grove Press, 2003), p. 49.

11. The mamluk army was much bigger than Hulagu's, but the Mongol's terrible success made them the Goliath in every confrontation.

12. Morgan, 146.

CHAPTER 10

1. Morgan, pp. 16–18.

2. See Akbar Ahmed's interesting discussion of these differences between the two religions in *Islam Today*, pp. 21–22.

3. Muhammed ibn-al-Husayn al-Sulami, *The Book of Sufi Chivalry: Lessons to a Son of the Moment* (New York: Inner Traditions International, 1983). These stories appear in the forward, pp. 9–14. The ghazis apparently borrowed the story about Omar from a traditional older story about a pre-Islamic king named Nu'man ibn Mundhir.

4. Alexandra Marks, writing for the *Christian Science Monitor* on November 25, 1997, said the Coleman Barks's translation of Rumi, *The Essential Rumi* (San Francisco: HarperCollins, 1995), had sold at that point, a quarter of a million copies worldwide.

5. See Paul Wittek, *The Rise of the Ottoman Empire* (London: Royal Asiatic Society of Great Britain and Ireland, 1965) pp. 33–51.

6. Details of Ottoman society come largely from Stanford Shaw's *History of the Ottoman Empire and Modern Turkey* (Cambridge: Cambridge University Press, 1976), especially pp. 55–65, 113–138, and 150–161.

7. Zahirud-din Muhammad Babur, *Babur-nama*, translated by Annette S. Beveridge, (1922; Lahor: Sang-e-Meel Publications, reprinted 1987), p. 121.

8. Waldemar Hansen, *The Peacock Throne, The Drama of Mogul India* (New York: Holt, Rinehart, and Winston, 1972) pp. 113–114, 493–494.

9. Marshall Hodgson, *Rethinking World History* (Cambridge: Cambridge University Press, 1993) p. 97.

CHAPTER 11

1. See C. M. Woolger, "Food and Taste in Europe in the Middle Ages," pp. 175–177 in *Food: The History of Taste*, edited by Paul Freedman, (Berkeley: University of California Press, 2007).

2. Peter Russel, *Prince Henry the Navigator* (London: Hispanic and Luso Brazilian Council, 1960).

3. Daileader, Lecture 15, *Early Middle Ages* (Chantilly, Virginia: The Teaching Company, 2004).

CHAPTER 12

1. Great Britain was born after King James VI of Scotland inherited the crown of England. He and his successors held both crowns separately until the Act of Union in 1707. Only after that date is it correct to speak of "the British."

2. For a detailed inside picture of life in the Ottoman harem, see Alev Croutier's *Harem: The World Behind the Veil* (New York: Abbeville Press, 1989), especially pp. 35–38, 103–105, 139–140.

3. James Gelvin points out these global interconnections in *The Modern Middle East*. See pp. 55–60.

4. Nick Robbins, "Loot: In Search of the East India Company," an article written for openDemocracy.net in 2003. Find it at http://www.opendemocracy.net/theme_7-corporations/article_904.jsp.

5. Gelvin, pp. 84–86.

6. As reported by Frederick Cooper, deputy commissioner of Amritsar, in a dispatch excerpted by Reza Aslan, *No god but God* (New York, Random House, 2006), pp. 220–222.

7. Jamil Abun-Nasr, *A History of the Maghrib in the Islamic Period*. (Cambridge: Cambridge University Press, 1988), pp. 249–257.

CHAPTER 13

1. Ernest Renan, *"La Reforme intellectuelle et morale"* (Paris: Calmann-Levy, 1929).

2. Hamid Dabashi, *Iran: A People Interrupted* (New York: New Press, 2007), pp. 58–59.

CHAPTER 14

1. Mark Elvin coins this phrase in *Pattern of the Chinese Past* (London: Eyre Methuen Ltd, 1973), which includes an analysis of why China failed to develop high-level technology in the fourteenth to nineteenth centuries, when it had the prosperity to do so.

2. Dabashi, pp. 60–61.

3. Gelvin, p. 129.

4. Joseph Mazzini, *On the Duties of Man*. Included in its entirety in Franklin, *Readings in Western Intellectual History* (New Haven, Connecticut: Yale University Press, 1978), p. 561.

5. Garry Wills discusses this idea in *Lincoln at Gettysburg: The Words That Remade America* (New York: Simon and Schuster, 1993). Shelby Foote (in a radio interview I heard) quipped that "the Civil War made us from an *are* into an *is*."

6. Gelvin, p. 82.

7. Hamit Bozarslan, writing about the Ottoman Empire for the Online Encyclopedia of Mass Violence at http://www.massviolence.org/_Bozarslan-Hamit, includes this quote from Ziya Gökalp's *Yeni Hayat, Dogru Yol.*

8. Quoted by Taner Akçam in *Türk Ulusal Kimligi ve Ermeni Sorunu* (Istanbul: Iletisim Yayinlari, 1992), pp. 175–176.

CHAPTER 15

1. Suroosh Irfani, *Revolutionary Islam in Iran: Popular Liberation or Religious Dictatorship* (London: Zed Books, 1983), p. 50.

2. Article 22, Covenant of the League of Nations.

3. Gelvin, p. 86.

4. Benjamin Shwadran, *The Middle East, Oil and the Great Powers* (New York: Frederick A. Praeger, 1955), pp. 244–265.

CHAPTER 16

1. See http://countrystudies.us/algeria/48.htm. The statistics come from the Federal Research Division of the Library of Congress Country Studies/Area Handbook Series sponsored by the U.S. Department of the Army.

2. Frank Thackery and John Findling, *Events That Changed the World in the Twentieth Century* (Westport and London: Greenwood Press, 1995). (See Appendix D, "States Achieving Independence Since 1945.")

3. The phrase came from American Jewish playwright Israel Zangwill. What he actually wrote, however (in 1901), was "Palestine is a country without a people, the Jews are a people without a country." Whether anyone actively used the phrase as a basis for a "slogan" is a matter of dispute.

4. Benny Morris, *Righteous Victims: A History of the Zionist-Arab Conflict, 1881–1999,* (New York: Alfred A. Knopf, 1999), pp. 14–17.

5. Theodor Herzl, *The Jewish State: An Attempt at a Modern Solution to the Jewish Question*, 6th edition (New York: The Maccabean Publishing Company, 1904), p. 29.

6. Nizar Sakhnini, writing for al-Awda at http://al-awda.org/zionists2.html includes this quote from Weizmann's *Trial and Error* (New York: Harper and Brothers, 1949), pp. 93–208.

7. Qutb's *Milestones* can be found online in its entirety at http://www.young muslimsonline.ca/online_library/books/milestones/hold/index_2.asp.

CHAPTER 17

1. For a concise Arafat bio, see http://nobelprize.org/nobel_prizes/peace/laureates/1994/arafat-bio.html.
2. David Cook, *Understanding Jihad*, p. 130.
3. Irfani, *Revolutionary Islam in Iran*, pp. 98–100, 121, 131.
4. Dabashi, pp. 164–166.
5. Quoted by Thabit Abdullah in *Dictatorship, Imperialism, and Chaos: Iraq Since 1989* (New York: Zed Books, 2006) p. 76.

BIBLIOGRAPHY

Abdullah, Thabit. *Dictatorship, Imperialism, and Chaos: Iraq Since 1989.* New York: Zed Books, 2006.

Abiva, Huseyin and Noura Durkee. *A History of Muslim Civilization from Late Antiquity to the Fall of the Umayyads.* Skokie, IL: IQRA' International Educational Foundation, 2003.

Abu Khalil, As'ad. *Bin Laden, Islam, and America's New "War on Terrorism."* New York: Seven Stories Press, 2002.

Abun-Nasr, Jamil M. *A History of the Maghrib in the Islamic Period.* Cambridge: Cambridge University Press, 1988.

Ahmad, Eqbal. *Confronting Empire: Interviews with David Barsamian.* Cambridge, Massachusetts: South End Press, 2000.

Ahmed, Akbar. *Islam Today: A Short Introduction to the Muslim World.* New York and London: I. B. Tauris, 1999.

Alger, Neil. *The Palestinians and the Disputed Territories.* San Diego: Greenhaven Press, 2004.

Ali, ibn Abi Talib. *Nahjul Balagha* [Peak of Eloquence]. Translated by Sayed Ali Reza. Elmhurst, New York: Tahrike Tarsile Qur'an Inc., 1996.

Ali, Maulana Muhammad. *The Early Caliphate.* Reprinted in Lahore, Pakistan: The Ahmadiyya Anjuman Isha'at Islam, 1983.

Ali, Tariq. *The Clash of Fundamentalisms: Crusades, Jihads and Modernity.* London: Verso, 2003.

Arberry, A. J., translator. *The Qur'an Interpreted.* New York: Macmillan, 1955.

Armstrong, Karen. *Holy War: The Crusades and Their Impact on Today's World.* New York: Anchor Books, 2001.

_____. *Muhammad: A Biography of the Prophet.* San Francisco: HarperCollins, 1992.

Aslan, Reza. *No god but God.* New York: Random House, 2006.

Catherwood, Christopher. *A Brief History of the Middle East: From Abraham to Arafat.* New York: Carroll and Graf, 2006.

Chittick, William. *The Inner Journey: Views from the Islamic Tradition.* Sandpoint, Idaho: Morning Light Press, 2007.

Cook, David. *Understanding Jihad.* Berkeley, California: University of California Press, 2005.

Croutier, Alev Lytle. *Harem: The World Behind the Veil.* New York: Abbeville Press, 1989.

Dabashi, Hamid. *Iran: A People Interrupted.* New York: The New Press, 2007.

Diouf, Sylviane A. *Servants of Allah: African Muslims Enslaved in the Americas.* New York: New York University Press, 1998.

Dunn, Ross. *The Adventures of Ibn Battuta.* Berkeley and Los Angeles: University of California Press, 1989.

Farsoun, Samih and Naseer Aruri. *Palestine and the Palestinians: A Social and Political History.* Boulder, Colorado: Westview Press, 2006.

Finkel, Caroline. *Osman's Dream: The History of the Ottoman Empire.* New York: Basic Books, 2006.

Fischel, Walter J. *Ibn Khaldun in Egypt.* Berkeley, California: University of California Press, 1967.

Fisher, William Bayne, et al editors. *The Cambridge History of Iran.* Cambridge: Cambridge University Press, 1993.

Frank, Irene and David Brownstone. *To the Ends of the Earth.* New York: Facts on File, 1984.

Fromkin, David. *A Peace to End All Peace.* New York: Owl Books, 2001. First published 1989 by Henry Holt.

Gelvin, James L. *The Modern Middle East: A History.* New York: Oxford University Press, 2005.

Gerner, Deborah J. and Jillian Schwedler. *Understanding the Contemporary Middle East.* Boulder, Colorado: Lynne Rienner Publishers, 2004.

Gettleman, Marvin and Stuart Schaar, editors. *The Middle East and Islamic World Reader.* New York: Grove Press, 2003.

Goitein, S. D. *Jews and Arabs: A Concise History of Their Social and Cultural Relations.* Mineola, New York: Dover Publication, 2005.

Gordon, Matthew S. *The Rise of Islam.* Westport, Connecticut: Greenwood Press, 2005.

Hansen, Waldemar. *The Peacock Throne: The Drama of Moghul India.* New York: Holt, Rinehart and Winston, 1970.

Heikal, Mohammed. *Iran: the Untold Story.* New York: Pantheon, 1982.

Hiro, Dilip. *The Longest War: The Iran-Iraq Military Conflict.* New York: Routledge, 1991.

_____. *War Without End: The Rise of Islamist Terrorism and Global Response.* Revised edition. London, England: Routledge, 2002.

Hodgson, Marshall. *Rethinking World History.* Cambridge: Cambridge University Press, 1993.

Hourani, Albert. *A History of the Arab Peoples.* Cambridge, Massachusetts: Harvard University Press, 1991.

Howarth, Stephen. *The Knights Templar.* New York: Barnes and Noble, 1982.

Ibn Khaldun. *The Muqaddimah: An Introduction to History.* Translated by Franz Rosenthal. Edited by N. J. Dawood. Princeton, New Jersey: Princeton University Press, 1969.

Imber, Colin. *The Ottoman Empire.* New York: Palgrave-Macmillan, 2002.

Irfani, Suroosh. *Revolutionary Islam in Iran; Popular Liberation or Religious Dictatorship.* London: Zed Books, 1983.

Kamrava, Mehran. *The Modern Middle East: A Political History Since the First World War.* Berkeley and Los Angeles: University of California Press, 2005.

Kennedy, Hugh. *The Great Arab Conquests: How the Spread of Islam Changed the World We Live In.* New York: Da Capo Press, 2007.

_____. *When Baghdad Ruled the Muslim World: The Rise and Fall of Islam's Greatest Dynasty.* New York: Da Capo Press, 2005.

Kinross, Lord. *The Ottoman Centuries: The Rise and Fall of the Turkish Empire.* New York: William Morrow, 1977.

Laiou, Angeliki E. and Roy Parviz Mottahedeh, editors. *The Crusades from the Perspective of Byzantium and the Muslim World.* Washington, D.C.: Dumbarton Oaks, 2001.

Lewis, Archibald Ross, editor. *The Islamic World and the West, AD 622–1492.* New York: John Wiley & Sons, 1970.

Lewis, Bernard, editor and translator. *Islam: From the Prophet Muhammad to the Capture of Constantinople.* New York and Oxford: Oxford University Press, 1987.

Lewis, Bernard. *The Middle East: A Brief History of the Last 2,000 Years.* New York: Simon & Schuster, 1995.

_____. *What Went Wrong? Western Impact and Middle Eastern Response.* New York: Oxford University Press, 2002.

Lings, Martin. *Mohammed: His Life Based on the Earliest Sources.* Rochester, Vermont: Inner Traditions International, 1987.

Maalouf, Amin. *The Crusades through Arab Eyes.* New York: Schocken Books, 1984.

Matroudi, Abdul Hakim al-. *The Hanbali School of Law and Ibn Taymiyah.* London and New York: Routledge, 2006.

Mazzini, Joseph. *On the Duties of Man.* Reprinted in *Main Currents in Western Thought: Readings in Western European Intellectual History from the Middle Ages to the Present.* Edited by Franklin Le Van Baumer. New Haven, Connecticut: Yale University Press, 1978.

Morgan, David. *The Mongols.* Malden, Massachusetts: Blackwell Publishing, 2007.

Moussalli, Ahmad S. *Moderate and Radical Islamic Fundamentalism: The Quest for Modernity, Legitimacy, and the Islamic State.* Gainesville: University Press of Florida, 1999.

Muir, Sir William. *Annals of the Early Caliphate.* London: Smith, Elder & Co. 1883.

Nasr, Kameel. *Arab and Israeli Terrorism: The Causes and Effects of Political Violence, 1936–1993.* Jefferson, North Carolina: McFarland & Co., 1997.

Nasr, Seyyed Hossein. *Ideals and Realities in Islam.* Boston: Beacon Press, 1966.

Nizam al-Mulk. *The Book of Government: Or Rules for Kings: The Siyasatnama or Siyar al-Muluk.* Translated from the Persian by Hubert Darke. London: Routledge & Paul, 1960.

Nutting, Anthony. *Nasser*. New York: Dutton, 1972.

Ojeda, Auriana, editor. *Islamic Fundamentalism*. San Diego: Greenhaven, 2003.

Potok, Chaim. *Wanderings*. New York: Ballantine Books, 1978.

Qummi, Sheikh Abbas. *Nafasul Mahmum [The Sigh of the Aggrieved]: Relating to the Heart Rending Tragedy of Karbala*. Translated by Aejaz Ali Bhujwala. Qom, Iran: Ansariyan Publications, 2005.

Rahman, Fazlur. *Islam*. Chicago: University of Chicago Press, 2002. First published 1979 by University of Chicago Press.

Robinson, Frances, editor. *The Cambridge Illustrated History of the Islamic World*. Cambridge: Cambridge University Press, 1996.

Rogerson, Barnaby. *The Heirs of Muhammad: Islam's First Century and the Origins of the Sunni-Shia Split*. Woodstock and New York: The Overlook Press, 2007.

Roshan, Rauf. *Remembrances of Doctor Tabibi*. Fremont, California: Tabayatee Faizi International, 1998.

Roux, Georges. *Ancient Iraq*. New York: Penguin Books (Pelican), 1966.

Rumi. *Divan-i-Shamsi-Tabriz: Forty-eight Ghazals*. Edited and translated by Iraj Anvar. Rome, Italy: Semar Publishing, 2002.

Runciman, Stephen. *A History of the Crusades*. Cambridge: Cambridge University Press, 1951.

Said, Edward. *The Question of Palestine*. New York: Vintage Books, 1980.

Salami, Ibn al-Husayn al-. *The Book of Sufi Chivalry: Lessons to a Son of the Moment*. New York: Inner Traditions International, 1983.

Shaban, M. A. *Islamic History: A New Interpretation*. Cambridge: Cambridge University Press, 1971.

Shaw, Stanford J. *History of the Ottoman Empire and Modern Turkey*. Cambridge: Cambridge University Press, 1976.

Sheikh, M. Saeed. *Islamic Philosophy*. London: Octagon Press, 1982.

Shwadran, Benjamin. *The Middle East, Oil and the Great Powers*. New York: Frederick A. Praeger, 1955.

Smith, Wilfred Cantwell. *Islam in Modern History*. Princeton, New Jersey: Princeton University Press, 1957.

Stewart, P. J. *Unfolding Islam*. Reading, U.K.: Garnet, 1994.

Tabari, al-. *Mohammed at Mecca*. Translated by Montgomery Watt and M.V. Mc-Donald. Albany, New York: SUNY Press, 1988.

Trofimov, Yaroslav. *The Siege of Mecca: The Forgotten Uprising in Islam's Holiest Shrine and the Birth of al-Qaeda*. New York: Doubleday, 2007.

von Grunebaum, G. E. *Classical Islam: A History 600 AD to 1258 AD*. Chicago: Aldine Publishing Company, 1970.

Wiet, Gaston. *Baghdad: Metropolis of the Abbasids*. Translated by Seymour Feiler. Norman, Oklahoma: University of Oklahoma Press, 1971.

ACKNOWLEDGMENTS

I owe a debt of gratitude to Susan Hoffman, who as director of the Osher Lifelong Learning Institute at San Francisco State, convinced me to teach a class on Islam and the West in 2006. Those lectures were one of the seeds out of which grew this book—a growth spurred also by Neils Swinkel, who taped some of those lectures and Matt Martin, station manager at KALW radio, who aired the edited tapes as a weekly series.

Next, let me thanks my agent, Carol Mann. When I told her I was vaguely thinking of writing something called "world history through Islamic eyes," she cut in to say, "That's it! That's your next book! *West of Kabul* was the ant's-eye view; this will be the bird's-eye view." And she was right—this is a bird's-eye view of my enduring preoccupation, the conjunction and disjunction of East and West.

And thank you, Lisa Kaufman, my insightful editor, whose notes and line edits have been like having not just a second set of eyes but a second and more exacting brain to apply to this project.

Also, I received priceless feedback on this book while it was still a work in progress from my brother Riaz Ansary, who knows more about the doctrines and early history of Islam than I ever will, from my brilliant sister, Rebecca Pettys, and from my friends Joe Quirk and Paul Lobell. Layma Murtaza generously allowed me to study correspondence and magazines her family inherited from her grandfather Dr. Abdul Hakim Tabibi, a disciple of Sayyid Jamaluddin-i-Afghan. Farid Ansary has contributed with a lifetime of stories, anecdotes, poetry quotations, and wit. Wahid Ansary has done his best to clue me in to the fine points of our religion, and then there is my friend Akbar Nowrouz: Akbar-jan, where would I be without all the Islamic-wisdom stories you send to my e-mail?

But above all, thank you to my wife, Deborah Krant, my first reader, first critic, and indispensable partner; thank you to Elina Ansary, for helping me so much with the maps; and thank you, Jessamyn Ansary, for being so endlessly supportive.

INDEX

Tamim Ansary is the author of *The Invention of Yesterday*, the memoir *West of Kabul, East of New York* and coauthor with Afghan land mine victim Farah Ahmadi of the *New York Times* bestseller *The Other Side of the Sky*. He has been a major contributing writer to several secondary school history textbooks. He writes a monthly column for Encarta. com and has published essays and commentary in the *San Francisco Chronicle, Salon, Alternet,* TomPaine.com, *Edutopia, Parade, L.A. Times,* and elsewhere. Ansary, director of the San Francisco Writers Workshop, lives in San Francisco.

PublicAffairs is a publishing house founded in 1997. It is a tribute
to the standards, values, and flair of three persons who have
served as mentors to countless reporters, writers, editors, and
book people of all kinds, including me.

I. F. STONE, proprietor of *I. F. Stone's Weekly*, combined a commitment to the First Amendment with entrepreneurial zeal and
reporting skill and became one of the great independent journalists in American history. At the age of eighty, Izzy published *The
Trial of Socrates*, which was a national bestseller. He wrote the
book after he taught himself ancient Greek.

BENJAMIN C. BRADLEE was for nearly thirty years the charismatic editorial leader of *The Washington Post*. It was Ben who
gave the *Post* the range and courage to pursue such historic
issues as Watergate. He supported his reporters with a tenacity
that made them fearless and it is no accident that so many
became authors of influential, best-selling books.

ROBERT L. BERNSTEIN, the chief executive of Random House
for more than a quarter century, guided one of the nation's pre-
mier publishing houses. Bob was personally responsible for
many books of political dissent and argument that challenged
tyranny around the globe. He is also the founder and longtime
chair of Human Rights Watch, one of the most respected human
rights organizations in the world.

.   .   .

For fifty years, the banner of Public Affairs Press was carried by its
owner Morris B. Schnapper, who published Gandhi, Nasser, Toynbee, Truman, and about 1,500 other authors. In 1983, Schnapper
was described by *The Washington Post* as "a redoubtable gadfly."
His legacy will endure in the books to come.

Peter Osnos, *Founder*